The Laws of Yesterday's Wars 2

International Humanitarian Law Series

VOLUME 64

The International Humanitarian Law Series is a series of monographs and edited volumes which aims to promote scholarly analysis and discussion of both the theory and practice of the international legal regulation of armed conflict.

The series explores substantive issues of International Humanitarian Law including:

- Protection for victims of armed conflict and regulation of the means and method of warfare
- questions of application of the various legal regimes for the conduct of armed conflict
- Issues relating to the implementation of International Humanitarian Law obligations
- national and international approaches to the enforcement of the law and
- the interactions between International Humanitarian Law and other related areas of international law such as Human Rights, Refugee Law, Arms Control and Disarmament Law, and International Criminal Law.

The titles published in this series are listed at *brill.com/ihul*

The Laws of Yesterday's Wars 2

From Ancient India to East Africa

Edited by

Samuel White

BRILL
NIJHOFF

LEIDEN | BOSTON

Cover illustration: Illustration of ancient warriors of Japan, World History Archive, copyright ANP

The Library of Congress Cataloging-in-Publication Data is available online at https://catalog.loc.gov

Typeface for the Latin, Greek, and Cyrillic scripts: "Brill". See and download: brill.com/brill-typeface.

ISSN 1389-6776
ISBN 978-90-04-47320-1 (hardback)
ISBN 978-90-04-47321-8 (e-book)

This book is printed on acid-free paper and produced in a sustainable manner.

Contents

Foreword

I am delighted to have been invited to contribute this Foreword to *The Laws of Yesterday's Wars: From Ancient India to East Africa*, the second volume in Samuel White's edited series of historical analyses of the regulation of warfare within specific selected cultures. The selections for this volume, like those for Volume I, follow no obvious geographic, cultural, theological or other discernible pattern although the essays in this volume are arranged more or less chronologically (laws of warfare from Ancient India through the centuries before and straddling the Common Era (Carthagian and Roman Empires, Islam during Mohammedan times) to more recent centuries (Eastern Native Americans, Japanese during the *Bushido* era and East African peoples)). That observation is not a criticism. What Samuel White has managed to do in two successive edited volumes is create a growing data set from which to compare and contrast approaches to constraint on the waging of war. His Conclusion to this volume, in which he engages in his own comparative analysis across the now combined total of fifteen case studies, is demonstrative of the potential richness of the comparative analysis to come – after the publication of the intended future companion volumes. I am sure I am not alone in looking forward to future companion volumes while savouring what is already here.

I have always been intrigued by the historical development of constraints on the waging of war and particularly on the antecedents to multilateral constraint within particular cultural, spiritual and social traditions. Twenty five years ago Gerry Simpson and I co-edited a volume entitled *The Law of War Crimes: National and International Approaches*. In that volume I attempted to trace the evolution of an international criminal law regime including constraints on the waging of war and particularly disciplinary measures for violations of those constraints. I am not suggesting here that my analysis then was in any way equivalent to the breadth and depth of analysis undertaken by Samuel White and his contributors. On the contrary, when I read back over what I wrote in 1997 I realise how relatively cursory my analysis was and how much more substantive, rigorous and meaningful others', including Samuel's, contributions to contemporary scholarship really are. But my early interest in this subject matter certainly laid a foundation from which my interest was piqued when the manuscript for Samuel's Volume I landed in my inbox. More recently I co-edited with Suzannah Linton and Sandesh Sivakumaran *Asia Pacific Perspectives on International Humanitarian Law* in which we assembled a diverse group of scholars from the Asia Pacific Region to provide authentic regional perspectives on this body so regularly the preserve of voices from

Europe and North America. In that co-edited volume, we were thrilled to include chapters from Xue Ru on 'Humanitarianism in Chinese Traditional Military Ethics' and from Manoj Kumar Sinha on 'Military Practices in Ancient India'. We shared a similar motivation to Samuel in including these contributions but, again, our breadth was decidedly narrower given our specific geographic focus.

My invitation to contribute stems less from my personal interest in the subject matter of this volume and much more from my role as editor-in-chief of Brill Nijhoff's International Humanitarian Law Series. The manuscripts for both Volumes I and II were reviewed, as all proposed manuscripts for inclusion in the Series are, and publication was unanimously recommended in both cases. The subject matter of these two volumes (and also that of future accompanying volumes) is precisely the sort of material that the International Humanitarian Law Series should include. The author of the Foreword for Volume I stated that '[t]his work is largely one of historical study rather than of Law' and that is an accurate statement *stricto sensu*. However, the history of warfare, including constraints on the waging of war – whether the result of legal regulation in a positivist sense or of norms emanating from the customs and usages of war of the result of some other cultural, spiritual and/or social influence – is a valued and worthwhile study to help us understand various contributing influences on the development of the law as well as to expose some of the overly-simplistic assumptions or, worse, the myths international humanitarian lawyers often help inadvertently promote about the development of this particular body of law.

One example of overly simplistic assumptions about the origins of international humanitarian law is that the 1864 Geneva Convention, as the first binding multilateral treaty, was the starting point and that subsequent 19th Century treaty law consolidated the newly emergent international legal constraints. In one sense the proposition is not fallacious - but it certainly lacks nuance. Twice in the 1868 St Petersburg Declaration 'the laws of humanity' are identified as the necessary counterweight to the necessities of war. Similarly, the 1899 and 1907 Hague Conventions and Declarations are replete with the call to acknowledge and respect the overarching protection of 'the principles of international law, as they result from the usages established between civilized nations, from the laws of humanity, and the requirements of the public conscience'. The essays in this volume, and indeed in Volume I, help provide substance to the meaning of concepts such as 'the laws of humanity', 'usages established between nations' and 'the requirements of the public conscience'. These concepts lay in the normative imposition of constraints on the waging of war that nations applied to their own military operations and had come to expect of their opponents. These concepts were not suddenly created by the emerging multilateral treaty law of the late 19th and early 20th Centuries.

The importance of the scholarship in this and related volumes is not only as an exposer of overly-simplistic assumptions although that is a worthwhile contribution in and of itself. Samuel's Introduction to the volume includes the assertion that: '[t]he cultural norms and customs that developed in many communities outside of Europe actually reflect a more nuanced approach to mitigating war's effects than the customs and codes developed in Europe'. The International Committee of the Red Cross (ICRC) has long advocated for deeper and more sensitive understanding of the history of constraints on the waging of war within cultures as a key hook for the promotion of respect for international humanitarian law within military and security forces with that cultural background. This motivation is both understandable and admirable and we see it explicitly referred to in the chapters in this volume by Ahmed Al-Dawoody on 'Islamic Laws of War' and also by Kenneth Wyne Mutuma and Eve Massingham on 'East African Laws of War'. Mutuma and Massingham cite the ICRC's important work on the history of the laws of war in Melanesian cultures in the 2009 publication *Protection under the Palm: Wars of Dignity in the Pacific* as a key comparator to Somali approaches to war. No doubt future related volumes in this series within a series will cover Melanesian cultural approaches to the laws of war to supplement Alexander Gillespie's chapter in Volume 1 on 'Maori Warfare and New Zealand Wars'. My key point here though is that, while other chapters may not be as explicit about this particular motivation as Al-Dawoody, Mutuma and Massingham all of whom have worked with the ICRC, the lack of explicit reference does not preclude the potential contribution that all the chapters offer.

Exposing overly-simplistic notions is one thing but myth-busting takes the contribution to a different level altogether. I have become increasingly sensitive to the importance of exposing what Frédéric Mégret calls international humanitarian law's 'original sin' – that humanity as a constraint on the waging of war was a narrowly colonialist construct intended to extend legal protections only to 'civilised' combatants to the exclusion of so-called 'uncivilised savages'.

The language of the early multilateral treaties provides all the clues necessary to expose the myth of inclusivity based on our shared humanity. The Preamble to the 1868 St Petersburg Declaration explains that States gathered in the then Russian capital to consider 'forbidding the use of certain projectiles in time of war between civilized nations' and that 'the progress of civilization should have the effect of alleviating as much as possible the calamities of war'. This new, multilateral prohibition on exploding bullets for anti-personnel use (not extending to anti-materiel use) would only apply to wars between States Parties and certainly not to wars with non-States Parties or 'savages'. Remember that the British military developed the dum dum bullet for its military campaigns in India because conventional full metal jackets did not stop advancing natives quickly enough. The Solferino rallying cry of *tutti fratelli* – we are all brothers – was perfectly acceptable for opposing French, Italian and Austro-Hungarian troops but the *tutti* of 1859 was a distinctive shade of white and never comprehensive enough to cover people of colour in other parts of the world. The 19th Century, with its dehumanisation of those who look different, has its own 21st Century parallels. In Samuel's Conclusion to the volume, he talks of 'sharp wars' which have lacked the constraining 'straightjacket' of law and which have often been used to justify campaigns of terror. In very recent times the world has witnessed the US self-declared 'Global War on Terror' and its legal excesses emanating from dehumanisation of the enemy. Samuel's response is important: 'As this work has demonstrated, however, there has always been an attempt to humanise combatants'. This, for me, is at the heart of one of the most important contributions of the work included in the present volume and those of its ilk. Each of the chapters here demonstrate that the particular culture of focus demanded of its military a respect for the humanity of its adversaries – a respect that European nations had no intention of reciprocating in the early development of international humanitarian law.

I applaud the contributions in this volume and eagerly anticipate the publication of future companion volumes. This is important work and I commend it to all who share an interest in constraining the conduct of war.

Tim McCormack
Professor of International Law, The University of Tasmania
Special Adviser on War Crimes to the Prosecutor of the International Criminal Court
Editor-in-Chief of Brill Nijhoff's International Humanitarian Law Series

Acknowledgement

Like anything, these works do not just occur in isolation; thanks are required to the multiple individuals and teams that worked on the project.

To the contributors who saw the goal of the project, and who saw it through – thank you.

To the individuals who read, re-read and begrudgingly read for a third time the entire manuscripts, made helpful comments, and who still seemed to be willing to read it a fourth time – thank you.

To Professor Tim McCormack, Lindy Melman and the Brill team, who assisted with the entire publishing process, and to Ms Helen Jeffcoat, who compiled the index – thank you.

To my mother & father, who from my birth have fostered a love and respect of the different cultures of the world – thank you.

Finally, and most importantly, to my wife & daughter – thank you for making it all worth it.

Notes on Contributors

Editor

Samuel Camden Duckett White
has served as both a Royal Australian Infantry Corps and an Australian Army Legal Corps officer in a range of tactical, operational and strategic postings. He is currently a Postdoctoral Research Fellow & RUMLAE Associate Researcher at the University of Adelaide, as well as an Adjunct Research Fellow at the University of New England. In 2021, he was recognised for his scholarship by the International Committee of the Red Cross as being an 'Emerging Voice' in international humanitarian law.

He holds a Bachelor of Arts and Bachelor of Laws (Hons) from the University of Queensland; a Master of Laws (with First Class Honours) from the University of Melbourne; and a Master of War Studies from the University of New South Wales. He is admitted to practice in the State of Queensland and the High Court of Australia and was Associate to Justice Logan RFD of the Federal Court of Australia, Supreme & National Courts of Papua New Guinea and President of the Defence Force Discipline Appeals Tribunal in 2018.

Contributors

Ahmed Al-Dawoody
is the Legal Adviser for Islamic Law and Jurisprudence at the International Committee of the Red Cross (ICRC) in Geneva, Switzerland. He also teaches at the Geneva Academy of International Humanitarian Law and Human Rights a course on the Islamic law of armed conflict. Prior to joining the ICRC, he was an Assistant Professor in Islamic Studies and Islamic law and jurisprudence at Al-Azhar University in Cairo. He was the Assistant Director of Graduate Studies for the Institute for Islamic World Studies and the coordinator of the MA program in Contemporary Islamic Studies at Zayed University in Dubai, United Arab Emirates. He has taught in Egypt, the USA, the UK, the UAE and Switzerland. He earned his PhD from the University of Birmingham, UK; his MA from Leiden University, the Netherlands; and BA from Al-Azhar University, Egypt. He has published more than two dozen articles and book chapters on Islamic Law and is the author of *The Islamic Law of War: Justifications and Regulations* (Palgrave Macmillan, 2011).

David Feeney
is a Senior Fellow at the Australian Strategic Policy Institute (ASPI), an independent, non-partisan think tank established by the Commonwealth Government to provide advice for Australia's strategic and defence leaders. He is also a member of the NIOA Advisory Board, a 100% Australian defence company, and a member of the Defence Council Victoria (DCV). David has previously served as Senator for Victoria (2008–2013) and Member of the House of Representatives (2013–2018), during which time he held various defence-related portfolios in both Government and Opposition. Mr Feeney was a contributing author in Peter J Dean, Stephan Fruhling and Brendan Taylor (eds.), 2016, *Australia's American Alliance* (Melbourne University Publishing, Carlton) and in Tom Frame (ed.), 2017, *The Long Road. Australia's Train Advise and Assist Missions* (UNSW Press, Sydney).

Prior to entering Parliament, Mr Feeney served in various roles in the Australian Labor Party, including Assistant National Secretary, Campaign Director for South Australia, Campaign Director for Victorian Labor, and Director of Strategy for the former Premier of Victoria, the Hon. Steve Bracks. He holds a Master of Public Policy and Management (MPPM) from Monash University, a Graduate Diploma in Arts (Advanced) from the University of Melbourne, and is a Graduate of the Australian Institute of Company Directors (GAICD). David commenced his PhD studies at Melbourne in 2021. David is married to Liberty Sanger, Principal Lawyer at Maurice Blackburn Lawyers, and they are parents to Ned and Matilda.

Anna Kretowicz
has worked as an Associate to a Justice of the High Court of Australia and is a candidate for the Bachelor of Civil Law at Oxford University. She holds a Bachelor of Laws (with First Class Honours), a Bachelor of Science, and was awarded a University Medal (2020) from the University of Queensland. She has a keen interest in national security laws, laws regulating the media, and their interaction with private law rights and freedoms. She has worked as a research assistant at the University of Queensland and Griffith University, including on projects on contract law in the South Pacific, and the use and effectiveness of technology in the courtroom to record and take evidence of vulnerable victims.

Wayne E. Lee
is the Bruce W. Carney Distinguished Professor of History at the University of North Carolina, and the former chair of the Curriculum in Peace, War, and Defense. His most recent book is *The Other Face of Battle: The Experience of*

Combat in America's Forgotten Wars (Oxford, 2021), co-authored with David Preston, David Silbey, and Anthony Carlson. Other books include *Waging War: Conflict, Culture, and Innovation in World History* (Oxford, 2016); *Barbarians and Brothers: Anglo-American Warfare, 1500–1865* (Oxford, 2011); and *Crowds and Soldiers in Revolutionary North Carolina* (Florida, 2001). In addition, he has edited two volumes on world military history (both 2011, one is now in a 2020 second edition) and has published many articles and book chapters on subjects ranging from the American Revolution to Native American warfare to Ottoman fortifications to Mongol conquest methods. He is currently working on a world history of making "conquest" stick. He has an additional career as an archaeologist, having done field work in Greece, Albania, Hungary, Croatia, and Virginia, including co-directing two field projects. He was a principal author and a co-editor of *Light and Shadow: Isolation and Interaction in the Shala Valley of Northern Albania,* winner of the 2014 Society for American Archaeology's book award. In 2015/16 he held the Harold K. Johnson Visiting Chair of Military History at the U.S. Army War College, and in 2021/22 he was the Colin S. Gray Visiting Chair of Strategic Studies at the U.S. Air Force's School of Advanced Air and Space Studies.

Eve Massingham
is a Senior Research Fellow with the School of Law, The University of Queensland. Eve's current research focuses on the diverse ways in which the law constrains or enables autonomous functions of military platforms, systems and weapons. She is the co-editor of *Ensuring Respect for International Humanitarian Law* (Routledge, 2020) and she has published a number of book chapters and journal articles in the fields of international humanitarian law and international law and the use of force. Prior to joining the University of Queensland, Eve worked for the International Red Cross and Red Cross Movement for ten years, including as the International Committee of the Red Cross' Regional Legal Adviser for East Africa and as an International Humanitarian Law officer for Australian Red Cross. She was Associate to Justice Collier at the Federal Court of Australia and has also served as an Australian Army Reserve Officer. Eve holds a Bachelor of Law (Hons) from Queensland University of Technology, a Master of International and Community Development from Deakin University, an LLM (Distinction) from King's College London and a PhD from the University of Queensland.

Kenneth Wyne Mutuma
is a senior lecturer at the University of Nairobi, School of Law. He has more than ten years teaching experience and lends his knowledge and experience in IHL

to academia, government and civil society in both East and Southern Africa. Kenneth has previously served as a legal officer for the Nairobi and Pretoria Delegations of the International Committee of the Red Cross. In addition, he has worked with the Nelson Mandela Foundation developing the capacity of governmental bodies and civil society in the areas of conflict resolution and ethical leadership. Kenneth holds several academic qualifications including a PhD on the challenges of outsourcing war to private entities. He also serves as the editor of the *Eastern Africa Journal on International Humanitarian Law*.

Zuzana Špicová
(Charles University, Prague) is a scholar of Sanskrit narratives, especially the *Mahābhārata*. In her Ph.D. thesis, "'For Bhīṣma's Destruction': Ambā, Śikhaṇḍinī and Śikhaṇḍin in the *Mahābhārata*", she presented a narratological analysis of the narratives concerning Bhīṣma's death and the complex characters who can be seen as his killers, and argued that evaluating subjective narrators is crucial for understanding the *Mahābhārata*. In her research, she applies current narratological and comparative approaches to both ancient and modern texts. She is predominantly interested in narratives about the warrior class, in autobiographical narratives and narrators, and in the possibilities of analysing ancient texts through the lens of rhetorical narratology. She also translates from Sanskrit and Bangla into Czech: she has translated some works of Śaratcandra Caṭṭopādhyāẏ, most notably *Debdās*, and is currently working on translating a couple of episodes from the *Mahābhārata*.

Introduction

Samuel Camden Duckett White

These volumes find their origin in a rather odd place. On one unexceptional evening, I was watching the HBO show, *Vikings*. The eponymously named show follows the mythic origins of Scandinavian raiders, who as they expand to find new land and new resources, come up against 'civilised' European society. For the most part, these Scandinavian men and women maintain their culture of warbands, raiding and looting. Yet, some do not – Rollo becomes a Francophile, adopting the culture and the warfighting of the Franks in return for land and titles. This is all to say that after a few seasons of slowly less and less violence, by the time we come across a scene where a warband of Vikings defile and destroy a small French homestead, we are reminded of the brutality of the times. Outraged that these raiders would do such a thing to innocent peasants, I said to myself 'surely that was a war crime even under Viking law'.

This mini-series started in trying to address the question of Viking laws of war. It then grew to address a wider question: how international is international humanitarian law? The start of the answer can be found in *The Laws of Yesterday's Wars: From Indigenous Australians to the American Civil War*.[1] This Volume (Volume 1) approached the laws of yesterday's wars from a wide cross-section of history and culture, in an aim to find any common ground. Evidently, the concept of 'law' will change from culture to culture. In some cultures, the customs were codified; in others, they remained oral. Yet in all they were binding.

So what were the results from Volume 1? How international is international humanitarian law? The answer, as all good legal ones seem to be, is that it depends. The laws of war as codified in the *Geneva Conventions* demonstrate an intellectual history based in Europe. Yet it is clear that societies generally have sought to regulation conduct in war. To this end, international humanitarian law is very much international. The clearest example of this are the laws of war of First Nations Australians and the Mexica. These two cultures had no linkages to Europe until their clash of civilisations, where the norms that had evolved in the non-European nations were found to be incompatible on the battlefield with the lethality of European methods and customs of war.

1 (Brill Nijhoff, 2021).

 | DOI:10.1163/9789004473218_002

This 'inevitable' colonial expansion seems to have influenced legal historical thinking. In the 8th Edition of *Brownlie's Principles*, there is a paragraph that reads:

> In terms of intellectual history international law was thus European in history. Thence it travelled with the colonizers to the Americas, to Asia, to Africa and eventually to Oceania.[2]

There is a lot to unpack in these two sentences.

The idea that international law was European (and, within this concept, Northern European) in history flies in the face of continents occupied by sovereign nations – such as pre-colonial Australia or pre-Columbus North America. The earlier was discussed in Volume 1,[3] and the latter in this Volume.

The argument in *Brownlie's Principles* falls prey to the 'straight line history of eternal progression',[4] where a Great White Man (Grotius, Vitoria, Augustine) discovered international law and it was developed progressively into the modern era. For many parts of European law, this is without a doubt correct – see the progression of Roman,[5] Medieval,[6] and Renaissance[7] laws of war in this Series. But it is clear that, outside of Europe, intricate and detailed customs of war existed that perfectly reflected the environment that they evolved in. The cultural norms and customs that developed in many communities outside of Europe actually reflect a more nuanced approach to mitigating war's effects than the customs and codes developed in Europe.

The hope for this work is to demonstrate a history of international law outside the usual confines of its 'development' by Europeans and its later 'contributions'. Anna's Chapter on traditional Japanese laws of war is particularly pointed, noting many of the cultural norms lost in the post-isolationist reforms

2 Ian Brownlie and James Crawford, *Brownlie's Principles of Public International Law* (8th edn, Oxford University Press, 2012) 4.

3 Ray Kerkhove & Samuel White, 'Indigenous Australian Laws of War' in Samuel White (ed.) *Laws of Yesterday's Wars* (Brill Nijhoff, 2021) 1–36.

4 Alonso Dunkelberg, 'It's a Trap! Re-Thinking Samuel Moyn's *Humane* Beyond the North Atlantic' (2021) 12 *Journal of International Humanitarian Legal Studies* 345–360.

5 Samuel White, 'Roman Laws of War' in in Samuel White (ed.) *Laws of Yesterday's Wars: Volume II* (Brill Nijhoff, 2021).

6 Samuel White 'The Late Middle Ages' in Samuel White (ed.) *Laws of Yesterday's Wars* (Brill Nijhoff, 2021) 101–127.

7 Kyle Walker, 'The Renaissance' in Samuel White (ed.) *Laws of Yesterday's Wars* (Brill Nijhoff, 2021) 127–150.

of the 18th century. Specifically, utilising the European laws of war were a way that Japan could protect itself by claiming quasi-Western statehood status.

Fukuzawa Yukichi, in his 1875 *Outline of the Theory of Civilization,* encouraged Japan to embrace 'European civilization' not because of its superiority but as a means to an end. Indeed, European culture had 'many defects' including the fact that 'war is the worst thing in this world but Western states always go to war'.[8] It was for this reason that Japanese law professors were embedded with Imperial troops, and reports were published in English[9] and French.[10] This form of lawfare was perhaps clearest in the words of Professor Ariga Nagao, legal embed with the Imperial Army:

> The Chinese, from the point of view of the [European] laws of war, can be compared to the Turks, the Arabs, the Red Skins. However, the Japanese Empire, in its war against one such nation, sought to comply with the laws of war that it would have followed with regards to France, England or Germany. But without sacrificing its military interests. Therefore, in my opinion, it is of great scientific interest to examine to what degree and through which procedures could it put these laws in practice. In fact, the Japanese nation is not the only one that, possessing a civilized army, can find itself in the necessity to engage in hostilities against a Far East people, not used to the customs of war. In the future, a European or American power may find itself in the same situation and then, the precedent of Japan in 1894–1895 will certainly be of great use.[11]

Here, Japan has rejected its pre-European laws of war and adopted those of Europe as a security measure, cementing its 'civilised' status. Yet the claim by Professor Nagao that the cultures of the Far East were not used to the customs of war is curious (particularly noting the Code of Bushido). As Dr Špicová's novel and ground-breaking Chapter demonstrates, there is a demonstrable history in the 'Far East' of customs of war. Indeed, outside of the analysis of the Australian continent, the *Mahābhārata* represents some of the earliest written works on the laws of war.

---

8 Susumu Yamauchi, 'Civilization and International Law in Japan During the Meiji Era' (1868–1912) (1996) 24 *Hitotsubashi Journal of Law and Politics* 7.

9 Sakuye Takahasi, *Cases on International Law during the Chino-Japanese War* (1899).

10 Ariga Nagao, *La Guerre Sino-Japonaise Au Point de Vue Du Droit International, Par Nagao Ariga* (1896).

11 Ibid, 9.

This work respresents the own views of the authors and should not be associated with any affiliate organisations. It is a work of legal analysis in so much as it is a work of legal history. Any errors, therefore, I am happy to say are ours alone and are always grateful for being raised. There are additional Volumes of this work that are planned for the near future, and it is hoped that each Volume adds to the breadth and depth of analysis that can occur in this field. For those that are reading this, if you wish to contribute to this Series, you are always welcomed. For those who do not find themselves in a position to contribute, then I hope you enjoy the scholarship of those who have.

CHAPTER 1

Ancient Indian Laws of War

Zuzana Špicová

1 Introduction

Warfare of ancient India is a very broad and rich subject. Our introduction to ancient Indian laws of warfare will be based on the most famous and influential sources which share a set of concepts (such as *dharma*[1]), thoughts and beliefs (such as *karman*[2] and the existence of heavens and hells), and depict a society which is divided into four basic classes or *varṇas*: *brāhmaṇas* (priests, intellectuals), *kṣatriyas* (rulers, warriors), *vaiśyas* (farmers, merchants) and *śūdras* (labourers). Men belonging to these *varṇas* have their specific laws, rules and obligations – specific *dharmas*. For this chapter, the most important are the *kṣatriyadharma*, a set of rules for the warrior *varṇa*, and the *rājadharma*, a set of rules specifically for kings.

There are various literary sources dealing with ancient Indian warfare and these two sets of *dharmas*: prescriptive lawbooks, such as Manu's *Dharmaśāstra*,[3] textbooks on economy and politics, such as Kauṭilya's

1 *Dharma* is notoriously difficult to translate but in this paper, it can be translated as 'law', 'religion', 'duty' and 'justice'. This paper is only concerned with the laws of wars in the Hindu tradition, and *dharma* will therefore be only considered from the Hindu point of view.

2 *Karman* literally means 'an act'. Very simply put, the *karman* law says that every act of a being will inevitably bear certain fruits in this life and/or in the next one.

3 *Dharmaśāstras* and *dharmasūtras* are prescriptive lawbooks dealing with a variety of subjects, from punishments for theft to duties of men from different *varṇas* to military laws. The most prominent of them is supposedly the *Mānavadharmaśāstra* or *Manusmṛti* (probably between third and fifth century AD). For more on the *Mānavadharmaśāstra* and its position in the *dharmaśāstra* literature, see Olivelle's Introduction to his translation of the *Mānavadharmaśāstra* (*Manu's Code of Law: a critical edition and translation of the Mānava-Dharmaśāstra*. Edited and translated by Patrick Olivelle, with the editorial assistance of Suman Olivelle. New York: Oxford University Press, 2005: 3–70), and for more on the *dharmasūtras*, see Olivelle's Introduction to his translation of the *dharmasūtras* (*Dharmasūtras the law codes of Āpastamba, Gautama, Baudhāyana, and Vasiṣṭha*. Edited and translated by Patrick Olivelle. Oxford: Oxford University Press, 1999: xxi–xliii).

 | DOI:10.1163/9789004473218_003

Arthaśāstra,[4] or on military education – *Dhanurvedas*,[5] and works of literature, most notably the *Mahābhārata*[6] and the *Rāmāyaṇa*[7] which contain prescriptive parts as well as narrative parts that show us how the authors presented military operations, laws and breaches of them. Wars were also depicted or mentioned in the preceding Vedic literature,[8] several *purāṇas*[9] and other works of narrative literature of ancient India, not to mention travelogues and

4 The *Arthaśāstra* of Kauṭilya (also known as Cāṇakya or Viṣṇugupta) is a treatise on politics, economy, warfare and other subjects, and had a great influence on later literature which often quotes it. See Olivelle's Introduction to his translation of the *Arthaśāstra* (*King, Governance, and Law in Ancient India. Kauṭilya's* Arthaśāstra. Translated by Patrick Olivelle. New York: Oxford University Press, 2013: 1–60), and Brekke, Torkel. "Wielding the Rod of Punishment – War and Violence in the Political Science of Kautilya." In Torkel Brekke (ed.). *The Ethics of War in Asian Civilization: A Comparative Perspective*. Oxon, UK: Routledge, 2006.

5 *Dhanurveda*, literally 'science of archery', is a literary genre dealing with warfare – from the rules of making a good bow to training of a warrior to military strategy. One of the most famous extant *dhanurvedas* is *Vasiṣṭha's Dhanurveda* which is relatively late (seventeenth century), and there are also *dhanurveda* parts in some *purāṇas*, e.g. in the *Agnipurāṇa* (249–250). For an overview of the *dhanurveda* literature, see Chakravarti, P. C. *The Art of War in Ancient India*. Ramna, Dacca: The University of Dacca, 1941: IX–XI.

6 The *Mahābhārata* is a lengthy ancient Sanskrit text which contains (among other things) narrative parts, especially the story of the fight between the Pāṇḍavas (the 'heroes') and the Kauravas (the 'villains'), and prescriptive parts, especially the discourses of the grandfather and patriarch of the Kaurava clan, Bhīṣma, in the twelfth and thirteenth books of it. The *Mahābhārata* chiefly focuses on *kṣatriyas*, and is therefore an amazing source of both prescriptive and descriptive information on the warrior *varṇa*. For this reason, most of the literary examples of the rules of wars, breaches of them and its consequences will be drawn from the *Mahābhārata*.

7 The *Rāmāyaṇa* is an ancient Sanskrit text, mostly narrative, about the king Rāma whose wife Sītā was kidnapped by a demon king Rāvaṇa. Similarly to the *Mahābhārata*, the *Rāmāyaṇa* focuses on the *kṣatriya varṇa*, but the fights depicted in it are often of a different kind: in the *Mahābhārata*, there are mostly battles on an open field and duels between noble chariot fighters, but in the *Rāmāyaṇa*, the main battle is a siege of Laṅkā, and the warriors are chiefly monkeys–who are using nails, rocks and trees as their weapons–on Rāma's side, and demons (*rākṣasas*) who often heavily rely on magical tricks, on Rāvaṇa's side.

8 Especially the oldest one, the *Ṛgveda*, contains information about several battles, and the youngest, the *Atharvaveda*, as well. For an overview of the wars depicted in the *Ṛgveda*, see e.g. Thapliyal, Uma Prasad. *Wars and War-Tactics in Ancient India*. Manohar: Routledge, 2021: 18–19.

9 *Purāṇas* are texts later than the *Mahābhārata* and the *Rāmāyaṇa*, and are often dubbed 'encyclopaedias of Hinduism' as they contain not only various stories, but also prescriptive parts about a gamut of topics, including warfare.

reports of foreign visitors and pilgrims.[10] Some information can also be drawn from inscriptions of Indian kings.[11]

These sources are of different dates spanning three millenia,[12] their authors (about whom we usually know very little anyway) were of different backgrounds and pursued different goals. For instance, Kauṭilya (traditionally considered a *brāhmaṇa* author) is visibly detached from the real battlefield and much more interested in subtleties of strategy and defeating the enemy with any means necessary, while Bhīṣma[13] in his dialogue to Yudhiṣṭhira in the twelfth and thirteenth books of the *Mahābhārata* shows signs of a *kṣatriya* author combining prescriptive laws with his own experience from the battlefield, and *Vasiṣṭha's Dhanurveda* focuses mostly on the education and training

10 Alexander's Indian campaign, and therefore Indian warfare in general, are mentioned in several Greek and Roman sources, including Arrian's *Indica* or Curtius's *Historiae Alexandri Magni.* The few extant parts of Megasthenes's *Indika* inform us about life in the Mauryan times. Generally speaking, historical battles between Indian and Greek armies are better documented than between any two Indian armies of that time. There are also Chinese sources, especially the Buddhist pilgrims Faxian and Xuanzang, but they mostly focus on other things than warfare.

11 There are inscriptions of various kings, beginning with Aśoka, informing us, among other things, about the wars they won and the extent of their kingdoms.

12 For a historical overview of the sources and the norms of war in Hinduism in general, see Roy, Kaushik. "Norms of War in Hinduism." In Vesselin Popovski, Gregory Reichberg and Nicholas Turner (eds.). *World Religions and Norms of War.* Tokyo: United Nations University Press, 2009, pp. 30–59, and for narratives about violence in Hinduism, see Patton, Laurie. "Telling Stories about Harm: an Overview of Early Indian Narratives." In J. R. Hinnells and R. King (eds.). *Religion and Violence in South Asia: Theory and Practice.* New York: Routledge, 2007, pp. 10–38. For an introduction to violence in Buddhism, see Deegalle, Mahinda. "Norms of War in Theravada Buddhism." In Vesselin Popovski, Gregory Reichberg and Nicholas Turner (eds.). *World Religions and Norms of War.* Tokyo: United Nations University Press, 2009, pp. 30–59, and Gethin, Rupert. "Buddhist Monks, Buddhist Kings, Buddhist Violence: on the Early Buddhist Attitudes to Violence." In J. R. Hinnells and R. King (eds.). *Religion and Violence in South Asia: Theory and Practice.* New York: Routledge, 2007, pp. 59–78, and in Jainism, see Dundas, Paul. "The Non-Violence of Violence: Jain Perspectives on Warfare, Asceticism and Worship." In J. R. Hinnells and R. King (eds.). *Religion and Violence in South Asia: Theory and Practice.* New York: Routledge, 2007, pp. 39–58.

13 Bhīṣma is a character of the *Mahābhārata* and not a 'real' author, but inside the text, he represents a specific view on the *kṣatriyadharma*, and his teachings in the twelfth and thirteenth books of the *Mahābhārata* are highly influential and in accordance with the implied author of the text. There are other characters who present distinctly different views on these matters. For this reason, I will distinguish between the voices of characters when presenting certain laws, especially in the *Mahābhārata* and the *Rāmāyaṇa*.

of a warrior more than on general strategy or conveying his own battlefield experience. There is also often a considerable difference between the sources in terms of prohibited weapons or conducts: one source may completely forbid something (the *dharmaśāstras* and *dharmasūtras*), another one allow it when absolutely necessary (some of the prescriptive parts of the *Mahābhārata*) and yet another one recommend it as a great strategic advantage (Kauṭilya's *Arthaśāstra, Agnipurāṇa*). There were apparently two major streams of military advice, one more idealistic and focusing on just war, and the other one more practical, focused on winning by any means, and it can often be observed how these two streams interrelated in the narrative portions of the texts, especially the *Mahābhārata*.

II Methods and Means of Warfare

Ancient Indian Army

Ancient Indian armies should, at least theoretically, consist only of male *kṣatriyas* of appropriate age. As other *varṇas* have different duties, they should not fight: it is especially noted about *brāhmaṇas*.[14] Even though this was the ideal situation, theoretical works also count with other types of soldiers. Apart from a small army of hereditary (*maula*) *kṣatriya* warriors which Kauṭilya[15] strongly recommends to have, mercenaries (*bhṛta*) are mentioned, corporate troops (*śreṇi*), troops provided by an ally (*suhṛd*), troops captured or won from the enemy (*dviṣad*) and those provided by a tribal chief (*āṭavika*).[16] From these types of troops, it is obvious that other classes were also employed in the army.[17]

Even a *brāhmaṇa* could become a warrior if he was not able to support himself with the occupations prescribed for him. Manu sums it up thus:

14 E.g. in *Mahābhārata* 1.11.12–15. All references are to the Pune Critical Edition (*Mahābhārata: Critical Edition. 24 vols. With Harivaṃśa*. Edited by Vishnu S. Sukthankar, et al. Poona: Bhandarkar Oriental Research Institute, 1933–1970). I used the Critical Edition and John D. Smith's online searchable version: https://bombay.indology.info/mahabharata/welcome.html.

15 *Arthaśāstra* (*The Kauṭilīya Arthaśāstra*. Edited by R. P. Kangle. Bombay: University of Bombay, 1960) 7.8.27 and 9.2. For translation, see Olivelle 2013: 301 and 352–354.

16 For an overview of these types see also Chakravarti 1941: 2–10.

17 Even *śūdras* are explicitly allowed to fight if in trouble, and people residing in the king's country should also help him in battle according to the *Agnipurāṇa* 249.8. See also Chakravarti 1941: 81.

> *ajīvaṃs tu yathoktena brāhmaṇaḥ svena karmaṇā|*
> *jīvet kṣatriyadharmeṇa sa hy asya praty anantaraḥ||*
> *ubhābhyām apy ajīvaṃs tu kathaṃ syād iti ced bhavet|*
> *kṛṣigorakṣam āsthāya jīved vaiśyasya jīvikām||*
>
> When a Brahmin is unable to earn a living by means of the activities specific to him given above, he may live by means of the Kṣatriya Law, for the latter is the one right below him. If it be asked: what happens if he is unable to earn a living by either of these two means? Taking up agriculture or cattle-herding, he should earn a living by the occupation of a Vaiśya.[18]

There are also many examples of famous *brāhmaṇa* warriors in literature (Rāma Jāmadagnya, Droṇa, Aśvatthāman) and in history (e.g. Puṣyamitra Śuṅga, a king and a former general of the Mauryas).[19] As *brāhmaṇas* should not fight and *kṣatriyas* should not kill them, this situation is often pondered as a crucial ethical question by the *kṣatriya* characters of the *Mahābhārata* (see Protected people).

Generally speaking, ancient Indian army was fourfold (*caturaṅga*): it contained infantry, cavalry, chariots, and elephants. According to the *Mahābhārata,* the smallest unit of an army was a *patthi* which comprised of one chariot, one elephant, three cavalrymen and five footmen, and the largest, an *akṣauhiṇī,* 21 870 chariots, the same number of elephants, 65 610 cavalrymen and 109 350 footmen.[20] Apart from these forces, it is recommended to also have a very wide net of spies and a lot of money when one wants to start a war.

Infantry, which was numerically the largest part of the ancient Indian army, was shown as relatively unimportant in the narrative portions of literature which focus almost exclusively on individual heroes, mostly chariot fighters, who are able to slay hosts of unnamed footsoldiers, and even authors of textbooks on warfare sometimes considered infantry uninteresting.[21] Kauṭilya describes the tasks for cavalry, elephants and chariots (adding also the tasks for a crown prince and labour corps) in detail, but for infantry, he only mentions

18 *Mānavadharmaśāstra* 10.81–82, translation by Olivelle 2005: 212. The same is proposed by Bhīṣma in the *Mahābhārata* 12.79.2.

19 Chakravarti 1941: 79–80 gives a list of famous *brāhmaṇa* generals, similarly also Ramachandra Dikshitar, V. R. *War in Ancient India*. Madras, Bombay, Calcutta, London: Macmillan and Co., 1944: 194–195.

20 *Mahābhārata* 1.2.15–23.

21 For an overview, see Chakravarti 1944: 16–17.

"carrying weapons in all places and times, and engaging in military exercises."[22] On the other hand, some sources – such as Puṣkara in the *Agnipurāṇa* – claim that it is strong infantry which ensures victory.[23] Cavalry also does not have a prominent position in the narrative portions of the *Mahābhārata* and the *Rāmāyaṇa,* but it was an important part of the ancient Indian army nevertheless, prized especially for its swiftness. War elephants were often dealt with in detail, especially their capture and training.[24] They were considered to be a great advantage but they could also become a huge problem in battle if they turned back and destroyed one's own army instead of the enemy's.

Chariots, on the other hand, were seen as extremely important in older times, and the *Mahābhārata* focuses almost exclusively on fights between heroes fighting on chariots and on presenting strategy connected to them. There are various options for a single chariot, but the most basic one is a single warrior shooting arrows and a single charioteer – this is the picture we get from the *Mahābhārata.* Gradually, chariots seem to have fallen into disuse in real fights but their importance in Indian thought and imagery remained high even then.[25] Chariots were eventually exchanged for ships in the fourfold system.

Just and Unjust War

What makes a war just in ancient Indian context? Theoretical literature is not concerned much with the just/unjust causes of a war. The *maṇḍala* (circle) system of neighbouring kings, as presented by Kauṭilya,[26] has the king as the *vijigīṣu* – desiring for a conquest – in the centre, so the main premise seems to be that a king who is powerful enough should always seek to enhance his kingdom. On the other hand, the main heroes of the narrative literature always have an explicitly just cause for their wars (typically to rid the earth of terrible demons), or at least a good explanation of them.[27]

---

22 The tasks are presented in 10.4.13–18, translation by Olivelle 2013: 381–382.

23 *Agnipurāṇa* 228.7.

24 See e.g. *Arthaśāstra* 2.2.6–16, translation in Olivelle 2013: 102.

25 For the evidence of the gradual fall into disuse, see Chakravarti 1941: 26–27.

26 For the basics of this system, see the sixth book of the *Arthaśāstra*, English translation in Olivelle 2013: 271–276. This system is also mentioned in the *Mānavadharmaśāstra* 7.154, *Agnipurāṇa* 233.14–20 and other literature, and used in the narrative literature.

27 For the just causes of the war in the *Rāmāyaṇa*, see Balkaran, Raj, and A. Walter Dorn. "Violence in the "Vālmīki Rāmāyaṇa": Just War Criteria in an Ancient Indian Epic." *Journal of the American Academy of Religion,* September 2012, Vol. 18, No. 3. Oxford University Press, 2012, pp. 659–690, especially pp. 664–667, and in the *Mahābhārata*, see Allen, Nick. "Just War in the Mahābhārata." In R. Sorabji and D. Rodin (eds.). *The Ethics of War: Shared*

A just war, *dharmayuddha*, is more about the means of warfare than about the causes of a battle. The most important underlying rule of ancient Indian warfare is the idea of fairness. This works on the level of kings and their armies as well as on the level of individual warriors. Fairness is one of the first principles the armies of the Kauravas and the Pāṇḍavas agreed upon before the great battle in the *Mahābhārata*:[28] if there is a verbal attack, one should respond with a verbal attack, chariots should only fight against chariots, elephants against elephants, cavalrymen against cavalrymen and footsoldiers against footsoldiers. One should also always fight against those who are equal to him in strength and age, and after properly challenging them first. These rules are repeated in the prescriptive portions by Bhīṣma as well: on a battlefield, a single warrior should always fight only against another single warrior, a chariot fighter against a chariot fighter, an army against an army, and one should never fight against a different type of a warrior: a cavalryman should never fight against a chariot fighter and so on.[29]

According to Bhīṣma in the *Mahābhārata*, a king should always fight justly, in accordance to *dharma*, and only when his opponent fights deceitfully or uses cunning methods, one can retaliate in kind.[30] The sense of fairness is paradoxically one of the most common excuses to fight against someone unfairly: if your opponent uses unfair measures, you can do the same, if he uses illusion, he should be killed with illusion,[31] and when one side fights unfairly, it justifies the other side to fight unfairly as well. On the other hand, it is also noted that even a deceitful king should be defeated fairly, if possible, and that a fair death is considered to be better than an unfair victory.[32]

A just war, battle or duel should always be properly announced to the enemy. According to Bhīṣma in the *Mahābhārata*, a warrior should always give a fair warning to his enemy in a duel,[33] and when a king attacks another (presumably kingless) country, he should announce that he is their king and will protect the

Problems in Different Traditions. Hants: Ashgate Publishing Limited, pp. 138–149. For just war in Hinduism in general, see Subedi, Surya P. "The Concept in Hinduism of 'Just War'". *Journal of Conflict & Security Law*, October 2003, Vol. 8, No. 2. Oxford University Press, 2003, pp. 339–361, or Brekke, Torkel. "The Ethics of War and the Concept of War in India and Europe." *Numen*, 2005, Vol. 52, No. 1, Religion and Violence. Brill, 2005, pp. 59–86...

28 The rules are laid down in *Mahābhārata* 6.1.26–34.

29 *Mahābhārata* 12.96.7–10.

30 *Mahābhārata* 12.96.9; 12.101.4–5.

31 E.g. Kṛṣṇa to Yudhiṣṭhira, *Mahābhārata* 9.30.6–14 who also reminds him that even the gods used special means to kill various demons.

32 *Mahābhārata* 12.96.16.

33 *Mahābhārata* 12.96.7c.

subjects of that country, and ask them to either give him a tribute, or to meet him in battle.[34] Challenging someone is repeated again and again throughout the narrative portions, and there are some repeating *formulae* used for it. Not to accept such a challenge is very rare and the hero who does so usually has a good explanation, such as a preceding vow to engage in a duel with someone else, or a claim that he cannot fight against the challenging hero because of his status. Giving a fair warning before attacking someone's city is shown consistently throughout the *Mahābhārata* without any special commentaries, so it seems to be a completely commonplace event.

A fair warning is obviously a problem when there is a need for a surprise attack. If a war is properly announced, Kauṭilya calls it an open war, and gives two other options – a covert war and a silent war – without any moral judgement:

> *prakāśayuddhaṃ nirdiṣṭe deśe kāle ca vikramaḥ|*
> *vibhīṣaṇam avaskandaḥ pramādavyasanārdanam||*
> *ekatra tyāgaghātau ca kūṭayuddhasya mātṛkā|*
> *yogagūḍhopajāpārthaṃ tūṣṇīṃ yuddhasya lakṣaṇam||*
>
> Attacking at an announced place and time is open war. Causing fright, surprise attack, striking during carelessness or calamity, and withdrawing and charging at the same place are the kinds of covert war. Employing secret measures and instigations through clandestine operatives are the marks of silent war.[35]

What is here translated as a 'covert war', *kūṭayuddha*, can also be translated as a treacherous war, and it is dealt with moral objections as the very opposite of *dharmayuddha* in other literature. Even when the heroes in the narrative portions are explicitly said to be just, stratagems are often used by them, and they are even advised to fight in such a way.[36] Kṛṣṇa explicitly tells Yudhiṣṭhira – who is the son of the god Dharma – to put *dharma* aside to win[37] and counsels him to lie, otherwise his army will be destroyed.[38] Even in the *Agnipurāṇa*,

34 *Mahābhārata* 12.96.2.

35 *Arthaśāstra* 7.6.40–41, translation by Olivelle 2013: 296.

36 Among other examples see e.g. the advice given in *Mahābhārata* 7.155.28 or 7.164.67–70.

37 *Mahābhārata* 7.164.68.

38 This is when Yudhiṣṭhira has to lie to be able to defeat his teacher Droṇa in *Mahābhārata* 7.164.98–99. It should be noted that this lie is explicitly condemned in the text: as a result of the lie, Yudhiṣṭhira's chariot, which used to hover over the ground, falls, and he also has to spend some time in hell because of that.

Rāma uses the same terms as Kauṭilya and advises to only have an open war when one is strong, and a covert or treacherous war in other circumstances.[39]

Strategies and Battles

It is the primary duty of male *kṣatriyas* to fight. It is often recognised – mostly by *kṣatriya* characters themselves – as a difficult and cruel duty[40] but, on the other hand, as necessary and ultimately good because *kṣatriyas*, and especially kings, must protect their subjects, punish the sinful and protect those who are good. This is noted in virtually every work dealing with kingship or *kṣatriyas* in general, e.g. by Manu:

> *yathoddharati nirdātā kakṣaṃ dhānyaṃ ca rakṣati|*
> *tathā rakṣen nṛpo rāṣṭraṃ hanyāc ca paripanthinaḥ||*

> As a weeder plucks the weeds and protects the corn, so the king should protect his realm and kill his adversaries.[41]

A *kṣatriya* king should never avoid war when he needs to protect his subjects. On the other hand, even though a *kṣatriya* king's highest duty was to protect his subjects, he was always advised to avoid war, if possible. In the words of Manu:

> *sāmnā dānena bhedena samastair athavā pṛthak|*
> *vijetuṃ prayatetārīn na yuddhena kadā cana||*
> *anityo vijayo yasmād dṛśyate yudhyamānayoḥ|*
> *parājayaś ca saṃgrāme tasmād yuddhaṃ vivarjayet||*
> *trayāṇām apy upāyānāṃ pūrvoktānām parikṣaye|*
> *tathā yudhyeta saṃyatto vijayeta ripūn yathā||*

> He should strive to triumph over his enemies through conciliation, gifts, and fomenting dissension, employed collectively or separately, but never through war. Victory and defeat in battle are uncertain for the two combatants; he should, therefore, avoid war. When the aforementioned three

39 *Agnipurāṇa* 242.13.

40 E.g. by Yudhiṣṭhira in the *Mahābhārata* 12.98.1.

41 *Mānavadharmaśāstra* 7.110, translation by Olivelle 2005: 160. Similar quotes about the *kṣatriyas* and kings having protection of their subjects as their highest law can be found in almost every source several times.

> strategies fail, then let him, always on guard, pursue war in such a manner that he will triumph over his enemies.[42]

The importance of trying to avoid war is stressed in the narrative literature as well. Almost the whole fifth book of the *Mahābhārata* is devoted to the exchange of envoys as the Pāṇḍavas (the heroes) are trying to avoid war with the Kauravas, and there are even discussions among the Kauravas in which many of them are trying to argue for peace. A king should always try to deal with the enemy using the three strategies (conciliation, gifts and dissension), and only if these fail, he should cautiously go to war.[43] On these strategies, Kauṭilya writes:

> *grāmāraṇyopajīvivrajavaṇikpathānupālanam ujjhitāpasṛtāpakāriṇāṃ cārpaṇam iti sāntvam ācaret*||
> *bhūmidravyakanyādānam abhayasya ceti dānam ācaret*||
> *sāmantāṭavikatatkulīnāparuddhānām anyatamopagraheṇa kośadaṇḍabhūmidāyayācanam iti bhedam ācaret*||
> *prakāśakūṭatūṣṇīṃ yuddhadurgalambhopāyair amitrapragrahaṇam iti daṇḍam ācaret*||

> Protecting people living in villages and wild tracts; protecting herd stations and trade routes; handing over those who have been jettisoned, who have deserted, and who have committed hostile acts—that is how he should practice conciliation. Giving land and property; giving girls in marriage; and giving safety—that is how he should practice gift-giving. Demanding treasure, troops, land, and inheritance by supporting a neighbor, a tribal chief, a pretender from the royal family, or a prince in disfavor—that is how he should practice dissension. Attacking the enemy by open, covert, and silent warfare, and through the employment of the means for capturing a fort —that is how he should practice warfare.[44]

When war is inevitable, a sixfold strategy is universally advised:

> *saṃdhiṃ ca vigrahaṃ caiva yānam āsanam eva ca*|
> *dvaidhībhāvaṃ saṃśrayaṃ ca ṣaḍguṇāṃś cintayet sadā*||

42 *Mānavadharmaśāstra* 7.198–200, translation by Olivelle 2005: 164.

43 E.g in *Mānavadharmaśāstra* 7.198–200.

44 *Arthaśāstra* 7.16.5–8, translation by Olivelle 2013: 321. Manu similarly notes that the three strategies should be tried before using military force, in *Mānavadharmaśāstra* 7.107–109.

> He should constantly think about the sixfold strategy: forging alliances, waging war, marching into battle, remaining stationary, pursuing a double stratagem, and seeking asylum.[45]

The *Mahābhārata* shows us the way a battle in the open field was conducted (or, at least, imagined to have been conducted by the authors). Apart from the main battle between the Kauravas and the Pāṇḍavas at Kurukṣetra, there are various other battles and duels, and they are predominantly fought on open fields as well. Even when one would expect a siege, the enemy king usually leaves the city and meets the hero on an open field. Such is the case of Arjuna's son Babhruvāhana[46] or the Magadha king Jarāsaṃdha.[47] The general idea of this type of battle is that the non-combatant subjects should be harassed as little as possible when *kṣatriyas* fight.[48] The king usually comes out of the city either with his army or alone, fighting against the enemy's army in a battle or with the enemy king himself in a duel.

If the king refuses to leave his city, a siege is necessary. For this eventuality, Manu recommends:

uparudhyārim āsīta rāṣṭraṃ cāsyopapīḍayet|
dūṣayec cāsya satataṃ yavasānnodakendhanam||
bhindyāc caiva taḍāgāni prākāraparikhās tathā|
samavaskandayec cainaṃ rātrau vitrāsayet tathā||
upajapyān upajaped budhyetaiva ca tatkṛtam|
yukte ca daive yudhyeta jayaprepsur apetabhīḥ||

45 *Mānavadharmaśāstra* 7.160, translation by Olivelle 2005: 162–163. The discourse on the sixfold strategy continues here till 7.180. See also *Arthaśāstra*, especially 7.1.2, but the whole seventh chapter of the *Arthaśāstra* deals with the sixfold strategy.

46 This story can be found in *Mahābhārata* 14.78–82.

47 This story can be found in *Mahābhārata* 2.13–22.

48 This is corroborated by the Greek ambassador Megasthenes in the first fragment of the *Indika*. Megasthenes observed that "for whereas among other nations it is usual, in the contests of war, to ravage the soil, and thus to reduce it to an uncultivated waste, among the Indians, on the contrary, by whom husbandmen are regarded as a class that is sacred and inviolable, the tillers of the soil, even when battle is raging in their neighbourhood, are undisturbed by any sense of danger, for the combatants on either side in waging the conflict make carnage of each other, but allow those engaged in husbandry to remain quite unmolested. Besides, they neither ravage an enemy's land with fire, nor cut down its trees." In McCrindle, J. W. *Ancient India as Described by Megasthenês and Arrian; Being a Translation of the Fragments of the Indika of Megasthenês Collected by Dr. Schwanbeck, and of the First Part of the Indika of Arrian*. London: Trübner & Co, 1877: 33.

> After laying siege to the enemy, he shall remain stationary—he should plunder his realm; constantly ruin his supplies of fodder, food, water, and fuel; demolish reservoirs, ramparts, and moats; launch surprise assaults against him; frighten him at night; forment sedition among the seditious; keep close watch over enemy activity; and when omens are propitious, fearlessly launch the attack with the determination to win.[49]

This type of battle is shown in the *Rāmāyaṇa*: a siege of the city of Laṅkā. This battle is mostly fought with infantrymen and shows a greater involvement of the non-combatant subjects who cannot be excluded as easily from the battle during a siege.

III How Did the Society Regulate Itself

One of the most crucial concepts of ancient Indian thought is the concept of *dharma* which can be translated, among other possibilities, as law, justice, religion or rules. *Dharma* should be followed by everyone, including *kṣatriya*s and kings, and everyone is judged based on their adherence to *dharma* in general and to their own particular *dharma*. On the other hand, there is the concept of *adharma* which is the negation of *dharma*. The difference between *dharma* and *adharma* can sometimes be clear, but more often than not, it is subtle and open to discussion. The three most important ways of regulation of wars in ancient India were all based on the concept of *dharma* and its two important types, the *kṣatriyadharma* and the *rājadharma*, namely (1) influential lawbooks (*dharmasūtra*s, *dharmaśāstra*s), textbooks and other sources which prescribed and prohibited certain conducts, (2) *brāhmaṇa*s who could, in case of a breach of military law, censure the *kṣatriya*s in question, and (3) *kṣatriya*s themselves – from the importance of their self-image as *dharmic* heroes, propagated also by narrative literature and *kṣatriya* women, to the social pressure of their peers who could exclude the guilty party from their midst, or even attack, dethrone and kill him. These three options were of course highly interconnected.

In ancient Indian society, the punisher of any crimes and acts of *adharma* was mainly the king. There are several quite elaborate descriptions of punishments for various offences in texts such as the *Mānavadharmaśāstra* and the

49 *Mānavadharmaśāstra* 7.195–197, translation by Olivelle 2005: 164.

Arthaśāstra. There are, however, only very few punishments for kings – who are *kṣatriyas* par excellence – themselves. A king was supposed to regulate himself[50] and to always listen to wise *brāhmaṇas* and elders who are experts in *dharma*. There were consequences of his wrongdoings (see Consequences), but there are no textbooks which would easily present the punishments.

Kṣatriyadharma is a crucial element of *kṣatriyas* and of their self-regulation. The importance of never abandoning the *kṣatriyadharma* is stressed by Bhīṣma in the *Mahābhārata*:

> *na bhayān nāpy anukrośān na lobhān nārthakāmyayā*
> *kṣatradharmam ahaṃ jahyām iti me vratam āhitam*
>
> Not from fear, not from compassion, not from avarice, not for property or desire I will desert the *kṣatriyadharma*, that is my pledged vow.[51]

The nature of *dharma*, *adharma*, sin, peace and war is discussed on multiple occasions and at length.[52] Even the frame of probably the most famous and influential work of ancient Sanskrit literature, the *Bhagavadgītā* (which is a part of the *Mahābhārata*), deals with the hero Arjuna, who is desperate before a great battle against his relatives, and with his friend – Viṣṇu's *avatāra* Kṛṣṇa – who persuades him to follow the *kṣatriyadharma* and fight. An important part of the *kṣatriyadharma* is to die in battle because dying in bed from illness or old age is considered shameful and even a sin for a *kṣatriya* male.[53] *Vasiṣṭha's Dhanurveda* says:

> *tasmāddhairyyaṃ vidhāyaiva hantavyā paravāhinī|*
> *adharmmaḥ kṣatriyasyaiṣaḥ yad vyādhi maraṇaṃ gṛhe|*
> *yadājau nidhanaṃ yāti so' sya dharmmaḥ sanātanaḥ||*

50 E.g. in *Agnipurāṇa* 225.22. The same is said by the queen Gāndhārī in *Mahābhārata* 5.127.22–34.

51 *Mahābhārata* 5.178.11. If the name of the translator is not given, the translations are the author's.

52 E.g. in the discussion between Yudhiṣṭhira, Kṛṣṇa and Dhṛtarāṣṭra's envoy Saṃjaya in *Mahābhārata* 5.26–29.

53 This is noted several times in the *Mahābhārata*, especially by Bhīṣma, both before the battle in 6.17.11 and after the battle in the prescriptive parts in 12.98.23–27 with a vivid description of the painful and pitious state of one dying that way.

> The greatest virtue of the kaṣtriyas [sic] is to fight in the battle and die. The most disgraceful for him is the death through disease and physical ailments.[54]

A warrior who dies on the battlefield goes to heaven, especially if he fights for the *brāhmaṇas*, women, his subjects or other commendable cause.[55] *Kṣatriyadharma* therefore tells the warriors not only to fight, but also when to fight and how to fight.

IV Prohibited Actions

In ancient Indian warfare, there are some general rules and prohibited actions, groups of people one should not fight against, and prohibited weapons, but there are always exceptions to these rules. As some of the rules are repeated in virtually all sources, it can be presumed that they were universal. On the other hand, there are also some rules particular for certain texts, especially in the narrative literature, so some rules may have been agreed upon before any particular battle.

Protected People

There are people who should never be killed in general, and people who should not be harmed in times of war. Generally speaking, Manu forbids these classes of people to be harmed:

> *ācāryaṃ ca pravaktāraṃ pitaraṃ mātaraṃ gurum|*
> *na hiṃsyād brāhmaṇān gāś ca sarvāṃś caiva tapasvinaḥ||*

> He must never cause harm to his teacher, instructor, father, mother, elder, Brahmins, cows, and all who are given to austerities.[56]

As war is the duty of adult male *kṣatriyas*, everyone else is theoretically excluded from it and should not be harmed. These include especially non-*kṣatriyas*,

---

54 *Vasiṣṭha's Dhaurveda* 3.46, text and translation in *Vasiṣṭha's Dhanurveda Samhitā*. Translated by Purnima Ray. Delhi: J. P. Publishing house, 2003: 66.

55 This is again a very frequent occurrence throughout the literature, from *Vasiṣṭha*'s *Dhanurveda* (3.39–40, 3.65) and *Mānavadharmaśāstra* (8.349) to the *Mahābhārata* (e.g. Bhīṣma in 12.101.38).

56 *Mānavadharmaśāstra* 4.162, translation by Olivelle 2005: 132.

women, children and the elderly. A short list of protected people specifically for the times of war is given by the king of gods, Indra, in the *Mahābhārata*:

> *vṛddhaṃ balaṃ na hantavyaṃ naiva strī na ca vai dvijaḥ|*
> *tṛṇapūrṇamukhaś caiva tavāsmīti ca yo vadet||*
>
> An old man and a young boy should not be killed, nor a woman and a twice-born,[57] one with a mouth full of grass[58] and one who says: "I am yours."[59]

These people – especially *brāhmaṇas*, women, the young and the elderly – should be defended and never killed. One should also never kill envoys[60] (even though they are often used as spies as well) and members of non-combatant staff in battle:

> *na sūteṣu na dhuryeṣu na ca śastropanāyiṣu|*
> *na bherīśaṅkhavādeṣu prahartavyaṃ kathaṃ cana||*
>
> Charioteers, horses, those who bring weapons, drummers or conch-blowers should never be attacked.[61]

Everyone is only protected if they are non-combatants. As soon as they engage in the battle – even if they are *brāhmaṇas* – it is fair to strike them.[62] In the *Mahābhārata* and the *Rāmāyaṇa,* we can see the protected people on a battlefield being killed, both when they actually take up arms – predominantly *brāhmaṇa* warriors – and when they do not, especially charioteers. The loss of a charioteer is often shown as a moment of great grief and confusion for the warriors, and it makes them very vulnerable both practically (they have to drive their chariots themselves, jump onto a friend's chariot or fight on the

57 This term theoretically includes all the three highest *varṇas*, but practically only *brāhmaṇas*.

58 Having grass in one's mouth apparently signified surrender, see e.g. Ramachandra Diksitar 1944: VI or an endnote in Fitzgerald 2004: 745–746 who connects grass in one's mouth with presenting oneself as a cow, i.e. someone who should not be killed.

59 *Mahābhārata* 12.99.47.

60 E.g. *Gautamadharmasūtra* 10.18; *Mahābhārata* 12.86.25–26; *Rāmāyaṇa* (*Rāmāyaṇa of Vālmīki*. Edited by Mehta, J. M. et al. Baroda: Oriental Institute, 1960–75) 5.56.126–127.

61 *Mahābhārata* 6.1.32 (rules before the battle).

62 E.g. *Mānavadharmaśāstra* 8.350–351; *Baudhāyanadharmasūtra* 1.18.12–13 or *Āpastambadharmasūtra* 1.29.7.

ground) and emotionally as close friendships are implied between some warriors and their charioteers.

*Non-*kṣatriyas *as Non-combatants*

In keeping with the idea of fairness, a king should only fight against another king,[63] not against someone who is not a king and not a *kṣatriya*. The group of non-*kṣatriyas* includes specifically *brāhmaṇas* and the rest of the king's potential subjects (*vaiśyas* and *śūdras*). A *kṣatriya* hero can also refuse to fight against anyone whom he considers below him. Similarly heroes may refuse to fight against someone who is crippled or even ugly.[64]

Brāhmaṇas are especially protected to such an extent that when a *brāhmaṇa* comes between two armies, they should stop fighting.[65] Killing a *brāhmaṇa* was considered one of the most heinous crimes possible, both in times of peace and war. *Brāhmaṇas* are often in lists of people who should never be killed[66] and Manu gives several options of severe penances for a person who kills a *brāhmaṇa*.[67] On the other hand, this rule only applies to non-combatant *brāhmaṇas*. As they could adopt the *kṣatriyadharma*, there had to be an exception to this rule: when a *brāhmaṇa* takes up weapons and attacks, he can be killed without commiting the sin of killing a *brāhmaṇa*.

There are various instances of warrior *brāhmaṇas* in the *Mahābhārata* and the *Rāmāyaṇa*: the teacher Droṇa and his son Aśvatthāman or Rāma Jāmadagnya being the most prominent ones. When the *kṣatriya* Bhīṣma is about to fight against his *guru*, the *brāhmaṇa* Rāma Jāmadagnya,[68] he quotes a *śloka* by a certain Marutta which says that it is allowed to punish an arrogant *guru* who does not distinguish between what should and should not be done. He will therefore fight against him but will not kill him, especially as Rāma Jāmadagnya is a *brāhmaṇa* old in ascetic practices. He further argues thus:

udyateṣum atho dṛṣṭvā brāhmaṇaṃ kṣatrabandhuvat|
yo hanyāt samare kruddho yudhyantam apalāyinam|
brahmahatyā na tasya syād iti dharmeṣu niścayaḥ||

63 *Mahābhārata* 12.97.7 by Bhīṣma.

64 This is included in Bhīṣma's specific list in *Mahābhārata* 6.103.73.

65 *Mahābhārata* 12.97.8.

66 E.g. in *Baudhāyanadharmasūtra* 1.18.11 or Indra's list in Bhīṣma's discourse in *Mahābhārata* 12.99.47, together with the old, the young and women.

67 *Mānavadharmaśāstra* 11.73–90.

68 *Mahābhārata* 5.178.23–38.

> When someone sees a *brāhmaṇa* with raised arms like a *kṣatriya* and kills him, angry in battle, when he is fighting and not fleeing, he will not be guilty of killing a *brāhmaṇa*. This is a fixed opinion in *dharmas*.[69]

Bhīṣma also argues that when someone acts somehow, others will reply in kind, and that also applies to *brāhmaṇas* behaving like *kṣatriyas*: *brāhmaṇas* cannot claim their privileges when they voluntarily enter a battle. Nevertheless, he asks Rāma Jāmadagnya for permission to fight against him and receives it.[70] Later, he repeats again that he is not aiming at the *Vedas*, Rāma's *brāhmaṇa*-hood or his ascetic merit but at Rāma's *kṣatriya*-hood because a *brāhmaṇa* becomes a *kṣatriya* when he takes up arms.[71] Even with all this reasoning and quotes of authorities, Bhīṣma feels guilty after he manages to actually hit his *guru*, curses the *kṣatriyadharma*, and claims that it was a sin.[72]

There are other instances where the characters argue that killing even one's guru is necessary for *kṣatriyas*.[73] Killing of the *brāhmaṇa* warrior Droṇa, who is also the teacher of the main 'heroes' and 'villains',[74] is the main goal of the seventh book of the *Mahābhārata*, and there is a great amount of characters noting that Droṇa is not a real *brāhmaṇa* because he engages in *kṣatriyadharma*.[75] When his death draws nearer, his forefathers and other eminent *brāhmaṇas* come to him to tell him that the fight was a breach of *dharma*, that he should put down his weapons, and that fighting is not right for him, who is a *brāhmaṇa* well versed in the *Vedas* and *Vedāṅga*, in the truth and in *dharma*.[76] In a word, the narrative literature abounds with examples of the problematic nature of warrior *brāhmaṇas* without presenting an easy solution.

---

69 *Mahābhārata* 5.178.27.

70 *Mahābhārata* 5.180.12–17. This is reiterated in the next book when Yudhiṣṭhira comes to ask his elders – including Bhīṣma – for the same permission.

71 *Mahābhārata* 5.180.23–25.

72 *Mahābhārata* 5.180.36–38.

73 E. g. Sātyaki in *Mahābhārata* 7.164.30.

74 It is often noted that the roles of 'heroes' and 'villains' cannot be easily defined here because both the Kauravas and the Pāṇḍavas have their heroic moments, but also their moments of *adharma* (see e.g. Nayak, Meena Arora. *Evil in the Mahabharata*. New Delhi: Oxford University Press, 2018: 280) and breaches of laws of wars. However, when the implied author of the Sanskrit *Mahābhārata* as we have it today and his way of presenting the story are taken into account, the Pāṇḍavas can be called the heroes and the Kauravas the villains.

75 E.g. by Bhīma in 7.165.28, and by Dhṛṣṭadyumna – Droṇa's eventual killer – in 7.168.25.

76 *Mahābhārata* 7.164.89–92.

Other *varṇas* are also to be protected, and new subjects should be immediately consoled and won over,[77] never harassed by the victor. According to Manu,

> *jitvā saṃpūjayed devān brāhmaṇāṃś caiva dhārmikān|*
> *pradadyāt parihārārṃś ca khyāpayed abhayāni ca||*
> *sarveṣāṃ tu viditvaiṣāṃ samāsena cikīrṣitam|*
> *sthāpayet tatra tadvaṃśyaṃ kuryāc ca samayakriyām||*
> *pramāṇāni ca kurvīta teṣāṃ dharmān yathoditān|*
> *ratnaiś ca pūjayed enaṃ pradhānapuruṣaiḥ saha||*
> *ādānam apriyakaraṃ dānaṃ ca priyakārakam|*
> *abhīpsitānām arthānāṃ kālayuktaṃ praśasyate||*

> After the victory, he should pay homage to gods and righteous Brahmins; grant exemptions; and issue proclamations of amnesty. After ascertaining the collective wishes of them all, he should install there a relation of the enemy king and draw up a treaty; make the Laws commonly held among them authoritative; and honor the new ruler, together with his chief officials, with precious gifts. When carried out at the appropriate time, the unwelcome seizure of desirable property and their welcome distribution are both commendable.[78]

The Young, the Elderly and the Women

Another group which should not fight, and therefore should not be killed as well, are the young and the elderly.[79] Not only one should never kill them, according to the *Mānavadharmaśāstra,* a good king should even forgive them their offences.[80] In the beginning of the sixth book of the *Mahābhārata* in which the great war starts, the narrator says that the whole earth was empty, because all the men (and horses, chariots, and elephants) were assembled on the battlefield, leaving only the young and the elderly behind.[81]

---

77 *Mahābhārata* 12.97.11. *Agnipurāṇa* 236.22–23 similarly states that when a king attacks a country, he should not humiliate its subjects.

78 *Mānavadharmaśāstra* 7.201–204, translation by Olivelle 2005: 164–165.

79 *Baudhāyanadharmasūtra* 1.18.11; *Mahābhārata* 12.99.47 by Indra, 12.286.4 by Parāśara; *Vasiṣṭha's Dhanurveda* 3.64.

80 *Mānavadharmaśāstra* 8.312.

81 *Mahābhārata* 6.1.7.

There is an obvious question about who is a minor and who is elderly. In the *Mahābhārata,* this question is a puzzling one. On the battlefield, there are boys as young as sixteen and men older than eighty-five; five generations of the Kaurava warriors take part in the battle,[82] and the only explicitly excluded male members of the Kaurava dynasty were the blind Dhṛtarāṣṭra and Vidura whose mother was a *śūdra* woman. This is, however, a work of literature, and the real ages of *kṣatriya* males excluded from battle would be different in reality, and also change in various times and places.

Since war in ancient India was a male issue, women were considered a protected group: they did not fight and they were not to be killed. Killing a woman was deemed a crime resulting in a loss of caste – and therefore in social ostracism – by Manu.[83] Women are noted as a protected group in the *Mahābhārata* several times,[84] as well as in the *Baudhāyanadharmasūtra*[85] and *Vasiṣṭha's Dhanurveda*[86] together with other people unable to protect themselves. Even the usually deadly practical Kauṭilya considers women protected as he presumes that daughters cannot be tortured:

> *apatya samādhau tu kanyāputradāne dadat tu kanyām atisaṃdhatte||*
> *kanyā hy adāyādā pareṣām evārthāyākleśyā ca||*
>
> In giving an offspring as a hostage, however, as between a daughter and a son, the man who gives a daughter is the one who outwits; for a daughter is not an heir, is intended only for others, and cannot be tortured.[87]

The role of *kṣatriya* women was first of all to give birth to heroes, and then to remind their husbands and sons of their duty to fight, and to mourn them if they were slain.[88] A good example can be found in the *Mahābhārata* again: the Pāṇḍavas are reminded of their duties by their mother Kuntī[89] and wife Draupadī (throughout the third to fifth books), and the whole eleventh

82 Bāhlīka, the paternal uncle of the 'grandfather' Bhīṣma, would probably be the oldest, and Abhimanyu, the son of Arjuna, or some of his peers, the youngest.

83 *Mānavadharmaśāstra* 11.67. There are, however, many other crimes on this list, and women are not a specifically protected group here.

84 E. g. in Indra's list in *Mahābhārata* 12.99.47.

85 *Baudhāyanadharmasūtra* 1.18.11.

86 *Vasiṣṭha's Dhanurveda* 3.65.

87 *Arthaśāstra* 7.17.15–16, translation by Olivelle 2013: 324.

88 E.g. mothers Subhadrā and Draupadī, and wife Uttarā for Abhimanyu in *Mahābhārata* 7.55.

89 Kuntī uses the story of a *kṣatriya* mother called Vidurā and her reluctant son to remind her own son Yudhiṣṭhira of his *kṣatriya* duties in *Mahābhārata* 5.130–135.

book is dedicated to women crying for their slain relatives after the battle. Women can both encourage their menfolk to fight, but they can also try to discourage them like the queen Gāndhārī who argues that there is nothing good in war[90] or the goddess Gaṅgā who repeatedly asks both her son Bhīṣma and the *brāhmaṇa* warrior Rāma Jāmadagnya not to fight one another,[91] but in vain.

Not killing women is repeated throughout the narrative parts of the *Mahābhārata* and the *Rāmāyaṇa* as well: Yudhiṣṭhira forbids Bhīma from killing the demoness Hiḍimbā and it is clear that he considers killing women unacceptable and against *dharma* under any circumstances:

> *kruddho 'pi puruṣavyāghra bhīma mā sma striyaṃ vadhīḥ|*
> *śarīraguptyābhyadhikaṃ dharmaṃ gopaya pāṇḍava||*

> Even though you are angry, Bhīma, tiger among men, do not kill a woman. Rather than protecting the body, protect *dharma,* o Pāṇḍava.[92]

On the other hand, there is also a prominent example of a hero killing a woman in the *Rāmāyaṇa*.[93] The hero Rāma is asked to kill a demoness Tāṭakā by an authoritative sage called Viśvāmitra, who presents the unwilling hero with several examples of great men killing women for the greater good. Rāma eventually obliges and kills the demoness.

A woman on an active battlefield is something unheard of in the prescriptive literature and extremely rare in the narrative literature. The only two notable examples are the goddess Gaṅgā who briefly serves as her son's – Bhīṣma's – provisional charioteer during his fight against Rāma Jāmadagnya,[94] and, arguably, the hero Śikhaṇḍin who is considered to be a woman by Bhīṣma during the main battle of the text.[95] Bhīṣma explicitly refuses to kill a woman before the battle at Kurukṣetra. He already mentioned a woman among the people he will not fight against, but here he stresses that he will not fight against a woman, someone who has formerly been a woman, someone with a woman's

90 *Mahābhārata* 5.127.39.
91 *Mahābhārata* 5.179.22–31.
92 *Mahābhārata* 1.143.2.
93 The story can be found in *Rāmāyaṇa* 1.23–25. For more on this issue, see Balkaran and Dorn 2012: 666–667, 675.
94 *Mahābhārata* 5.183.15.
95 Bhīṣma mentions this several times throughout the *Udyogaparvan* and the *Bhīṣmaparvan,* beginning with 5.169.19.

name or appearance, and therefore cannot kill Śikhaṇḍin because this is his great oath.[96] He also adds that:

> *yadi bhīṣmaḥ striyaṃ hanyādd hanyād ātmānam apy uta|*
> *nainaṃ tasmādd haniṣyāmi dṛṣṭvāpi samare sthitam||*
>
> If Bhīṣma kills a woman, he will indeed kill himself, therefore I will not kill him even if I see him ready in battle.[97]

Bhīṣma, arguing that Śikhaṇḍin used to be a woman, refuses to fight against him, and is subsequently killed with his help. A perceived woman is thus considered protected by him even though (s)he is actively participating in male *kṣatriyadharma* – women are therefore probably the only group that should be protected in all circumstances, even when they take up arms.

Prohibited Weapons

There was a great variety of weapons in ancient India, the most important of which were bows and arrows. Which weapons were prohibited and which were not was apparently a matter of discussion, because where Manu – in accordance with the idea of *dharmayuddha* – prohibits weapons anointed with poison,[98] Vasiṣṭha[99] and Kauṭilya[100] give various instructions and recipes to make the poisons as deadly as possible, which would be considered one of the means of *kūṭayuddha*.

Manu states that:

> *na kūṭair āyudhair hanyād yudhyamāno raṇe ripūn|*
> *na karṇibhir nāpi digdhair nāgnijvalitatejanaiḥ||*
>
> When he is engaged in battle, he must never slay his enemies with weapons that are treacherous, barbed, or laced with poison, or whose tips are ablaze with fire.[101]

96 *Mahābhārata* 5.193.62–65.
97 *Mahābhārata* 5.193.65.
98 *Mānavadharmaśāstra* 7.90, translation by Olivelle 2005: 159.
99 *Vasiṣṭha's Dhanurveda* 1.69–71.
100 *Arthaśāstra* 14.1, translation by Olivelle 2013: 421–424.
101 *Mānavadharmaśāstra* 7.90, translation by Olivelle 2005: 159.

There is a longer list of prohibited weapons in the *Mahābhārata*. The narrator Saṃjaya says that the battle was completely *dharmic* and noble and that there were no *adharmic* weapons used:

> *āryaṃ yuddham akurvanta parasparajigīṣavaḥ||*
> *śuklābhijanakarmāṇo matimanto janādhipāḥ|*
> *dharmayuddham ayudhyanta prekṣanto gatim uttamām||*
> *na tatrāsīd adharmiṣṭham aśastraṃ yuddham eva ca|*
> *nātra karṇī na nālīko na lipto na ca vastakaḥ||*
> *na sūcī kapiśo nātra na gavāsthir gajāsthikaḥ|*
> *iṣur āsīn na saṃśliṣṭo na pūtir na ca jihmagaḥ||*
> *ṛjūny eva viśuddhāni sarve śastrāṇy adhārayan|*
> *suyuddhena parāṁl lokān īpsantaḥ kīrtim eva ca||*

> ... they fought a noble fight as they sought to defeat one another; those wise lords of men, of unblemished descent and deed, did battle according to *dharma*, holding their end in view. They employed no form of warfare contrary to *dharma* or to the rules of weaponry: no barbed arrows or reed-arrows, no poison-smeared arrows or poison-injecting arrows, no needle-arrows or monkey-arrows, no arrows of cow-bone or elephant-bone, no double-arrows or infected arrows, no crooked-flying arrows. The weapons they all used were straight and pure, for all desired to gain the world of heaven, and glory too, through fair fight ...[102]

These types of weapons either cause unnecessary suffering (such as the barbed weapons) or give the person using them an unfair advantage (poison-smeared). Bhīṣma similarly mentions poison-smeared (*lipta*) and barbed (*karṇī*) arrows as prohibited in his list,[103] both barbed arrows (*karṇī*) and poisoned arrows (*digdha*) are also mentioned in the *Baudhāyanadharmasūtra*.[104] Even though they are mentioned as explicitly prohibited, some of them are shown as used during the battles of the *Mahābhārata* and the *Rāmāyaṇa* on several places, especially barbed arrows: barbarians are said to have used barbed (*karṇī*), reed (*nālīka*) and iron (*nārāca*) weapons.[105] Similarly, the Pāṇḍavas shoot these

102 *Mahābhārata* 7.164.9–13, translation by Smith, John D. *The Mahābhārata: An Abridged Translation*. London: Penguin Group, 2009: 472.

103 *Mahābhārata* 12.96.11a.

104 *Baudhāyanadharmasūtra* 1.18.10.

105 *Mahābhārata* 8.59.11a.

three types of arrows in the end of the third book,[106] not on a person, but on a deer. It is interesting to note that immediately after this, they lose track of the deer and fall into misfortune.

Prohibited Times and Places

There are several pieces of advice telling a king which place is the best for a battle based on the time of the year or his strongest part of the army in the *Arthaśāstra* and other works.[107] There are, however, no mentions of places where one should not fight. Given the premise that non-combatants should be harassed as little as possible in times of war, it can be argued that any place with non-combatants is prohibited to some extent. When there is a properly announced battle in the *Mahābhārata,* the heroes or armies always leave the city and fight somewhere outside of it, mostly at Kurukṣetra. This is not applicable to the siege war where the citizens of the city in question are by definition present, as shown in the sixth book of the *Rāmāyaṇa*. Furthermore, some sources – especially Puṣkara in the *Agnipurāṇa* – include ways of punishing an enemy which explicitly includes destroying villages and poisoning waters.[108] Even Puṣkara forbids destroying properties of gods.[109]

Concerning time, Bhīṣma counsels Yudhiṣṭhira to march during the months of *Caitra* or *Mārgaśīrṣya* but adds that it is possible to march immediately if his enemy is weakened.[110] In the narrative literature, the fight usually stops at sunset but there are also exceptions to it: in the *Rāmāyaṇa,* the fight continues even after the sunset, and there are two night fights in the *Mahābhārata* as well: one on the fourteenth night of the battle, and Aśvatthāman's explicitly *adharmic* night raid, depicted in the tenth book. In all of these night battles, malevolent beings seem to have advantages.

There are some occurrences of a ceasefire in the *Mahābhārata,* especially when an important hero falls. When the grandfather of both the enemy parties was killed, a truce was quickly negotiated:

---

106 The story, including the *yakṣa*'s questions and Yudhiṣṭhira's answers, can be found in *Mahābhārata* 3.295–299, the arrows in 3.295.13 and 3.295.29.

107 Bhīṣma also gives his list of good times and places for the four types of forces in *Mahābhārata* 12.101.18–22, similarly also *Agnipurāṇa* 228 and 233.1.11.

108 *Agnipurāṇa* 234.2. Originals cited from *Agnipurāṇam*. With Hindi translation by Ācārya Śivaprasād Dvivedī. Delhi: Caukhambā Saṃskr̥ta Pratiṣṭha, 2009, and translations from *Agni-purāṇa II*. Translated and annotated by N. Gangadharan. Delhi: Motilal Banarsidass, 1998.

109 *Agnipurāṇa* 236.22–23.

110 *Mahābhārata* 12.101.9–10.

sa saṃjñām upalabhyātha bhāradvājaḥ pratāpavān|
nivārayām āsa tadā svāny anīkāni māriṣa||
vinivṛttān kurūn dṛṣṭvā pāṇḍavāpi svasainikān|
dūtaiḥ śīghrāśvasaṃyuktair avahāram akārayan||
vinivṛtteṣu sainyeṣu pāraṃparyeṇa sarvaśaḥ|
vimuktakavacāḥ sarve bhīṣmam īyur narādhipāḥ||
vyupāramya tato yuddhād yodhāḥ śatasahasraśaḥ|
upatasthur mahātmānaṃ prajāpatim ivāmarāḥ||

When the powerful Droṇa received the news, he ordered his troops to turn away, sir. When the Pāṇḍavas saw the Kauravas turning away, they also sent envoys on swift horses to their troops to order a truce. When the soldiers were returning, all the kings together unfastened their armour and went to Bhīṣma. Hundreds of thousands of soldiers then left the battle and came to the great-souled man like the immortals to Prajāpati.[111]

Prohibited Conduct

Generally speaking, there are no complete lists of prohibited conducts in the prescriptive literature, but we can learn about them from the lists of protected people, prohibited weapons and from the narrative literature, especially when there are breaches. The rules of conduct in ancient Indian warfare stem from the idea of fairness: one should never attack someone if he has an unfair advantage. Manu sums these rules up thus:

na ca hanyāt sthalārūḍhaṃ na klībaṃ na kṛtāñjalim|
na muktakeśaṃ nāsīnaṃ na tavāsmīti vādinam||
na suptaṃ na visannāhaṃ na nagnaṃ na nirāyudham|
nāyudhyamānaṃ paśyantaṃ na pareṇa samāgatam||
nāyudhavyasanaprāptaṃ nārtaṃ nātiparikṣataṃ|
na bhītaṃ na parāvṛttaṃ satāṃ dharmam anusmaran||

He must never slay a man standing on the ground, an effeminate man, a man with joined palms, a man with loose hair, a seated man, a man declaring "I am yours," a sleeping man, a man without his armor, a naked man, a man without his weapons, a non-fighting spectator, a man engaging someone else, a man with damaged weapons, a man in distress, a

111 *Mahābhārata* 6.115.25–28.

> badly wounded man, a frightened man, or a man who has turned tail—recalling the Law followed by good people.[112]

These rules are repeated in most of the sources, in the prescriptive lawbooks and in both the prescriptive and the narrative parts of the narrative literature. Generally speaking, a *kṣatriya* killing another *kṣatriya* who is in distress would be in breach of the fairness rule when there are several warriors attacking a single one, when the opponent is disadvantaged (is asleep, intoxicated, without a chariot, arms or armour) or is engaged in a duel with another. Other rules are not to fight against a coward (who is afraid, fleeing or capitulating), and one can or even should refuse to fight against someone who is imperfect (impotent, missing a limb, ugly, lower *varṇa*)[113] or someone who is childless, and who would not therefore be able to reach heaven. These can be captured but should not be killed.[114]

Several Warriors Killing a Single One

A single warrior should only fight against a single warrior.[115] One of the most famous examples of a breach[116] of this rule is the killing of Abhimanyu in the seventh book of the *Mahābhārata*. Abhimanyu, a young son of the hero Arjuna and nephew of Kr̥ṣṇa himself, manages to break the enemy's (Kauravas') ranks on the thirteenth day of the battle and to fight valiantly in fair duels. Eventually, the Kauravas lose their patience: the cunning Gandhāra king Śakuni advises to stop fighting in duels and to kill him together instead,[117] and Droṇa comes with the strategy to rid him of his horses, chariot, bow and charioteers, make him turn away and then strike him from behind,[118] naming situations in which a *kṣatriya* should never be killed. Six prominent warriors shoot arrows at the single boy who has lost his chariot and weapons, and he is eventually killed in a final duel with clubs. The fact that his death was against *dharma* is repeatedly mentioned by the narrator, Saṃjaya, as well as by celestial beings who strongly protest from the sky:

---

112 *Mānavadharmaśāstra* 7.91–93, translation by Olivelle 2005: 159.

113 The most famous case is in the *Mahābhārata* 1.126.30–33 when the wise Kr̥pa asks Karṇa to announce his parentage and *varṇa* so he can fight against Arjuna whom he challenged. Karṇa is unable to do so, and Arjuna will therefore not fight against him.

114 *Mahābhārata* 12.97.3.

115 E. g. *Mahābhārata* 12.96.7–10.

116 There are other examples, e.g. the Kauravas attacking Arjuna in 4.57.

117 *Mahābhārata* 7.47.16.

118 *Mahābhārata* 7.47.26–30.

abhikrośanti bhūtāni antarikṣe viśāṃ pate|
dṛṣṭvā nipatitaṃ vīraṃ cyutaṃ candram ivāmbarāt||
droṇakarṇamukhaiḥ ṣaḍbhir dhārtarāṣṭrair mahārathaiḥ|
eko 'yaṃ nihataḥ śete naiṣa dharmo mato hi naḥ||

The beings lamented in the mid-air, o lord of the earth, when they saw the fallen hero like the moon dropped from the sky: "Killed by six great Kaurava warriors,[119] headed by Droṇa and Karṇa, lies this single one. We think this is not *dharma*."[120]

After Abhimanyu's death, his father Arjuna swears to kill Jayadratha whom he deems responsible, in a single day, or otherwise to kill himself. Abhimanyu's death also serves as a justification of the Pāṇḍavas' following breaches of *dharma*, bearing with the basic rule which says that if the enemy fights unfairly, one is allowed to do the same.

Killing Someone Engaged with Another

One of the most common and obvious rules which is repeated in various sources is that one warrior should always fight against one warrior in a duel[121] and one should never fight against someone who is already engaged with someone else. Its obvious nature can be observed in the fight between Bhīṣma and Śālva in the first book of the *Mahābhārata*:[122] Bhīṣma kidnaps three princesses of Kāśi[123] and all the assembled kings pursue him to get them back. Bhīṣma fights against all of them at once, but when one of them, Śālva, challenges him to stop and fight with him, the two heroes engage in a duel and the rest of the kings simply stop and observe without engaging in the fight anymore.[124] After the duel ends with Śālva's defeat, everybody returns to their respective kingdoms without challenging Bhīṣma anymore.[125]

119 For easier understanding, I translate '*Dhārtarāṣṭra*' as a Kaurava, and '*mahāratha*' as a great warrior.

120 *Mahābhārata* 7.48.20–21.

121 *Mahābhārata* 12.96.7.

122 The story can be found in *Mahābhārata* 1.96.

123 This is a legal, although sometimes disputed, way of acquiring wives.

124 *Mahābhārata* 1.96.30.

125 In a retrospective episode in the fifth book of the *Mahābhārata* (5.170.15–21), Bhīṣma narrates this situation differently. He omits the duel against Śālva and claims to have defeated all of the kings at once and very easily. For an explanation of this difference, see Špicová, Zuzana. "Bhīṣma, an (Un)reliable Narrator." In Robert P. Goldman and James

When a hero is engaged in a duel with another hero, other warriors can only be observers. To kill someone who is fighting in a fair duel with somebody else is considered against *dharma*. A famous example can be found in the seventh book of the *Mahābhārata*:[126] two heroes, Bhūriśravas (a Kaurava) and Sātyaki (a Vṛṣṇi fighting for the Pāṇḍavas), engage in a duel and Sātyaki is about to be killed. Kṛṣṇa, who is his relative, repeatedly asks Arjuna to intercede and protect Sātyaki. Arjuna eventually shoots at Bhūriśravas and severs his arm. Bhūriśravas complains and reproaches Arjuna for severing his arm while Bhūriśravas could not see him and was not engaged in combat with him, reminds him of his teachers and elders, and reiterates the laws of battle:

> *na pramattāya bhītāya virathāya prayācate|*
> *vyasane vartamānāya praharanti manasvinaḥ||*
> *idaṃ tu nīcācaritam asatpuruṣasevitam|*
> *katham ācaritaṃ pārtha tvayā karma suduṣkaram||*
> *āryeṇa sukaraṃ hy āhur āryakarma dhanaṃjaya|*
> *anāryakarma tv āryeṇa suduṣkarataraṃ bhuvi||*

> The wise do not strike someone who is intoxicated, fearful, devoid of a chariot, begging for his life, in distress or running away. But why did you do this low and very wicked deed, followed by bad people, son of Pṛthā? A good deed done by a noble person is called a noble deed, Dhanaṃjaya,[127] but an ignoble deed by a noble person is called the most wicked in this world.[128]

Bhūriśravas claims that Arjuna has abandoned *kṣatriyadharma* and also blames Kṛṣṇa whose idea he – correctly – assumes it to be. Bhūriśravas then sits on the battlefield with the resolve to die. Warriors from the whole Kaurava army blame Arjuna and Kṛṣṇa of a wicked act. Arjuna defends himself, saying that he had sworn an oath that no ally of his will be killed within the range of his arrow, and therefore his act was not wrong. On the other hand, it was the killing of his son Abhimanyu which was wrong and against *kṣatriyadharma*. Sātyaki stands up, takes his sword and prepares to kill Bhūriśravas, and even

Hegarty (eds.). *Proceedings of the 17th World Sanskrit Conference, Vancouver, Canada, July 9–13, 2018, Section 4:* Epics, Vancouver: University of British Columbia, 2019.

126 The story can be found in the *Mahābhārata* 7.117–118.

127 Another name of Arjuna.

128 *Mahābhārata* 7.118.8–10.

though heroes from both armies try to prevent him, he does so. A discussion amongst the warriors starts, and Sātyaki defends his act, pointing again to the killing of Abhimanyu, and to the fact that Bhūriśravas disrespected him by kicking him in the chest – and Sātyaki had sworn an oath to kill everyone who would disrespect him thus.

There are other examples of a breach of this particular rule, the most famous of which is Rāma engaging in the fight between the two monkey brothers, Vālin and Sugrīva in the *Rāmāyaṇa* and in the *Rāmopākhyāna* of the *Mahābhārata.*[129] Rāma and Lakṣmaṇa befriend a group of monkey warriors including Sugrīva who then asks Rāma for his help in defeating his brother Vālin who usurped his kingdom. Sugrīva goes to claim his throne and engages in a duel with Vālin. The monkeys are fighting using trees, rocks, fists, nails and teeth and both are equally strong. Rāma also cannot recognise Sugrīva from Vālin as they look both very similar to him. When Sugrīva is given a garland from Hanumān, Rāma draws his bow from behind, aims for Vālin and shoots him in the heart. Vālin, throwing up blood and falling down, sees Rāma in the distance and reproaches him for this act. In the *Mahābhārata*, the problem of Rāma acting against *dharma* is skipped, but in the *Rāmāyaṇa,* Vālin has a long speech, blaming Rāma for abandoning *dharma*, calling him a hypocrite, an *adharmic* person in the garb of *dharma* for killing someone who was engaged with another. He also says that a slayer of a king, a *brāhmaṇa* or a cow, as well as a thief, a person who enjoys killing other beings, an atheist and a younger brother who marries before an older brother go to hell, apparently counting Rāma amongst those enjoying killing other beings without a proper cause. Rāma, however, claims that he only punished Vālin's sins by killing him, as was his duty as a *kṣatriya.*[130]

Killing a Distracted Opponent

Similarly to the rule against killing non-combatants, it is also prohibited to kill someone who is not fighting at the moment: the most frequently mentioned cases are someone who is sleeping[131] or intoxicated or mad,[132] also an

---

129 In the *Mahābhārata,* the story is narrated by the *ṛṣi* Mārkaṇḍeya, this part in 3.264, and in the *Rāmāyaṇa,* Rāma's involvement in the duel is narrated in 4.12–18. For a discussion on this in the context of just war, see Balkaran and Dorn 2012: 668, 675–676.

130 *Rāmāyaṇa* 4.17–18.

131 *Mānavadharmaśāstra* 7.92; *Vasiṣṭha's Dhanurveda* 3.64; *Mahābhārata* 10.5.9 (by Kṛpa in the narrative parts), 12.101.24 (by Bhīṣma in the prescriptive parts).

132 *Baudhāyanadharmasūtra* 1.18.11; *Vasiṣṭha's Dhanurveda* 3.64; *Mahābhārata* 6.1.31 (rules before the battle), 7.118.8 (Bhūriśravas to Arjuna); *Rāmāyaṇa* 6.67.38 (Rāma to Lakṣmaṇa).

opponent who is unconscious,[133] thirsty,[134] exhausted,[135] in times of eating or drinking,[136] or generally unprepared.[137]

Killing of sleeping enemies is the main topic of the tenth book of the *Mahābhārata* where Aśvatthāman, wanting to revenge the *adharmic* death of his father Droṇa, enters the camp of the enemies at night and slaughters everyone indiscriminately: those who were sleeping as well as those who managed to wake up. His act is explicitly condemned by various characters and he is later severely punished, not only for the night attack, but also for killing children. There are also several examples of killing a tired opponent. During the fight between Bhīma and Jarāsaṃdha, Kṛṣṇa notices that Jarāsaṃdha is getting tired, and tells Bhīma never to press a tired opponent because he might die. Bhīma understands and does exactly the opposite, killing Jarāsaṃdha.[138]

Killing a Disadvantaged Opponent

It is also prohibited to kill a disadvantaged opponent: someone who is standing on the ground – without a chariot, other vehicle or horses –[139] while his enemy is on a chariot, a horse or an elephant, someone who is devoid of armour (does not have it or it was destroyed),[140] does not have weapons (his weapons have broken, he put them down voluntarily),[141] has fallen into misfortune,[142] is ill,[143] missing a limb[144] or wounded.[145] One should also not kill someone who has no son[146] or only has a single son.[147]

In the narrative portions of the *Mahābhārata*, Bhīṣma refuses to fight against Rāma Jāmadagnya when his opponent is chariotless and armourless:

133 *Vasiṣṭha's Dhanurveda* 3.41.
134 *Mahābhārata* 12.101.24 by Bhīṣma.
135 *Mahābhārata* 12.101.24 by Bhīṣma, 12.286.4 by *ṛṣi* Parāśara.
136 *Mahābhārata* 12.101.25 by Bhīṣma.
137 *Mahābhārata* 12.286.4 by *ṛṣi* Parāśara.
138 *Mahābhārata* 2.21.20–2.22.6.
139 *Gautamadharmasūtra* 10.18; *Mahābhārata* 10.5.9 by Kṛpa, 12.96.13 by Bhīṣma.
140 *Baudhāyanadharmasūtra* 1.18.11; *Mahābhārata* 6.1.31 (rules before the battle), 6.103.72 by Bhīṣma, 8.66.63 by Karṇa, 12.96.7 and 12.97.3 by Bhīṣma.
141 *Vasiṣṭha's Dhanurveda* 3.61, 3.64; *Āpastambadharmasūtra* 10.10–11; *Gautamadharmasūtra* 10.18; *Mahābhārata* 6.1.31 (rules before the battle), 6.103.72 by Bhīṣma, 8.66.62–63 by Karṇa, 10.5.9 by Kṛpa, 12.97.3, 12.96.7 and 12.96.13 by Bhīṣma.
142 *Mahābhārata* 8.66.62 by Karṇa, 12.96.10 by Bhīṣma.
143 *Mahābhārata* 12.286.4 by *ṛṣi* Parāśara.
144 *Vasiṣṭha's Dhanurveda* 3.41.
145 *Mahābhārata* 12.96.12 by Bhīṣma.
146 *Mahābhārata* 12.96.12 by Bhīṣma.
147 *Mahābhārata* 6.103.73 by Bhīṣma.

tam ahaṃ smayann iva raṇe pratyabhāṣaṃ vyavasthitam|
bhūmiṣṭhaṃ notsahe yoddhuṃ bhavantaṃ ratham āsthitaḥ||
āroha syandanaṃ vīra kavacaṃ ca mahābhuja|
badhāna samare rāma yadi yoddhuṃ mayecchasi||

I replied to him then when he came on the battlefield: "I am not able to fight someone standing on the ground when I am standing on a chariot, sir. Ascend a chariot, hero, and put on your armour, strong-armed one, if you want to fight against me in battle, Rāma."[148]

Even though there are some instances of heroes refusing to fight against someone who has lost his chariot,[149] there are also cases in which this rule is disregarded: Arjuna on a chariot kills Karṇa who is standing on the ground. Karṇa tries to remind him of the rules of war and asks him to wait for a moment so he can repair his chariot and fight with him properly.[150] Arjuna is, however, reminded of Karṇa's former misdeeds by Kṛṣṇa, disregards his plea and kills him nevertheless.

Killing an Opponent Who Doesn't Fight Anymore

One should also never kill or even pursue an opponent who is not ready or not fighting,[151] fleeing from the battle,[152] who has climbed on a mound or a tree,[153] who is capitulating (saying "I am yours")[154] or asking for asylum,[155] begging or crying,[156] generally someone who is afraid,[157] who was already defeated[158] and in similar circumstances. The rules concerning a conquered rival are fairly

148 *Mahābhārata* 5.180.1–2.

149 E.g. Śikhaṇḍin refuses to fight against Kṛpa in this situation in *Mahābhārata* 8.53.13.

150 *Mahābhārata* 8.63–65.

151 *Gautamadharmasūtra* 10.18; *Mahābhārata* 12.286.4 by *ṛṣi* Parāśara; *Rāmāyaṇa* 6.67.38 by Rāma.

152 *Āpastambadharmasūtra* 10.10–11; *Vasiṣṭha's Dhanurveda* 3.42, 3.64; *Mahābhārata* 6.1.31 (rules before the battle), 6.103.72 by Bhīṣma, 8.62–65 by Karṇa, 10.5.10 by Kṛpa, 12.286.4 by *ṛṣi* Parāśara; *Rāmāyaṇa* 6.67.38 by Rāma.

153 *Gautamadharmasūtra* 10.18.

154 *Mahābhārata* 6.103.72 by Bhīṣma, 10.5.10 by Kṛpa, 12.97.3 by Bhīṣma; *Rāmāyaṇa* 6.67.38 by Rāma.

155 *Vasiṣṭha's Dhanurveda* 3.41; *Mahābhārata* 10.5.10 by Kṛpa.

156 *Āpastambadharmasūtra* 10.10–11; *Gautamadharmasūtra* 10.18; *Mahābhārata* 12.286.4 by *ṛṣi* Parāśara; *Rāmāyaṇa* 6.67.38 by Rāma.

157 *Baudhāyanadharmasūtra* 1.18.11; *Vasiṣṭha's Dhanurveda* 3.41, 3.64; *Mahābhārata* 6.103.72 by Bhīṣma, 10.5.10 by Kṛpa, 12.286.4 by *ṛṣi* Parāśara.

158 *Mahābhārata* 10.5.10 by Kṛpa.

universal: he should not be killed but merely captured, and should have an option to be released. As Kauṭilya puts it,

> *āryaprāṇo dhvajāhṛtaḥ karmakālānurūpeṇa mūlyārdhena vā vimucyeta||*
>
> An Ārya individual who is captured in battle must be freed either by appropriate work during a specified period or by paying half the price.[159]

Bhīṣma in the *Mahābhārata* agrees that an enemy king should not be killed or seriously wounded but left alive if possible, or even taken into the victorious king's house and persuaded to become his friend.[160] Bhīṣma is also shown to spare a defeated opponent in the narrative parts: after he defeats Śālva, he kills his charioteer and horses, but he does not kill the king himself and allows him to return to his city.[161] In both the narrative literature and in history, the defeated king was often either reinstalled, or, when killed, his son was anointed a king instead.[162]

These rules for a warrior in distress are among the most ignored in the narrative literature. The *Mahābhārata* has examples of almost all of these rules breached: there is nobody taken captive during the Kurukṣetra war. A *rākṣasa* (demon) Ghaṭotkaca does not spare the fearful or the fleeing,[163] and similarly Kr̥pa and Kr̥tavarman are systematically killing those who are running away from Aśvatthāman's attack.[164] Warriors who are in meditation and not fighting anymore are also killed in the *Mahābhārata*, and their deaths are similarly contentious: Sātyaki kills Bhūriśravas[165] and Dhr̥ṣṭadyumna kills Droṇa.[166] Both heroes are condemned by their peers, but both are able to argue their cases.

Unfair Fighting

There were also rules about fighting with specific types of weapons. As the warriors of the *Mahābhārata* were predominantly chariot fighters, most of the rules and their breaches concern them. There is, however, one prominent fight

159 *Arthaśāstra* 3.13.19, translation by Olivelle 2013: 209.

160 *Mahābhārata* 12.97.4 by Bhīṣma, similarly *Agnipurāṇa* 236.62–65.

161 *Mahābhārata* 1.96.38–39.

162 E.g. in the *Mahābhārata* 2.20 the king Jarāsaṃdha appoints his heir before the fight against Kr̥ṣṇa, Arjuna and Bhīma. His son Sahadeva then pays tribute to the Pāṇḍavas' king Yudhiṣṭhira and eventually fights for him at Kurukṣetra.

163 *Mahābhārata* 7.154.39c.

164 *Mahābhārata* 10.8.99–103.

165 *Mahābhārata* 7.118.

166 *Mahābhārata* 7.165.

in which the warriors use clubs: the final duel between Bhīma and Duryodhana in the ninth book of the *Mahābhārata*. When the Pāṇḍavas come to challenge their cousin and main enemy Duryodhana, he reiterates the rules of battle:

ekaikena ca māṃ yūyam āsīdata yudhiṣṭhira|
na hy eko bahubhir nyāyyo vīra yodhayituṃ yudhi||
nyastavarmā viśeṣeṇa śrāntaś cāpsu pariplutaḥ|
bhṛśa vikṣatagātraś ca hatavāhanasainikaḥ||

Approach me one against one, Yudhiṣṭhira. It is not proper for one to fight with many in a battle, especially one that is devoid of armour, tired and immersed in water, with severely wounded limbs and whose horses and soldiers were killed.[167]

Yudhiṣṭhira agrees and lets Duryodhana choose which one he will fight against in a fair duel, and Duryodhana chooses his old enemy, Bhīma. The stakes are extremely high: whoever wins this duel will rule the kingdom.[168] As both of the heroes are equally skilled, Kṛṣṇa is afraid that Bhīma might lose if he fights fairly, and tells Arjuna that they should use *adharmic* means to win this fight. Arjuna signals to Bhīma that he should aim for Duryodhana's thighs and he does so, and even puts his foot on Duryodhana's head after he falls. For the latter, he is severely reproached by Yudhiṣṭhira. Duryodhana's father Dhṛtarāṣṭra explicitly calls the killing *adharmic*,[169] and the teacher of both Duryodhana and Bhīma, Kṛṣṇa's brother Balarāma, condemns Bhīma for striking below the navel which he says is against the rules of battle, as attested by textbooks.[170] As always, the discussion returns to the question of a personal oath (Bhīma swore to smash Duryodhana's thighs) and preceding *adharmic* acts of Duryodhana.

Kṣatriyas in Distress as an Advantage

Even though the prescriptive sources mostly condemn when someone fights against a *kṣatriya* in distress, there are also *ślokas* which recommend fighting like that as it gives the attacker an advantage. This current is prominently present in Kauṭilya's *Arthaśāstra* and in the *Agnipurāṇa*. For instance, Rāma in the *Agnipurāṇa* advises that:

167 *Mahābhārata* 9.31.49–50.

168 The fight, including the negotiations about the act and Duryodhana's intent to get revenge, can be found in the *Mahābhārata* 9.54–63.

169 *Mahābhārata* 5.59.1.

170 *Mahābhārata* 9.59.5–6.

śrāntaṃ mundaṃ nirākrindaṃ hanyād aśrāntavāhanam|

… one should attack the fatigued, slow and the one whose aid has been cut off without causing fatigue for his force.[171]

The *Agnipurāṇa* offers several pieces of advice on 'covert' war or treacherous war (*kūṭayuddha*), which are often very much against the laws of wars prescribed by the *Mānavadharmaśāstra* or prescriptive parts of the *Mahābhārata*, such as attacking the enemy who is resting or sleeping.[172] This way of fighting can be observed in the narrative literature as well. For instance, the villain of the *Mahābhārata*, Duryodhana, quotes the priest of the gods, Bṛhaspati, who said that enemies should be slain by every means,[173] showing that this current was already well established during the times of the *Mahābhārata*. Similarly, when Aśvatthāman ponders his next move in the *Mahābhārata*, he remembers an old *śloka* by wise and *dharma*-minded men which says:

pariśrānte vidīrṇe ca bhuñjāne cāpi śatrubhiḥ|
prasthāne ca praveśe ca prahartavyaṃ ripor balam||
nidrārtam ardharātre ca tathā naṣṭapraṇāyakam|
bhinnayodhaṃ balaṃ yac ca dvidhā yuktaṃ ca yad bhavet||

The power of the enemies who are thoroughly fatigued, wounded, and eating, departing and entering, should be attacked, as should those fallen asleep in the middle of the night, when devoid of a leader, with broken weapons or with force divided in two. [174]

This current is not limited to the 'villains' of the narrative literature. Especially Kṛṣṇa, the *avatāra* of the god Viṣṇu, is consistently shown to give this type of advice to the Pāṇḍavas, and it is Kṛṣṇa's advice which eventually makes them victorious.

171 *Agnipurāṇa* 242.19, translation by Gangadharan 1998: 631. This part of the *Agnipurāṇa* is also almost *verbatim* present in the *kūṭayuddha* part of Kāmandaka's *Nītisāra* (*Nîtisâra of Kâmandaka with the commentary Jayamaṅgala of Śaṅkarârya*. Edited by T. Ganapati Sâstrî. Trivandrum: Trivandrum Sanskrit Series, No XIV., 1912) in 29.54–62.

172 *Agnipurāṇa* 242.18–27.

173 *Mahābhārata* 2.66.7–8.

174 *Mahābhārata* 10.1.51–52.

V Defences

There are no proper defences in the prescriptive literature and only very little in the narrative parts. When there is something apparently *adharmic* about to happen, the concerned hero typically tries to convince his opponent that his act would be against *dharma* and unbecoming for such a great hero. When Arjuna and Kṛṣṇa are about to kill Karṇa whose chariot is stuck in the mud, he gives a list of people a hero should not fight against and says:

tvaṃ ca śūro 'si kaunteya tasmāt kṣama muhūrtakam|
yāvac cakram idaṃ bhūmer uddharāmi dhanaṃjaya||
na māṃ rathastho bhūmiṣṭham asajjaṃ hantum arhasi|
na vāsudevāt tvatto vā pāṇḍaveya bibhemy aham||
tvaṃ hi kṣatriyadāyādo mahākulavivardhanaḥ|
smṛtvā dharmopadeśaṃ tvaṃ muhūrtaṃ kṣama pāṇḍava||

> You are a hero, Kaunteya, therefore wait for a little moment while I take out the wheel from the ground, Dhanaṃjaya.[175] Do not kill me who is standing on the ground and unarmed, and you on a chariot. I am not afraid of Vāsudeva[176] or of you, son of Pāṇḍu. You are a *kṣatriya* heir, greatly increasing your great clan. Remembering the instructions of *dharma*, wait for a moment, son of Pāṇḍu![177]

These words, however, have no effect here, and usually have no effect at all, and Karṇa is indeed killed in this *adharmic* manner. If something *adharmic* already happened, there can also be discussions amongst the heroes if it really was *adharmic* or not, and there can be complaints[178] or even attempts to kill the person who commited the unjust deed.

---

175 I.e. Arjuna.

176 I.e. Kṛṣṇa.

177 *Mahābhārata* 8.66.63–65.

178 E.g. Duryodhana complains about all the unjust killings in *Mahābhārata* 9.60.27–38 but is immediately reminded of his own unjust actions by Kṛṣṇa. Divine beings enter the discussion and rule that Duryodhana is, in fact, right, and that Bhīṣma, Droṇa, Karṇa and Bhūriśravas were killed unjustly (9.60.51–56). This is still not the end of the discussion as Kṛṣṇa replies even to them and explains why it was necessary to fight like this (9.60.57–63).

VI Consequences

There are generally three groups of potential consequences to any breaches of the proper conduct in battle. A warrior who was not the king could be punished by the king, and a vassal king by a superior king. For warriors who were independent kings, there were (1) practical political consequences, such as a rebellion or a *coup*, (2) religious and (super)natural consequences, such as going to hell or the lack of rain in their kingdoms, and (3) social and practical punishments, such as exclusion from the group of kings.

Practical Political Consequences

A king finds himself in a precarious position because people hate a cruel king but they despise a mild king, so he has to be both.[179] Practical political consequences are mostly warnings that when a king or another *kṣatriya* behaves improperly, he may lose his kingdom. A threat could come from discontented *brāhmaṇas*, other kings in his circle (*maṇḍala*), or from his subjects.

The always practical Kauṭilya warns that:

> *yastūpanatān hatvā baddhvā vā bhūmidravyaputradārān abhimanyeta tasyodvignaṃ maṇḍalam abhāvāyottiṣṭhate||*
> *ye cāsyāmātyāḥ svabhūmiṣv āyattās te cāsyodvignā maṇḍalam āśrayante||*
> *svayaṃ vā rājyaṃ prāṇān vāsyābhimanyante||*
>
> When, however, a man kills or imprisons those who have surrendered and covets their land, property, sons, and wives, his circle, becoming alarmed, will rise up to destroy him. Those ministers who, living in their own lands, are subject to him, moreover, will also become alarmed and seek refuge with the circle. Or else, they will plot against his kingdom or life.[180]

Bhīṣma similarly notes that when a king wins a new land in battle and behaves poorly towards his new subjects, they will side with his enemies[181] which will lead to him losing the kingdom. These warnings and consequences of an

179 *Mahābhārata* 12.103.33.

180 *Arthaśāstra* 7.16.30–32, translation by Olivelle 2013: 323. The text reads "*badvdhā*" instead of "*baddhvā*" and "*vā 'syābhimanyante*" instead of "*vāsyābhimanyante*" which I consider to be typos.

181 *Mahābhārata* 12.97.12–13.

adharmic conduct are described in the narrative portions of the *Mahābhārata* as well: when Kṛṣṇa, Bhīma and Arjuna come to punish Jarāsaṃdha,[182] Kṛṣṇa stresses that Jarāsaṃdha kidnapped other kings with the plan to eventually sacrifice them to Śiva, acting towards those from the same *varṇa* as if they were animals. Kṛṣṇa further argues that the proper sacrifice for a *kṣatriya* is battle and that Jarāsaṃdha deprived the kings of a death of a hero, and challenges him to fight in a duel against either of them. Jarāsaṃdha replies that capturing kings in battle is perfectly *dharmic* but accepts the challenge nevertheless, and is of course killed.

The most apparent consequence seems to be that when an opponent is acting unjustly, one can also adopt unjust means. In the narrative literature – especially in the *Mahābhārata* – it creates an ever worsening cycle of breaches of *dharma,* and also a cycle of revenges. The killing of Abhimanyu leads his father Arjuna to kill Jayadratha, and the way Abhimanyu was killed also serves as a ready-made answer to anyone from the other army who mentions any transgressions against *dharma* on the side of the Pāṇḍavas: where were you with your objections when Abhimanyu was being killed? By acting against *dharma,* one allows others to act in the same way towards him.

Religious and Super(Natural) Consequences

There were also religious and (super)natural consequences of any breaches, and these are often repeated especially in the *Mahābhārata*: someone who does not follow the rules of *dharma* is sinful, will eventually die[183] and end up in hell. When Aśvatthāman gets ready to slay the sleeping army of the enemy, Kṛpa warns him that this deed will definitely lead him to hell.[184] Aśvatthāman is aware of a religious punishment but insists that he will kill his father's killers even if it means ending up in hell or being reborn as an insect.[185]

Manu gives examples of possible afterlife consequences of someone who would harm a *brāhmaṇa* in great detail:

> *brāhmaṇāyāvagūryaiva dvijātir vadhakāmyayā|*
> *śataṃ varṣāṇi tāmisre narake parivartate||*
> *tāḍayitvā tṛṇenāpi saṃrambhān matipūrvakam|*
> *ekaviṃśatim ājātīḥ pāpayoniṣu jāyate||*
> *ayudhyamānasyotpādya brāhmaṇasyāsṛg aṅgataḥ|*

---

182 This story is in the *Mahābhārata,* 2.20.

183 *Mahābhārata* 12.96.17–21.

184 *Mahābhārata* 10.5.12.

185 *Mahābhārata* 10.5.25.

> *duḥkhaṃ sumahad āpnoti pretyāprājñatayā naraḥ||*
> *śoṇitaṃ yāvataḥ pāṃsūn saṃgṛhṇāti mahītalāt|*
> *tāvato 'bdān amutrānyaiḥ śoṇitotpādako 'dyate||*

> If a twice-born merely threatens a Brahmin with murderous intent, he will meander in the Tāmisra hell for one hundred years. If he strikes him deliberately in anger with even a blade of grass, he will be reborn in evil wombs for twenty-one births. If a man foolishly draws blood from the body of a Brahmin who is not attacking him, he will experience intense suffering after death. A man who draws blood will be eaten by others in the next world for as many years as the number of dust particles from the earth that the spilled blood lumps together.[186]

There are also instances of various offences which led heroes from the *Mahābhārata* to hell – even the just king Yudhiṣṭhira had to spend a little time in hell because of his *adharmic* killing of the teacher Droṇa.[187]

Concerning the (super)natural consequences, they are largely based on the idea that there is a special bond between a king and his kingdom. *Adharma* generally weakens the king and the country.[188] Not only the king's actions influence the behaviour of his subjects, but they can also influence the rain, the crops, even the longevity of his subjects. When the king is just and acts according to *dharma*, his kingdom is perfect and free of problems: in the description of the kingdom of Daśaratha, we are informed that all of his subjects were happy, truthful, long-lived and just and there were no liars or atheists,[189] and there are similar descriptions of kingdoms under the reign of *dharmic* kings, such as Yudhiṣṭhira or Rāma. On the other hand, when the kingdom has no king[190] or the king behaves improperly, it can lead to several problems: when a king called Lomapāda acted unjustly, the *brāhmaṇas* of his kingdom left him which resulted in no rain in the kingdom, as narrated in the story of Ṛṣyaśṛṅga in the *Mahābhārata*.[191]

---

186 *Mānavadharmaśāstra* 4.165–168, translation by Olivelle 2005: 132. Similarly also 11.207–209, 12.55.

187 *Mahābhārata* 18.3.14.

188 *Mahābhārata* 12.97.2.

189 The description can be found in *Rāmāyaṇa* 1.6.

190 E.g. after Daśaratha's death, Vasiṣṭha paints a grim picture of a kingless kingdom in *Rāmāyaṇa* 2.61.9–21. Similarly, when Vicitravīrya dies in *Mahābhārata* 5.145.16–40, there is no rain in the kingdom.

191 *Mahābhārata* 3.110.19–21.

Social and Practical Punishments

Practical punishments for breaches of *dharma* in war are fairly rare. Killing a *brāhmaṇa*, for instance, makes a *kṣatriya* socially excluded: Bhīṣma says that whoever kills a *brāhmaṇa* or similarly transgresses *dharma* will become only a nominal *kṣatriya*, will not be praiseworthy and will become unacceptable in an assembly.[192] There are also various instances of assemblies of kings discussing and punishing each other's wrongdoings in the narrative literature, and also the idea that when a *kṣatriya* wins unfairly, he kills himself and is sinful.[193]

Puṣkara in the *Agnipurāṇa* presents two possible kinds of punishment, public and private, and continues:

> *luṇṭhanaṃ grāmaghātaś ca śasyaghāto 'gnidīpanam||*
> *prakāśo 'tha viṣaṃ vahnirvividhair puruṣair vadhaḥ|*
> *dūṣaṇañ caiva sādhūnām udakānāñ ca dūṣaṇam||*
>
> Public punishment (consists of) looting and the destruction of villages (of the enemy country), destruction of the food grains and setting fire. (The private punishment consists of) killing and poisoning or setting fire or by engaging several men, dishonouring pious men and poisoning waters.[194]

A punishment of fighting against a non-combatant is depicted in the *Mahābhārata*: a hero named Śrutāyudha, son of Varuṇa, has a special boon from his father that nobody could kill him thanks to a divine weapon, but he cannot use it on a non-combatant. During the Kurukṣetra war, he hurls it on Kr̥ṣṇa, and the weapon kills Śrutāyudha himself.[195] It is also Kr̥ṣṇa who punishes Aśvatthāman for killing children: the punishment for this evil deed is to roam the earth for three thousand years alone with no human company, reeking of purulence and blood.[196]

Punishments for Desertion

The only deed which results in all three of these consequences is desertion. Manu writes that fleeing from battle will be severely punished:

---

192 *Mahābhārata* 12.97.8–9.
193 *Mahābhārata* 12.96.15.
194 *Agnipurāṇa* 234.2–3, translation by Gangadharan 1998: 606.
195 *Mahābhārata* 7.47.35–56.
196 *Mahābhārata* 10.16.8–12.

yas tu bhītaḥ parāvṛttaḥ saṃgrāme hanyate paraiḥ|
bhartur yad duṣkṛtaṃ kiṃ cit tat sarvaṃ pratipadyate||
yac cāsya sukṛtaṃ kiṃ cid amutrārtham upārjitam|
bhartā tat sarvam ādatte parāvṛttahatasya tu||

> When a man is killed in battle by the enemy as he turns tail frightened, he takes upon himself all the evil deeds committed by his master; while any good deeds that a man killed as he turns tail has stored up for the hereafter, all of that his master takes from him.[197]

When Bhīṣma talks about the battle, he stresses that the leader should make his soldiers swear not to desert one another and ask those who are afraid to leave before the battle. These men are no heroes, should have never been born and gods send disasters on them. When someone flees from a battle, he kills himself and his people and loses his fame.[198] Bhīṣma also advises that the fearful stay in the rear during the battle so they are not in immediate danger but at least show the numbers to the enemy.[199] However, anyone who wants to save his own life by deserting his fellows during the battle will not only be cursed by gods, but they should also be killed with sticks or stones or burnt with fire. Such a person should be killed not like a hero or even a man, but like an animal.[200] Bhīṣma also holds that whoever turns away from fear in battle and is killed goes to hell.[201] Puṣkara in the *Agnipurāṇa* adds that it is said that someone like this gets the fruit of killing a *brāhmaṇa* on every step, and that gods are lost for him.[202]

Conclusion

In the history of Sanskrit laws of wars, two streams of teachings, which were often interconnected in the narrative literature, can be distinguished: a more idealistic prescriptive stream which firmly prohibited killing disadvantaged opponents and propagated the just war, *dharmayuddha*, and a more practical stream of covert or treacherous war, *kūṭayuddha*, which recommended attacking these because it was presented as a tactical advantage. Bearing with the

197 *Mānavadharmaśāstra* 7.94–95, translation by Olivelle 2005: 159.
198 *Mahābhārata* 12.101.29–38.
199 *Mahābhārata* 12.101.43.
200 These ways of death are very non-*kṣatriya*. *Mahābhārata* 12.98.21–22.
201 *Mahābhārata* 12.99.39.
202 *Agnipurāṇa* 236.54–55.

idea of fairness, even those who propagated the ideal *dharmayuddha* agreed that if an enemy uses treacherous means of warfare, one can do the same.

Virtually all prohibited actions are recommended in some sources, and all prohibited weapons are used or recommended to use somewhere. There are protected groups of people – especially *brāhmaṇas*, non-combatants, the young, the elderly and women – but they are only protected as long as they do not take up arms and fight, perhaps with the exception of women. It is also prohibited to attack a disadvantaged, distracted or defeated opponent when *dharmayuddha* is pursued. Pursuing *dharmayuddha* is, however, presented as a very difficult thing. The general picture we get from narrative literature, especially from the *Mahābhārata*, is that it is virtually impossible to win a war using only just means. After the battle at Kurukṣetra, the king Yudhiṣṭhira, son of the god Dharma, asks Bhīṣma about *dharma* and victory. First, he asks how he can win according to *dharma*,[203] but even he eventually asks:

yathā jayārthinaḥ senāṃ nayanti bharatarṣabha
īṣad dharmaṃ prapīḍyāpi tan me brūhi pitāmaha

Tell me, o grandfather, how those wishing for victory lead the army, even when suppressing *dharma* a little, o bull among Bharatas.[204]

203 *Mahābhārata* 12.96.1.

204 *Mahābhārata* 12.101.1.

CHAPTER 2

Carthaginian Laws of War

David Feeney

In the period *c.* 550–400 BC[1] the city-state of Carthage, located on the North African coast near modern Tunis, established an extensive empire spanning the Western Mediterranean. Founded by Phoenician settlers in the ninth century BC, Carthage emerged as the most demographically and economically significant Phoenician city in the West, and from 550 was able to assert itself as the preeminent of the Phoenician settlements there. From this point modern historians refer to the Phoenician populations of the western Mediterranean basin as 'Punic' (from the Latin *punicus*, from *Poenus*, inhabitant of Carthage). Ancient Greek and Latin sources variously name these Punic populations as 'Libyphoenicians'[2] or Phoenicians,[3] but they also use terms such as *mastienoi, bastuli, bastulo poeni* and *blastophoinikes* to designate Punic populations in the Iberian Peninsula.[4]

Carthage is often described as a thalassocracy, and the origin of the city's military power is to be found in its fleet. From the mid sixth century BC it was the city's fleets of warships that enabled Carthage to establish its leadership over the other Punic/Phoenician city-states of the western Mediterranean. These city-states were mostly Tyrian foundations dating back to the eighth and seventh centuries BC, several of them more ancient than Carthage.[5] The pattern of Phoenician settlement across the western Mediterranean meant that these cities were found on the coast, sited on defensible promontories, offshore islands

1 All dates hereafter are BC.

2 The term Libyphoenician is usually, but not exclusively, applied to Punic populations in North Africa, and encompasses deeply Punicised Libyan populations integrated into Punic city-states in North Africa, such as Hippo Acra or Lepcis. For a detailed discussion of the term see: Sandrine Crouzet, 2003, 'Les statuts civi ques dans l'Afrique punique. De l'historographie moderne a l'historiographie antique', *Melanges de l'Ecole francaise de Rome, Antiquite*. Tome 115, No. 2, pp. 655–703.

3 Diod. 13.80.6, 14.47.5, 14.65.3; Polyb. 9.11; Livy, 28.37.5; 28.46.12. The term 'Phoenician' is used to describe Punic populations, including sometimes, but not always, Carthaginians.

4 Jose Luis Lopez Castro, 2008, 'Fenicios Occidentales, Mastienos, Blasto-Fenicios y Bastulo-Punicos en el I Milenio a.C.', *Varia, 9, 1st Congreso Internacional de Arqueologia Iberica Bastetana*, Universidad Autonoma de Madrid, pp. 197–209.

5 The Phoenician colonies at Lixus in Morroco, Gadir (Cadiz) in Spain, and Utica in Tunisia all pre-dated Carthage.

 | DOI:10.1163/9789004473218_004

or at river mouths and lagoons.[6] Proximity to the sea ensured that these cities remained culturally, socially, politically and militarily closer together. By ship, the Punic cities of the central Mediterranean were only separated by one- or two-days travel. Carthage could rely on notions of nautical proximity to draw the Punic cities of the West under the protection of its fleet, and thereby into its control. C R Whittaker, in his influential 1978 article *Carthaginian imperialism*, observed that Carthaginian "control" over these Punic city-states should be understood as arising from unequal treaties, with Carthage defining their foreign relations and obtaining privileged economic conditions, in exchange for offering military protection.[7] Carthage more resembled the leader of a league of city-states founded by Tyre than a true imperial power.

1 Means and Methods of Warfare

a *The Carthaginian Empire*

The military protection offered by Carthage to its dependent Punic allies in *c.* 550 took the form of the city's fleet of galleys, manned by Carthaginian oarsmen, sailors and citizen militia.[8] The Punic city-states, being located on the coast, could rely on the Carthaginian fleet to swiftly counter a number of potential threats. These included pirates (i.e. the battle of Alaila in *c.* 535[9]); the encroachment of Greek settlers into regions already settled by Punic populations, as in western Sicily (Pentathlos at Lilybaion[10] in *c.* 580; Doreius at Mount Eryx in *c.* 500)[11] and the Syrtes region (*c.* 520[12]); and assisting Punic cities when they came into conflict with indigenous neighbours (Gadir, *c.* 520?).[13]

---

6 Offshore islands include Motya, Sulci, Gadir; capes and promontories include Nora, Tharros, Bithia, Panormos, Lixus, Lepcis, New Carthage and Carthage itself.

7 C R Whittaker, 1978, 'Carthaginian imperialism', in P D A Garnsey and C R Whittaker, *Imperialism in the Ancient World*, Cambridge University Press, pp. 59–90.

8 Herodotos reports that the Carthaginians deployed 60 warships against the Phokaian Greeks conducting piracy from Alalia in Corsica in c. 535 BC (1.165). If these warships were biremes – the typical Phoenician galley of the period – then this would represent a force of around 7,000–7,500 oarsmen, sailors and marines.

9 Herod. 1.165.

10 Paus. 10.11.3.

11 Herod. 5.42–48; Franco de Angelis, 2003, *Megara Hyblaia and Selinous, The Development of Two Greek City-States in Archaic Sicily*, Oxford University School of Archaeology, Monograph 55, Oxford, pp. 152–160.

12 Herod. 5.42–44, 46–48.

13 Justin, 44.5; Ruth Pliego Vazquez, 2019, 'Carthaginians in Turdetania: Carthaginian Presence in Iberia before 237 BCE', in Gonzalo Cruz Andreotti, *Roman Turdetania*,

Subsequent to establishing its leadership over the Punic city-states, Carthage undertook a series of military campaigns throughout *c.* 520–450 aimed at territorial conquest in Sardinia and Tunisia. Ancient sources mention the Carthaginian general Malchus[14] campaigning in Sicily, Sardinia and Tunisia,[15] followed by his successor Mago "the general of the Carthaginians, after having been the first, by regulating their military discipline, to lay the foundations of the Punic power".[16] In "regulating their military discipline", Mago presumably ensured that Carthage's citizen militia possessed the panoply and simple drill needed to fight effectively as a hoplite phalanx, supplemented by the urban militias of Carthage's various Punic allies.[17] At this time the hoplite panoply and fighting style predominated not only among the Greeks, but also among the Etruscans, Romans and Campanians of Italy.[18]

b *Sardinia and Tunisia*

By *c.* 450 Carthage's fleet and citizen army had succeeded in conquering much of Sardinia and Tunisia, and the city established provincial systems of rule, including governors and garrisons, the extraction of tribute and taxes, and the reorganisation of the territory.[19] The *chora* of Carthage expanded beyond the peninsula of the city itself to encompass the north coastal *Tell*, the lower *Bagradas* (modern Medjerda) river valley, Cape Bon, and the adjacent *Sahel* on the east coast. The peninsula of Cape Bon was known in antiquity

---

Romanization, Identity and Socio-Cultural Interaction in the South of the Iberian Penenisula between the 4th and 1st centuries BCE, Brill, pp. 89–107; Manuel Alvarez Marti-Aguilar, 2018, 'The Network of Melqart: Tyre, Gadir, Carthage and the Founding God', in Toni Naco del Hoyo and Fernando Lopez Sanchez (eds), *War, Warlords and Interstate Relations in the Ancient Mediterranean*, Brill, Leiden and Boston, pp. 113–150.

14 'Malchus' is a name used by convention by modern historians; the original medieval manuscripts of Justin wrote Mazeus, Maceus and Maleus.

15 Justin, 18.7.

16 Justin, 19.1.; Dexter Hoyos, 2019, *Carthage's Other Wars*, Pen & Sword, pp. 33–55.

17 Mago may also have begun adding to Carthaginian military strength by hiring mercenaries and allied auxiliaries. Enrique Gozalbes Cravioto, 2017, 'Los inicios del ejercito cartagines (siglo VI a.C.)', *Aqvila Legionis*, Vol. 20, pp. 9–30.

18 Martin P Nilsson, 1929, 'The Introduction of Hoplite Tactics at Rome: Its Date and Its Consequences', *The Journal of Roman Studies*, Vol. 19, pp. 1–11; A M Snodgrass, 1965, 'The Hoplite Reform and History', *The Journal of Hellenic Studies*, Vol. 85, pp. 110–122.

19 Whittaker, 1978, pp. 88–90. The Carthaginian province in western Sicily is often named the *eparchia* in the ancient sources, a Latinized word from the Greek ἐπαρχία, which can be loosely translated as the rule over a province or territory. Carthage charged taxes (*phoroi*) in Sicily; Diod. 13.59.3, 13.114, 14.47.5–6. This was a fixed tax on the population and harbour duties: App. *Sic.* 2.6.

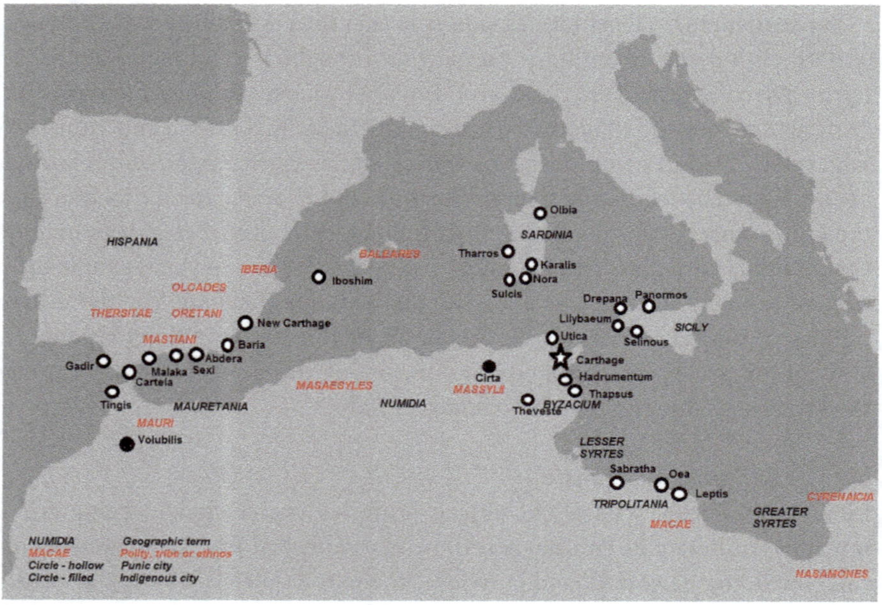

MAP 1 The Carthaginian 'empire', *c.* 300 BC

as the 'Fair Promontory' and became famous for its lush villa plantations.[20] The olive groves, vineyards, orchards and farms of this *chora* fed the metropolis, and the Carthaginian aristocracy acquired rich agricultural estates worked by large numbers of slaves.[21] The intensive occupation and transformation in the settlement pattern of the Carthaginian *chora* is archaeologically visible.[22] The indigenous Libyan population continued to live in this countryside after the Carthaginian conquest and settlement.[23]

---

20 Diod. 20.8.3–4; Polyb. 1.29.7. Several Carthaginian sites have been identified on Cape Bon. Complex garrisoned forts/watch points/navigation beacons have been located at Ras ed-Drek and Ras Fortass. The town at Kelibia has been identified as ancient Aspis/Clupea and dated to the fifth century BC. The cliff-top town at Kerkouane had a population of around 2–3,000, with towers that may have served as watch points, and a kilometre-long defensive double wall to the landward.

21 cf. Justin, 21.4.6.

22 Rachael A Sycamore and Brian G Buchanan, 2016, 'Rediscovering the rural landscape of Carthage's hinterland: a reassessment of the Carthaginian Countryside survey', *Libyan Studies*, pp. 1–11; Roald Doktor, 2009, 'Carthage and its hinterland', in S Helas and D Marzoli (eds.), *Phönizisches und punisches Städtewesen*, Iberia Archaeologica 13, Philipp Von Zabern, Mainz, pp. 179–189.

23 This is evident from the continuity in Libyan Haouanet style tombs dating to pre- and post- Carthaginian conquest: Nathan Pilkington, 2013, *An Archaeological History of*

Beyond Carthage's expanded *chora*, the city conquered the Tunisian *Tell*, a much larger area extending up to 100 km to the west and south of the city. Here the towns and villages of the native Libyans (Polybius calls them *Libyes*, Livy calls them *Africani*) were subjects of Carthage, required to pay tribute and taxes, provide men for Carthage's wars, and were ineligible to acquire civic rights.[24] In *c.* 400 Socrates observed that the Carthaginians were the rulers and "the Libyans" were the ruled.[25] The Libyans were thereafter the most numerous and important population under Carthaginian direct rule. These Libyan farmers appear to have lived in conditions that approached serfdom, having to hand over at least a third of their harvest to the Carthaginian state, and in times of stress, such as during the First Punic War, considerably more.[26] Perhaps Aristotle and Polybius noted the similarities between the Carthaginian and Spartan constitutions because these two societies shared a distinctive characteristic – that the Libyans and *helots* of Sparta were both serfs owned by the state, mostly tied to labour on farms owned by individuals of a privileged citizen class?[27]

The Carthaginian conquest of much of the interior of Sardinia meant the occupation of the island's most fertile districts. Here the native chiefdoms disappeared and the territory was reorganised to enable the expansion of agricultural production, with the foundation of new Punic agricultural towns (i.e., Othoca, Neapolis, Monte Luna/Santu Teru) and the formation of elite-owned estates.[28] By *c.* 400 the Sardinian countryside was worked by a socially integrated peasantry that was largely of native descent, but included labour

Carthaginian Imperialism, Thesis submitted in partial fulfillment of the requirements for the degree of Doctor of Philosophy in the Graduate School of Arts and Sciences, Columbia University, p. 239.

24 Ancient *Libya* corresponded to North Africa west of the Nile, although its narrower usage referred only to the northern half of today's Tunisia, blending on its west into the highlands and valleys of *Numidia*, roughly modern Algeria, and beyond that *Mauretania*, roughly today's Morocco. The many tribes and groups of this region were Berbers – Amazigh in their own language – and were farmers and pastoralists. The Libyans are usually regarded as being distinct from Numidians and Mauri because they occupied more fertile areas, the Medjerda Valley stretching over one hundred miles southwest from Carthage was some of the richest agricultural lands in the Mediterranean, and its sedentary Libyan inhabitants lived in towns, villages and farms.

25 Xen. *Memorabilia* 2.1.10.

26 Polyb. 1.72.1–5.

27 On *helots* and state serfs, see: Fisher, N R E, 2003, *Slavery in Classical Greece*, Classical World Series, Bristol Classical Press, London, pp. 22–33.

28 P van Dommelen, 1998, *On Colonial Grounds, A comparative study of colonialism and rural settlement in first millennium BC west central Sardinia*, Archaeological Studies Leiden University, The Netherlands, pp. 115–157.

secured through immigration from North Africa and the importation of chattel slaves.[29] Van Dommelen summarised “it is assumed that the indigenous inhabitants were ‘deculturalized’ and that a new ‘integrated’ Sardinian-Punic society was created”.[30] Carthaginian political and cultural domination in both Tunisia and Sardinia meant that indigenous inhabitants there experienced processes of elite integration, ‘Punicisation’, hybridization and assimilation. The Carthaginian state strictly regulated foreign trade in Sardinia and Tunisia, and granted trading rights in various seaports as acts of political favour.[31]

c *Sicily*

Sicily in the period *c.* 550–265 was a multipolar, unstable, violent environment inhabited by numerous autonomous city-states. The island was a cross roads, wealthy thanks to its fertile agriculture and advantageous geographical position, linking the Punic world with the markets and manufactures of southern Italy, western Greece, Corinth and Athens. Sicily was densely populated by urbanised communities of Punics, Greeks (Sikeliots) and indigenous groups.[32]

---

29 On immigration from Africa, note Cicero: “*From the Punic, mixed with the African, arose the Sardinians who were not settlers who freely went to settle in Sardinia, but only the refuse of settlers that one gets rid of*”: Cic. *Pro Scauro*, 19.42–43 (authors translation). Fourth century BC tombs in the Campidano plain show the same architectural and stylistic features (i.e. red paint) as Punic *hypogea* in the Tunisian Sahel and Cape Bon, which supports the hypothesis that many if not most of the Punic settlements in the Campidano were used by Carthage to install settlers from Africa, with the intention of promoting cereal cultivation: see Piero Bartoloni, 2017, ‘L’età dell’egemonia cartaginese’, in Michele Guirguis (ed.), *La Sardegna Fenicia e Punica, Storia e Materiali*, Corpora delle antichità della Sardegna, Regione Autònoma de Sardigna, Ilisso Edizioni, Nuoro, pp. 78–100. A 2020 study in Sardinia’s genome history asserts that Sardinia experienced relative genetic isolation through the Bronze Age/Nuragic period; after this the study found gene flow from eastern Mediterranean and North African sources in two Punic sites, Monte Serai and Villamar and concludes: “*These results … are not unexpected given that the Punic centre of Carthage on the North-African coast itself has roots in the eastern Mediterranean. Interestingly, the Monte Serai individuals, predating the Villamar individuals by several centuries, show less North-African ancestry. This could be because they harbour earlier Phoenician ancestry and North-African admixture may have been unique to the later Punic context, or because they were individuals from a different ancestral background altogether*”: Joseph H Marcus *et. al*, 2020, ‘Genetic history from the Middle Neolithic to present on the Mediterranean island of Sardinia’, *Nature Communications*, Vol. 11:939, pp. 1–14.

30 Van Dommelen, 1998, p. 129.

31 Polyb. 2.22.8; Whittaker, 1978, pp. 344–348.

32 At the time that Sicily was settled by Punic and Greek colonists in the eighth and seventh centuries BC the island was inhabited by the Elymoi in the west, the Sikanoi in the centre and the Sikeloi in the east. These indigenous groups largely retreated into the interior, where they coalesced in their own city-states led by their own dynasts, the most important of whom was Ducetius in the mid-fifth century BC, see: Trinity Jackman,

Near constant warfare, accompanied by the destruction and re-settlement of sites, the forced migration of defeated populations, and the settlement of foreign mercenaries meant that ancient Sicily was a far more multicultural milieu than the ancient sources concede.[33] There were close trade relations between Carthaginians and Sikeliots in peacetime.[34] Thucydides stated: "The Sicilian cities have enlarged populations made out of all sorts of mixtures, and there are constant changes and rearrangements in their citizen bodies".[35]

In order to mitigate their security concerns, the Punic cities of Sicily sought the protection of Carthage. The Punic cities of Sicily – Motya, Panormos, Soloeis and Drepanon – all shared particularly strong cultural, religious and language affinities with the Carthaginians.[36] The indigenous Elymi of Segesta petitioned to become Carthaginian tributaries in 410 so as to secure protection from their expansionist neighbour, the Sikeliot city-state of Selinunte.[37] The larger Greek city-states of Sicily were often torn by civil conflict (*stasis*) between oligarchs, democrats and tyrants. Further, the city-state of Syracuse almost constantly sought to control the other *poleis* and weld them into a coalition capable of driving Carthaginian power from Sicily altogether. The border in Sicily delimiting the Punic and Sikeliot zones of the island were fixed by treaty, shifting back and forth depending on the fortunes of war, but were usually either the river Lykos (modern Platani) or the more easterly river Himera (modern Salso). The Carthaginian high-water mark was the treaty of 405 with Dionysius I of Syracuse, whereby the Sikeliot city-states of Selinunte, Himera, Akragas, Gela and Camarina were demilitarized and deemed tributaries of Carthage.[38]

2006, 'Ducetius and fifth-century Sicilian tyranny', in Sian Lewis (ed.), *Ancient Tyranny*, Edinburgh University Press, pp. 33–48.

33 Kathryn Lomas, 2006, 'Tyrants and the polis: migration, identity and urban development in Sicily', Sian Lewis (ed.), *Ancient Tyranny*, Edinburgh University Press, pp. 95–118.

34 E.g. Diod. 13.81.4–5: Carthage importing oil and wine from Sicily; Diod. 14.1.3: Carthaginian artisans living in Syracuse; Diod. 14.46.1.3; pogrom of Carthaginians living in Syracuse; Diod. 14.53.4; Greek inhabitants of Motya fighting against Dionysius I; Diod. 16.9.4–6, Plut. Dion. 25.12; Dion's close personal ties with the Carthaginian elite; Herod. 1.165: Hamilcar is guest-friend of Terillos tyrant of Himera.

35 Thuc. 6.17.

36 Josephine Quinn, 2018, *In Search of the Phoenicians*, Princeton University Press, New Jersey, pp. 91–131; on the 'Circle of the Tophet' in the central Mediterranean and the small group of Phoenician migrants that practised ritualised child sacrifice see: Josephine Crawley Quinn, 2012–2013, 'Tophets in the 'Punic World'', *Studi Epigrafici e Linguistici*, 29–30, pp. 23–48.

37 Diod. 14.43.3.

38 Diod. 13.114.1.

After 405 the long-standing hegemonic influence of the Carthaginian state in western Sicily appears to have hardened into an imperial territory, the *eparchia*.[39] The legends on Carthaginian coins (*b'rst* = "in the territories", i.e. "in the Sicilian domains" of Carthage) are indicative of strengthening Carthaginian authority over western Sicily.[40] The Carthaginians founded or re-founded five additional cities in western Sicily in the fourth century BC. The most important of these was the fortress/port of Lilybaion (Latin: Lilybaeum), originally built as a new home for refugees from the nearby city of Motya, it is likely that immigrants from Carthage significantly supplemented its population. Strategically placed on Cape Boeo, the westernmost point of Sicily, Lilybaion soon became a hub for commercial traffic between North Africa, Sicily, Italy and Greece. Perhaps the most striking aspect of the city were its formidable defences.[41] Selinunte was captured by the Carthaginians in 409, after which it arose anew as a Carthaginian tributary,[42] a more heavily Punic city than we might expect if its population consisted only of survivors, and it likely included new settlers from North Africa. It may have been the Carthaginian colony[43] named *Rosh Melkart* by the Carthaginians.[44] A third foundation was at Eryx, originally a native Elymoi settlement, it was conquered by the Carthaginians in 396 and they colonized the site sometime before the First Punic War.[45] In

39 *Eparchia* is a Latinized word from the Greek ἐπαρχία, which can be loosely translated as the rule over a province or territory; Whittaker, 1978, pp. 59–90.

40 Sandro Filippo Bondi, 2009, "Sicilia e Sardegna nel mondo punico: relazioni, funzioni, distinzioni", pp. 457–465, in Carmine Ampolo (ed.), *Immagine e immagini della Sicilia e di altre isole del Mediterraneo antico*, Vol. I, Edizioni Della Normale, Pisa, pp. 457–465; Jonathan R W Prag, 2008, "Siculo-Punic Coinage and Siculo-Punic Interactions", *Bollettino di Archeologia On Line*, Volume Speciale, Roma 2008, International Congress of Classical Archaeology, Meetings between Cultures in the Ancient Mediterranean, pp. 1–10.

41 Zirone, 2004–2005.

42 Diod. 13.59, 114.

43 Fentress, 2013, pp. 157–178.

44 Pilkington, 2019, pp. 154–155. Maria Giulia Amadasi Guzzo, 1997, '*RʔŠ MLQRT, « les élus de Melqart »?*', Antiquités africaines, Vol. 33, pp. 81–85.

45 Pilkington, 2019, p. 156. Several land and sea battles were fought in the vicinity of Eryx in the late fifth and early fourth centuries BC: Diod 13.80, 14.47–48, 14.55. The Elymoi of Eryx allied with Dionysius I of Syracuse in 397: Diod. 14.47 and 14.48. Eryx was then "taken by treachery" by the Carthaginian general Himilcon in 396: Diod. 14.55. On the settlement at Eryx, see: Beatrice Lietz, 2010, 'La Dea Di Erice Nel Suo Contesto Mediterraneo: Un'identità Contesa', in Enrico Acquaro, Antonino Filippi and Stefano Medas (eds.), *La Devozione Dei Naviganti il Culto di Afrodite Ericina nel Mediterraneo, Atti del convegno di Erice 27–28 novembre 2009*, Athenaion, Lugarno, pp. 89–94. The powerful fortifications at Eryx are now dated to the 4th century BC, in the period of the Punic *eparchia*, see: Donata Zirone, 2003, 'Problemi Relativi Alla Datazione Dellemura Di Erice', *Quartegiornate Internazionali*

407 Carthage planted the colony of Thermae Himerenses on the *chora* of the destroyed Sikleiot city of Himera with "volunteers from their citizens and the other inhabitants of Libya",[46] and they may have founded Halaesa at around the same time: these two colonies secured the Carthaginian position on Sicily's north coast.[47]

Carthaginian interest in much of the hinterland of western Sicily was not based on that region's agriculture, but instead on its fortified hilltop settlements that created a defensive buffer zone for the main object of Carthaginian economic interest on the island, namely its ports. There is archaeological evidence for Carthaginian garrisons at Adranon, and Diodorus and Plutarch mentions a garrison at Herakleia Minoa in 357.[48] It is generally understood that these garrisons were placed into fortresses that were maintained, at least in part, on the production of the *chora* that they probably managed.[49] Such fortresses safeguarded the Carthaginian *epikrateia* in western Sicily, and were intended to slow any major incursion launched from eastern Sicily

d *Carthaginian Colonies*

Aristotle observed in *c.* 340 that "The government of the Carthaginians is oligarchical, but they successfully escape the evils of oligarchy by enriching one portion of the people after another by sending them to their colonies. This is their panacea and the means by which they give stability to the state".[50] As we have seen, the Carthaginians planted colonies throughout its expanded *chora* in Tunisia, and also in western Sicily. Significant numbers immigrated to Sardinia to populate its rich agricultural areas, and inhabit new foundations such as Olbia. The Punic city of Iboshim on the island of Ibiza was founded in the seventh century BC by Phoenicians from southern Iberia, but in the fifth century BC it was reinforced with new groups of Punic settlers from North

Distudi Sull'area Elima, (Erice, 1–4 dicembre 2000), Scuola Normale Superiore Di Pisa, Laboratorio di Storia, Archeologia e Topografia del Mondo Antico, Pisa, pp. 1357–1384.

46 Diod. 13.79.8; cf. Cic. *Verr.* 2.35.

47 Diod. 14.16.4.

48 Diod. 16.9; Plut. Dion 25. A certain Synalus (Diodorus names him Paralus) is described by Plutarch as governor of Minoa, which lay "in the dominion of the Carthaginians". Interestingly, Synalus was a friend of Dion. Barracks at Adranon: see Nunzio Allegro, 2014, 'Greci e Punici tra il Belice e Platani. Il caso di Rocca Nadore', in Marina Congiu, Calogero Micciché and Simona Modeo (eds.), *Viaggio in Sicilia Racconti, segni e città ritrovate, Atti del X Convegno di Studi*, Salvatore Sciascia, Rome, pp. 249–265.

49 Anna Chiara Fariselli, 1999, 'The impact of military preparations on the economy of the Carthaginian state', in Giovanna Pisano (ed.), *Phoenicians and Carthaginians in the Western Mediterranean*, Studia Punica 12, Universita degli Studi di Roma, Rome, pp. 59–67.

50 Arist. *Pol.* 1273b.

Africa.[51] Similarly, Carteia, located near Gibraltar, received immigrants from North Africa.[52]

Other colonies were founded to strengthen Carthaginian control of the coastline south of Carthage. In Byzacium, the colonies of Hadrumentum and Acholla[53] exploited a region renowned for its rich yields of wheat and oil.[54] In Tripolitania the cities of Lepcis, Sabratha and Oea may have been Carthaginian colonies founded on the sites of older Phoenician *emporia*. The wealth derived from maritime trade, agriculture and trans-Saharan trade meant the city of Lepcis alone paid Carthage a tribute of 1 talent a day – some 9 tons of silver a year.[55] Carthaginian control of Byzacium, the Lesser Syrtes and the Greater Syrtes is hinted at by the reports of the native tribal groups there such as the Macae, Nasamones, Garamantes and Gaetuli all fighting in Carthaginian armies as either allies or mercenaries.[56]

e *The Independent Tribes of North Africa*

In North Africa the independent Numidian tribes had formed two supra-tribal confederations, probably by around 237.[57] The Masaesyles inhabited western Algeria, and the Massylii eastern Algeria/western Tunisia. These were dominated by overlords who styled themselves as kings, but who nonetheless had to impose their authority on lesser chieftains and sub-tribes. The Carthaginian

51 Diod. 5.16.2–3; Benjami Costa y Jordi H Fernandez, 1997, 'Iboshim Phoenissa et Poena. La isla de Ibiza en epoca fenicio-punica', *Espacio, Tiempo y Forma*, Serie 1, Prehistoria y Arqueologia, 10, pp. 391–445.

52 Mela 2.96. Carteia may have been a colony originally planted by the Punic city-state of Gadir (modern Cadiz): see Manuel Alvares Marti-Aguilar, 'Tyrian Connections: Evolving Identities in the Punic West', in Gonzalo Cruz Andreotti, *Roman Turdetania, Romanization, Identity and Socio-Cultural Interaction in the South of the Iberian Penenisula between the 4th and 1st centuries BCE*, Brill, pp. 108–129.

53 Livy 33.48.1; Plin. *NH* 5.24.

54 David J Mattingly, 1994, *Tripolitania*, University of Michigan Press, Ann Arbor.

55 Livy, 34.62.2–3.

56 David J Mattingly, 1994, *Tripolitania*, University of Michigan Press, Ann Arbor, pp. 26–28. Macae: Silius Italicus 2.60, 3.275, 5.194, 9.11, 89, 222 and 15.670. Nasamones: Silius Italicus 1.408, 3.320, 13.481. Garamantes: Livy, 29.33.

57 Carthage had warred with some Numidians in 256/255 during the First Punic War: Polyb. 1.31.2. Gaia is king of the Massylii at the start of the Second Punic War in 218; his brother Naravas made an alliance with Hamilcar Barca during the Mercenary War 240–237 (Polyb. 1.78.1f), and reportedly married Hamilcar's daughter. Carthaginian punitive campaigns into Numidia in 238/237 (Oros. 4.9.9; Diod. 26.23) may have established the Massylii as a pro-Carthaginian supra-tribal authority. Thereafter the Massylii were allies of Carthage, and Carthaginian interventions into Numidia (Diod. 25.10) likely defended/consolidated the Massylian kingdom.

state sought to influence these kingdoms through active diplomacy, alliances and intermarriage[58] so as to exert its influence to either employ (as allied auxiliaries or mercenaries) or deflect Numidian military resources.[59]

By 218 the Moors or Mauri, who inhabited the lands of Mauretania to the west of Numidia, had formed a single nation under King Baga.[60] Apparently, there was no formal alliance between the Mauri and Carthage, yet Carthaginian agents were evidently able to recruit Mauri mercenaries.[61] The use of Punic as the language of the Mauri elite signals deep and long-standing relationships between Mauretania and the Punic world, and the circulation of knowledge, technologies and people, but there is no need to hypothesize any Carthaginian military occupation, or the foundation of Punic colonies, let alone Carthaginian administrative control. Mauretania was an independent kingdom on the periphery of the Punic world, its indigenous people deeply influenced by centuries of interaction with Punic seafarers, traders and diplomats.[62]

f *The Balearic Islands*

The westernmost island chain of the Mediterranean Sea were divided into two pairs by Classical authors; the southern two islands, Ibiza and Formentera, were called the Piyuses or Pine Islands, while the northern two islands of Mallorca and Menorca were known as the Balearic Islands (or, more rarely, the Gymnasiae).[63] The Piyuses were first settled by the Phoenicians in the eighth century BC,[64] and by the fourth century BC the city of Iboshim on Ibiza had developed into a large, wealthy trading city, while the whole of the island

---

58 Naravas and Hamilcar's daughter: Pol. 1.78.1–10; Syphax and Sophonisba: cf. Livy, 29.23.

59 Louis Rawlings, 'Warlords, Carthage and the Limits of Hegemony', in Toni Naco del Hoyo and Fernando Lopez Sanchez (eds), *War, Warlords and Interstate Relations in the Ancient Mediterranean*, Brill, Leiden and Boston, pp. 151–180.

60 Livy, 29.30.2.

61 cf. Pol. 15.11.1.

62 Emanuele Papi, 'Punic Mauretania?', pp. 203–218, in Quinn J.C. & Vella N.C. (eds.), *The Punic Mediterranean: identities and identification from Phoenician settlement to Roman rule*, Cambridge University Press, 2014.

63 Alexander Smith, 2020, 'Balearic Insularity in a Global Mediterranean: Considering Circular Domestic Structures of Late Iron Age Menorca', in Anna Kouremenos, *Mediterranean Archaeologies of Insularity in an Age of Globalization*, Oxbow Books, pp. 151–178.

64 The islands of Ibiza and Formentera may have been uninhabited prior to Phoenician settlement: Alexander Joel Smith, 2009, *Indigeneity and Colonial Response: The Metamorphoses of Balearic Culture in the Late Iron Age*, Thesis, B A Braneis University, Providence, Rhode Island, p. 23; Carlos Gomez Bellard, 2008, 'Ibiza: the Making of New Landscapes', in Peter van Dommelen and Carlos Gomez Bellard (eds.), *Rural Landscapes of the Punic World*, Equinox, London, p. 46.

was exploited agriculturally, mostly for olive oil and wine production. In contrast, the Balearic Islands were not colonised by the Phoenicians/Punics, and remained exclusively inhabited by its indigenous peoples, the *Baleares*.[65]

While from the seventh century BC the *Baleares* began interacting with the nearby Punic population, and the islands became part of Carthage's economic network, they remained free of Carthaginian territorial control. Contact with the Punic world stimulated processes of change, stratification and centralization among the *Baleares* (labelled by archaeologists the 'Post-Talayotic Period, *c*. 550–123 BC'). The main economic focus of the *Baleares* moved from the agricultural lands of the interior towards the coast. Sites like Puig de Sa Morisca in south-western Majorca, with differentiated residential areas, defensive walls and towers, and a high concentration of Punic pottery and other Punic finds, suggest that a more powerful native political elite arose, the native chiefdoms increased their coercive power, social differences and social hierarchy and dependency, and were able to assemble a larger agricultural surplus for exchange with the foreigners.[66] Carthage controlled trade and exchange with the Balearians, and so held exclusive access to the Balearians' main export – its military manpower.

II System of Governance

a *The Constitution of Carthage*

Carthage was a city-state, an aristocratic republic, ruled by elected city officials, councils of aristocratic notables, and citizen assemblies. The philosopher Aristotle noted with approval Carthage's stable, oligarchic "mixed constitution", likening it to that of Sparta.[67] It was the only non-Greek constitution that Aristotle assessed, let alone praised. "Carthage also appears to have a good constitution … and a proof of a well-regulated constitution is that the

65 The indigenous culture of the *Baleares* is labelled by modern archaeologists as Late Talayotic.

66 Fernando Prados Martinez, Helena Jimenez and Jose Javier Martinez Garcia (eds.), 2017, *Menorca Entre Fenicis i Punics, Menorca Entre Fenicios y Punicos*, Universidad de Murcia, Publicaciones del Cepoat No. 2, Cercle Artistic de Ciutadella Publicacions des Born, 25; Alejandra Falmes Alba, 2015, 'Visibility and Perception in the Building of a Prehistoric landscape, the Case of Calvia (Mallorca, Balearic Islands)', *Complutum*, Vol. 26, No. 1, pp. 173–188.

67 Robert Drews, 1979 (Spring), 'Carthage and the Spartan Eunomia', *The American Journal of Philology*, Vol. 100, No. 1, Tekmhpion, A Special Issue in Hoor of James Henry Oliver, pp. 45–58.

populace willingly remain faithful to the constitutional system, and that neither civil strife has arisen in any degree worth mentioning, nor yet a tyrant."[68] The Greek geographer Eratosthenes asserted that the Carthaginians and Romans could not be considered "barbarians" because they had such excellent constitutions.[69] Polybius took the view that the good governance Eratosthenes observed at Carthage and Rome was a result of their mixed constitutions, a form of *politeia* restricted for him to just three cities: "The constitution of the Carthaginians seems to me to have been well framed from the first as regards its general distinctions. For they had kings, and the *gerousia* (i.e. senate) was an aristocratic body, and the multitude were masters of matters appropriate to them, and the way in which the whole system worked was very similar in general to that of the Romans and the Spartans."[70] Punic Carthage, notwithstanding its eastern ancestry, came to acquire the traits of a Mediterranean *polis*.

Carthage's government was headed by two *sufetes* (Hebrew "*shophet*"; "judges") elected for a 1-year term, who had wide judicial and administrative powers, much like Roman consuls and Greek *archons*.[71] The *sufetes* were in charge of convening and presiding at the two assemblies of the city; the Council of Elders (called a *gerousia* by Greeks and a *senatus* by Romans) and the People's Assembly. As in Rome, the Council of Elders made the majority of important policy decisions for the state, including declaring war and making peace.[72] While in theory the People's Assembly, comprised of all citizens, enjoyed supreme sovereignty, in practice, the wealthy aristocracy dominated the Council of Elders and the elected public offices, which were not paid. Aristotle, writing in *c.* 335, asserts that election relied on the eminence of one's family and that wealth, however it was procured, was of the greatest importance in obtaining the power required for election.[73]

The Punic city-states of the Western Mediterranean, located in southern Spain, Sardinia, western Sicily and the North African coast, as well as on islands

68 Arist. *Pol.* 2.1272b.

69 Strabo, 1.4.

70 Polyb. 6.51.1–2.

71 Nicolaas Verhelst, 2021, 'The Carthaginian Sufetes: (re-)assessing the literary, epigraphical and archaeological sources', *Carthage Studies 12*, pp. 31–80; Brett Kaufman, 2017, 'Political Economy of Carthage: The Carthaginian Constitution as Reconstructed through Archaeology, Historical Texts and Epigraphy', in Pavel S Avetisyan and Yervand H Grekyan (eds.), *Bridging Times and Spaces, Papers in Ancient Near Eastern, Mediterranean and Armenian Studies*, Archaeopress Publishing Ltd, Oxford, pp. 201–213.

72 Polyb. 3.33.1–4, 15.19.1–3, 8.

73 Arist. *Pol.* 1273a31.

like Ibiza and Malta, all seem to have possessed constitutions that closely mirrored that of Carthage itself.[74]

b *The Carthaginian Aristocracy*

There is a Greco-Roman *topos* that portrays the Carthaginian aristocracy as entrepreneurial, avaricious sea merchants, untrustworthy (*Punica fides*), and generally unwarlike.[75] This *topos* sometimes endures in modern scholarship, where it is suggested that the merchants of Carthage preferred to hire mercenaries to do the serious fighting for them, while they remained focussed on profitable trade. Consideration of the evidence, however, quickly demonstrates this *topos* to be inaccurate. In fact, the Carthaginians were at least as warlike as other Mediterranean states of the time. On several occasions the ancient sources record Carthaginian citizen armies fighting with valour (against Agathocles of Syracuse in 310–308 and M Atilius Regulus in 256/255), and in the fourth century BC the city of Carthage fielded an elite force – the Sacred Band – that was recruited from amongst the city's aristocracy.[76] The most significant aristocratic families in the history of Carthage, the Magonids of the late sixth and early fifth century BC[77] and the Barcids of the third century BC, were military families, not merchants.[78] Aristotle reports: "Indeed among some peoples there are even certain laws stimulating military valour; for instance at Carthage, we are told, warriors receive the decoration of armlets of the same number as the campaigns on which they have served".[79] Like the Greeks and Romans, the Carthaginians took great pride in displaying the spoils of war in their city. Booty looted from Sikeliot cities in the fifth and fourth centuries BC was either sold on the spot or carried back to Carthage in triumph.[80] The Carthaginians seized the famous bronze 'brazen bull of Phalaris' from Akragas in 406 and displayed it in their city until 146 BC, when the Roman Scipio Aemilianus returned it to Akragas.[81]

---

74 On the epigraphic evidence for sufet/shophet magistrates and "people's assemblies" in Punic cities see: Nathan Pilkington, 2019, *The Carthaginian Empire 550–202 BCE*, Lexington Books, pp. 141–171.

75 cf. Diod. 5.38.2–3, 16.79.2; Polyb. 6.52; Plut. *Tim.* 28.11.

76 Diod. 16.80.4.

77 Justin, 18.19.

78 Arthur M Eckstein, 2006, *Mediterranean Anarchy, Interstate War and the Rise of Rome*, University of California Press, pp. 158–176.

79 Arist. *Pol.* 7.1324b.

80 Diod. 13.90.3–4.

81 Diod. 9.18–19: brazen bull of Phalaris. Diod. 13.90.4: "*The most valuable pieces, accordingly, Hamilcar sent to Carthage, among which, as it turned out, was the bull of Phalaris*".

The Carthaginian aristocracy were landowners more than seafarers, enriched by the city's bulk commodity trade in grain, olive oil and wine with Athens, Corinth and other city-states in the Mediterranean.[82] The huge estates of Hanno the Great in North Africa were alleged to have required the toil of 20,000 slaves[83]; the Barca family-owned large olive plantations sixty miles southeast of Carthage.[84] The wealth of the Carthaginian state and its aristocracy rested upon agriculture, lands worked by great numbers of native Libyan serfs or chattel slaves procured through the Mediterranean slave trade. Moreover, the peacefulness of seafaring and maritime trade in ancient times should not be exaggerated, as merchants were typically also potential pirates, raiders and slavers, and it is clear that the Carthaginians were regarded as notorious raiders and slavers by their Graeco-Roman contemporaries.[85]

c *Carthaginian Generals*

The Carthaginian constitution had a unique feature, in that it split civil and military authority among its elected magistrates. While the most senior magistrates were the *sufetes*, they did not possess military authority, unlike Roman consuls or Greek *strategoi*. Instead, the Carthaginians elected generals to undertake specific military tasks or command in a theatre of operations. The election of generals seems to have been a prerogative of the citizen's assembly.[86] It seems that after *c.* 255 the assembly merely ratified the army's own

82 North African, Sardinian and Sicilian grain were the mainstays of the grain trade of the western Mediterranean: see Lionel Casson, 'The Grain Trade of the Hellenistic World', *Transactions and Proceedings of the American Philological Association*, Vol. 85, 1954, pp. 168–187.

83 Justin, 21.4.6.

84 Livy, 33.48.1; Pliny, *NH* 17.93.

85 The Punic economy traded extensively in slaves, and the volume of their slave trade seems to have reached greater proportions than that of other Mediterranean peoples: see S Moscati, *Il Mondo de Fenici*, Milano, 1966, p. 164 & 347. Ancient sources like Herodotus and Homer characterize Phoenicians as dangerous pirates and kidnappers. The two Romano-Carthaginian treaties that have survived suggest that many slaves were taken by Carthage through organized brigandage; the treaty of 509 BC forbade the Carthaginians from building forts in Latium and to spend the night on land, suggesting pirates and slavers preying on the neighbourhood in search of captives; the treaty of 326 BC prevents Carthage from selling captured people from towns allied to Rome in Roman markets. This suggests Punic slave-raiding groups from North Africa were raiding the Italian coast in search of human spoils. On the relationship between piracy and the Hellenistic slave trade see: Philip de Souza, 1999, *Piracy in the Graeco-Roman World*, Cambridge University Press, Port Melbourne, pp. 60–65.

86 Diod. 11.20.1; Polyb. 3.13.4, 1.82.12.

choice.[87] During the Mercenary War the generals Hamilcar Barca and Hanno quarrelled, and the army was asked to reject one of them.[88] When Hamilcar Barca was killed in Iberia, his son-in-law Hasdrubal was "acclaimed as general by the army and by the Carthaginians alike".[89] Later, when a successor for Hasdrubal needed to be found, Polybius records that the Carthaginians "at first waited for a pronouncement on the part of the troops, and when news reached them from their armies that the soldiers had unanimously chosen Hannibal as their commander, they hastened to summon a general assembly of the commons, which unanimously ratified the choice of the soldiers".[90] This pattern may reflect the fact that a kind of "mobile citizen's assembly" was held to be present because of the number of citizens present in the Carthaginian army.

Generals were not elected for a discrete term of office, but rather for the duration of a military campaign, unless they were dismissed or resigned. Hence, Carthaginian generals often held long-term commands: Hannibal Barca was supreme general of Carthage for twenty years. This certainly increased their experience, and enabled generals to create workable command structures, especially important since the Carthaginian army was made up of such disparate ethnic and linguistic elements. The sources suggest that the office of 'general' was very often monopolised by a small number of aristocratic families in Carthage, families with a 'military tradition'; this certainly appears to be true of the Mago family in the fifth century BC and the Barcid family in the third century BC. This served to provide Carthaginian generals with the "sort of informal military training of commanders which was necessary in ancient societies with no concept of formal military academies."[91]

The powers of the Carthaginian generals were very wide. The Greek rhetorician Isocrates (436–338) noted "we know that while the Carthaginians and the Lacedaemonians, who are the best governed peoples of the world, are ruled by oligarchies at home, yet, when they take the field, they are ruled by kings."[92] Carthaginian generals could command forces at land or sea as they saw fit, exercise military authority over all Punic territory, were empowered to make alliances and agreements on behalf of the state, and even found new cities.

87 cf. Xanthippos: Pol. 1.33.4–5.

88 Pol. 1.82.5, 12.

89 Diod. 15.12.1.

90 Polyb. 3.13.3–4.

91 Jonathan P Roth, 2007, 'Chapter 12: War', in Philip Sabin, Hans Van Wees and Michael Whitby (eds.), *The Cambridge History of Greek and Roman Warfare, Vol. 1: Greece, the Hellenistic World and the Rise of Rome*, Cambridge University Press, Melbourne, pp. 372–373.

92 Isoc. 3.24.

Carthaginian generals also exercised administrative powers; during the First Punic War it was Carthaginian generals that enforced the Carthaginian's harsh taxation of their Libyan subjects.[93]

Notwithstanding the wide authority of Carthaginian generals, there should be no doubt that they remained subordinate to the government at Carthage. The Council of Elders may have been required to ratify decisions made by its general in the field, and it was alive to the threat of corruption and abuse that a general may represent. In the fifth century BC Carthage established a formal mechanism to review the actions of generals. "One hundred judges were chosen from the senate, who were to demand of the generals, when they returned from war, an account of their proceedings, in order that, under this control, they might exercise their command in war with a regard to the judgements and laws at home".[94] Generals were thus able to be tried by the Council of Elders, although any such trial might lead to sedition.[95] Diodorus observed that in war the Carthaginians "advance their leading men to commands, taking it for granted that these should be first to brave danger for the whole state; but when they gain peace, they plague these same men with suits, bring false charges against them through envy, and load them down with penalties."[96] In one case a general starved himself to death before facing trial.[97] Unsuccessful generals could suffer dismissal, fines or even execution by crucifixion: Hanno was crucified following defeat at the hands of the Roman fleet at the Aegates Islands in 241.[98] Being a Carthaginian general that suffered defeat could cost one his life. While the Carthaginian treatment of its generals appears harsh in comparison to Rome (i.e. Varro after Cannae[99]), it was not so unusual when compared to the Greek world in the Classical Period. Athenian generals chosen by the *demos* could be tried at any time *during* their generalship for treason, corruption or other crimes and be executed or obliged to flee into exile.[100]

93 Diod. 24.10.2.

94 Justin, 19.2.5–6.

95 Malco: Justin. 18.7.

96 Diod. 20.10.3.

97 Diod. 14.76.4.

98 Dismissal: Zon. 8.5; Diod. 23.9.2. Fines: Diod. 23.9.2. Crucifixion of Hanno: Zon. 8.17. A general named Hannibal was crucified by his own men after a defeat during the First Punic War: Polyb 1.11.5.

99 Livy, 22.61.14–15.

100 Between 431 and 322 some 28 Athenian generals were deposed in Athens. Of the 21 trials that ensued in 14 the verdict was death (5 escaped and fled into exile); see D Hamel, 1998, *Athenian Generals. Military authority in the Classical Period*, Mnemosyne Supplement 182, Brill, Leiden, pp. 115–140.

d *Carthaginian Staff and Officers*

There are several occasions when a conflict required or was entrusted to more than a single general. In some cases these generals appear to have identical powers,[101] whereas on other occasions one general is clearly superior to the others.[102] In the Second Punic War, for example, Hannibal Barca was clearly the supreme general, although there were several other generals commanding fleets and/or armies in other theatres of conflict.

Carthaginian generals commanded and controlled their armies with the assistance of a number of senior officers. The sources also refer to senior naval officers, using the Greek terms *trierarch* or *navarch* interchangeably. While in the Classical Greek world a *trierarch* refers to a "captain of a trireme" and a *navarch* is a "leader of ships", the terms appear to denote "admiral" in the Carthaginian context. Polybius describes Hasdrubal, son-in-law and heir of Hamilcar Barca, as *trierarch* in command of the Carthaginian fleet.[103] Another Carthaginian officer named Hannibal is a *trierarch,* "who commanded the Carthaginian squadron of triremes in Italy".[104]

The sources depict Hannibal leading his army with the assistance of a 'council' of senior Carthaginian officers,[105] and there are many instances of Hannibal delegating command of sections of his army to such officers, both in battle and in independent operations. In Hannibal's army during the Second Punic War many of his most senior lieutenants were his family connections or friends (i.e., Hannibal Monomachus and Mago 'the Samnite').[106] Other Carthaginian officers entrusted with important commands, such as Marhabal son of Himilco, Carthalo,[107] Gisgo,[108] and Himilco,[109] were also likely Carthaginian aristocrats as well as professional soldiers.

Aside from Carthaginian officers, Hannibal was accompanied in both Hispania and Italy by *synedroi*, who were probably members of the Carthaginian senate, perhaps serving in a capacity not unlike that of Spartan *ephors*.[110] Three of these – Mago, Myrcan and Barmocar – were important enough to be

101 At the Crimisus in 339: Plut. Tim. 25.3; against the Romans in North Africa during the First Punic War: Polyb. 1.30.1, 1.32.5.
102 Diod. 13.80.2; Polyb. 1.82.12.
103 Polyb. 2.1.9.
104 Polyb. 7.2.
105 Polyb. 3.71.5, 85.6, 9.24.4–8.
106 Polyb. 9.24.5–6, 25.
107 Livy, 22.15.8; 22.49.13; 58.7.
108 Plut., *Vit. Fab. Max.* 15.2.
109 Livy, 22.30.1.
110 *Synedroi*: Polybius, 3.20.8, 71.5. *Gerousiastai*: Polybius, 7.9.1.

mentioned along with Hannibal in the treaty of 215 with Philip V of Macedon.[111] Presumably, these aristocrats represented the Carthaginian state, and they perhaps had responsibilities in matters of diplomacy and logistics. Carthaginian generals commanded their multinational armies in the Punic language rather than Greek; we know that Xanthippos commanded through interpreters[112] and that the Punic language was the *lingua franca* for the Carthaginian army at the time of the outbreak of the Mercenary War in 241.[113]

III The Carthaginian Military

a *The Carthaginian Fleet*

The operational limitations of ancient galleys and the resulting strategic implications are articulated in several publications, including A W Gomme's *A Forgotten Factor of Greek Naval Strategy*, Boris Rankov's *The Second Punic War at Sea* and Louis Rawling's *The Carthaginian Navy: Questions and Assumptions*.[114] The short endurance and low sea keeping qualities of oared warships tied them to friendly bases and shores and limited their range of operations. Fleets typically confined their activities to the Mediterranean's optimal sailing months of May-September. Carthage's geographical position in the central Mediterranean meant that the city's fleets were well placed to move between North Africa, Sicily, Sardinia, southern Iberia and Ibiza. For example, the ports at Lilybaion, Drepanon and Panormos in western Sicily were all strongly fortified and possessed large anchorages, and were well suited to serve as landing points for forces crossing from Carthage. Ancient fleets were used to escort sailing ships and galleys transporting forces and materiel, to undertake raids upon enemy coasts, or to support sieges of enemy strongpoints. These fleets, being comprised of oared galleys specialised for sea fighting, such as triremes

111 Polyb. 7.9.1.

112 Diod. 23.16.1.

113 Polyb. 1.80.6; Gregory Daly, 2002, *Cannae. The Experience of Battle in the Second Punic War*, Routledge, London & New York, p. 88.

114 A W Gomme, 1933, 'A Forgotten Factor of Greek Naval Strategy', *Journal of Hellenic Studies*, Vol. 53, pp. 16–24; Boris Rankov, 1996, 'The Second Punic War at Sea', in Tim Cornell, Boris Rankov and Philip Sabin (eds.), *The Second Punic War. A Reappraisal*, London, pp. 49–58; Louis Rawlings, 2010, 'The Carthaginian Navy: Questions and Assumptions', in Garrett Fagan and Matthew Trundle (eds.), *New Perspectives on Ancient Warfare*, History of Warfare, Vol. 59, Brill, pp. 253–287; also Philip De Souza, 2007, 'Naval Battles and Sieges', in Philip Sabin, Hans Van Wees and Michael Whitby (eds.), *The Cambridge History of Greek and Roman Warfare*, Cambridge University Press, pp. 434–460.

or larger quinqueremes, might engage in sea battles with enemy fleets. These sea battles typically occurred near the shore or in key straits, given the operational role of fleets of galleys.

Carthaginian fleets were not standing forces, but rather were launched on an *ad hoc* basis, much like the city's land armies. Carthage was home to first-rate harbour and port facilities, and these are described in detail by Appian,[115] for which there is firm archaeological evidence.[116] Carthage's military port was built over several phases of construction, with a sequence of timber and stone buildings, and while the original harbour dates to the fourth century BC, the harbour described by Appian was later. The stone shipsheds have been dated to "*no earlier than the late third century and possibly as late as the mid second century BC*."[117] The total number of shipsheds fitted into the military harbour at Carthage is estimated to have been 170, with 30 in the island and 140 along the perimeter. These shipsheds served as individual bays in which to hold galleys out of the water, so that they could be stored in a state of readiness.[118] The excavation of two warship wrecks at Punta Scario, Sicily,[119] provided information concerning Carthaginian shipbuilding techniques, including the discovery of Punic letters and incised guide lines on the ship's timbers, suggesting that a literate workforce had used prefabricated parts and serial construction to construct oared galleys.[120]

115 App. *Pun.* 95–96; cf. Strabo 17.3.14–15.

116 Henry Hurst and Lawrence E Stager, 1978, 'A Metropolitan Landscape: The Late Punic Port of Carthage', *World Archaeology* 9.3, pp. 334–346; Henrik Gerding, 2013, 'Carthage', in David Blackman, Boris Rankov, Kalliopi Baika, Henrik Gerding and Jari Pakkanen, *Shipsheds of the Ancient Mediterranean*, Cambridge University Press, pp. 307–318.

117 Henry Hurst, 1999, 'The Sanctuary of Tanit at Carthage in the Roman Period: A Reinterpretation', *Journal of Roman Archaeology*, Supplementary Series 30, p. 13.

118 Ideally war galleys were kept out of the water when not in service, so as to keep their hulls dry, keeping them light for better performance when at sea, and to avoid the effects of shipworm: see Alwin G. Steinmayer Jnr and Jean MacIntosh Turfa, 1996, 'Effects of shipworm on the performance of ancient Mediterranean warships', *The International Journal of Nautical Archaeology* 25.2, pp. 104–121.

119 Honor Frost, 1973, 'First season of excavation on the Punic wreck in Sicily', *The International Journal of Nautical Archaeology and Underwater Exploration* 2.1, pp. 33–49; Honor Frost, 1974, 'The Punic wreck in Sicily', *The International Journal of Nautical Archaeology and Underwater Exploration* 3.1, pp. 35–54; Honor Frost, 1987, 'How Carthage Lost the Sea', *Natural History* 96.12, pp. 58–66.

120 Honor Frost, 1989, 'The Prefabricated Punic Warship', in E Lipinski and H Devijver, *Punic Wars, Orientalia Lovaniensia Analecta 33, Studia Phoenicia 10*, Louvain, pp. 127–136. Another fascinating discovery was that of baskets of *Cannabis sativa*: Honor Frost, 2011, 'Don't Forget the Dunnage: targeting plants on ships', *Nautical Archaeology* 40.1, pp. 194–198.

Rather than timber, bronze or even money, manpower was the principal constraint on the size of fleets in the ancient world. On the basis of the literary evidence, W W Tarn concludes that in the fifth and fourth centuries BC the ordinary establishment of the Carthaginian fleet was around 120 triremes, requiring some 20,400 oarsmen and sailors and an additional 2,400 marines. Tarn believes that the city was capable of launching a fleet of 200 warships in a "supreme national effort", which would require some 40,000 oarsmen, sailors and marines.[121] According to Polybius the Carthaginian and Roman fleets launched during the First Punic War comprised 200 or more of the larger quinqueremes, which would represent a gargantuan commitment of manpower, some 60,000 oarsmen alone. Polybius reports that the Carthaginian fleet at the battle of Cape Ecnomus in 256 numbered 350 "decked ships": if these were quinqueremes then such a fleet would have required 105,000 oarsmen alone, besides sailors, officers and marines.[122]

It is generally assumed that most of the oarsmen, sailors and officers serving in Carthaginian galleys were citizens,[123] while embarked marines seem to have been detached from the land forces.[124] Carthaginian citizens serving as oarsmen were likely augmented by drafts from other Punic cities such as Utica, Hippo Acra and Panormos. Panormos was the best harbour in Sicily, able to host two-hundred warships, and possessed shipyards able to repair whole fleets.[125] Appian, describing Hippo Acra in 148, notes that it was "a large city, with walls, citadel, harbor, and dockyards handsomely built by Agathocles".[126] Hippo Acra seems to have maintained a squadron of warships, and this may have been typical of Carthage's Punic allies, just as it was for Rome's *socci navales*. It is suggestive that the *columna rostra* set up to mark Duilius' victory at Mylae in 260 mentions both captured Carthaginian and *socii* ships.[127] The Punic cities of Iberia certainly provided crews (and perhaps also ships) during the Second Punic War.[128] All of the Punic cities of the western Mediterranean

121 W W Tarn, 1907, 'The Fleets of the First Punic War', *The Journal of Hellenic Studies* 27, pp. 48–60.

122 Polyb. 1.25.

123 Polyb. 1.27.1.

124 cf. Polyb. 1.9.10, 1.60.3.

125 Diod. 11.20.2–3: Carthaginian fleet of 200 warships suffers storm damage and repaired at Panormos.

126 App. *Pun.* 110. Agathocles stormed Hippo Acra "after getting the better of it's people in a naval battle" and it was probably there that he constructed the "*pentekonters and light ships*" described at Diod. 20.55.5.

127 *CIL* i2 2.25.

128 Livy, 23.26.

enjoyed a seafaring tradition, were participants in maritime trade and possessed ports and seafarers. The demand for oarsmen was such that Carthage likely recruited them wherever it could, and Livy notes that when the main Carthaginian fleet was in Tarentum in 211 it was crewed by "men of all races".[129]

While speculative, Carthage may have found the manpower for its galley fleets in much the same way that Athens did during the fourth century BC. Athens, like Carthage a maritime city, recruited its oarsmen from among its own citizenry, specifically from among the class named *thetes*, who were not liable for service as hoplites, but had to serve as rowers. The *thetes* of Athens were poorer citizens, craftsmen and casual labourers, who owned little or no land. Many of *thetes* in Athens lived on state pay; they were paid from state funds for their service as oarsmen, and this became an important livelihood for a significant number of the Athenian poor.[130] In addition, the citizen conscripts of Athens were often of such poor quality that the state hired professional oarsmen on the open market, often referred to as 'mercenary oarsmen'.[131] Like Athens in the fourth century BC, the Carthaginian galley fleet in the third century BC prided itself on ramming tactics, which required speed and manoeuvrability, and this required skilled oarsmen. For this reason, Carthage may have sought to develop among its poorer citizens a supply of skilled oarsmen. Just as Athens conscripted the *thetes* as rowers, perhaps Carthage also relied upon its poorer landless citizens, who may, in turn, have come to rely (at least in part) upon state pay.[132]

Contrary to popular belief, the oarsmen in galleys were not recruited from among prisoners of war, slaves or criminals. The ancient galley needed a crew that was experienced, motivated, willing to fight both at sea and during amphibious operations ashore. Given that approximately 300 of the 400 men of a *quinquereme* crew served as oarsmen, it was absurd to have some 75% of a crew drawn from such a disloyal and potentially rebellious source. Only later in the Renaissance period did Mediterranean galleys come to rely on slave and criminal labour. The few occasions when the ancients do report the

129 Livy, 26.20.9–10.

130 A H M Jones, 1955, 'The Social Structure of Athens in the Fourth Century', *The Economic History Review*, New Series, Vol. 8, No. 2, pp. 141–155.

131 Vincent Gabrielsen, 1995, 'The Athenian Navy in the Fourth Century BC', in Robert Gardiner & Prof. John Morrison (ed.), *The Age of the Galley*, Conway Maritime Press, pp. 234–240.

132 Carlos G.Wagner, 2006, 'Ciudad y Ciudadania en la Cartago Punica', in Francisco Marco Simon, Francisco Pina Polo and Jose Remesal Rodriguez (eds.), *Republicas y Cuidadanos: Modelos de Participacion Civica en el Mundo Antiguo*, Universitat de Barcelona, Barcelona, pp. 103–113.

recruitment of freed slaves and captives as oarsmen are moments of dire crisis, and resonate simply because they are so rare.[133]

b *Soldiers of Carthage*, c. *550–300*

As we have seen, the origins of Carthaginian power are to be found in its fleet. However, the Carthaginians soon found that the city needed to field land armies too if it was to annexe territories in North Africa and Sardinia, or successfully contend with the Greek city-states of Sicily. In 480 and then throughout the years 410 to 241 Carthage fought a series of wars in Sicily, particularly against the expansionist tyrants of Syracuse Dionysius I (406–367) and Agathokles (317–289), and finally against Rome (First Punic War 264–241). These wars made ever-greater demands upon Carthage for manpower, money and resources. In 410–404 the Carthaginians defeated the Greeks in Sicily, consolidating the city's control in the west of the island, and imposing tribute on eastern parts of the island. Thereafter, Carthaginian military involvement in Sicily was usually either in response to appeals for assistance (i.e. Syracuse 345, Katane and Leontinoi in 341/340) or to repel sudden Greek invasions of Punic Sicily (i.e. Dionysius I in 399, Timoleon in 341).

Experience meant that the Carthaginians understood that any strong Greek power able to unite eastern Sicily was likely to then attack the Carthaginian position on the island without warning, regardless of existing diplomatic agreements, and with substantial military force.[134] For this reason, Carthage intervened in affairs in eastern Sicily with the aim of ensuring that the several Greek city-states there remained autonomous under their own leaders, opposed to the restoration of any Syracusan hegemony, and on good diplomatic terms with the Carthaginians.[135] The success of Timoleon in 344 and Agathokles in 312/311 in re-establishing Syracusan power and invading Punic Sicily represented moments when this Carthaginian policy in Sicily failed.

In periods of peace, the Carthaginian state seems to have maintained garrisons in key places in Sicily, as well as in Sardinia and North Africa. Polybius and Appian refer to an officer named a *boetharchos* (Βοήθαρχος), a Greek term that denotes a military officer in charge of territory. These were likely military governors in Carthaginian provinces who commanded the permanent garrisons

133 Jan M Libourel, 'Galley Slaves in the Second Punic War', *Classical Philology*, Vol. 68, No. 2, Apr. 1972, pp. 116–119.

134 Motya in 398/397: Diod. 14.44–6; Dionysius' sudden attack in 368: Diod. 15.73; Christopher de Lisle, 2021, *Agathokles of Syracuse. Sicilian Tyrant and Hellenistic King*, Oxford Classical Monographs, Oxford University Press, pp. 209–214.

135 Carthage supports Dion against Dionysius II in 357/356: Diod. 16.9.4–6; Plut. *Dion* 25.

there in peacetime. The purpose of these garrisons seems to have been to maintain general security and support Carthaginian rule; in Sicily the several garrisons on the border of the *epikrateia* had the task of deterring or delaying any major incursion until Carthage could organise a military response.[136]

The response of the Carthaginian state to any major incursion in Sicily was to muster the expeditionary forces needed to repel the enemy. Diodorus provides a snapshot of how Carthage did this when, in 397, the city was preparing such an expedition. Carthage sent representatives "with large sums of money" to recruit mercenaries (*xenologein*) from the Balearics and Iberia, while they themselves canvassed Libya registering (*katagraphontes*) soldiers from among the Libyans, Phoenicians, and (presumably Carthaginian) citizens; they also summoned (*metepemponto*) troops from allied peoples and kings in North Africa, including the Nomades, Marausii, and peoples living in the area of Cyrene, while hiring others (*misthōsamenoi*) in Italy.[137] Carthage's military forces were hence recruited in three distinct ways: Italian, Iberian, and Balearic warriors are hired as mercenaries, North African allies sent auxiliary contingents, and there was a registration of men from among the subject Libyan and allied Punic populations, as well as at Carthage itself. Mustering such expeditions was slow, and typically took a year or even longer after hostilities had begun. Diodorus speaks of "great preparations" prior to the first Carthaginian intervention into Sicily in 480.[138] In its military campaign in Sicily in 409–396 the Carthaginian expeditions included *mechanemata* (presumably siege equipment) and *bele* (missiles and projectiles).[139] Arms production, particularly of siege engines, seems to have occurred exclusively at Carthage. The burden for keeping Carthaginian expeditions in Sicily provisioned seems to have fallen on Punic Africa and Sardinia, with grain being shipped into ports close to the areas of conflict.[140]

The most important and reliable source of military manpower to field heavy infantry for Carthage were its own citizens and Libyan subjects. Carthage remained abreast of tactical and technological military developments, and as we have already seen were greatly influenced by the Greeks. There is every reason to understand that the base of the Carthaginian military structure in the

136 Polyb. 1.79.2; App. *Lib.* 68.306, 71.318–319, 74.341 (in 149 BC).

137 Diod. 13.80.2–3.

138 Diod. 11.1.4–5.

139 Diod. 13.54.1–3, 13.79.8, 13.80.1–6, 13.96.5, 14.54.4–6.

140 Anna Chiara Fariselli, 1999, 'The impact of military preparations on the economy of the Carthaginian state', in Giovanna Pisano (ed.), *Phoenicians and Carthaginians in the Western Mediterranean*, Studia Punica 12, Universita degli Studi di Roma, Rome.

fourth century BC remained its citizens, as it was too for Greek and Etruscan city-states. The citizen militia provided the infantry core of Carthaginian armies, armed in the hoplite panoply,[141] but added to these were Libyan conscripts.[142] At the battle at Crimissus in 339 some 75% of the hoplite infantry were Libyans, the remainder being Carthaginians. Diodorus reports that the Carthaginians "made a levy from among their noblest citizens and made suitable drafts among the Libyans".[143] We can reasonably assume that these Libyan conscripts were mustered, drilled and equipped by the Carthaginian state and commanded by Carthaginian officers. At Crimissus the Carthaginian and Libyan hoplite infantry were indistinguishable in their panoply and drill.[144] At the outbreak of the Mercenaries War in 241 the largest portion of the Carthaginian army was Libyan.[145] It was the native Libyan subjects of Carthage that supplied the heavy infantry core of Carthaginian armies, and this would remain true during the First and Second Punic Wars. In 218 some 12,000 of the 20,000 heavy infantry Hannibal brought to Italy were Libyan, the remainder being Iberians.[146]

The conscription of Libyan manpower offset the fact that the city of Carthage itself had a relatively small citizen body, lacking the class of small farmers that was typical of Greek city-states and Rome. The surrender of 200,000 cuirasses to Rome during the Third Punic War[147] suggests Carthaginian armouries held supplies intended for its subject levies, as these are far too many for the city's population alone. Gregory Daly notes that; "Perhaps Carthage was reluctant to give her subjects the responsibility of providing their own weapons when they served as soldiers – after all, a subject people with the right to bear arms could pose a significant threat to their masters."[148] There were several serious

141 cf. Polyb. 1.33; Plut. *Tim.* 28.1.

142 In 410 Carthage was able to swiftly deploy 5,000 Libyan infantry to protect Segesta from Selinuntian attacks: Diod. 13.44.1. This was the first occasion that such a body of Libyans had been deployed by Carthage since the city had annexed large parts of Tunisia in the years *c.* 470–450. It seems from Diodorus that these Libyan troops were "on hand" and available for speedy redeployment to Sicily.

143 Diod. 16.73.

144 Plutarch mentions "ten thousand footmen bearing white shields, whom they guessed to be all Carthaginians" (*Tim.* 27.4), while Diodorus informs us that the Carthaginian 'Sacred Band' numbered only 2,500, while the remaining hoplites were presumably Libyans.

145 Polyb. 1.67.13, 7.

146 Polyb. 3.56.4.

147 Polyb. 36.6.7; Appian, *Pun.* 80.

148 Gregory Daly, 2002, *Cannae. The Experience of Battle in the Second Punic War*, Routledge, London & New York, p. 86.

Libyan revolts against Carthaginian rule; in 395,[149] again in 379/78 (Libyans and Sardinians revolt)[150] and most seriously during the Mercenary War 240–238.

Notwithstanding the recruitment of Libyans (and mercenaries) Carthaginian citizens continued to serve in the phalanx overseas after 339, and are reported in 311 and 310.[151] Thereafter, however, Carthaginian citizens are usually found serving as officers and staff, commanding subject Libyans, Numidian allies or mercenaries. It is noteworthy that in 311 Carthage supported its expedition to Sicily with a fleet of 130 triremes, which would have required some 22,000 oarsmen. It would appear that manning the fleet became the chief role of the Carthaginian citizen body. After 310 the Carthaginian citizenry is only mobilised for land warfare *in extremis*, when the city itself was threatened, such as during Agathokles invasion of Africa, and later during the Mercenary War and the Roman invasions of North Africa during the Punic Wars.[152]

c *The Hellenistic Period (323–31 BC) and the Homogenisation of Weapons and Panoply in the Western Mediterranean*

The military campaigns of Philip II and Alexander the Great of Macedon triggered a revolution in strategy, tactics, doctrine, weapons and troop types that influenced warfare throughout the Mediterranean for centuries. The campaigns of King Pyrros of Eperios in Italy and Sicily during 280–275 meant that both Rome and Carthage experienced first-hand the onset of a modern, all-arms Hellenistic army, one comprising shock cavalry, war elephants, skirmishers and heavy infantry fighting in the "Macedonian style", that is as close order pikemen wielding the *sarissa*.[153]

The demands of warfare in the Hellenistic period meant the need for larger armies that were required to remain in the field for longer periods, wintering in camps rather than dispersing, renewing military operations in the spring. The Carthaginians remained keen recruiters of mercenaries when mustering their forces for war, but this was entirely typical of the Hellenistic period, and mirrored the behaviour of the Greek Leagues and the 'Successor' kingdoms in Greece, Asia and Egypt. It was the Romans themselves who were unusual for

149 Diod. 14.77.

150 Diod. 15.24.2–3, 15.73.1.

151 In 311 some 2,000 citizens including many nobles and 10,000 Libyans: Diod. 19.106.2. In 310, Diod. 20.10.5–6.

152 Agathokles in Africa: Diod. 20.10.5–6, 20.12.3. First Punic War: Polyb. 1.32, 1.33.6, 1.34.6. The Mercenary War: Polyb. 1.73.1–2, 1.75.2, 1.87.3–6.

153 Sekunda, Nicholas, 2019, *The Army of Pyrrhus of Epirus, 3rd Century BC*, Men-at-Arms No. 528, Osprey, London.

their complete reliance on citizen militia and allied levies rather than mercenary manpower. Warfare became more complex, as the decisive clash of armies was now accompanied by campaigns of manoeuvre and long sieges, extensive skirmishing, foraging and raiding. New troop types emerged to meet these requirements. The constant need for funds and provisions to support standing armies and garrisons took on an enormous importance.

There were important military influences upon Carthage (and Rome) besides Greece and the Successor kingdoms. Encounters with warriors from Celtic, Iberian and Italic societies engendered processes of interaction, imitation and adoption of new equipment and fighting styles. Beginning in the late fourth century BC there began a steady homogenisation of military equipment and fighting styles in the Western Mediterranean, encompassing both Carthage and Rome, both of which abandoned the hoplite phalanx.[154]

The use of open-style helmets such as the Celtic-style Montefortino type became common, enabling better sight and sound for the wearer. It was now important for heavy infantry to have better sight and sound on the battlefield, given the new emphasis of individual combat and more complex tactical manoeuvres. Celtic-style chain mail armour (*lorica*), Samnite and Iberian style round breastplates and pectoral armour (*pectorales* or *kardiophilakes*) and Greek-style iron, bronze or linen cuirasses became common. While the main hoplite weapon, the thrusting spear (Greek: '*dory*'; Latin: '*hastae*') continued to be found in the equipment of heavy infantry, it was steadily superseded in importance by the cut-and-thrust sword (i.e., the Greek *xiphos*, Iberian *falcata*). Heavy infantry now carried heavy throwing spears (*pilum* or the Iberian all-iron *soliferrum*) and lighter spears and javelins (*longche*). In this way, heavy infantry in the West came to combine the roles of Classical period skirmishers and close-order hoplites. The increasing use of javelins and *pila* encouraged the use of Celtic-style shields (*scutum*), because these enabled troops to protect themselves from missile fire and engage in hand-to-hand fighting. Fighting in a close order phalanx gave way to fighting in more flexible, open-order formations – labelled manipular tactics by the Romans, but not greatly different from the fighting styles of Celtic and Iberian warriors.[155] Borrowing from the

154 Michael T Burns, 2003, 'The Homogenisation of Military Equipment Under the Roman Republic', in A D Merryweather (ed.), *Romanisation? Digressus Supplement 1*, Proceedings of a post-graduate colloquium, The Institute of Classical Studies, University of London, 15 November 2002, pp. 60–85.

155 Fernando Quesada Sanz, 2006, 'Not so different: individual fighting techniques and battle tactics of Roman and Iberian armies within the framework of warfare in the Hellenistic Age', in P Francois, P Moret, S Pere-Nogues (eds.), *L'Hellenisation en Mediterranee*

Celts, Iberians and Italic peoples, the panoply and method of fighting of the heavy infantryman of the western Mediterranean evolved from that of a hoplite to one that could inflict damage from a distance with javelins, form a line to fight hand-to-hand with sword or spear, and move swiftly and operate flexibly across rugged terrain.

Hellenistic armies of the eastern Mediterranean also adopted this new panoply and fighting style, but to a much more limited extent. While the Macedonian-style phalanx armed with the long pike remained central to the armies of Macedonia and the Successors, nonetheless there did appear a new type of soldier – the *thureophoroi*. These were dual-purpose infantry, armed with an oval shield (*theuros*), throwing spears and swords, able to fight either as open order skirmishers or in a battle line. *Thureophoroi* were not so different from the Roman *hastati* or Celtic and Samnite warriors. It is speculated that the Greek *theuros* shield was based upon the *scutum* shields encountered during the Celtic invasion of Greece in 281–279, or perhaps the Italic *scutum* encountered in the Pyhrric Wars of 280–275.[156] Later, in the 160s, the Successor kingdoms moved to equip and drill their own forces in the "Roman manner" (as it had then become known) – but by that time the progress of the Roman legions in the eastern Mediterranean was irresistible.[157]

d *Carthaginian Pikemen? Carthaginian Infantry in the Punic Wars*

Given the influence of the Hellenistic World on Carthaginian society and warfare, several historians have asserted that the Carthaginians also adopted the 'Macedonian-style' phalanx, that is, pikemen in close order formation wielding the *sarissa* (Greek: σάρισα, a long spear or pike about 13–20 feet in length). The erroneous notion that at least some of the heavy infantry of Carthage fought the Punic Wars in the manner of Macedonian pikemen was promoted by John Warry's *Warfare in the Classical World* (1980) and Peter Connolly's *Greece and Rome at War* (1981), and has been promulgated ever since by several authors

Occidentale au temps des guerres puniques, Actes du Colloque International de Toulouse, 31 mars-2 avril 2005, Pallas 70, pp. 245–263.

156 Nicholas Secunda and Philip de Souza, 2007, 'Chapter 11: Military Forces', in Philip Sabin, Hans Van Wees and Michael Whitby (eds.), *The Cambridge History of Greek and Roman Warfare, Vol. 1: Greece, the Hellenistic World and the Rise of Rome*, Cambridge University Press, Melbourne, p. 341.

157 Nicholas Sekunda, 2001, *Hellenistic Infantry Reform in the 160's BC*, Leopard's Head Press, Gdansk; Luke Euda-Sarson, 2002 (May), 'The Evolution of Hellenistic Infantry Part 1: The Reforms of Iphikrates', *Slingshot*, Vol. 222, pp. 30–36; Luke Euda-Sarson, 2002 (July), 'The Evolution of Hellenistic Infantry Part 2: Infantry of the Successors', *Slingshot*, Vol. 223, pp. 23–28.

in more recent studies of ancient military history and the Punic Wars, such as J E Lendon (2005),[158] Brian Todd Carey *et. al.* (2007)[159] and Richard A Gabriel (2008).[160]

While Polybius often refers to bodies of Punic infantry as a 'phalanx',[161] he uses the term broadly to describe men fighting *en masse* or in formation, and so we find him using the term to describe Roman *hastati*.[162] Asclepiodotus even describes bodies of cavalry and light infantry as 'phalanxes',[163] suggesting that by the second century BC the term 'phalanx' had become synonymous with 'unit'. Sometimes it is asserted that while the Lacedaemonian mercenary Xanthippos commanded the Carthaginian army in 255 he may have introduced the *sarissa*. However, there is no suggestion in the sources that Xanthippos re-armed or transformed the fighting style of the various contingents of the Carthaginian army.[164] The Spartans themselves did not re-equip their army in the 'Macedonian style' until the Cleomenean War (229/228–222). Xanthippos had no difficulty commanding the Iberian and Celtic contingents in the Carthaginian army, who were certainly equipped and fought as heavy infantry in their own native style.

Ancient military systems disappear slowly, as evidenced by the fact that a remnant of the hoplite panoply persisted in Roman armies throughout the Republican period in the form of the *triarii* – the 600 veterans that formed the 'third line' of the 4,500-strong all-arms Roman legion. A remnant of the hoplite panoply may also have endured in Carthaginian armies. At least a portion of the soldiery mustered at Carthage – whether Carthaginians or Libyans is

158 "[By 197 BC] the Romans had been fighting the Macedonian phalanx for more than a century. Pyrrhus defeated the Romans with it in the early third century, the Carthaginians in Africa in the middle of the century did as well, and Hannibal did the same later.": J E Lendon, 2005, *Soldiers and Ghosts. A History of Battle in Classical Antiquity*, Yale University Press, New Haven and London, p. 204.

159 "The backbone of the Punic heavy infantry was made up of Liby-Phoenicians who fought in a Greek-style phalanx. There is some debate concerning how these troops were armed, either with long pikes in the Macedonian fashion, or with the shorter thrusting spears favoured by hoplites.": Brian Todd Carey, Joshua B Allfree & John Cairns, 2007, *Hannibal's Last Battle. Zama and the Fall of Carthage*, Pen & Sword Military, Barnsley, Great Britain, p. 11.

160 "Metal helmets, greaves, linen cuirasses, round shields, two handed pikes, and short swords, all typical of the Greek army of Alexander and Pyrrhus, were the Carthaginian infantry's standard kit.": Richard A Gabriel, 2008, *Scipio Africanus. Rome's Greatest General*, Potomac Books Inc., Washington, p. 55.

161 cf. Polyb. 1.33.6; 15.12.7.

162 Polyb. 15.12.7.

163 Asclep. 1.4.

164 Polyb. 1.32.7.

unknown and perhaps unknowable – continued to be equipped in the manner of hoplites until the final destruction of Carthage in 146. The Chemtou and Kbor Klib monuments in North Africa are understood to have been built by the Numidian kings in *c.* 150, perhaps to celebrate the triumph of Roman and Numidian arms during the Second Punic War, and depict the arms and armour of defeated Carthaginian troops.[165] The friezes display Hellenistic-style linen cuirasses (*linothorax* with shoulder pieces and *pteruges*) and both oval *scutum* and round *aspis* shields. Perhaps depicting such *aspis* shields as architectural decoration was a stylist convention of the period.[166] However, it is possible that civic formations of Carthaginians continued to be equipped in the manner of hoplites. Perhaps these were the Carthaginian equivalent of the Roman *triarii* and the Macedonian *hypaspists*?[167]

The literary evidence, however, points to the fact that by the Second Punic War the Carthaginians built their armies around a Libyan heavy infantry core that closely resembled their Roman enemies in arms and tactical deployment. In describing the battle of Illipa in 206, Livy notes that the 'Carthaginian' and 'African' heavy infantry[168] were "fairly matched in courage and arms" with their Roman opponents; at one critical stage "the veteran Carthaginians and Africans, the strength of the enemy army, had not even reached the point when they could throw their spears".[169] This strongly suggests that the 'Carthaginians' and 'Africans' were equipped and fought like their Roman adversaries; neither hoplites nor pikemen would "*throw their spears*" prior to engaging. It is because Libyan (and Carthaginian) infantry fought in this manner that Hannibal's 'Africans' could so readily be re-equipped with Roman spoils, the best of Roman arms, after the battles of Trebbia and Trasimene.[170] Indeed, Livy describes a re-equipment so complete that "One might have taken

165 Duncan Ross, 2005, *Kbor Klib and the Battle of Zama*, BAR International Series 1399, Archaeopress.

166 Minor M Markle, 1999 (April-June), 'A Shield Monument from Veria and the Chronology of Macedonian Shield Types', *Hesperia*, Vol. 68, No. 2, pp. 219–254.

167 Macedonian *hypaspists* normally employed the spear, hoplite shield and related equipment, see: Minor M Markle III, 1977 (Summer), 'The Macedonian Sarissa, Spear, and Related Armour', *American Journal of Archaeology*, Vol. 81, No. 3, pp. 323–339.

168 Livy refers both '*Poeni*' and '*Carthaginenses*' serving as line infantry in the Carthaginian armies in Hispania during the Second Punic War. These are usually understood to be civic levies from the Punic cities of Hispania, but perhaps they included infantry recruited from the citizens of Carthage (Livy, 28.14.4). Just as Carthaginians and Libyans were equipped and fought in the same manner at the Crimissus in 339, so too is it likely that they were equipped and fought in the same manner during the Second Punic War.

169 Livy, 28.14.18.

170 Polyb. 3.87.3; 1.14.1; Livy, 22.46.4.

the Africans to be a Roman battle line, for they were armed with captured weapons, some taken at the Trebbia, but most of them at Trasimene".[171] It is hard to imagine how these soldiers could be mistaken for Romans unless they fought with the oblong *scutum* shield. It is inconceivable that a *scutum* shield could be combined with the long Macedonian *sarissa*. If the Libyans fought as hoplites (with the large, round *aspis* shield) or as pikemen then it is impossible that they could have been mistaken for a Roman battle line. The accounts of the fighting at *Trasimene* supports the notion that the Libyan infantry fought as swordsmen; it is difficult to believe that troops armed as either hoplites or pikemen could have charged downhill from ambush to attack the Romans from all sides.[172] Instead, Libyan heavy infantry is described as carrying throwing spears (Greek: '*longche*'; Latin: '*lancea*'[173]). Polybius describes Carthaginian infantry as '*longchophoroi*' on several occasions,[174] which has sometimes been misinterpreted as 'pikemen', but it is in fact a term used to denote light-armed troops armed with javelins and throwing spears. Nor could Hannibal's Libyans have been re-equipped so readily with Roman arms and armour if they were trained to fight as close-order pikemen. Nor is it plausible that Hannibal embarked upon the task of re-equipping them to fight in a completely new manner with new equipment in 217, while in the middle of a campaign, in enemy territory. "*Successful armies are copied, unsuccessful ones are not, it is a platitude, but it is nonetheless correct.*"[175]

For the Libyan and Roman battle lines to look similar required not only that they were equipped in a similar panoply, but that they also used a similar tactical deployment. Like Roman legionaries, Carthaginian infantry were organised into small, maniple-type formations; the ancient sources sometimes refer to such formations as *speirai*.[176] The fact that the Sacred Band numbered 2,500[177] suggests it was organised in units of 500 men. Polybius describes how in 210 the Carthaginian commander Mago divided his *syntagma* (formation or unit) of 1,000 men into two.[178] Livy refers to Numidian *turmae*, the Roman military term for squadrons of 30–36 horsemen.[179] Carthaginian formations made extensive use of standards and officers to command and control the

171 Livy, 22.46.4.
172 Polyb. 3.84.1–4; Livy, 22.4.
173 Livy, 28.14; App. *Pun.* 93.
174 Polyb. 3.73.7; 3.91.2.
175 Ian Stephenson, 2008, *Hannibal's Army*, Stroud, Tempus Publishing Ltd, p. 114.
176 Polyb. 3.114.4.
177 Diod. 16.80.4.
178 Polyb. 10.12.2.
179 Livy, 25.17.3 and 27.26.8.

battle line; Livy frequently mentions standards in Carthaginian armies or taken by the Romans as trophies.[180] Greek and Macedonian armies did not use standards at all during the Hellenistic period[181]– the very presence of standards in the Carthaginian army suggests the absence of troops equipped and drilled as pikemen. The primary sources describe fresh Carthaginian and Celtic troops relieving tired comrades.[182] The presence of standards and the ability to replace or reinforce tired infantry on the battle line with fresh troops, in a manner similar to that of the Roman *triplex acies* ('triple line') formation, strongly suggest that the Carthaginians organised their Libyan heavy infantry into a system of units and sub-units.

Philip Sabin, Alexander Zhmodikov and Fernando Quesada Sanz have studied the combat experience at the level of the individual and small-unit during clashes between massed heavy infantry in the third century BC.[183] Infantry melees were characterised by "*a brief and localized flurry of hand-to-hand combat*" followed by a "*safety distance*" which featured missile exchanges.[184] The Roman *pila*, Iberian *saunion/soliferreum* and the various Hellenistic javelins (*longchai*) were all throwing spears of various types, and were hurled in mass volleys by line infantry of the period.[185] The sources describe infantry contests in which missiles were used on a protracted basis.[186] References to 'repeated charges' and to steady advances and withdrawals before the final rout accord

180 cf. Livy, 27.40.11, 27.48.16, 27.49.8, 30.18.14. Punic standards; S Gsell, 1928, *Histoire Ancienne de l'Afrique du Nord*, vol. 2, 3rd edition, pp. 390–391; Gregory Daly, 2002, *Cannae. The Experience of Battle in the Second Punic War*, Routledge, London & New York, pp. 81–92.

181 Nicholas Sekunda, 2006, *Hellenistic Infantry Reform in the 160's BC*, Studies on the History of Ancient and Medieval Art of Warfare, Vol. V, Monograph Series AKANTHINA, Gdansk, p. 29.

182 Livy, 27.2.8; 30.18; Caesar, *BG* 3.5; 7.85.

183 Philip Sabin, 2000, 'The face of Roman battle', *Journal of Roman Studies*, Vol. 90, pp. 1–17; Alexander Zhmodikov, 2000, 'Roman Republican heavy infantrymen in battle (IV-II centuries BC)', *Historia* 49.1, pp. 67–79; Fernando Quesada Sanz, 2006, 'Not so different: individual fighting techniques and battle tactics of Roman and Iberian armies within the framework of warfare in the Hellenistic Age', in P Francois, P Moret, S Pere-Nogues (eds.), *L'Hellenisation en Mediterranee Occidentale au temps des guerres puniques*, Actes du Colloque International de Toulouse, 31 mars-2 avril 2005, Pallas 70, pp. 245–263; Philip Sabin, 2007, *Lost Battles. Reconstructing the Great Clashes of the Ancient World*, Hambledon Continuum, London; Koon, Sam, 2011, 'Phalanx and Legion: the "Face" of Punic War Battle', in Hoyos, Dexter (ed.), 2011, *A Companion to the Punic Wars*, Wiley-Blackwell, pp. 77–94.

184 Alexander Zhmodikov, 'Roman Republican heavy infantrymen in battle (IV–II centuries BC)', *Historia* 49.1, pp. 67–79.

185 Livy, 9.13; 28.2; Caesar, *BG* 1.25; 1.52; 2.23; *BC* 3.46; 3.93.

186 Livy, 34.14; Caesar, *BG* 1.26; 2.27; 4.32; 5.33–35; *BC* 1.45–6.

very well with the image of sporadic surges forward from a shifting, stand-off position. Some battles fought between such infantry were short in duration, while there were others that lasted two, three or even more than four hours.

Roman sub-units like centuries and maniples were tactically similar to the *speirai* or bands of warriors that gathered around the standards of native chieftains and leaders. Celtic, Iberian, Bruttian and Lucanian warriors would have performed much like Roman maniples on the battlefield. The key individuals would be the 'natural fighters', chieftains, junior leaders and military officers, who would encourage a concerted lunge forward. For this reason, the Roman's formal structure of sub-units, officers, discipline and drill was a strong advantage. The unit and sub-unit system of Roman legions, together with the drill and discipline that supported it, is what gave the Romans the edge in their clashes with Celtic, Iberian and Celtiberian warriors, rather than any great difference in equipment or fighting style. Fernando Quesada Sanz observes:

> [the] ... classical sources do not emphasize the differences in weapons and their employment when comparing Romans and Iberians, as they do when comparing Romans and Macedonians, rather they focus on organization, on discipline, on moral issues, and in the different concepts concerning war (e.g. Livy, 28.32.9–12). It is not the type or the handling of weapons on which they concentrate, but rather on the inability of the Iberians to handle large armies and organize campaigns (Polybius, 2.32–33). Livy is explicit in this respect when describing the battle of Hibera in 216 BC (Livy, 23.29.6): the difference between the Roman and Carthaginian armies (whose main body was formed of Iberian line troops) laid not in the number or in the type of soldiers (genere militum), but in morale.[187]

Ian Stephenson, author of *Hannibal's Army*, concluded after reviewing the archaeological and literary evidence that the pike or *sarissa "was not carried by Hannibal's army during his invasion of Italy, nor from our evidence does it appear to have been used by any other Carthaginian force during the Second Punic War ... Rather we see what appear to be similarly equipped armies engaged, the outcome relying upon factors other than the primary armament of close-order heavy infantry"*[188] The conclusion must be that the Carthaginians never organised

187 Fernando Quesada Sanz, 'Not so different: individual fighting techniques and battle tactics of Roman and Iberian armies within the framework of warfare in the Hellenistic Age', in P Francois, P Moret, S Pere-Nogues (Eds.), *L'Hellenisation en Mediterranee Occidentale au temps des guerres puniques*, Actes du Colloque International de Toulouse, 31 mars-2 avril 2005, Pallas 70, 2006, pp. 245–263.

188 Ian Stephenson, *Hannibal's Army*, Stroud, Tempus Publishing Ltd, 2008, p. 114.

their forces to fight in the 'Macedonian style', and that in fact by the Second Punic War the Carthaginian and Roman armies were very similar in arms, armour, organisation and fighting styles.

e *Mercenaries of Carthage*

In order to field larger armies and support its Carthaginian and Libyan phalanx with specialist troops, such as cavalry and slingers, Carthage hired mercenaries.[189] Carthage sourced such men from throughout the Western Mediterranean basin, and regularly recruited Greeks, Iberians, Balearians, Celts[190] (presumably from northern Italy), Ligurians, Campanians (from central Italy), and, on occasion, also Etruscans,[191] Sardinians[192] and Sikels (from central Sicily).[193] No attempt appears to have been made by Carthage to standardise these mercenary troops, who were neither armed nor trained to fight in a uniform manner. Instead, they fought according to their traditional customs. For example, the Balearians fought as infantry skirmishers armed with slings, the Celts as heavy infantry with long swords and large, oblong *scutum* shields, the Campanians as hoplite spearmen or cavalry. Such troops were organised on the basis of nationality, since it would have made no sense to deploy troops together who did not understand one another or lacked similar weapons and combat styles.

In order to muster these mercenaries, the city of Carthage required an extensive network of recruiting agents, mints to pay them, and a sophisticated infrastructure to transport them to Carthage, where military expeditions were assembled prior to deployment to Sicily. The recruitment of these mercenaries was undertaken by high-ranking envoys sent from Carthage with significant sums of money to where these fighting men were to be found, whether it be to the Balearian chiefs, Iberian kings or the well-established mercenary markets

189 Jonathan P Roth, 2007, 'Chapter 12: War', in Philip Sabin, Hans Van Wees and Michael Whitby (eds.), *The Cambridge History of Greek and Roman Warfare, Vol. 1: Greece, the Hellenistic World and the Rise of Rome*, Cambridge University Press, Melbourne, p. 368.

190 The term 'Celts' is used here to describe the inhabitants of 'Cisalpine Gaul' (i.e. northern Italy, the Po valley) as well as 'Transalpine Gaul' (i.e. western Europe). The Celtic inhabitants of the Po valley and Western Europe were known to the Romans as 'Gauls' (Latin: '*Galli*') and to the Greeks as '*Galatai*' or '*Keltoi*'.

191 cf. Diod. 19.106.2.

192 Diod. 14.95.1. It is surprising how rarely there are references to the Carthaginians using soldiers or levies raised in Sardinia. Perhaps the Punic city-states in Sardinia were obliged to furnish supplies of grain (cf. Diod. 11.20.4, 14.77.6) rather than levies, while the Nuragic chiefdoms of the Sardinian interior declined to be a source of mercenary manpower (except in 480? Hdt. 7.165).

193 Diod. 14.75.6.

of Greece.[194] The period that elapsed from a mercenary's original recruitment to their deployment in Sicily seems to have typically be a year or more. At the conclusion of the military campaign mercenaries were generally brought back to Carthage and discharged, whereupon they may have returned home, or sought further employment.

Mercenaries are sometimes described as Carthaginian "cannon fodder", but when one considers the cost, time and effort invested in recruiting and then transporting these troops to Sicily, this cannot be the explanation for their employment. Rather, these contingents added specialist skills to the Carthaginian and Libyan phalanx, such as the Balearians, who were valued as missile troops, able to clear enemy walls of defenders[195] and even repel Greek hoplites with their accurate fire.[196]

Iberians were regarded as being among the best fighting material to be found in the western Mediterranean,[197] and were valued as fierce, disciplined infantry, effective in assaulting enemy walls or facing Greek hoplites in battle.[198] They were probably recruited through pacts with the kings and chiefs of the polities of southern and eastern Spain, no doubt facilitated by the Punic city-states of Iberia. Iberians fought with a panoply that included a heavy thrusting spear, the unique *soliferreum* all-iron throwing spear, the distinctive falcata-type sword, plumed helmets, circular shields, greaves, and bronze cuirasses or pectoral armour.[199]

Plutarch reports that after the battle of Crimissus, where 3,000 Carthaginian citizens were slain,[200] the Carthaginians "voted not to risk the lives of citizens in the future but to enlist foreign mercenaries, especially Greeks who, they thought, would answer the call in large numbers because of the high rate of

194 Carthaginian recruiting agents were "certain citizens who were held in high esteem" or even explicitly described as members of the city's Council of Elders: Diod. 13.80.2, 14.47.3. Large sums of gold and silver: Livy, 30.21.3–4. Carthaginian recruiting agents in Greece: Polyb. 1.32.1.

195 Diod. 5.18.3, 13.54.7.

196 Diod. 19.109.1–4.

197 Thuc. 6.90.3.

198 Iberians storm the defences of Selinunte: Diod. 13.56.4, 13.62.2. Iberians versus Greek hoplites: 13.110.5–6. Diodorus reports that the Iberians had their own encampment: Diod. 13.85.1. On another occasion, when the Carthaginians had fled and the army collapsed, the "Iberians alone massed together with their arms and dispatched a herald to treat about taking service with him [Dionysius]". Dionysius was so impressed that he promptly hired the Iberians and they remained in his service for many years: Diod. 14.75.8–9.

199 Fernando Quesdada Sanz, 2010, *Armas de la Antigua Iberia de Tartessos a Numancia*, La Esfera de los Libros, Madrid, pp. 171–180.

200 Plut. *Tim.* 28.10.

pay and the wealth of Carthage".[201] Greek hoplites were prized as mercenaries throughout the Mediterranean in the late Classical period, and they were perfectly willing to serve non-Greek paymasters, being extensively employed by both the Persian Empire and the Carthaginians.[202] Greek mercenaries feature in both peacetime garrisons[203] and armies until the end of the First Punic War.[204] Sicily was a magnet for Greek mercenaries throughout *c.* 500–241 BC: the island was not only the scene of major wars between Carthage and Syracuse, but was also cursed with incessant warfare between rival Greek polities, factional strife (*stasis*) within *poleis*, and where tyrants often maintained their rule over their fellow citizens by employing bodies of mercenaries to serve as their enforcers and bodyguards. After 241, however, Sicily came to enjoy peace and political stability as a Roman province, and no longer served as a beacon to draw Greek mercenaries west.

Campanian mercenaries in Diodorus are differentiated by name from most other troops in the Carthaginian army, and are called *equites*, and were regarded as elite troops. A notorious company of 800 Campanian cavalry (*hippeis*) were hired by the Carthaginians in Sicily in 410, and later installed as garrison troops in western Sicily – the Campanians seem to have preferred land to payment and repatriation home.[205] The Carthaginians sought out Campanian mercenaries, valuing them as fierce fighters, both as cavalry and as hoplite infantry.[206] Syracusan tyrants too made extensive use of Campanian mercenaries, often paying them with land grants or citizenship.[207] Mercenaryism was an

201 Diod. 16.81.

202 Matthew Trundle, 2004, *Greek Mercenaries, From the Late Archaic Period to Alexander*, Routledge, London and New York.

203 Herakleia Minoa in 357: Diod. 16.9; Plut. *Dion* 25.

204 cf. Polyb. 1.43.4 and 1.48.3.

205 Diod. 13.44.1–2, 13.55.7–8, 13.62.5–6, 13.80.2–5; Aldina Cutroni Tusa, 2012, 'La zecca di Entella tra Campini e Cartaginesi', *Annali della Scuola Normale Superiore di Pisa. Classe di Lettere e Filosofia*, Serie 5, Vol. 4, No. 1, pp. 3–12, 307–309; Ian Lee, 2000, 'Entella: The Silver Coinage of the Campanian Mercenaries and the Site of the First Carthaginian Mint', *The Numismatic Chronicle*, Vol. 160, pp. 1–66.

206 Campanian warriors wore typical Oscan dress and armour, such as the triple-disc cuirass, but were armed with the traditional hoplite's long thrusting spear and large round shield. Reconstructions based on Campanian vases and coins of the Mamertini; see Head, Duncan (drawings by Ian Heath), 1982, *Armies of the Macedonian and Punic Wars, 359–146 BC*, A Wargames Research Group Publication, pp. 166–167.

207 Campanian mercenaries served in Sicily in the armies of Carthage and the tyrants of Syracuse in great numbers. One notorious company of 800 Campanian cavalry served Athens, Carthage and Dionysius I in the years 413–368: cf. Diod. 13.44.1–2, 13.55.7–8, 13.80.2–5, 13.85.3–4, 13.88.5, 14.8.5–9.4, 15.73.2; Ian Lee, 2000, 'Entella: The Silver Coinage of the Campanian Mercenaries and the Site of the First Carthaginian Mint 410–409 BC',

important alternative to the acquisition of land in Campania itself, which was in the hands of the aristocratic classes of *equites*.[208] After 241 Campanian and Italic mercenaries were unavailable to Carthage; the treaty that ended the First Punic War specifically barred Carthaginian recruitment of mercenaries in Italy.[209]

The Balearic Islands was understood to produce the finest slingers in the western Mediterranean, warriors renowned for their skill, range and accuracy with their simple but terrible weapons.[210] Balearian slingers were recruited into Carthaginian armies from at least the end of the fifth century BC.[211] It is said that when Carthage first began employing them they were paid in wine and women, as the Balearians did not use money.[212] By the third century BC, however, we hear of Carthaginian agents with large sums of money recruiting Balearian mercenaries. Although Strabo reports that when the Carthaginians first came into contact with the *Baleares* they were armed with fire-hardened javelins,[213] the vast majority were slingers. Strabo reports that the slings of the islanders were made of black tufted rush, hair or sinew, and they carried several slings of different sizes, designed for long, medium and short range.[214] The Balearians did not use lead shot, but rather preferred to use stones, much larger than those of other slingers, each weighing up to half a mina (436 g), giving rise to the claim that Balearian slingshot could have a force like a catapult.[215]

In 218 Carthage had some 1,500 Balearic slingers serving in its armies in Hispania and Africa,[216] and perhaps another 1,500 accompanied Hannibal on his march to Italy. This from a total *Baleares* population of perhaps only

---

The Numismatic Chronicle, Vol. 160, pp. 1–66. The Sicilian tyrants relied heavily on mercenary soldiers in order to maintain control of their territories. Polybius believed that tyrants and mercenaries had a symbiotic relationship: 11.13.3–8. Large numbers of Greek and Italic mercenaries were enrolled as citizens by tyrants such as Dionysius of Syracuse and Agathokles. Agathokles discharged mercenaries emerged as the 'Mamertines' that controlled Messana and much of north-eastern Sicily.

208 Francesca Mermati, 2017, 'The Campanians', in Gary D Farney and Guy Bradley (eds.), *The Peoples of Ancient Italy*, De Gruyter, pp. 385–418.

209 During the Mercenary War (241–238) Rome relaxed this treaty provision, and allowed Carthaginian agents to recruit mercenaries in Italy, but it was in force again after 238.

210 Diod. 5.18.4; Strabo, 3.5.1.

211 Diod. 13.80.1–5; Adolfo J Dominguez Monedero, 'Los Mercenarios Balearicos', in Benjami Costa and Jordi H Fernandez (eds.), *Guerra y Ejercito en el Mundo Fenicio-Punico*, Eivissa, pp. 163–189.

212 Diod. 5.17.4.

213 Str. 3.5.1; cf. Livy, 21.55.6.

214 Str. 3.5.1; Diod. 5.18.3.

215 Diod. 5.18.3.

216 Polyb. 3.33.11, 16; Livy, 21.21.12; 22.2.

30,000 people![217] Carthage continued to recruit *Baleares* slingers throughout the Second Punic War. In 208 Hannibal's brother Mago crossed to the Balearic islands "with a large sum of money" to recruit mercenaries,[218] and he returned in 206, recruiting a further 2,000 from the island of Menorca and dispatching them to Carthage. In 205 Mago departed Menorca only after levying yet more.[219] Mago's hostile reception at Majorca in 206 was probably because the *Baleares* chieftains were unwilling to send any additional men to serve in Carthage's armies (28.37.6–9).[220]

Carthage had a long history of employing Celtic warriors in its Sicilian wars,[221] and they also appear in the armies of the Sikeliot tyrants Dionysius I and Dionysius II.[222] Celtic warriors eager for plunder and glory had provided a ready source of mercenary manpower from earliest times. In the Second Punic War Hannibal relied heavily on Celtic manpower, and during 218–216 perhaps 40% of his army in Italy was comprised of Celtic recruits. Most of these were recruited from the *Insubres* and the *Boii*, respectively inhabiting territories north and south of the Po River[223] and formal allies of Carthage.[224] The Celtic recruits in Hannibal's army were probably mercenary volunteers, and the alliance between Hannibal and the *Boii* and *Insubres* probably provided diplomatic support for Carthaginian agents to recruit Celtic

217 Diod. 5.17.

218 Livy, 27.20.7.

219 Livy, 28.46.7–8. On the hypothesis that Mago warred with local *Baleares* chieftains to levy men into his army, see: María Luisa Sánchez León, 2003, 'La ciudad de Mago (Maó, Menorca): continuidades y rupturas', *Mayurqa*, Vol. 29, pp. 97–109.

220 Fernando Prados Martinez, Helena Jimenez and Jose Javier Martinez Garcia (eds.), 2017, *Menorca Entre Fenicis i Punics, Menorca Entre Fenicios y Punicos*, Universidad de Murcia, Publicaciones del Cepoat No. 2, Cercle Artistic de Ciutadella Publicacions des Born; Adolfo J Dominguez Monedero, 'Los Mercenarios Balearicos', in Benjami Costa and Jordi H Fernandez (eds.), *Guerra y Ejercito en el Mundo Fenicio-Punico*, Eivissa, pp. 176–177.

221 cf. Diod. 11.1.5.

222 Jan Bouzek, 2014, 'The Celtic Mercenary Reconsidered', in Christopher Gosden, Sally Crawford and Katherine Ulmschneider (eds.), *Celtic Art in Europe*, Oxbow Books, pp. 223–233. Dionysius I made alliance with the Celtic *Senones* in *c.* 386/385: Justin 20.5.1–6. Dionysius I even sent a Celtic contingent to help Sparta in 369/368: Xen. *Hellenica* 7.1.20, 31. See Timothy P Bridgman, 2003, 'The 'Gallic Disaster': Did Dionysius I of Syracuse Order It?', *Proceedings of the Harvard Celtic Colloquium*, Vol. 23, pp. 40–51.

223 Polyb. 2.22.1; 17.4.7.

224 Polyb. 7.9. Polybius (3.44) describes how Magilius and other Celts invited Hannibal to Italy, and (3.66.7) mentions Hannibal's alliances with many of the Celts in Cisalpine Gaul. The treaty between Carthage and Philip V of Macedon (7.9.6) is evidence that these were genuine alliances rather than informal arrangements, as Celtic and Ligurian allies are specifically mentioned.

mercenaries, rather than establishing any kind of levy. These tribes remained autonomous, and fielded their own tribal armies with which to fight Rome when necessary.[225]

Polybius refers to the Celtic infantry fighting in *speirai*, probably tribal units of irregular size.[226] Celtic warriors were famed for fighting naked[227] or only wearing trousers,[228] with long slashing swords, large oval scutum shields and javelins. Celtic noblemen, chieftains and their senior retainers typically fought as cavalry.[229] Celtic cavalry were well equipped, frequently wearing helmets and mail shirts, round or oval shields, armed with the traditional Celtic long sword and heavy thrusting spear or lance, the use of either from the saddle being facilitated by the stability provided by the four-horned saddle favoured by the Celts, who also used short spurs to urge on their horses.[230] Hannibal commanded some 4,000 Celtic cavalry at Cannae.

Ligurians are first reported serving as Carthaginian mercenaries in 480,[231] and thereafter they routinely appear in the city's armies, fighting in the Sicilian Wars[232] and in the First Punic War.[233] At the outbreak of the Second Punic War there was a force of Ligurians serving under Hasdrubal in Hispania.[234] The treaty between Hannibal and Philip V of Macedonia describes the Ligurians as formal allies of Carthage.[235] Livy makes several references to the Ligurian tribes aiding Carthage and supplying warriors.[236] There were numerous Ligurian tribes, and these remained stubborn enemies of Rome throughout the Second Punic War, with Ligurians found in Hannibal's army at Zama in 202.[237] Romans regarded the Ligurians as warlike and proud, with more endurance than their Celtic neighbours, although smaller in stature.[238] The Ligurians fought exclusively on foot, were tough and flexible, being capable raiders and ambushers as

225 i.e., Silva Litana in 216: Livy, 23.24.6–11.
226 Polyb. 3.114.4.
227 Polyb. 2.28.7–8, 3.114.2–4.
228 Livy, 22.46.6.
229 cf. Ducarius: Livy, 22.6.3–4; Celts more effective as cavalry than infantry: Str. 4.4.2.
230 Livy, 22.6.3–4.
231 Diod. 5.17.1.
232 cf. Diod. 14.95.1; 15.73.3.
233 Polyb. 1.17; 17.4–6; 19.9; Diod. 23.8.
234 Polyb. 3.33.16.
235 Polyb. 7.9.6.
236 Livy, 21.22.2; 38.3; 58.2; 59.10; 27.39.2; 48.7–49.8; 28.46.8–11; 29.5.3–9; 30.33.5.
237 Polyb. 15.11.1.
238 Diod. 5.39.2.

well as able to fight close quarters as line infantry, armed with javelins, *scutum* shields and medium-length swords.[239]

The ancient sources like Diodorus often create the impression that the Carthaginian armies in Sicily included vast numbers of barbarian mercenaries, but in fact the numbers were likely far more modest. The Balearian contingent in Sicily in 311 numbered "at least a thousand".[240] As we have seen, the Campanians in 410 were 800 strong. Iberian mercenaries were no doubt more plentiful, but can only have numbered several thousand at any one time, given the constraints of recruitment, availability and transport. Throughout the wars in Sicily during 410–289 the central component of Carthaginian armies remained the Carthaginian and Libyan phalanx. Carthaginian generals would not be careless with the lives of their mercenary troops, acquired at such cost and effort to fulfill particular purposes. But nor would they hesitate to deploy them in situations where they might have been more circumspect with the lives of citizens, such as when assaulting a breach in a city's walls.

f *Allied Auxiliaries from North Africa*

The armies of Carthage deployed from earliest times contingents of Numidian light cavalry, either recruiting them as mercenaries or as allied contingents. The term 'Numidian' was often used by Greco-Roman authors as a 'catch-all' term for the horsemen of North Africa, all of which fought from horseback as light armed cavalry with javelins. In fact, Carthage recruited such horsemen not only from the neighbouring Numidian tribes, but also the Mauri (in modern Morrocco), the Macae (inhabiting the littoral of the Greater Syrtes), Nasamones (of the Greater Syrtes), the Garamantes (of modern Fezzan) and the Gaetuli (itself a blanket term to describe the little-known pastoral tribes of the pre-desert). In 407 the Carthaginians "summoned soldiers from the peoples and chieftains who were their allies, Maurusians and Numidians and certain peoples who dwell in the regions toward Cyrene".[241] Numidian cavalry seem to have typically served under their own princes, such as Navaras,[242] Tychaeus[243] and Masinissa.

239 Diod. 5.39.7; Strabo, 4.6.2. Marco Severino, 1982 (September), 'The Ancient Ligurians: Part 2 – Dress, arms and equipment', *Slingshot, Official Journal of the Society of Ancients*, No. 103, pp. 9–11; Richard Wellington Husband, 1911 (October), 'Kelts and Ligurians', *Classical Philology*, Vol. 6, No. 4, pp. 385–401.

240 Diod. 19.109.1.

241 Diod. 13.80.3.

242 Polyb. 1.78.1–11.

243 Polyb. 15.3.5.

Numidian Cavalry were the finest and most feared skirmisher cavalry in the western Mediterranean, famed for their endurance[244] and their persistent, deadly harassing tactics. These horsemen were not the fastest of cavalry, but their small horses were small, lean, hardy ponies that were agile and very manoeuvrable, able to scramble through or over terrain that brought other, larger mounted units to a halt.[245] Born horsemen, the Numidians rode bareback, without bit or bridles or saddles, instead relying on their knees plus a riding crop\stick to control their mounts. Numidian cavalry were expert ambushers, able to hide in undergrowth or folds in the landscape, and make sudden attacks upon unsuspecting enemies. As skirmishers, Numidians harassed the enemy with a rain of javelins, outflanking and surrounding them, but scattering to avoid enemy charges. They retired swiftly from an enemy charge, but returned quickly to the attack. This method of skirmishing combat was used regardless of whether the enemy was on foot or mounted, the aim being to cut off the victim and force him to stand or run; the Numidian cavalry were particularly deadly and effective when pursuing a broken and flying foe.[246]

The Carthaginians also recruited light-armed infantry skirmishers from among independent and allied tribes in North Africa.[247] Armed with a small, light round bossless shield, javelins and daggers, relying upon distance and agility for defence,[248] these warriors were noteworthy for their livid all-body tattoos, body-paint and elaborate hairstyles.

g *Iberians in the Second Punic War*

Carthaginian conquests in the Iberian Peninsula in 237–219 meant that Carthage secured access to enormous sources of military manpower. By 218 Carthage was in a position to not only hire Iberian mercenaries, but also to levy troops from subject Iberian communities. On the basis of archaeological and literary evidence, Fernando Quesada Sanz has demonstrated that Carthaginian conquests in Iberia were accompanied by a swift evolution in the panoply of Iberian and Celtiberian warriors. The round shield (*caetra*) and spear were supplanted by the oblong *scutum* shield, *Montefortino*-type helmets, javelins, and ever greater numbers of native dagger and sword types.[249] These

244 Polyb. 3.71.10; App. *Pun.* 11, 71.

245 Livy, 35.11.6–11; Str. 17.3.7; Aelian 3.2.

246 William Horsted, 2021, *The Numidians 300 BC–AD 300*, Men-at-Arms No. 537, Osprey Publishing.

247 cf. Livy, 22.37.8.

248 Livy, 23.36.

249 The most important new offensive weapon during this 'Late Phase' was the sword. Iberian swords were of two basic types. The straight-bladed sword (identical to the Roman *gladius*

changes reflect that the panoply was modified and adapted to a new situation of high-intensity warfare, protracted military operations, set piece battles and sieges,[250] and immersion in the Carthaginian military, which needed ever-greater numbers of heavier infantry types in the Second Punic War.[251] The integration of Iberian and Celtiberian troops in Carthaginian armies was a much easier accomplishment than might be first imagined because the city's generals only had to improve on weapons and discipline, not the basic approach to battle. Livy describes a battle between a force of Celtiberians enlisted by the Carthaginians and a Roman force in 207, where it is apparent that both are similarly equipped and share the same fighting style.

> There were in the army of the Celtiberians 4,000 heavy-armed troops and 200 cavalry. These constituted a full legion, and were the pick of their forces, and so Mago placed them in the front line, setting the rest, the light-armed troops, in reserve. He then led them all from the camp, formed up in this manner, and barely had they gone beyond their palisade when the Romans hurled their javelins at them. The Spaniards crouched down in the face of the enemy barrage, and then rose to hurl theirs in turn. The Romans, in their usual close formation, received them

hispaniensis), about 60 cm long, had two cutting edges and a point. More common was an elegant curved sword, known to moderns as the *espada falcata*, an Iberian variation of the Greek *kopis*, and most common in the south and east of Hispania. The *espada falcata* had a small blade of between 35–52 cm, and was a cut as well as thrust weapon. Another development in offensive weapons during the third century BC was the *biglobular* dagger (prototype of the Roman *pugio*), a type with short, tapering, triangular blade, waisted and with a midrib only in the final series. This dagger is typically Celtiberian in origin – the earliest series go back to the fourth century BC, but it became widespread in the Iberian Peninsula after *c.* 237. The distinctive all-iron throwing spear, the *soliferrea*, and the heavy throwing spear the *saunion* (identical to the Roman *pila*), javelins and thrusting spears were also popular.

250 Louis Rawlings, 1996, 'Celts, Spaniards, and Samnites: warriors in a soldier's war', Tim Cornell, Boris Rankov & Philip Sabin (ed.), *The Second Punic War, A Reappraisal*, London, pp. 81–96.

251 Fernanado Quesada Sanz, 1997, *El Armamento Iberico: Estudio Tipologico, Geografico, Funcional, Social y Simbolico de las Armas en la Cultura Iberica (Siglos VI–I a.C.)*, Monographies Instrumentum 3.1 and 3.2, Editions Monique Mergoil, Montagac; F Quesada Sanz, 2004, 'Innovaciones de raiz helenistica en el armamento y tacticas de los pueblos ibericos desde el siglo III a.C.', in M Bendala, P. Moret, and F Quesada Sanz (eds.), *Formas e imagines del poder en los siglos III y II a.C: Modelos helenisticos y respuestas indigenas*, Cuadernos de Prehistoria y Arqueologia de la Universidad Autonoma de Madrid, 28–29 (CuPAUM 28–29), Madrid, 2002–2003, pp. 69–94.

> with shields locked tightly together; then they closed in and proceeded to fight with the sword.[252]

Iberian skirmishers were also prominent in the Second Punic War, and were reportedly better than the 'Moors'.[253] Livy calls the Iberian skirmishers 'targeteers',[254] being armed with the distinctive small round shield (*caetra*) and javelins. Celtiberians and Lusitanians are also found among Hannibal's light infantry operating in mountainous terrain.[255]

h *Italians in the Army of Hannibal Barca during the Second Punic War*

In the Second Punic War the Carthaginian general Hannibal adopted a strategy aimed at shattering the Roman hegemony in Italy, seeking to cripple Roman prestige and authority through battlefield victories, and so encourage the city-states and tribal polities of Italy to renounce their subordinate alliances with Rome. After Cannae in 216, Hannibal secured a number of significant defections; the Apulian cities of Arpi, Salapia, and Herdonia, the Hirpini and Caudini tribes of Samnium, many of the Lucanian and Bruttian communities, and, most importantly of all, the influential and wealthy Campanian city of Capua. To these Hannibal added the Italiot cities of Tarentum, Metapontium and Thurii and the Messapians in the years 213–212. All these cities and groups formed a patchwork of pro-Carthaginian allies which entered into formal treaties with Hannibal and Carthage. These treaties guaranteed their local autonomy and independence, and Hannibal secured neither tribute nor military levies in exchange. Instead, Hannibal achieved the strategic denial of these resources from Rome, and the right to recruit military volunteers from among allied communities.

Effectively isolated by sea from Carthaginian bases in North Africa and Iberia, Hannibal needed to sustain his military forces in Italy from local resources. A strong army-in-being was critical to Hannibal's survival and success. While most of Hannibal's losses throughout 218–216 fell upon his Celtic warriors, nonetheless wounds, desertion and disease must have taken a toll upon his whole force. Yet despite such losses, and the lack of significant reinforcements from Carthage, Hannibal succeeded in keeping a powerful army-in-being in Italy. Moreover, in the years between 216–211 Hannibal was able to divide his forces into a main field army commanded by himself, and a smaller

252 Livy, 28.2.
253 Livy, 23.26.11.
254 Livy, 21.21.12, 23.26.11.
255 Livy, 21.57.5.

field army led at first by his brother Mago and then later an officer named Hanno. Throughout 216–209 Hannibal maintained a high tempo of military operations in southern Italy, continuing to attack major towns like Neapolis, Nola, Nuceria and Tarentum, and he continued to fight important battles against the Romans, such as those around Nola in 216–214 and at Herdonia and Numistro in 210. Hannibal is also reported as installing significant garrisons in key towns such as Arpi, Salapia and several Samnite towns. Thus, it appears from the literary evidence that during the period 215–209 Hannibal must have had as many as 60,000–70,000 men in arms between Campania and Bruttium. How had Hannibal's army in Italy actually expanded? Dexter Hoyos surmises:

> The answer must be that [Hannibal] replaced losses among his original troops with mostly Italian recruits. Mercenaries from abroad may have made their way to him too but cannot have been all that numerous, while for Italians in the Punic army there is a fair amount of evidence ... Samnite spokesmen as early as 215 put it to him that all their young men were serving with him (no doubt an exaggeration). In 214 his lieutenant in the south, Hanno had 17,000 largely Bruttian and Lucanian infantry and 'a few Italians' in his 1,200 cavalry, when the proconsul Ti Sempronius Gracchus badly defeated him at the river Calor near Beneventum. This was not Hannibal's own army but it suggests that he too could recruit locally. By 207, when his area of control had shrunk to little more than Lucania and Bruttium, he is fact recorded sending Hanno, still in harness, to raise fresh levies from the Bruttians ... The population of the Italian defector-states, then, probably did supply manpower to Hannibal's army, not in separate allied contingents but as volunteers under direct Punic command. This surely suited him much better, for otherwise he would have had to cajole semi-autonomous contingents out of his allies, with the inevitable headaches that that would have entailed.[256]

The patchwork of allies across southern Italy only provided Hannibal with military manpower only for so long as they were successfully defended from Rome. After 216 Hannibal was no longer freely marauding across enemy territory. Instead, he needed to reduce the stubborn Roman enclaves that endured in southern Italy and protect his allies from Roman reprisals and reconquest.[257]

---

256 Dexter Hoyos, 2005, *Hannibal's Dynasty. Power and politics in the western Mediterranean, 247–183 BC*, Routledge, Oxon, pp. 128–129.

257 Dexter Hoyos, 2005, *Hannibal's Dynasty. Power and politics in the western Mediterranean, 247–183 BC*, Routledge, Oxon, pp. 132–133.

i *Siege Warfare*

Carthage was a thoroughly capable practitioner of siege warfare. The Roman engineer Vitruvius and the Greek philosopher Athenaeus both attributed the invention of the battering ram to the Carthaginians.[258] While this is absurd, it is revealing that the ancients found such a tale plausible. In 410 the Carthaginian army landed in Sicily with "machinery for sieges, missiles, and all other equipment".[259] The Carthaginians possessed, via their Phoenician cousins, a knowledge of Near Eastern siege craft, and used battering rams, wheeled siege towers and relays of assaults by mercenaries to devastating effect. At Himera in 409 the Carthaginians "camped around the city" and successfully undermined the city's walls.[260] Dionysius I of Syracuse (r. 406–367) responded by hiring skilled craftsmen – some of whom came from Punic Sicily – to design engines of war for him.[261] These made advances in artillery, deploying arrow-shooters and perhaps inventing torsion catapults.[262] The wars between Carthage and the Greeks in Sicily featured siege warfare and witnessed the rapid development of new technologies and stratagems.

In the Hellenistic period the Carthaginians were significantly more advanced than their Roman adversaries in siege craft. The Roman use of artillery "was the result of confiscation rather than manufacture".[263] In 209 when the Romans captured New Carthage (modern Cartagena) in Iberia they discovered an arsenal of "120 catapults of the largest dimensions, and 281 smaller ones; 23 large scale and 52 smaller-scale ballistas; a large number of the larger and smaller scorpions, and of weapons and projectiles".[264] Plainly the Carthaginians maintained a sophisticated siege train in Iberia, built and maintained by specialist engineers and officers, with which they swiftly reduced native Iberian and Celtiberian fortifications.

It is sometimes suggested that the Carthaginians were weak in siege warfare, based on the difficulty Hannibal experienced in taking walled cities in Italy during the Second Punic War. In fact, Hannibal demonstrated a capability

258 Vitr. *De arch.* 10.13.1–2; Ath. *Mech.* 9.4–10.4.

259 Diod. 13.54.7.

260 Diod. 13.59.8.

261 Skilled craftsmen from the *epikrateia*: Diod. 14.41.3–4.

262 Diod. 14.42.1; Everett L Wheeler and Barry Strauss, 2007, 'Chapter 7: Battle', in Philip Sabin, Hans Van Wees and Michael Whitby (eds.), *The Cambridge History of Greek and Roman Warfare, Vol. 1: Greece, the Hellenistic World and the Rise of Rome*, Cambridge University Press, Melbourne, p. 241.

263 Duncan B Campbell, 2003, *Greek and Roman Artillery 399 BC – AD 363*, New Vanguard No. 89, Osprey Publishing, p. 22.

264 Livy, 26.47.6.

to undertake siege warfare, and an ability to build siege weapons as and when he needed them. In his attempts to capture Nola he ordered his soldiers to bring up all the equipment needed for an assault.[265] At Acerrae Hannibal made preparations for a siege and assault, and the town was circumvallated by the Carthaginians.[266] In his operations to capture Casilinum Hannibal used mantelets (*vineae*) and dug saps,[267] while in other siege operations in Italy the Carthaginians built and deployed artillery, siege engines[268] and high wooden siege towers.[269] Of course, Hannibal did not need to drag his siege engines around with him, but rather would build them on-site[270]; wood was readily available and Hannibal's professional army no doubt included officers and engineers who were 'siege experts', able to oversee the construction of siege engines and siege works.[271] The chief limitation in enabling Hannibal to undertake extensive siege operations in Italy were considerations of food supply; he lacked a logistical supply base from which to keep his army fed if it were to remain in one place for an extended period.[272]

j *Carthaginian Cavalry*

The advent of heavy cavalry was a reasonably recent development in warfare at the time of the Punic Wars. The use of heavy cavalry that delivered a shock charge with lance and edged weapons, rather than fighting as mounted skirmishers, was first perfected by Alexander the Great (the Macedonians themselves having encountered such cavalry among the Scythians and Thracians in the Balkans). Unlike the Persian cavalry (and traditional Greek cavalry), who preferred to fight at a distance with the javelin and bow, as mounted skirmishers, Alexander's heavy cavalry were trained to fight at close quarters with lance and sword. Presumably they were also skilled in the use of the javelin. Typically, cavalry of this type were organised into squadrons which varied in size from 180 to 225 men.[273] The deployment of bodies of heavy cavalry on the battlefield was a feature of Hellenistic warfare.

---

265 Livy, 23.16.11–12.
266 Livy, 23.17.4–6.
267 Livy, 23.18.8–9.
268 Livy, 25.11.10; Pol. 8.34.1–2; App. *Hann.* 6.33.
269 Livy, 23.37.2–3.
270 cf. Livy, 29.7.4.
271 John F Shean, 'Hannibal's Mules: The Logistical Limitations of Hannibal's Army and the Battle of Cannae, 216 BC', *Historia*, Vol. 45, No. 2, 1996, pp. 159–187.
272 Paul Erdkamp, 1998, *Hunger and the Sword. Warfare and Food Supply in Roman republican Wars (264–30 BC)*, J C Gieben, Amsterdam, pp. 156–187.
273 Robert E Gaebel, *Cavalry Operations in the Ancient Greek World*, University of Oaklahoma Press, Norman, 2002, p. 161.

Carthage probably began to field heavy cavalry equipped in the new Hellenistic fashion only in around 300. There were Greek heavy cavalry serving in the Carthaginian armies fighting Agathokles' forces in both Africa[274] and Sicily.[275] The Carthaginians sourced their heavy cavalry from the aristocracies of Carthage and the Punic cities, from Greek allies and mercenaries (until 241), and Campanians (until 238). Polybius speaks of how, during the Mercenary War, Carthage *"mustered and drilled their civic cavalry"*, these no doubt being from the city's wealthy and noble families.[276] Libyphoenician cavalry are reported by both Polybius and Livy.[277] Because heavy cavalry was the most expensive arm to field, with the need for suitable horses, it made sense for the Carthaginians to shift the burden onto its allies as far as was possible, without denying their own aristocratic citizens the opportunity to serve in a manner fitting their station. These cavalrymen were likely armed in the typical manner of the Hellenistic period, with lance and shield, and armoured with either a mail coat or metal cuirass.

In the Second Punic War, Carthaginian armies relied upon Celtic and Iberian cavalry. In the years 216–212 Hannibal was able to recruit small numbers of cavalry from among his allies in Italy, such as the Lucanians, Apulians, Capuans and Tarentines.

Hellenistic period heavy cavalry had limitations. They required flat, open terrain to be effective. Importantly, ancient cavalry lacked stirrups, and so they needed to keep their seat and control their mount using their legs. For this reason, heavy cavalry could not strike with their target with the lance while charging without the leverage provided by stirrups. In melee, cavalry were vulnerable to being unhorsed. This is no doubt why heavy cavalry are often described as dismounting to engage in hand-to-hand combat. Heavy cavalry did not launch frontal charges against unbroken infantry formations, but rather protected the flanks of the infantry line, attacked enemy cavalry, charged through gaps in the enemy battle line, assailed enemy skirmishers, and attacked the flanks and rear of the enemy battle line. It was common for heavy cavalry to attack in conjunction with light-armed infantry.[278] Robert E Gaebel emphasises that such limitations should not be exaggerated;

274 Clinon: Diod. 20.38.1–6.

275 Deinocrates: Diod. 19.103, 20.29.5.

276 Polyb. 1.73.

277 Polyb. 3.33.15; Livy 21.22.3.

278 Robert E Gaebel, 2002, *Cavalry Operations in the Ancient Greek World*, University of Oaklahoma Press, Norman; Gregory Daly, 2002, *Cannae. The Experience of Battle in the Second Punic War*, Routledge, London & New York, pp. 73–76.

> The type of close mounted combat that the written sources depict is entirely consistent with the riding skills that result from sitting a horse without saddle and stirrups as well as the collected style of riding recommended by Xenophon and commonly depicted in the figured evidence. All else being equal, the bareback rider will be more skilled than one using a saddle. He will have a deeper seat with a lower centre of gravity; he will of necessity develop a better sense of balance, since no security will be offered by the shape of the saddle or lateral support from stirrups; and he will have better control by virtue of the close contact between his legs and the sides of the horse.[279]

The Carthaginian expansion in Iberia after 237 meant that it was able to recruit cavalry from among the subject and allied communities there, who were famous for their horsemanship. The warrior aristocracies of Iberia had been engaged in endemic inter-regional warfare long before the Barcid conquests began in 237, and there was a strong equestrian ideology among the Iberian and Celtiberian elites, where the horse enjoyed great importance in social and symbolic life.[280] For this reason, it is no surprise that Iberian cavalry were typically well mounted, on tough, strong horses. It may have been the Iberians that invented the horseshoe in the fourth century BC, which improved the military potential of cavalry. The Iberians decorated their mounts with care, using bells and a prominent, distinctive frontal ornament attached to the brow.[281]

Iberian light cavalry were typically equipped with javelins and the small, round *caetra* shield (which could be slung over the back or on the side of the horse when not in use), they were effective raiders, scouts, foragers and mounted skirmishers. It seems that prior to 237 the Iberians and Celtiberians did not employ bodies of heavy cavalry as tactical units on the battlefield. It may have been that in the pre-Barcid period the main feature of the horse in Iberian society was to serve as a potent symbol of prestige, distinction and wealth for native elites, rather than serving as a 'warhorse' on the battlefield. Quesada observes that the archaeological record reveals only a small number

---

279 Robert E Gaebel, *Cavalry Operations in the Ancient Greek World*, University of Oaklahoma Press, Norman, 2002, p. 165.

280 Fernando Quesada Sanz, 1997, '¿Jinetes o caballeros?. En torno al empleo del caballo en la Edad del Hierro Peninsular', *La Guerra en la Antigüedad*, Catálogo de la Exposición, Madrid, pp. 185–194; Mª del Mar Gabaldón Martínez and Fernando Quesada Sanz, 1998, '¿Jinetes y caballos en el Más Allá ibérico?. Un vaso cerámico en el Museo Arqueológico de Linares', *Revista de Arqueología*, n. 201, pp. 16–23.

281 Martin Almagro-Gorbea, 2005, 'Ideologia Ecuestre en la Hispania Prerromana', *Gladius*, Vol. 25, pp. 151–186.

(4.5%) of Iron Age tombs in Iberia contain spurs, gear and harness associated with warhorses.[282] In reconciling the archaeological record with the iconography, Quesada suggests that in the pre-Barcid period Iberian horsemen normally dismounted to enter into combat. At Cannae in 216 they are reported as colliding with the Romans, dismounting, and fighting on foot.[283] Hence, the native aristocracy and their retainers, forming the most lavishly equipped warriors in any Iberian force, are better described as 'mounted infantry' rather than as cavalry in the modern sense. Yet the Barcids also introduced the deployment of bodies of true cavalry into Iberia, and Iberian heavy cavalry were also found in Carthaginian armies.[284] The famous 2nd/1st century BC *'vase of the armoured warriors'* found at Liria (Valencia, Spain) depicts Iberian cavalry wearing corselets of mixed construction, including scale cuirasses, iron ring mail and thickly-woven esparto grass matting. With large oval or round shields, a long thrusting lance and falcata-type swords, these were genuine shock cavalry.

k *From Chariots to War Elephants*

Traditionally, the Carthaginians deployed four-horse chariots – in 480 the chariotry were lost in the sea crossing to Sicily, and so were never deployed, but there were 400 against Dionysius in 397,[285] 300 chariots in Sicily in 343, and supposedly 2,000 at Tunis in 310. Chariotry was not only derived from the Carthaginian's heritage from the Near East, where the use of chariots continued in the Persian Empire and later the Seleucids, but also persisted among the Greeks and Libyans of Cyrene,[286] and perhaps too the Garamantes of the Fezzan.[287] The four-horse chariots of the Carthaginians and Libyans had

282 Fernando Quesada Sanz, 1997, '¿Jinetes o caballeros?. En torno al empleo del caballo en la Edad del Hierro Peninsular', *La Guerra en la Antigüedad*, Catálogo de la Exposición, Madrid, pp. 185–194.

283 Polyb. 3.115.2–4; Livy, 22.47.1–3.

284 Fernando Quesada Sanz, 1998, 'Aristocratas a caballo y la existencia de una verdadera 'caballeria' en la cultura iberica: dos ambitos conceptuales differences', in C Aranegui (ed.), *Los Iberos, principes de Occidente*, Actas del Congresso Internacional, Barcelona, pp. 169–183; Fernando Quesada Sanz, 2005, 'El Gobierno del Caballo Montado en la Antiguedad Clsica con Especial Referencia al Caso de Iberia. Bocados, Espuelas y la Cuestion de la Silla de Montar, Estribos y Herraduras', *Gladius*, Vol. 25, pp. 97–150.

285 Diod. 14.54.4–6.

286 Diod. 20.41.1; Polyaenus, *Strat.* 7.28.1.

287 cf. Hdt. 4.183. Herodotos claims that the Greeks of Cyrene learnt the technique of using four-horse teams for chariots from the Libyans. The contingents of war-chariots which served in the armies of Cyrene in the fifth and fourth centuries BC were probably provided by Libyans, and the Cyrenaean passion for chariot racing was certainly influenced by local Libyans, among whom the horse-drawn war-chariot was still in normal use, whereas it had long ago been abandoned in mainland Greece. There was a large chariot

three-man crews, and tactically seem to have been used to screen infantry from harassment, and to attack enemy infantry formations in battle, although they proved relatively ineffective.[288]

The Carthaginians probably first encountered war elephants when they fought King Pyrros in Sicily during 278–275, where he "… *totally routed the Phoenicians* …".[289] It seems that by 275 the Carthaginians came to appreciate that the war chariot was obsolete. Realising the military possibilities of the elephant, Carthage proceeded to raise an elephant corps from among the African "forest" elephants (*Loxodonta Africana cyclotis*) that roamed aplenty in the forests of the Atlas Mountains in Numidia and Mauretania.

Carthage deployed its first corps of 50 war elephants in 262 against Rome at Akragas in the First Punic War. While some believe the original elephant trainers may have been brought to Carthage from Syria or even from India, the practice of calling the mahouts 'Indians'[290] was probably a literary convention, as the word became synonymous with "elephant-rider".[291] By 255 the elephant corps had grown to 100 beasts, and in 251 the Carthaginians had some 140 war elephants with its army in Sicily. The Carthaginian figure Hanno the Great is reported commanding a corps of 100 war elephants during the Mercenary War and Hamilcar Barca used war elephants extensively in both the Mercenary War and in his Iberian campaigns. War elephants had quickly become a standard component of Carthaginian armies in the Hellenistic period.

War elephants were very expensive to capture, they took many years to train for warfare, and they consumed enormous amounts of forage. For this reason, to keep a war stud of the beasts in Iberia brought the Barcids enormous prestige as well as a formidable military capability. To possess such a stable of war elephants was an attribute of a super-power in the Hellenistic period. Indeed, in 229 Hasdrubal 'the fair' commanded a corps of 200 war elephants, which would have required some 40–45 tons of fodder per day, and produced a full 25 tons of manure every day! Emphasising their association with war elephants, the Barcids occasionally used the image of an elephant on their coinage.

component to the army Ophellas of Cyrene brought to assist Agathokles invasion of Carthage in 308: Diod.

288 cf. Diod. 20.12.1.

289 Plut. *Pyrrh.* 22.4.

290 cf. 1.40; 3.461: Vegetius 3.24.

291 John M Kistler, 2007, *War Elephants*, University of Nebraska Press, Lincoln & London, pp. 97–140; Richard Glover, 1944 (February), 'The Elephant in Ancient War', *The Classical Journal*, Vol. 39. No. 5, pp. 257–269; William Gowers, 1947 (January), 'The African Elephant in Warfare', *African Affairs*, Vol. 46, No. 182, pp. 42–49.

While the Carthaginians may have obtained a small number of Indian elephants from the Near East, the great majority of their war elephants were African "forest" elephants (*Loxodonta africana cyclotis*). The African forest elephant was some 7–8 feet at the shoulder, and were smaller than the better-known African bush elephants (*Loxodonta africana Africana*, 13 feet) or the Indian elephants (*Elephus maximus*, 10 feet). The distinctive features of the forest elephant were the low posture of the head, the flat or concave line of its back, its small rounded ears, small, straight tusks and a ridged trunk that ended in two "fingers". The forest elephant was hunted to extinction in North Africa by the sixth century AD.[292]

The tactical deployment of these war elephants was a subtle military art. Elephants provided a disproportionate psychological factor on the battlefield – boosting the morale and confidence of the army that possessed them, and unnerving the enemy, particularly if the enemy troops had not faced war elephants before. The effect of war elephants on the Iberians and Celtiberians proved particularly devastating. Yet elephants have a highly-strung nervous system which is easily upset. Unlike a modern tank, an elephant is made of flesh and blood, and so when pelted with javelins and arrows may panic, turn and bolt. A wounded, maddened elephant that is out of control might become as great a danger to his own side as to the enemy. Nonetheless, when used effectively, war elephants were devastating on the ancient battlefield. The war elephant had a far greater shock value than cavalry; not only was he bigger, but he had weapons of his own with which he fought. He trampled the men he felled, or gored them with his tusks, or he might kick, and an elephant's kick will send a man flying.[293] In addition, the elephant may carry armed riders. Copying the Successor kingdoms, the war elephants of the Carthaginians likely carried *howdahs* ('towers' the ancients called them) with a crew of four men.[294] The Roman poet Juvenal ascribed towers to Hannibal's elephants, and several coins from ancient Italy depict elephants with towers. In the first century BC the Roman writer Lucretius said "*in process of time the Carthaginians taught fierce elephants, with towers on their backs, and with snake-like proboscis, to endure the wounds of war, and to throw vast martial battalions into confusion.*"[295] In describing the Carthaginian battle line at Illipa in 206, Livy says

292 Isidore of Seville, *Etymologiae*, 12.2.16.

293 Polyb. 1.74.

294 Livy, 37.40.

295 Lucretius (trans. John Selby Watson), *Lucretius on the Nature of Things*, London, Bell & Daldy, p. 239; John M Kistler, 2007, *War Elephants*, University of Nebraska Press, Lincoln & London, p. 120.

"Before the wings of the Carthaginian line stood the elephants, which from a distance, looked like castles".[296] These 'towers' were made of hides stitched over a wooden framework, its crews armed with arrows, javelins, or even long pikes. Polybius reports that Ptolemy's African forest elephants at Raphia in 217 were indeed equipped with towers.[297]

Some scholars, however, doubt that the Carthaginians ever used *howdahs* on their war elephants, believing that the African forest elephant may have been too small in stature to carry one. Certainly, only a trained war elephant would have been able to carry a *howdah*, and so, on those occasions that Carthage deployed elephants that had only been recently captured and had received minimal training, such as Zama, they may not have been fitted with towers. Carthaginian war elephants were sometimes partly protected by armour; Appian reports that the Carthaginian war elephants at Zama wore colourful coverings, perhaps dyed leather armour. The elephants fielded by the Numidian king Juba were both turreted and armoured, and the Numidians must have learnt their elephant techniques from Carthage.[298] The Carthaginians are said to have adopted from the east the practice of fixing iron points or spears on the tusks (which also served to protect the tusks of older elephants).[299]

But towers and crews were not essential. Get a good *mahout* to guide him into battle and the elephant was perfectly competent to do his own fighting – shock action applied *en masse*. Whereas it is correct to mass men against cavalry, because a horse will not charge home against a firm body of men, a charging war elephant is another matter. When a commander had not enough elephants to cover his front, like a screen of tanks, it was best to concentrate them on the wings. Elephants had a damaging effect on horses' nerves, and were an effective anti-cavalry screen. It was folly to use elephants against fortifications, however, as they cannot jump, and so could be immobilized by trenches.

---

296 Livy, 28.14.4.

297 Polyb. 5.84–85. For a contrary view, asserting that Ptolemy's turrented elephants were actually Indian elephants, see: Michael Charles, 2007, 'Elephants at Raphia: Reinterpreting Polybius 5.84–85', *Classical Quarterly*, Vol. 57, pp. 306–311.

298 Duncan Head (drawings by Ian Heath), 1982, *Armies of the Macedonian and Punic Wars, 359–146 BC*, A Wargames Research Group Publication, p. 187.

299 William Gowers, 1947 (January), 'The African Elephant in Warfare', *African Affairs*, Vol. 46, No. 182, p. 43.

IV Carthaginian Citizenship and Manpower

a *Carthaginian Citizenship*

Carthage's territorial expansion in Tunisia and Sardinia enabled the agricultural expansion that was the basis for the city's prosperity.[300] It is no accident that the heartland of the Carthaginian empire – North Africa, Sardinia and Sicily – would later form the bread basket of the Roman empire. The wealth of Carthage was proverbial; in 264 its revenues have been estimated at 2,200 talents a year; in 218 its revenues are estimated at 3,000 talents a year; in 193 it was still 1,500 talents a year. By comparison, the Athenian empire at its height had a revenue of around 1,000 talents a year; Rhodes in *c.* 200 had a revenue of 300 talents a year; Rome in *c.* 180 had revenues of around 2,250 talents a year.[301]

It is impossible to know the population of the Carthaginian empire, but we can attempt an estimate. On the eve of the First Punic War Carthage was one of the greatest cities of the Mediterranean basin, with an urban space of at most around 800 hectares inhabited by some 200,000 people. Cape Bon, with its towns and agricultural villages, was inhabited by around 70,000. Carthage's *chora*, the city's colonial foundations in the Bagradas valley, and the indigenous Libyan villages in the Tunisian *Tell* and *Sahel* may have added another 300–400,000 people. Nathan Pilkington estimates that overall, the territorial heartland of Carthage in Tunisia possessed a total population of 750–900,000, meaning some 150–175,000 men of military age. "To this can be added the small figure of 20,000 men of military age in its overseas colonies in Sicily and Sardinia, assuming a total population of 100–120,000 dependents. It is unlikely that Carthage possessed direct access to more than 200,000 men of military age at any point in its history."[302] In 247 the Roman census registered 241,700 Roman citizens – adult males. By 225 the number had grown to 273,000. The conclusion is that by the time of the outbreak of the First Punic War in 264, the republic of Rome probably controlled a larger manpower base than Carthage.

---

300 Veronique Krings, 2008, 'Rereading Punic Agriculture: Representation, Analogy and Ideology in the Classical Sources', in Peter van Dommelen and Carlos Gomez Bellard, Rural Landscapes of the Punic World', Equinox Publishing Ltd, London and Oakville, pp. 22–43.

301 In 264 Carthage's empire included western Sicily and Sardinia; in 218 Sicily and Sardinia were lost, replaced by an expanded Carthaginian empire in Iberia; in 193 Carthage was reduced to its North African holdings: Dexter Hoyos, 2003, *Hannibal's Dynasty. Power and Politics in the western Mediterranean 247–183 BC*, Routledge, pp. 27–28.

302 Nathan Pilkington, 2019, *The Carthaginian Empire 550–202 BCE*, Lexington Books, pp. 167–171; also Dexter Hoyos, 2003, *Hannibal's Dynasty. Power and Politics in the western Mediterranean 247–183 BC*, Routledge, pp. 27–29.

The exclusive nature of Carthaginian citizenship restricted the expansion of the city's armies. Carthage sought to overcome this through the employment of mercenaries, levying subject Libyans and procuring troops from its dependent allies. Several tyrants of Syracuse, such as Dionysius I, sought to escape this same restriction through forcible transfers of populations and offering their mercenaries citizenship. The expansion of the Roman manpower base, which enabled Rome's military and territorial expansion, was due to its willingness to extend citizenship, the establishment of numerous colonies of citizens on confiscated land, and an alliance system that fully incorporated allied contingents into their military structures. The exclusive nature of Carthaginian citizenship did not permit this. It was impossible for the Carthaginians to extend civic rights to their Libyan subjects, who were, in many respects, state serfs.

There is evidence that Carthage offered citizenship to outsiders in certain circumstances. Inscriptions from Carthage show Greek names, sometimes written in Greek and sometimes in a bilingual formula, as well as Phoenicians from the east and Punics from Sicily, Ibiza or Sardinia. Citizenship seems to have been a reward granted to foreigners for service on the battlefield. Andrew Hill offers an intriguing hypothesis concerning the several Carthaginians mentioned in the sources who boast toponymical nicknames, such as Hamilcar Rhodanus,[303] Mago Saunites[304] and Mago 'the Bruttian',[305] is evidence for "Carthage's wide-reaching recruitment programmes and perhaps the multi-generational settlement of some mercenaries".[306] Perhaps these nicknames had become hereditary family names, like the cognomen Barca, and were used in the time of the Second Punic War by the grand-children of Phoenician, Greek, Samnite and Bruttian mercenaries assimilated into the Carthaginian citizenry?

After the fall of Tyre to Alexander the Great in 332, Phoenicians from the eastern Mediterranean may have migrated to Carthage to seek new opportunities. Diodorus and Curtius both assert that the elderly, women and children of Tyre were sent to safety in Carthage to escape Alexander's siege of Tyre.[307] We may wonder how many of these returned to Tyre in the years after that city was stormed by the Macedonians, its defenders having been either slain, crucified or sold into slavery. The fall of the Persian Empire also meant that

303 Oros. 4.6; Justin 21.6.1–7; Frontin. Str. 1.2.3.
304 Polyb. 9.25.
305 Polyb. 36.5.
306 Andrew M Till, 2020, 'Hamilcar of Barce? Discerning Barcid Proto-History and Polybius' Mixellenes', *Journal of Hellenic Studies*, Vol. 140, p. 78.
307 Curt. 4.8, 4.15; Diod. 17.40, 17.41.

thousands of Greek mercenaries were unemployed and fearful of Alexander's retribution.[308] Diodorus reports that in 307 thousands of Greek, Etruscan and Samnite mercenaries in the service of Agathokles of Syracuse surrendered to Carthage on terms that saw them either transfer into Carthaginian service or settled on state land in Sicily.[309] Two of Hannibal's senior officers in the Second Punic War, the brothers Hippokrates and Epykides, were descended from one of these men. Both grew up in Carthage, sons of a Carthaginian woman, grandsons of a prominent Syracusan exile.[310]

The addition of favoured mercenaries to Carthage's citizen body may have added a number of military families to the city, but it cannot have significantly expanded the city's available manpower. The settlement of such immigrants did, however, establish a precedent that was able to be exploited by the Barcids. Between 337–219 the Barcids in Iberia adopted a military manpower model that was not tied to Carthage's citizen body, but which instead was typical of the contemporaneous Hellenistic kingdoms. As the Barcid conquests in Iberia expanded, so too did their demographic and financial base. This led to an expansion in the size and complexity of Barcid military forces, which in turn led to further territorial expansion. In 237 Hamilcar Barca's army numbered around 20,000. At the outbreak of the Second Punic War in 218 Hannibal Barca commanded some 130,000.[311] The Barcids founded new cities,[312] built forts and mines, expanded agricultural production, and encouraged the immigration of Punic populations from Africa.[313] They may also have settled discharged veterans on lands in Iberia. A number of communities in the interior of the Iberian Penninsula – in what would have been a frontier zone in the third century BC – persisted in minting Neo-Punic coins until the Augustan period. These so-called 'Lilyphoenician' coins are indicative of an enduring Punic identity[314],

308 At the Granicus in 334 Alexander refused to accept the surrender of Omares and the Greek mercenaries in Persian service, and they were surrounded "and butchered to a man": Arr. 1.16.2–6.

309 Diod. 20.69.3–5.

310 Pol. 7.2; Liv. 24.6.2. Hippokrates and Epykides were the grandsons of Arcesilaus, a friend of the Syracusan tyrant Agathocles. In 307 Agathocles was defeated in Africa by the Carthaginians, and he then abandoned his mercenary army (whose pay was in arrears) and fled to Syracuse; the abandoned soldiers were able to capture Agathocles' eldest son Agatharchus before he could escape with his father. Arcesilaus killed Agatharchus, prior to him and the surviving mercenaries surrendering to Carthage: Just. 22.8; Diod. 20.69.3.

311 Dexter Hoyos, 2003, *Hannibal's Dynasty. Power and Politics in the western Mediterranean 247–183 BC*, Routledge, p. 55, 107, n. 16.

312 cf. Diod. 25.12.

313 cf. Mela 2.96.

314 c.f. Liv. 33.21.7-8.

and may have been towns where the Barcids granted land parcels to military settlers, much like the 'allotment-holders' (*klerouchoi*) that Alexander the Great and his Successors settled in the former Persian Empire for loyal military service.[315] Upon arriving in Italy in 218, Hannibal promised his soldiery "land wherever they wished, in Italy, Africa, or Spain, which would be free from all taxation for the recipient and for his children; if any preferred money to land, he would satisfy his desires; if any of the allies wished to become Carthaginian citizens he would give them the opportunity"[316]

The First and Second Punic Wars (264–241 and 218–201) required that Carthage mobilise ever greater numbers of men in order to contest Roman manpower. The Carthaginians continued to draft, equip and drill the subject Libyans to provide heavy infantry, and mustered contingents of skirmishers and light cavalry from its Numidian allies and tributaries in North Africa[317] Carthage continued to recruit mercenaries from throughout the western Mediterranean. Aristocrats continued to serve in the city's armies as senior and junior officers and staff, but they appear to only have formed whole infantry units when Carthage itself was threatened. It must be remembered, however, that the Carthaginian fleet, which during the First and Second Punic Wars typically numbered 120 or more galleys,[318] was likely manned by citizens. The fact that the Libyphoenician cities are never mentioned in the ancient sources as fielding infantry suggests that perhaps these communities provided oarsmen and sailors (much like the Roman *socii navales*).[319] Manning the fleet must have been a considerable demand on Carthaginian (and Libyphoenician?) manpower.

---

315 Susana Perez Guijo, 2001, 'La Beturia: definicion, limites, etnias y organizacion territorial', *Flor.*, Vol. 2, No. 12, pp. 315–349; Alicia Jimenez, 2015, 'Punic after Punic times? The case of the so-called 'Libyphoenician' coins of southern Iberia', in Josephine Crawley Quinn and Nicholas C Vella (eds.), *The Punic Mediterranean. Identities and Identification from Phoenician Settlement to Roman Rule*, Cambridge University Press, pp. 219–242.

316 Liv. 21.45.5-6.

317 c.f. Pol. 1.78.

318 If these galleys were the larger quinqueremes or "fives" (as Polybius and Livy suggest) then a fleet of 120 warships would have required 36,000 oarsmen and a further 14–15,000 marines, sailors and officers.

319 There is no evidence that Libyphoenicians ever served as infantry in Carthaginian armies, although certain modern writers persist in believing that African line infantry were either Libyphoenicians or a combination of Libyans and Libyphoenicians (Connolly, 1998, p. 148; Warry, 1980, p. 122). Polybius only ever mentions a force of 450 Libyphoenician cavalry, described as "bridled and steady" (3.65.6), suggesting they were heavy cavalry. I would speculate that wealthier Libyphoenicians served in Carthaginian armies as cavalry, while the poorer allied citizens served as oarsmen and sailors.

b *Carthaginian Grand Tactical Doctrine*

By the time of the Second Punic War the strategic and tactical doctrine of the Carthaginians had grown sophisticated, having learnt the key lesson of Hellenistic warfare – the need to coordinate an all-arms combined force on both campaign and upon the battlefield. On the battlefield Carthaginian generals aimed to deploy a strong battle line in the centre, and to deliver a decisive blow with the cavalry on the wings; this was the approach of Xanthippos at Bagradas (255), Hannibal at Trebbia (218) and Cannae (216), and his brother Hasdrubal at Hibera (216/215?). This grand tactical approach meant that Carthaginian generals used light-armed troops aggressively to conduct ambushes, screen deployments, support cavalry, and join in the envelopment of the enemy's flanks and rear. Heavy infantry was used defensively; to hold the battle line and fix the enemy army in place while the decisive blow was struck on the flanks and rear of the enemy battle-line. The ability of such infantry to 'hold the line' against Roman infantry was the difference between success (Trebbia and Cannae) and failure (Hibera, Illipa). The Carthaginians relied upon armies that were unusually strong in cavalry and possessed war elephants, the latter to terrify the enemy and disrupt their battle line.

v Laws of War and Prohibited Actions

There were certain 'laws of war' that were unwritten, but which were customary and internationally understood norms, "laws common to all men" that operated throughout the "civilized" states of the Mediterranean, encompassing the Greeks, Persians, Punics and others. These norms were not codified in treaties or the laws of states, and they were not motivated by any humanitarian impulse, but largely grew out of religious customs. Carthage and other ancient states were deterred from ignoring these international norms by the practical fear that the wronged might extract vengeance, concern for the impacts of wider reputational damage at home and abroad, and the very real religious fear of divine sanctions being extracted by angry deities.

We should not be surprised that Greek and Punic societies shared common notions concerning the laws of war; they were entangled culturally and economically as well as militarily, and their cities were multicultural. In Syracuse Punic resident aliens held property,[320] while Greeks were resident in the Carthaginian-controlled west of Sicily.[321] There was a resident

320 Diod. 14.41.53.

321 Diod. 14.41, 14.53.4–5.

Greek community in Carthage itself; the Greek tyrant Terillos of Rhegion is described as a "guest-friend" (*xenia*) of the Carthaginian Hamilcar, who had a Syracusan mother,[322] while in 209 during the Second Punic War we find a senior Carthaginian officer who was a guest-friend of a Roman consul.[323]

The Carthaginians were a deeply religious people, worshipping Tyrian deities as well as Egyptian (Bes and Isis) and Greek (Demeter and Kore), and the city boasted many temples and shrines. Like the Greeks, the Punics were devoted to rites and ceremonies to appease the gods or win their favour. In 480 during the battle of Himera the general Hamilcar "remained in camp trying to obtain a favourable omen from sacrifices, burning whole carcasses on an immense fire; and at last, seeing, as he poured the wine upon the sacrificed victims, that his army was giving way, he leapt into the flames, was burnt to nothing, and in this way disappeared".[324] It seems the Carthaginians took the threat of divine sanctions very seriously indeed.

The laws of war dictated that temples, shrines and sacred places were not to be disturbed in wartime. Polybius regarded the plundering or destruction of temples as the most heinous war crime.[325] During the siege of Akragas in 406 the Carthaginians plundered the tomb of Theron for building materials. This sacrilege was then blamed for the subsequent plague that broke out in the Carthaginian army, killing the general Hannibal. His successor Himilco "seeing how the throng was beset with superstitious fear" ceased the sacrilege and "after the custom of his people by sacrificing a young boy to Cronus and a multitude of cattle to Poseidon by drowning them in the sea" was able to proceed with the siege.[326] In 395 a Carthaginian army besieging Syracuse was struck by plague, and Diodorus reports that "the gods were clearly fighting" against the Carthaginians.[327] The Carthaginians resolved that the plague was the divine wrath of the gods of Demeter, Kore and Zeus, because the army had plundered their temples. In order to make peace with these deities, they decided to establish temples to the Greek gods of Demeter and Kore in the city of Carthage itself, and they "*appointed their most renowned citizens to be priests of these goddesses*", and adopted the Greek rites to honour the statues they erected.

---

322 Hdt. 7.165.

323 Liv. 27.16.4.

324 Hdt. 7.167.

325 Oleg L Gabelko and Eugene G Teytelbaum, 2019, '"Waged War not only on men but on gods": Polybius' views on religious crimes in military conflicts of the Greco-Roman World', *Anabasis*, Studia Classica et Orientalia, Vol. 10, pp. 297–313.

326 Diod. 13.86.3.

327 Diod. 14.77.4.

The rules of war were critical to the conduct of siege warfare. The norms of ancient warfare were not motivated by any humanitarian sentiment. If a community failed to surrender then the besieging army was permitted to do whatever it wanted with the property and lives within. The besieging army would typically commence a siege by calling on the city to surrender. If it surrendered the city could secure terms, which ensured that it survived, albeit as a tributary or subject community, perhaps obliged to take on a garrison. For example, Diodorus reports in 406: "And first they [the Carthaginians] dispatched ambassadors to the Akragantini, asking them, preferably, to become their allies, but otherwise to stay neutral and be friends with the Carthaginians, thereby remaining in peace; and when the inhabitants of the city would not entertain these terms, the siege was begun at once".[328]

If a city refused to surrender, then it risked extermination. In 217 Hannibal arrived at Gereonium in Apulia, and sought to seduce the inhabitants into an alliance by promising them unspecified advantages. When they rejected his overtures, the Carthaginian general besieged and captured the town and massacred its inhabitants.[329] In 216 Hannibal's army surrounded Nuceria and "besieged the town for some time",[330] alternating between mounting assaults on the town's defences and inviting the inhabitants to surrender "by trying to win over either the commons or the ruling class", playing on political divisions within the community. Finally, Nuceria was starved into surrendering on terms, whereby the survivors departed their homes with only their clothes, becoming destitute refugees. Nuceria itself was sacked and razed by the victorious Carthaginians, while Hannibal "offered rewards and promotion to any of the townspeople who stayed behind and were willing to serve in his army".[331]

Sieges could end far more brutally. There were no protections for defeated soldiers or noncombatants. A victorious army was permitted according to custom to slaughter or enslave the entire population of a city taken by force. Cities of great wealth and antiquity faced the threat of annihilation when besieged. In 409 the Carthaginian general Hannibal resolved to storm the defences of Selinunte and so promised his Campanian and Iberian mercenaries "that he would give them the city to pillage, pushed the siege engines forward and

328 Diod. 13.85.2.

329 Polyb. 3.100.1–8; Livy, 22.18.7, 22.23.9; App. *Hann.* 15.

330 Livy, 23.15.3.

331 Livy, 23.15.3–6. Some of the lurid accounts of Hannibals treatment of the people of Nuceria – such as suffocating the Nucerian senators in the baths – are inventions of later Roman annalists seeking to illustrate Hannibal's vices and treachery, see: Arthur J Pomeroy, 'Hannibal at Nuceria', *Historia*, Vol. 38, No. 2, 1989, pp. 162–176.

assaulted the walls in waves with his best soldiers".[332] After nine days of fighting resistance collapsed and a general massacre ensued; Diodorus tells us that 16,000 inhabitants were killed and 5,000 enslaved. Only the women and children that took refuge in the city's temples were spared. The mercenaries "... mutilated even the dead according to the practice of their people, some carrying bunches of hands about their bodies and others heads which they had spitted upon their javelins and spears".[333] The city was sacked, much of it burnt or razed to the ground, and Hannibal even plundered "*the temples of their gods*".[334] Greek Selinunte was dead, and the Carthaginians refounded the city sometime later.[335]

The norms of war permitted the victor to treat captives taken in battle as they pleased. Typically, captives were sold into slavery, but they might also be ransomed or even recruited into the victorious army. Hannibal during his invasion of Italy famously released captives from Roman allied states without ransom, seeking to emphasise that his enemy was the republic of Rome, not its subordinate allies, and so undermine the loyalty of these polities to their Roman masters. Roman captives, however, were sold into slavery. After Cannae in 216, however, Hannibal moderated this policy, seeking to create the conditions for peace negotiations. Hannibal addressed his Roman captives and declared: "As his ancestors had capitulated before the valour of Rome, so his goal now was to see others in turn capitulating before his success and valour. Accordingly, he concluded, he was giving the prisoners the opportunity of ransoming themselves: the price would be 500 quadrigati per cavalryman, 300 per infantryman, and 100 per slave".[336] The Roman senate, however, refused to countenance any peace discussions or that any ransom be paid from either the state or private sources. Rome's leaders showed little regard for its prisoners of war, accusing them of cowardice for being taken captive, and fearing the ransom money would strengthen Hannibal. As a consequence, in the autumn of 216 the Carthaginians sold some 10,000 Roman citizens into slavery, most of them disappearing into Greece.[337] Such a development must have astonished

332 Diod. 13.55.5.

333 Diod. 13.57.3.

334 Diod. 13.57.5.

335 Nathan Pilkington, 2019, *The Carthaginian Empire 550–202 BCE*, Lexington Books, pp. 154–155.

336 Livy, 22.58.2–4.

337 Livy reports (34.50.6–7) that in 194 the Romans sought out those citizens in Greece who were in slavery. "There was a great number of them, captives in the Punic War, whom Hannibal had sold when they were not ransomed by their relatives. It is an indication of their number that Polybius writes that this cost the Achaeans one hundred talents,

the Carthaginians, who could never countenance allowing such a large body of citizens to be lost.

This may in part explain the presence of Roman deserters in the armies of Carthage during the Punic Wars. The Roman army, where savage discipline and heavy losses could be expected, suffered desertion from among its conscripts, and many of these joined the enemy. Hamilcar Barca refused to surrender deserters serving in his forces to the Romans when negotiating the peace treaty that ended the First Punic War in 241.[338] Hannibal in Italy commanded at least one contingent of 600 Roman deserters.[339] Such men were formidable soldiers, fighting to the death, because they knew if they surrendered or were captured by their countrymen they faced certain execution.[340]

The laws of war provided immunity to envoys and heralds, a practical custom to ensure that diplomatic communication could take place between enemies; Carthaginian envoys are reported dealing with both Greek and Roman adversaries.[341] The Carthaginians placed as much emphasis on a proper burial

although they had fixed the price per head to be paid to their owners at five hundred denarii. On that basis Achaea had one thousand two hundred. Calculate now, in proportion to this, how many there probably were in all Greece".

338 Hamilcar refuses to surrender the Roman deserters serving in his army, see: Nepos, *Ham.* 1.5. Many deserters joined the enemy, where they fought to the death rather than risk capture, flogging and execution. "Desertion was always a problem for the Roman army. Enemy leaders as separated by time and geography as Jugurtha, Tacfarinas and Decebalus recruited their best men from Roman deserters. According to Dio, men were even willing to desert and join the rebels within the city during the siege of Jerusalem in AD 70 (Dio. 65.5.4). Treaties concluding wars in the second century often seem to have included provision for the return of Roman deserters and prisoners (Dio. 68.9.5)."; Adrian Goldsworthy, *The Roman Army at War 100 BC-AD 200*, Oxford University Press, 1996, p. 113. As one historian has said, "... mutiny and insubordination were surprisingly prevalent in the Roman army"; William Stuart Messer, 1920, 'Mutiny in the Roman Army. The Republic', *Classical Philology*, Vol. 15, No. 2, pp. 158–175. In the peace of 201 BC Carthage was required to hand over all 'Roman prisoners, deserters and runaway slaves'. In 198 BC, Phillip V of Macedon employed a force of Roman deserters and Hannibal's veterans from Italy as his garrison at Sicyon; during the siege they fought fanatically against the Romans, fearing reprisals if taken captive: Liv. 32.23. In 200 BC Roman envoys visited Carthage to complain "... that the Roman deserters had not all been handed over; in fact reports said that a large number of them were living at Carthage without concealment": Liv. 32.36. In the Third Punic War (149–146 BC) the most fanatical defenders of doomed Carthage were Roman deserters, 900 in number at the conclusion of the siege, who barricaded themselves in the temple of Aesculpius and committed suicide: App. *Pun.* 130–131. Aemilius Scipio would not offer them any terms; he had used elephants to trample deserters in 167, and threw deserters and runaway slaves to beasts in shows at Rome: Val. Max. 2.7.12–4.

339 Liv. 27.28.1–13.

340 cf. Liv. 25.25.1; 28.3.12.

341 Diod. 15.17.5; Livy, 22.58.9.

of the fallen as did the Greeks and Romans, and so heralds might seek the return of bodies, even though making such a request was usually a humiliation. Hannibal Barca was typically scrupulous in his treatment of fallen Roman generals, giving them burial with honours and even sending their ashes to their families in Rome – in marked contrast to the manner that the Romans mistreated the corpse of Hannibal's brother Hasdrubal in 207.[342] In the Mercenary War of 240–237 the rebels tortured and massacred their prisoners of war and refused to return the bodies of fallen Carthaginians for burial. The rebels declared that any Carthaginian heralds approaching them would also be tortured and then killed.[343] For this reason the Mercenary War was sometimes known as the 'Truceless War'. Hamilcar Barca responded by henceforth having enemy prisoners trampled to death by his war elephants.[344]

VI Conclusion

From the mid-sixth century BC until the end of the Second Punic War in 201 the city-state of Carthage was one of the great powers of the Mediterranean basin. In the multipolar, violent anarchy that was the international environment of the period,[345] Carthage built a hegemony that spanned North Africa, Sicily, Sardinia and southern Iberia. An intensifying export trade in commodities such as grain, olive oil and fish sauce from the Punic world via Carthage to Athens, Corinth and the eastern Mediterranean city-states in *c.* 550–450 stimulated an agricultural expansion throughout the Punic world.[346] This commerce generated enormous wealth for the Carthaginian state and its political elites, and encouraged territorial expansion in Sardinia and Tunisia. In undertaking the defence of its extended sphere of interest, particularly in Sicily against Greek Syracuse, Carthage was obliged to field armies. Carthaginian warcraft was typical for its times; unsurprising given it was a trading city integrated into wider Mediterranean cultural and economic currents. Carthage conscripted

342 For example, the treatment of the corpse of Tiberius Sempronius Gracchus (*cos.* 215, 213): Liv. 25.16.8–25; Pol. 8.35.1; App. *Hann.* 35. Also the burial of Marcus Claudius Marcellus (*cos.* 222, 215, 214, 210, 208); Plut. *Marc.* 30.2 ff.; Liv. 27.28.2; Cic. *Cato Maior* 75; Val. Max. 5.1.

343 Polyb. 1.81.3.

344 Polyb. 1.82.1–2; Dexter Hoyos, 2007, *Truceless War. Carthage's fight for survival, 241 to 237 BC*, Brill, Leiden and Boston, pp. 160–175.

345 Arthur M Eckstein, 2006, *Mediterranean Anarchy, Interstate War and the Rise of Rome*, University of California Press.

346 Nathan Pilkington, 2019, *The Carthaginian Empire 550–202 BCE*, Lexington Books, p. 107.

its Libyan subjects to augment its citizen militia, so as to offset the fact that the city lacked a large rural population of farmers. In order to field large and effective armies, while protecting Carthage's citizens from grievous battlefield losses (such as those sustained at Crimissus in 339), the city employed mercenaries and allied auxiliaries. Carthage's allies included at various times the independent Numidian tribal kingdoms of North Africa, Sicilian cities, Iberian and Celtiberian communities, city-states and tribal groups in Italy, and several Celtic and Ligurian tribes in northern Italy.

Throughout its military history, Carthaginian armies faced a particular struggle in fielding enough heavy infantry of sufficient quality to face their chief enemies, the Greeks and the Romans. Heavy infantry comprised the core of any army during this period, and the Greek hoplite and the Roman legionary were the most formidable heavy infantrymen of their day. In order to compete, Carthage sought to add specialist troops to support its Libyan infantry core; war elephants, slingers, and Greek, Iberian and Celtic mercenaries. Carthaginian heavy and light cavalry – recruited from citizens, Punic allies, Numidians, Celts and Iberians – generally outclassed their adversaries and were intended to strike the decisive blow on the flanks of the enemy line. When Carthage was able to even just match Greek and Roman heavy infantry, its strength in cavalry and skirmishers enabled its armies to secure crushing victories (i.e. Bagradas, Trebbia, Cannae), but when its infantry battle line collapsed (i.e. Crimissus, Hibera, Ilipa) it experienced serious defeats.

Carthage absorbed the prevailing military ideas of its time. When the hoplite panoply and way of war – the decisive infantry battle – was dominant among Greeks, Etruscans and Romans, it also dominated in the Punic world. In the late fourth century BC warcraft became more complex. Alexander the Great ushered in a military revolution in the Hellenistic period which featured the appearance of new troop types, larger and more complex armies, and emphasised the importance of cavalry and combined-arms operations. In the western Mediterranean skirmishers and heavy infantry (hoplites) were superseded after *c.* 300 by dual-purpose infantry, men equipped with the weapons and panoply that enabled them to engage in both open-order skirmishing or close-order, hand-to-hand combat. Dual-purpose infantry evolved as regional variations among Celtic, Italic (especially Samnite) and Iberian traditions interacted and homogenised. By the mid third century BC this homogenisation of panoply and method of fighting is exemplified by the Roman *hastati* – soldiers armed with a Celtic-style shield, an Iberian-style sword and Samnite-style armour. Carthage too absorbed these new military ideas, its generals familiar with Celtic, Italic and Iberian weapons and fighting styles. Carthage's military evolved much as Rome's did. Between 237–218 the Carthaginian army in Iberia not only demonstrated that it had become a first-rate practitioner of 'modern' Hellenistic warfare, but it also nurtured Iberian and Celtiberian military manpower to serve in its armies as dual-purpose infantry.

Carthage was typically Hellenistic in another important respect. It perceived the Mediterranean as being dominated by a small number of super-states, and that warfare was undertaken because in this system Carthage was "contending for honour and empire".[347] Carthage did not aim to annihilate Rome. Instead, it imagined that the Second Punic War would end with a defeated Rome negotiating with a victorious Carthage a treaty that acknowledged a changed balance of power between the two powers. This was how Hellenistic powers ended wars. It was the republic of Rome that did not conform to Hellenistic norms in international relations. Rome would not accept defeat. Instead, it relentlessly waged 'just war' (*bellum iustum*) until its enemies 'placed themselves in the faith of the Roman people' (*deditio in fidem populi Romani*), effectively an unconditional surrender. Rome did not play by the same rules as other Hellenistic states. Hannibal believed Rome might make peace after Cannae in 216. He was wrong, and the Second Punic War only ended in 201 with the dismantling of the Carthaginian overseas empire, the surrender of the city's warships and elephants, and a prohibition of the city waging war without the permission of Rome.[348]

Greeks and Latins depicted the Phoenicians/Punics as merchants and sailors because they held that such maritime and commercial pursuits were inherently less noble, honest or reliable than virtuous farmers such as themselves. Stereotyped as merchants, prioritising profit over nobler pursuits (i.e. agriculture, war), the Punics are sometimes dismissed as being dependent on others for agricultural produce and military strength. In fact, the Carthaginian reliance upon mercenaries was entirely typical of Mediterranean powers in the Hellenistic period: it was Rome that was unusual in not employing them. The Carthaginians were both seafarers and farmers: the introduction of Levantine systems of viticulture, olive and wheat farming into North Africa and Sardinia meant that the Punic world later served as the bread basket of the Roman Empire. The most famous agricultural text of ancient times was produced by a Carthaginian (Mago's 28-book treatise), which the Romans used as a farming and gardening manual for centuries.[349] When one strips away the Greco-Roman stereotypes from the subject, we find that Carthage was a

347 Hannibal in a speech to prisoners in 216: Liv. 22.58.2–3.

348 Liv. 30.37.

349 Plin. *N.H.*, 18.22–23; Columella, *Rust.* 1.1.13; G E Fussell, 1967, 'Farming Systems of the Classical Era', *Technology and Culture*, Vol. 8, No. 1, pp. 16–44.

Hellenistic power, not some oriental anomaly; that it was an oligarchy ruled by an aristocracy that was at least as warlike as other Mediterranean powers; and that Carthage waged war with a mix of forces (citizens, subjects, allies and mercenaries) and in a manner that was typical of the era.

Rome defeated in swift succession the kingdoms of Macedon (Second Macedonian War 200–197) and the Seleucid Empire (Seleucid War 192–188), thereafter dominating the eastern Mediterranean. The Successor kingdoms proved to be significantly less formidable challenges to Roman military power than had the republic of Carthage during 264–201.

CHAPTER 3

Roman Laws of War

Samuel White

1 Introduction

Rome was not built in a day. Neither, too, did it remain the same in its thousand-year reign. This Chapter must therefore be specific in its analysis and addresses the rough range of the Roman Republic and the Julio-Claudian Empire – approximately 350 BC to 60 AD. This allows for analysis of the developments of the Roman Republic to be incorporated, without the fractured nature of the late Imperial period. These dates further exclude the impact of Christianity on the Empire[1] and the codes brought in by the Emperor Maurice in his *Strategica*[2] and the recordings of Ruffus.[3]

It further captures a rather Latin approach to the laws surrounding war from which modern international humanitarian law takes its etymology – the laws around the right to declare and wage war (*jus ad bellum*) and the laws for the conduct of operations in war (*jus in bello*). Combined, these made the *jus belli* – the laws of war. Misleading as it may be, these laws were not codified but were a matter of custom; custom that evolved and adapted as it contacted other cultures and methods of warfare. The malleability of Latin culture to more effective or efficient methods of war was indeed a defining feature of the Roman Empire – its so-called *interpretatio Romana*.[4] In particular, the absorption of Greco culture after its annexation shaped the Roman interpretation of the *jus in bello* forever. These Hellenistic tendencies, however, never overrode unique Latin cultural rules. Specifically, as will become clear, the idea of maintaining *fides* permeated throughout all international dealings.

1 See the jurists of Ignatius, Tertullian and Origen in L Cahil, *Love Your Enemies: Pacifism and the Just War Theory* (NYC: Cahill, 1994) 41–55.

2 See C.E. Brand, *Roman Military Law* (University of Texas Press, 1968) 195–196.

3 *Ex Ruffo Leges Militares.*

4 Tac. *Germ.* 43.4 – although this term related to the adoption of foreign deities, it is a fitting term for the osmosis that occurred in cultural and theological shifts.

 | DOI:10.1163/9789004473218_005

II Means and Method of Warfare

As the common ancestor of *Bronlie's* international law, Roman law has understandably been subject to literally millennia of discussion. At its core, however, are two schools of thought about the laws of war. William Harris summarises the first school of though, when he opined:

> in many respects, the Romans' behaviour resembles that of many other non-primitive ancient people's, yet few others are known to have displayed such an extreme degree of ferocity in war while reaching a high level of political culture.[5]

There is some merit to Harris' claim: the concept of 'no quarter' is often traced to the Roman style of war known as *guerre mortelle* – in which no privilege of ransom or mercy would be granted. A quick perusal of historical works demonstrates the devastation and massacres that occurred in the expansion and maintenance of Kingdom, Republic and Empire.[6] It also perhaps is linked to the uniquely Roman practice (in comparison to Hellenistic laws of war) of capturing, then executing, prisoners of war in the Forum (Rome's main public space).[7]

However, some have argued Roman customs to be the exact opposite. Coleman Phillipson highlights:

> [Latin practises] varied according as their wars were commenced to exact vengeance for gross violations of international law, or for deliberate acts of treachery. Their warlike usages varied also according as their adversaries were regular enemies … or uncivilized barbarians and bands of pirates and marauders … the belligerent operations of Rome, from the point of view of introducing various mitigations in the field, and adopting a milder policy after victory, are distinctly of a progressive character.[8]

5 *War and Imperialism in Republican Rome* (Oxford: Oxford University Press, 1979) 48.

6 See specifically the three volumes of Alexander Gillespie, *A History of the Laws of War: Volume 1 – Combatants and Captives* (Hart Publishing, 2011)*; A History of the Laws of War: Volume 2: Civilians* (Hart Publishing, 2011)*; A History of the Laws of War: Volume 3: Arms Control* (Hart Publishing, 2011).

7 Polybius, *The Rise of the Roman Empire* – see the incident of 270 BC.

8 Coleman Phillipson, *The International Law and Custom of Ancient Greece and Rome* (MacMillan & Co., 1911) 221–23.

Phillipson here, as will be seen, perhaps offers the more nuanced (and correct) interpretation. His argument of *relative* Roman civility is key to any discussion. Harris' argument however goes to core of modern sensibilities: classical Latin customs lacked the term for foreign civilian, and its cultural blindness to the distinction of combatant and non-combatant often leads to incorrect conclusions about a merciless savagery.

Key to the ability for civility was the discipline of the common Roman soldier. Although conscription was the initial means of recruitment (the Latin word for conscription *legio,* is the etymological root of *legion*), by the time of Julio-Claudian dynasty there were two main sources of recruitment for the military: volunteers and conscripts.[9] Regardless of service categories, however, legionaries were viewed as a distinct cultural subgroup within society, of specific and distinct legal status.[10]

This status, as will be expanded upon in the notion of defence of superior orders, was one that enabled utter discipline due to the *imperium* of their commander. Within the Republic, *imperium* was linked to those who bore military command and from it flowed *authoritas*. Generals and Governors of Roman provinces were appointed and granted the right to use *imperium* – the right to command – from which their *authoritas* flowed.[11] Critically, within the sacrosanct province of Italy, only the elected magistrates of the Roman Republic could hold *imperium,* and soldiers were required to be disarmed.[12] This acted as a necessary check and balance against the excess of armed forces against Roman citizens and the Republic.[13]

The consequence of crossing the small stream – the Rubicon –was that one's right to hold *imperium* ceased, for troops could not operate domestically on Italian soil. By crossing the Rubicon with his Legio XIII, Julius Caesar was illegally operating domestically and committing, under Roman law, insurrection,

---

9 During the period of Augustus (27 BC–14 AD), approximately 68 per cent of legionaries were of Italian origin; see Gillespie (n 6) *Volume 1*, 23.

10 Frederick Edwin Smith, *Points of View: Volume 2* (Books for Library Press, 1970) 2. This is reflected to this day in legal constructs around modern military service in Anglo-Saxon societies: see Samuel White, 'Taking the King's Hard Bargain' (2022) 96 *Australian Law Journal* (forthcoming).

11 On select occasions, *imperium maius* could be granted which superseded the *imperium* of commanders; see, for example, the *imperium maius* granted to Pompey Magnus in his clearance of pirates from the Mediterranean. See Victor Ehrenberg, 'Imperium Maius in the Roman Republic' (1953) 74(2) *American Journal of Philology* 113, 117; see generally how this has impacted modern military operations in Samuel White, *Keeping the Peace of the Realm* (LexisNexis, 2021).

12 Gillespie (n 6) *Volume 3*, 9.

13 Cicero, *Against Verres* 2.2, 8; 3.213.

treason and a declaration of war on the Roman Senate and Roman people. This provides the first, overarching framework for any analysis of Roman laws of war. As may seem common place to those whose culture followed the Latin structure, the delineation between foreigner/domestic was key to Roman thinking and heavily impacted on the nature of warfare.

Nature of Warfare – Just War

The Roman tradition held that peace, and war, were binary constructs: there could only ever be one of two states existing. Augustus Caesar exemplified this when, during his reign, he boasted to have closed the doors of the Temple of Janus (Janus being the god of two faces, or the god of binary constructs).[14] This act demonstrated that a state of peace, one of Janus' two faces, existed within the Empire.[15]

According to Roman tradition, a priesthood (the *fetiales*) oversaw the proper procedures for declaring war – procedures initially applied only to conflicts outside of internal territory against legally defined enemies. War could be properly declared afte following an escalating procedure called the rerum repetitio – a series of requests for restitutions.[16] Following these procedures made war just, and allowed for a state of war to be declared.

Just war (*bellum justum*), the doctrine most associated with Rome, was one of the cornerstones of Roman warfare and related to the rules revolving around the declaration and a state of war. In particular to the above discussion of foreign/domestic divides, just war was a state of affairs concerned with the external and was intrinsically linked to the idea of self-defence and border disputes.[17] It merits then to discuss the different forms of war, found throughout Roman jurisprudence. It is necessary so as to discuss the *jus in bello* in more detail, with specific reference to the forms of war.

---

14 Suetonius, *The Life of Augustus* (Loeb Classical Library, 1913) 22.

15 Livy, *The History of Rome* (Hackett Publishing Co, 2006) Book 1, [19].

16 Ibid, 1.32 recounts that the fetial (a Roman class of priest) would use a series of prescribed phrases, first at the enemy frontier, then over the border, then to the first person he saw, then on entering the gates of the target city, and again on entering the forum in the presence of local magistrates. If demands were not met, he would declare war and wait 33 days for any capitulation. At the end of the prescribed time, he would return to the border of the enemy, and throw a blood-tipped javelin across the border and into the soil of their territory. Interestingly, such a procedure was mirrored by the Mexican people; see Samuel White and Ray Kerkhove, 'Aztec Laws of War' in Samuel White (ed), *The Laws of Yesterday's Wars* (Brill, 2021) 63, 68.

17 Aristotle, *Politics*, 1333b37.

Defined Enemy

Implied within *bellum justum*, although not often discussed, is its applicability to civilised sovereign States – which necessarily requires a degree of externality. In order to be able to conduct just war, through the *fetiales*, a sedentary population with established borders was necessary. Those who did not fit into this concept of a regular, legally defined enemy (the *hostis justus*) were incompatible with the concept of just war. Accordingly, bandits, pirates and rebels (who primarily were internal threats) were not 'regular' or 'traditional' enemies, and the *jus in bello* could not apply to them.[18]

This was weaponised by the Roman state in an early form of lawfare. Recognition of statehood resulted in international obligations; as such, Gauls were noted as sovereign nations but the Germanic tribes across the Rhine were not until 300 AD. This meant that the customs and protections of Latin laws of war were not accessible to the Teutons.

Sieges

Ancient sources do not have much to say with respect to Roman sieges; the practice and procedures may have been viewed as given and thus did not merit any comment. The mentions of siege conduct that are left to us are therefore examples of exceptionalism – such as the final capture of New Carthage in 208 BC (discussed below)[19] or the fratricidal capture of Cremona in 69 AD.[20]

The preference for siege warfare was reinforced to Roman generals, whereby the ability 'to distress the enemy more by famine than the sword (was noted as) a mark of consummate skill'.[21] This was also economically incentivised: when a city fell, its booty fell to the troops; when it surrendered, to the commanders.[22] Commonly terms were offered by Roman commanders prior to siege warfare – sometimes generous, sometimes not.[23] Livy recounts to us the standard demand at the start of any siege:

---

18 See, for example, Wouter G Werner, 'From Justus Hostis to Rogue State: The Concept of the Enemy in International Legal Thinking' (2004) 17(2) *International Journal for the Semiotics of Law* 155, 158, 167.

19 Polybius, *The Rise of the Roman Empire* – XX.

20 Tacitus, *The Histories*, 156.

21 Vegetius, *The Military Institutions of the Romans* (Westport, Greenwood Press Westport) 11.

22 Tacitus, *The Histories*, 156; Livy, *The History of Rome* 4.49.9–50.6.

23 Livy, *War With Hannibal*, (Longdon, Penguin) 21.13.9; Polybius *The Rise of the Roman Empire* 248–9.

> Do you surrender the people, the city, fields, water, boundaries, shrines, utensils, all things divine and human in the domain of … the Roman people?'[24]

The Roman's adapted and continued the *realpolitik* cultural norm of offering terms before sieges, although they added to it their own unique take – the so-called 'battering ram rule'. This is perhaps best demonstrated in the warning Julius Caesar gave prior to laying siege in Bourges, warning the enemy to surrender before his battering rams hit the wall as:

> The alternative was infinitely worse: slavery for their wives and children, death for themselves – the universal fate of conquered people.[25]

If terms were not accepted, and the siege was eventually successful, then the specific act of *diripio* would begin. This reflected the practice of spoil distribution: 'when a city was stormed, its booty fell to the troops; when surrendered, to the commanders'.[26] To merely translate the term as a Latin concept of systematic sacking of a city fails to capture the brutality intended: Ziolkowski notes that the term originally referred to the act 'to tear apart, to mangle, to rip to pieces'[27] but came later to mean 'to deprive, to take away or to divest, with an emphasis on the unruly and violent part of the act'.[28] Livy highlights this, noting that in 204 BC a Roman garrison treated the inhabitants of a captured town as such:

> They all rob, plunder, beat, wound, slay; they defile matrons, maidens and freeborn boys, dragged from the embrace of parents. Every day our city is captured, ever day it is being plundered (*cotidie capitur urbs nostra, cotidie diripitur*).[29]

Again, the words here are not of the Roman's themselves but of a conquered people. The greatest emphasis must therefore fall upon the fratricidal capture of Cremona in 69 AD. Tacitus recounts:

---

24 Livy, *The History of Rome*, 1.38.1.

25 Julius Caesar's, *War Commentaries* (trans J. Warrington, London, Dent, 1955) 122.

26 Tacitus, *The Histories* (trans K. Wellesley, Lodon, Penguin, 1975) 156.

27 Adam Ziolkowski, '*Urbs Direptia,* Or How the Romans Sacked Cities' in John Rich and Graham Shipley (eds.) *War and Society in the Roman World* (Routledge, 1993) 70.

28 Ibid.

29 Livy, *The History of Rome*, 29.17.15–16.

> Forty thousand armed men burst into the town; the number of camp-followers and servants was even greater and they were more ready to indulge in lust and cruelty. Neither rank nor years protected anyone; their assailants debauched and killed without hesitation. Aged men and women near the end of life, despised as booty, were dragged off to be the soldiers' sport. Whenever a young woman or handsome youth fell into their hands, they were torn to pieces by the violent struggles of those who tried to secure them, and this in the end drove the despoilers (*direptores*) to kill one another.[30]

The unique Roman manner of this act – *urbs direptia* – and how it linked into the laws of war will be covered below.

Civil War

The final form of warfare were those within the State – *bellum civile* – was a particularly unique Roman construct. War was, as noted above, an armed conflict in a just cause against an external enemy. For this reason, Appian would remark:

> At Rome, the common people and Senate were frequently at odds with each other over the passing of laws and the cancellation of debts, or the distribution of land, or during elections, but there was never any outbreak of civil violence ... No sword was ever brought into the assembly, and no Roman was ever killed by a Roman, until Tiberius Gracchus, while holding the office of Tribune and in the act of proposing legislation, became the first man to die in civil unrest.[31]

The key point here is that it was unrest (*statis*)– not war (*bellum*). By general agreement, civil wars only began with Sulla's march into Rome in 88 BC,[32] beginning a period of destruction that was thought to be unequal with that caused by any foreign conqueror.[33] Generals tried to claim that they were justified in defence of the Republic, thus providing a level of legal protection to their actions. By implication, those on the other side were not to be afforded the protections of a distinct body of soldiers, being unlawful and unrecognised combatants. No laws of war applied in the *bellum civile* and as Cornelius

30 Tacitus, *The Histories*, 3.33.1–3.
31 Appian, *Civil Wars* 1.1–1.2.
32 David Armitage, *Civil War – A History in Ideas* (Yale University Press, 2017) 51.
33 Ibid.

Tacitus wrote – 'the roads were choked with heaps of dead ... after all, in civil war, you cannot make money out of prisoners'.[34]

There was also no *fides* to be maintained – as Lucan (39–65 AD) put it, civil wars were 'wars which would bring no triumphs'.[35] This tiny statement of fact from an Early Empire era historian is worth unpacking a little more. Roman ritual triumphs were the reward for victory, in a just war, against a recognised enemy. A victorious army thus proclaimed its general an *Imperator* – who in turn, through this authority, requested the Senate's permission for various rituals of thanksgiving. As wrote Valerius Maximus in the first century:

> no man though he might have accomplished great things eminently useful to the commonwealth in a civil war, was given the title of *imperator* on that account, nor were any thanksgivings decreed, nor did such a one triumph either in ovation of with chariot, for such victories have ever been accounted grievous, though necessary, as won by domestic not foreign blood.[36]

This convention was flaunted blatantly by Pompey Magnus and Julius Caesar respectively; however, Octavian (Augustus) Caesar was clear to mark his defeat of Mark Antony and Cleopatra with a triumph over domestic and foreign enemies.

III Prohibited Actions

The best source of Hellenistic laws of war were formulated by Plato in his *Republic* who devised a code for pan-Hellenic warfare. These restrictions ranged from prohibiting enslavement of Greek cities or the decoration of temples with spoils from defeated Greek armies, to limiting destruction of territory to crops, to exempting lands and dwellings.[37]

There are less sources to rely upon when it comes to Roman laws of war. Some Roman sources make comments about outrages to the laws of war; most however justify the breaches and nearly all seem to omit them in any histories written. Most analysis, therefore, has to occur through implication and points

34 Armitage (n 32) 107.

35 Lucan, *Bellum civile* 1.12.

36 *Memorable Deeds and Sayings* 2.8.7.

37 See David Feeny, 'Carthaginian Laws of War' in Samuel White (ed.) *The Laws of Yesterday's Wars: Volume II* (Brill Nijhoff, 2022).

of contention by Greek scholars who lived under Roman rule. Specifically, Polybius is perhaps the most useful for this Chapter. A prominent and educated citizen of Megalopolis, Polybius lived for two decades as a hostage in Rome. During this time, he mingled with leading statesmen and witnessed Roman military operations in Greece, Spain and Africa. The importance of his Greek background is that he writes for a Greek audience, and comments ont the customs of the Latins that are different to those of the Hellenes.

Polybius provided the most detailed discussions of Latin laws of war: keeping oaths; good faith (*fides*) in treaties and truces; the necessity of a declaration of war; the inviolability of ambassadors; sparing prisoners taken on the battlefield; the immunity of religious sanctuaries and their treasuries; and limiting destruction or capture to such elements that support the opponent's war effort, such as forts, harbors, cities, men, ships and crops—but sparing non-combatants or items of long-term value like fruit trees. Importantly, and reflecting Latin custom, Polybius was a rationalist and noted these rules were for the most part discretionary. The one exception, however, was *fides*.

Underlying Philosophy

As foreshadowed, Rome's rise to prominence brought its own version of laws of war that, like the Roman constitution, remained unwritten. Some coincided with Greek practice, while others reflected Rome's legalistic tendencies. Its armies scrupulously observed the inviolability of ambassadors and sanctuaries, unless an enemy's cults were seen as potential inspiration for later revolt. Above all, Romans prided themselves as people of good faith (*bona fides*) who kept their word. Indeed, the Latin fides is to be translated as an oath. It is the single most important concept for this chapter, as fides was conceived of as the underlying basis of all international relationships.[38] Sometimes the bona fides was expressly guaranteed by a special cause or stipulation, but more often it was implicit. Even Greek authors, who prided themselves on their cultural honour, begrudgingly accepted that there was no need for any witnesses if a Roman gave an oath.[39]

Two key concepts emerge from fides – the idea of 'just war' and that oaths would be maintained. As noted above, oaths sometimes contained implicit contracts and these formed the basis for prohibited conduct in war. All of this led to promoting *fides publica populi Romani* (trust towards the Roman state). This mantra was core to the aim of Roman laws of war and breaches of the

38 Phillipson (n 8) 117.

39 Polybius, *The Rise of the Roman Empire* 6.56.

faith formed the core conduct that was admonishments by Roman jurists. An example arises from the conduct of Caesar in Gaul. During a truce negotiation with two Germanic tribes, Caesar seized there negotiators hostage and attacked:

> Their fear was obvious from their screams and chaotic running around. Our soldiers, spurred on by the betrayal of the previous day, burst into the camp where those of the enemy who could quickly seize their weapons resisted for a short time ... Meanwhile the masses of other persons—women and children, for the Germans had left home and crossed the Rhine with their entire families—began to flee in every direction. Caesar sent the cavalry to run them down. When the Germans heard shouts rising behind them and saw that their people were being slaughtered, they threw their arms away ... and rushed out of the camp. When they reached the place where the Rhine and Meuse run together, they lost any remaining hope of getting away. A great number of them were killed. The rest threw themselves into the river and perished there, overcome by panic, exhaustion, and the power of the current. Every last one of our men survived, and only a few were wounded.[40]

Subsequently, the Roman senator Cato the Younger wanted Julius Caesar surrendered to the Germans for his violation of a truce and impacting on Rome's *fides publica*.[41] Of course, the move by Cato was political, but underpinned by the laws of war at the time. Livy, writing in dying years of the Republic and the rise of the Empire, highlights this. Livy recounts that the Senate admonished its diplomats over bad faith negotiations as a delaying tactic, during a campaign in Macedon. Specifically, the Senate stated:

> our ancestors did not wage war by ambush or night battle, nor by pretended flight and surprise return catch the enemy off his guard, so that they should glory in craftiness rather than real *virtus*[42]

The degree to which the Romans preferred to fight openly, and without tactics and trickery is controversial.[43]

---

40 Caesar, *Gallic Wars*, 4.14–4.15.

41 Plutarch, *Cato Minor* 51.1–5; *Caesar* 22.1–7; Suetonius, *Divus Iulius* 24.3; Drogula 2019: 199–200.

42 See Livy, *The History of Rome* 3.42.4; 3.60.8 for examples of where Rome did just that.

43 HH Scullard, *Scipio Africanus: Soldier and Politician* (Cornell University Press, 1970).

What is clear is that commanders sought to maintain – either as a matter of honour, or as a façade – the faith in Rome. This desire led to some rather paradoxical scenarios where Roman commanders would not accept the surrender of a city, as the corresponding obligations on Rome were too onerous and they would have breached their faith.[44]

If we interpret the Roman *jus in bello* through the lens of *fide publica,* then a pattern of restraint begins to emerge – although targeting of foreign cultural property was the norm, there are clear instances that if property was unlawfully or wrongly obtained (such that it was not taken through looting allies, or in violations of terms of surrender) then it would be ordered to be restored. This occurred such as the looting of the temples of Lorci by uncontrolled Roman army, following the Second Punic War.[45]

The golden thread running through this discussion, then, is the interrelation between *fides publica* and the sacking of cities. The *urbs direptia* was the most likely situation where troops would be undisciplined; where faith could be broken; and where prohibited conduct would be committed.

Siege Warfare – **fides populi** *and* **urbs direptia**

There are two references to *urbs direptia* in the literature of the time. The first relates to the sack of Victumulae by Hannibal in 218 BC:

> The next day they surrendered and received a garrison within their walls. Being commanded to give up their arms they complied: whereupon a signal was suddenly given to the victors to sack the town, as if they had taken it by storm (*ut tamquam vi captam urbem diriperent*). Nor was any such cruelty omitted which historians deem worth noting on such an occasion; but every species of lust and outage and outrage and inhuman insolence was visited upon the wretched inhabitants.[46]

Of note here is that it is Carthaginian, rather than Roman, troops that are committing the *urbs direpta.* Particular emphasis should be placed on the line that 'as if they had taken it by storm'. Hannibal's misdeed was not in the excessive force, which was common for a city taken by assault, but in breaking the faith and the customs of war.

44 Livy, *The History of Rome,* 21.57.13–14; Polybius, *The Rise of the Roman Empire* 28.14; Appian, *Civil Wars,* 6.10.56–60; Tacitus, *The Histories* 12.17.

45 Livy, *The History of Rome,* 29.8–9; 31.20.2; 38.9.13–14.

46 Ibid, 21.57.13–14y.

The second was by Polybius, the Greek slave turned Latinphile historian, who gives an account of the Roman capture of New Carthage by Cornelius Scipio in 209 BC. New Carthage was key strategic ground – the largest Punic logistical node in modern Spain and with over 10,000 male citizens who could fight. The passage of the sacking of New Carthage, although long, merits recounting for it is a Hellenistic interpretation of Roman behaviour to a Greek audience. The author (Polybius) highlights the particular aspects of Latin conduct that were most unlike Hellenic customs (emboldened below). This explains the manifest lack of any mention of rape of captured personnel. Polybius notes:

> When Scipio thought that a sufficient number of troops had entered the town, he gave leave to the larger number of them to attack those in it, according to the Roman custom, *with directions to kill everything they met, and to spare nothing; and not to begin looting until they got the order to do so. The object of this is, I suppose, to strike terror.* Accordingly, one may often see in towns captured by the Romans, not only human beings who have been put to the sword, but even dogs cloven down the middle, and the limbs of other animals hewn off. On this occasion the amount of such slaughter was exceedingly great, because of the numbers included in the city.
>
> Scipio himself with about a thousand men now pressed on towards the citadel. When he arrived there, Mago at first thought of resistance; but afterwards, when he was satisfied that the city was completely in the power of the enemy, he sent to demand a promise of his life, and then surrendered. *This being concluded, the signal was given to stop the slaughter: whereupon the soldiers left off slaying, and turned to plunder.*
>
> When night fell those of the soldiers to whom this duty had been assigned remained in the camp, while Scipio with his thousand men bivouacked in the citadel; and summoning the rest from the dwelling houses by means of the Tribunes, *he ordered them to collect all their booty into the market-place by maniples*, and to take up their quarters for the night by these several heaps ...
>
> Next morning the baggage of those who had served in the Carthaginian ranks, as well as the property of the city-folk and the craftsmen, having been collected together in the market-place, *the Tribunes divided it according to the Roman custom among their several legions.* Now the Roman method of procedure in the capture of cities is the following: Sometimes certain soldiers taken from each maniple are told off for this duty, their numbers depending on the size of the city; sometimes maniples are told

> off in turn for it: but there are never more than half the whole number assigned to the work. The rest remain in their own ranks in reserve, sometimes outside, at others inside the city, for taking such precautions as may be from time to time necessary. Sometimes, though rarely, four legions are massed together; but generally speaking the whole force is divided into two legions of Romans and two of allies. This being settled, all who are told off for plundering carry all they get, each to his own legion; and when this booty has been sold, *the Tribunes distribute the proceeds among all equally, including not only those who were thus held in reserve, but even those who were guarding the tents, or were invalided, or had been sent away anywhere on any service.* But I have spoken fully before, when discussing the Roman constitution, on the subject of the distribution of booty, showing how no one is excluded from a share in it, in accordance with the oath which all take upon first joining the camp.
>
> may now add that the arrangement whereby the Roman army is thus divided, half being engaged in gathering booty and half remaining drawn up in reserve, precludes all danger of a general catastrophe arising from personal rivalry in greed. For as both parties feel absolute confidence in the fair dealing of each in respect to the booty —the reserves no less than the plunderers —no one leaves the ranks, which has been the most frequent cause of disaster in the case of other armies.

As Ziolkawaski notes, at the heart of Polybius' account is the prohibition against unlawful / undisciplined sacking and plundering.[47] Some further observations can be made, however. The discipline of the soldiers was such that the rule against embezzlement seems to have been strict, and evidence of punishment of soldiers for ill-disciplined plundering litters the history books.[48] However, the power to require troops to give back plundered goods seems weaker in the Republic than it does under the Caesars.[49] This perhaps reflects the lesser *imperium* of Republican generals.

Underlying the conduct here was a desire to instil terror, as Polybius notes. But I suggest that it was perhaps more nuanced – an act that was done in order to fulfil the *fides.* Scipio had given an oath in accordance with the Roman custom prior to the siege. New Carthage had failed to respond, and the *urbs*

---

47 Ziolkowski (n 27) 76.

48 Livy, *The History of Rome,* 38.27.3.

49 Ibid, 37.32.12–14 where Regillus' restoration of goods to an allied city does not extend to taking plunder away from troops.

direptia was thus ordered. It was not lamented, nor critiqued as a breach of faith. Indeed, the sacking was actually the opposite – the inevitable and faithful enactment of a promise.

IV Defences

The above canvasses the underlying philosophical and legal foundations for prohibited conduct in Roman warfare. There are, of course, many other examples that can be given – prohibitions against mistreatment of the dead;[50] the sanctuary given to certain classes of people in places of worship;[51] and maintaining care over individuals taken slaves.[52] There is little benefit gained through a length exploration of these different iterations of *fides publica populi Romani*.

Of more interest to the readers might be the defences to these breaches. In 107 BC, Marius (Julius Caesar's uncle) had captured by surprise attack the Numidian city of Capsa. Specifically, Marius had reneged on the conditions of the town's surrender, and upon entering the city, burned it and massacred its inhabitants. This act of *urbs direptia* was noted to be *contra ius belli* – against the law of war.[53]

The historian Sallust sought to defend Roman general Gaius Marius against breaches of the *fides publica populi Romani*. Marius was, incidentally, Sallust' patron in the proper Roman sense of the word. Citing the city's strategic importance and the population's untrustworthiness, the breach of the faith was justified under the concept of military necessity.

An argument from 'military necessity' also appears at the siege of Jerusalem in AD 70. Titus, the Roman commander and later emperor, held a council of war to decide the fate of the Jewish Temple. Noted above, maintaining sanctuaries was implicit in the *bona fides* conduct of war. Yet, as a potential rallying point for the rebels, it had to be demolished.[54] These operations were justified under military necessity. The Roman concept of military necessity is a highly saturated field. This Chapter will focus on the lesser analysed, but potentially much more relevant, defence of superior orders.

50 See Cassius Dio, *Oration*, 75.9, 'the slain are deemed to no longer be foes, nor are hated and insult wreaked upon their bodies'; Cicero, *De Legibus*, 447–57.

51 Diodorus 13.58.2, 13.62.1–4; 13.90.1–5;13.108.2.

52 Arising from the principle of *postliminium*.

53 Sallust. *Iug.* 91.6–7.

54 Josephus, *Of the War* (Loeb Classical Library, 2009) 6.12.

Defence of Superior Orders

In many instances of Roman history, actions by individuals could be absolved if they were *remotion criminis* or *metastasis*[55] or as modern translations called it, the defence of superior orders. The position was posited by Justinian as:

> He who causes loss who orders it to be caused; but he is without blame, *culpa,* who is under the necessity of obeying.[56]

But what this modern translation meant for those individuals varied. There were two fundamental schools of thought when it came to superior orders under Roman law. Auctor held that the action did not shift the crime but merely the *culpa* or *causa;*[57] Cicero assigned superior orders as a shifting of the *factum,* or the *res ipsa* – that is, the behaviour had no link to the subordinate, as they were merely a subordinate. Quinitilian wavers between the two. Although he advocated for the *transferre crimen,* a passing of the crime, he stressed that it is only a question of deflecting the *culpa*. On this basis, the defence was one similar to following a law.

The three different advocates above diverge further when canvassing how the defence is to be applied. For Auctor, three questions that need be answered in order to rely on the defence: what was the power imbalance and the possibility of harm if the order is refused;[58] the second a question of fact – was there an order; and the third relating to whether the accused is to be blamed for finding himself in the situation more generally.[59]

There are examples of these differing perspectives. Felix Sulla, as consul, ordered a horseman to execute P Sulpicius.[60] The latter complied. When, after an inevitable regime change occurs, the horseman was brought to trial, where he invoked the order from the consuls. Sulpicius was found guilty and executed.

Cicero differed in his legal analysis of the defence of superior orders. In his opinion, by pleading *remotion criminis,* a soldier dissociated themselves from the entire affair. The only question to be asked was: whether, arising from the respective offices of who ordered and who actioned the order, there was anything to do but comply? Marcus Antonius (Mark Antony) requested when he lost the civil war against Augustus that his troops' offence of civil war be

55 The latter comes from the Greek concept of obeying one's father; Gellius, 2.7.

56 Lenel, *Palisgenesia Juris Civilis 1889*, I 1150.

57 Seneca *Troades* 290.

58 *Ad Herennium* 3.2.3.

59 Ibid, 2.16.23.

60 See David Daube, *The Defence of Superior Orders in Roman Law* (Clarendon Press, 1956) 6.

absolved on the basis that they were following the orders of a general. As such, they were mere agents of his command.[61] Whilst Octavian did not follow this reasoning, his successor Tiberius absolved Piso the Younger of the charge of civil war 'since he could not have declined his father's orders'.[62]

Yet there also existed within the jurisprudence agreement that some orders were inexcusable – in modern parlance, that they were manifestly unlawful.[63] Mnester, when Messalina's circle was overthrown, claimed to be merely following orders. It was held that his conduct was so infamous that it need not matter whether it was voluntary or enforced.[64] The term manifestly unlawful can be interchangeable with 'obviously contrary to law'[65] that one 'knows, or ought to know to be illegal'[66] or that which was an 'apparent and palpable illegal order'.[67] The adjective 'manifestly' thereby related to a reasonableness of such a belief, a concept relative to the times. It is therefore interesting that even with respect to Mnester, his conduct was held to be such. Of course, there is an undercurrent of *realpolitiks* that must be remembered. Yet it is a live issue that can be found within domestic and international law today.

V Conclusion

Maintaining the faith of the Roman people was fundamental to all international relations and conduct. As this Chapter has demonstrated, it could lead to rather perverse results where an acknowledged inability to maintain an obligation (such as to house and feed prisoners of war) would lead to rejecting surrender. So too could *fides* be interpreted and reinterpreted in a manner that was desirable for Rome – defined notions of friendship could grant a just cause for a just war, and breaches of *fides* could be exculpated on the basis of following orders.

61 Appian, *Civil Wars* 5.5.33.

62 Tacitus, *Annals* 3.17.

63 Samuel White, 'A Shield for the Tip of the Spear' (2021) 49(2) *Federal Law Review* 210.

64 Tacitus, *Annals*, 11.36.

65 Justice Brereton, *Inspector-General of the Australian Defence Force Report of Inquiry into Questions of Unlawful Conduct Concerning the Special Operations Task Group in Afghanistan* (Inquiry Report, 19 November 2020) 110.

66 *United States v Jones*, 36 Fed Cas 653 (No 15494) (CCD Pa 1813).

67 Stanley Yeo, 'Mistakenly Obeying Unlawful Superior Orders' (1993) 5(1) *Bond Law Review* 1, 7.

CHAPTER 4

Islamic Laws of War

Ahmed Al-Dawoody

I Introduction

For over fourteen centuries, Islamic law has developed incredibly detailed rules ranging from religious ordinances, dietary rules and restrictions, family law, commercial law, criminal law, international law, international humanitarian law (IHL), and constitutional law among other areas of Islamic law. According to recent studies, there are twenty-nine Muslim-majority States that include compulsory implementation of family, civil, commercial, or criminal Islamic laws in their legal systems.[1] Islamic law is the bedrock of the Islamic faith and the embodiment of the Islamic identity. It regulates the daily lives of hundreds of millions of Muslims and influences to varying degrees the Muslim-majority State practice, their domestic legislations and the international treaties they enter into. Islamic law has both religious and positive law elements and reflects diverse rules and interpretations partly, for the concern of this chapter, due to local and international societal changes as well as changes at the levels of both the modern nation Muslim-majority States and international society's structures. At present, most of the work of entities working in or in relation to armed conflict areas and conflict-related arenas such as the International Committee of the Red Cross, the United Nations High Commissioner for Refugees, Geneva Call and the International Criminal Court are focused in Muslim contexts. Moreover, the greatest majority of contemporary armed conflicts are non-international armed conflicts where many Islamic non-state armed groups (NSAGs) use Islamic law as the source of reference that regulates their use of force, their governance and their administration of justice.

Hence, this chapter studies the development of the Islamic law of war during the earliest and most authoritative period for the formulation of Islamic law, i.e., the lifetime of Prophet Muhammad. It argues that the Islamic rules developed by classical Muslim jurists regulating the use of force in the primitive war situations of this period still continue to constitute the source of

1 E.J. Powell, *Islamic Law and International Law: Peaceful Resolution of Disputes* (New York: Oxford University Press, 2020), p. 1.

 | DOI:10.1163/9789004473218_006

regulating and justifying certain means and methods of warfare by Islamic non-state arms groups, let alone shape the deliberations among Islamic law scholars. Therefore, it is unrealistic to ignore the role Islamic law can play on, first, better understanding of the contemporary patterns that govern the use of force by some State and non-state armed Islamic actors and, second, the humanization of contemporary armed conflicts in Muslim contexts as well as, third, the universalization of the principles of IHL. Since all the fighting that took place during the Prophet's lifetime were between Muslims and their non-Muslim adversaries, inter-Muslim fighting falls outside the realm of this study.

II The Religious and Political Structure in Arabia at the Advent of Islam

The religion of Islam emerged in the city of Mecca in 611 CE. At the time Mecca was the pilgrimage destination center for the Arab pagans who saw in the then new monotheistic religion a serious threat to their religious, economic, and political power as well as their unrivalled prestige in Arabia.[2] In the words of T. W. Arnold (d. 1930), the spread of Islam meant for the Meccans "the destruction of the national religion and the national worship, and a loss of wealth and power to the guardians of the sacred Ka'bah."[3] Islam's monotheistic call to the worship of one God necessitated the destruction of Meccans' businesses, which largely depended on the revenues from the pilgrims' visits to the shrines. Therefore, the Meccans were determined to terminate the new religion once and for all.[4]

The political system in Arabia was characterized by tribal or clan affiliation.[5] The tribes or the clans functioned as independent political entities and were the sources of the individual's security and sense of belonging. The leader of the tribe, usually an old, well-to-do, wise and of sound judgment man, used to function as the political and military leader. He lead the war, distributes the war booty, settles disputes between members of the tribe, meets envoys

2 John L. Esposito, *Unholy War: Terror in the Name of Islam* (Oxford: Oxford University Press, 2002), pp. 29–30.

3 T.W. Arnold, *The Preaching of Islam: A History of the Propagation of the Muslim Faith*, 2nd ed. rev. & enl. (London: Constable & Company, 1913), p. 14.

4 W. Montgomery Watt, *Muḥammad: Prophet and Statesman* (Oxford: Oxford University Press, 1961), p. 74.

5 See Afzal Iqbal, *Diplomacy in Early Islam*, 4th ed. (Lahore: Institute of Islamic Culture, 1988), pp. 42–43.

and delegations from other tribes and concludes alliances.[6] Each tribe used to have its own army and sometimes tribes formed alliances and concluded joint defense agreements and pacts of non-aggression.

When individuals were expelled from their tribe, they found themselves forced to seek refuge in another tribe for protection. Granting protection to refugees and asylum seekers emanates from the virtues of chivalry, hospitality, protection of the weak and nobility, which the Arab tribes used to take pride in as documented in their pre-Islamic poetry.[7] This protection constitutes part of what William Montgomery Watt has called Arab "tribal humanism."[8] The different tribes including the Prophet's were united in their hostility against the new religion of Islam. It is interesting to see tribalism still plays a big role in politics and in the stability (or instability) of many regimes in Muslim-majority States.

Hostilities towards the Muslims took place in different forms. To avoid different forms of persecution, torture and boycott of the new Muslim community, eighty-three Muslims fled to Abyssinia (modern day Ethiopia) in 615 CE in order to live under the protection of the negus, Christian King of Abyssinia. Persecution of the Prophet and the Muslims increased after the demise of both the Prophet's protector, his uncle Abū Ṭālib, and his wife Khadījah in 619.

The historian Ibn Isḥāq (d. 767 CE) described the systematic attempts by the Meccans to force Muslims to apostatize from Islam as follows: "every clan which contained Muslims attacked them [the Muslims], imprisoning them, and beating them, allowing them no food or drink, and exposing them to the burning heat of Mecca, so as to seduce them from their religion. Some gave way under pressure of persecution."[9] Such cases of forced apostasy under torture were considered excusable by the Qur'ān 16:106.

The Meccans also tried to tempt the Prophet to give up the call for the new religion and his response was: "By God, if they [the Meccan idolaters] put the sun in my right hand and the moon in my left so that I abandon this matter

6 See Yāsīn Ghaḍbān, *Madīnah Yathrib qabl al-Islām* (Amman: Dār al-Bashīr, 1993), p. 165.

7 Ahmed Al-Dawoody and Tilman Rodenhäuser, "The principle of non-refoulement under Islamic law and international law: complementing international legal protection in Muslim contexts" in the *Humanitarian Law and Policy* blog, 20 June 2021, available at: The principle of non-refoulement under Islamic law and international law: complementing international legal protection in Muslim contexts – Humanitarian Law & Policy Blog | Humanitarian Law & Policy Blog (icrc.org).

8 William Montgomery Watt, *Muhammad at Mecca* (Oxford: Oxford University Press, 1960), p. 24.

9 A. Guillaume, trans., *The Life of Muhammad: A Translation of Isḥāq's Sīrat Rasūl Allāh* (Oxford: Oxford University Press, 1955), p. 143.

[the religion of Islam], I will not until God establishes it or I perish."[10] When enmity escalated and particularly following a failed attempt on the life of the Prophet, most of the Muslims and Prophet Muhammad were forced to flee Mecca this time to Yathrib (later known as Medina) on 16 July 622 – the date that marks the beginning of the Islamic calendar – with the consequent confiscation of their land and properties by the Meccans.[11] In the Arab culture at the time, this *hijrah* (flight) meant already the existence of a state of war between the Muslims and the Meccans. It is worth adding here that the Meccans used the tribal/clan factor in their plot to assassinate Prophet Muhammad. They agreed "that each clan should provide a young, powerful, well-born, aristocratic warrior; that each of these should be provided with a sharp sword; then each of them should strike a blow at him [the Prophet] and kill him."[12] The logic behind this collaboration of the Meccan clans in the assassination attempt is that the Prophet's clan would not be able to seek revenge from all of these warriors' clans in case they would succeed in assassinating him.

Although no actual fighting took place during the period known in Islamic history as the Meccan period (611–622 CE) between the few hundreds of new Muslims and the Meccans, the *jus ad bellum* (conditions which justify the resort to armed force) of the Islamic law of war cannot be adequately studied without keeping this context in mind. It is worth mentioning here that during the Meccan period, Muslims were unable to build a Mosque for their worship and for a number of years they used to pray in secret and/or hide their Islamic affiliation and Islamic worship. Furthermore, the first and second *hijrahs* of the Muslims aimed at securing their lives and practicing their religion freely.

III The City-State Paradigm: System of Governance, Religion, Law and War

Medina (situated about 450 kilometers north of Mecca) was chosen as the destination for *hijrah* following invitations that the Prophet Muhammad received

10 Muḥammad Husayn Hykal, *Ḥayah Muḥammad*, 14th ed., (Cairo: Dār al-Maʿārif, 1977), p. 173.

11 See Muḥammad Ḥammīdullāh, *The Battlefields of the Prophet Muhammad, with Maps, Illustrations and Sketches: A Continuation to Muslim Military History* (New Delhi: Kitab Bhavan, 2003), pp. 16, 27–28; Abdulrahman Muhammad Alsumaih, "The Sunni Concept of Jihad in Classical Fiqh and Modern Islamic Thought" (PhD thesis, University of Newcastle Upon Tyne, 1998), pp. 191–192.

12 Guillaume, *The Life of Muhammad*, p. 222.

from a number of delegations from this war-torn city. These delegations came to Prophet Muhammad in Mecca and promised that they would protect him and the new Muslim community in the same way as they would protect themselves. Their aims behind this invitation were that the Prophet would be able to bring peace into their hostile city[13] and "unite"[14] the opposing factions. This meant accepting the political leadership of the Prophet by those invited him to Medina.

The inhabitants of Medina consisted of Arab pagan tribes and a number of Jewish tribes. The biggest and most prominent of these Jewish tribes were Banū al-Nadīr, Banū Qaynuqāʿ and Banū Qurayẓah whose adult males combined were estimated at around 2000.[15] These Jewish tribes usually worked as farmers, craftsmen and manufacturers of weapons and textile, gold and silver, fishermen and traders.[16] In addition to administration of the religious affairs, Jewish Rabbis functioned as teachers, arbitrators, judges and settled disputes among the Jewish community.[17] The Arab pagans were mainly farmers, unlike the Meccans traders, and used to perform the pilgrimage to the idols in Mecca.[18]

Before the *hijrah*, Medina had a long history of internecine hostility between the two main Arab tribes al-ʾ Aws and al-Kharzraj, on one hand, and between them and the Jewish tribes on the other. Nonetheless, there were pacts of non-aggressions concluded between the Arab pagans and the Jewish tribes. The struggle for dominance over Medina shifted in favor of the Arab tribes around the second half of the sixth century,[19] i.e., prior to the advent of Islam, and it seems that the Arab Christian of the Levant took sides with the Arab pagans.[20]

This means that prior to the *hijrah*, the inhabitants of Medina were not unified under any form of government. There was no central political or judicial authority in Median at the time as every tribe would recognize the authority of its leader only. However, it is quite remarkable that within the first year of the *hijrah* to Medina, the Prophet Muhammad established a State (described

13 Arnold, *The Preaching of Islam*, p. 47.
14 Guillaume, *The Life of Muhammad*, p. 198.
15 See Yāsīn Ghaḍbān, *Madīnah Yathrib qabl al-Islām* (Amman: Dār al-Bashīr, 1993), p. 87.
16 *Ibid.*, pp. 88, 114–115.
17 *Ibid.*, pp. 125–126.
18 *Ibid.*, p. 88.
19 *Ibid.*, p. 93.
20 *Ibid.*, p. 91.

in Western scholarship as the city-state) that was the foundation for the Caliphate State system that expanded in less than a century over territories in Asia, Africa and Europe.

The document known as the *Ṣaḥīfah al-Madīnah* (Constitution of Medina) unveils the nature of this newly established city-state system and its conception of nationhood, including who is in charge of the decision to wage war and the responsibilities of the inhabitants of Medina in case of an attack on their city. The authenticity of the document is generally recognized, and previous research shows that it dates back to the first few weeks of the *hijrah*, in 622 CE.[21]

The most prominent achievement that the Constitution of Medina made, at least for the purpose of this chapter, is that it established a concept of citizenship that transcends the tribal and religious affiliations. It formed strong ties of brotherhood between the two communities of Muslims – the Meccan Emigrants (*muhājirūn*) and the Medinan Helpers (*al-Anṣār*) – and established a treaty of peace and rapprochement with the Jewish community.[22] It makes all the Muslim inhabitants of Medina one *ummah* (nation) and all the Jewish inhabitants of Medina one *ummah* with the Muslims. It stipulates that "the Jews have [the right to ractice] their religion and the Muslims have their own religion."[23]

Second, it established a government system which made Prophet Muhammad the head of the city-state of Medina. It affirms that cases of disagreements or serious disputes between the inhabitants of Medina shall be referred to God and the Prophet.[24]

21 See Ahmed Al-Dawoody, *The Islamic Law of War: Justifications and Regulations*, Palgrave Series in Islamic Theology, Law, and History, Vol. 2, (New Work: Palgrave Macmillan, 2011, reprint July 2015), p. 19; 'Abd al-Raḥman ibn Khaldūn, *Tārīkh Ibn Khaldūn: Al-Musammā Dīwān al-Mubtadā' wa al-Khabar fī Tārīkh al-'Arab wa al-Barbar wa man Āṣarahum min Dhawī al-Sha'n al-Akbar*, ed. Khalīl Shiḥādah (Beirut: Dār al-Fikr, 2000), Vol. 2, pp. 422–423; Uri Rubin, "The 'Constitution of Medina' Some Notes," *Studia Islamica*, No. 62, 1985, p. 18; Mohammad Hashim Kamali, *A Textbook of Hadīth Studies: Authenticity, Compilation, Classification and Criticism of Ḥadīth* (Leicestershire: Islamic Foundation), 2005, p. 26.

22 See Al-Dawoody, *The Islamic Law of War*, p. 19; Ḥammīdullāh, *Battlefields*, pp. 16–17.

23 Guillaume, *The Life of Muhammad*, p. 233.

24 On the articles of the Constitution of Medina that attempted to bring about peace and end "conflict that had been plaguing the region for generations," see Yetkin Yildirim, "Peace and Conflict Resolution in the Medina Charter," *Peace Review*, Vol. 18, Issue 1, 2006, pp. 109–117.

Third, it designated Medina as a *ḥaram* (a sanctuary) for all the parties the Constitution of Medina addresses[25] which means a total prohibition of violence among the citizens of Medina.

Fourth, it stipulates a collective defence agreement between the Jews and the Muslims in the case of an attack on either of them and therefore it stipulates that none of the Jewish tribes should initiate a war without prior permission from the Prophet unless it is in revenge.[26]

Therefore, this system confirms that all the citizens of this newly established nationhood city-state system overrides the tribal affiliation system and that religious freedom is guaranteed for the Jewish community.[27]

IV *Jus ad bellum*: Offensive or Defensive Wars?

The Muslims' *hijrah* to Medina did not mean the end of the state of enmity between the Muslims and the Meccans, but in fact the beginning of an anticipated state of armed conflict. Very tellingly, the Constitution of Medina makes it clear that a state of war exists between the Muslims and the Meccans. In one of its articles, the Constitution of Medina stipulates that "no covenant of protection is given to the Quraysh [the then ruling tribe of Mecca] or any of its helpers".[28] Hence, in preparation for expected armed conflict, Prophet Muhammad, first, established in the Constitution of Medina a collective defence agreement with the Jewish tribes in case of foreign attacks on their city. Second, he made peace treaties with the tribes from outside of Medina such as Banū Ḍamarah[29] and Banū Mudlaj to ensure that they would not join the Meccans in case they attacked the Muslims in Medina.[30] The treaties with these tribes are described by Watt as "pacts of non-aggression."[31]

---

25 Muḥammad Ḥusayn Haykal, *The Life of Muḥammad*, trans. from the 8th ed. by Isma'īl Rāgī A. al-Fārūqī (n.p.: North American Trust Publication, 1976), p. 182; Ḥammīdullāh, *Battlefields*, p. 17.

26 Al-Dawoody, *The Islamic Law of War*, p. 21.

27 W. Montgomery Watt, *Muhammad at Medina* (Karachi: Oxford University Press, 1981), p. 241.

28 Guillaume, *The Life of Muhammad*, p. 233.

29 For a translation of this treaty see Watt, *Muhammad at Medina*, p. 354.

30 Maḥmūd Shākir, *Al-Tārīkh al-Islāmī: Qabl al-Ba'thah wa al-Sīrah*, 8th ed. (Beirut: Al-Maktab al-Islāmī, 2000), p. 164.

31 Watt, *Muḥammad: Prophet and Statesman*, p. 104; Watt, *Muhammad at Medina*, pp. 3–4.

Significantly, it is in this context of the early days of the *hijrah* that the first Qur'ānic revelation occurred, permitting Muslims a recourse to war.[32] This relevant Islamic *jus ad bellum* as follows:

> Permission to [engage in fighting] is given to those against whom war is waged because they have been wronged; verily God is able to give them victory. Those who have been expelled from their homes unjustly and only for saying: God is our Lord; had not God permitted people to defend themselves against [the aggression of] others, monasteries, churches, synagogues and mosques, wherein the name of God is oft-mentioned, would be pulled down; certainly God will support those who support Him; indeed God is All-Strong, All-Mighty.
>
> QUR'ĀN 22:39–40[33]

This text permits Muslims who managed to do the *hijrah* to resort to defensive war to protect themselves against aggression and violent religious persecution. Additionally, a subsequent text invites Muslims to recourse to war to rescue the fellow religiously persecuted Muslims who were unable to do the *hijrah* as follows:

> Would not you fight in the way of God for *al-mustaḍʿafīn* (the oppressed socially weak Muslims) from men, women and children who pray: Our Lord! Take us from this city of the oppressive people and appoint for us from Your side a guardian and appoint for us from Your side a protector. Those who have believed fight in the way of God and those who disbelieve fight in the way of Satan, so fight the allies of Satan; surely the plot of Satan is weak.
>
> QUR'ĀN 4:75–76

Recourse to armed conflict in this case has been equated with what we call today humanitarian intervention.[34] While these two texts and some others as

---

32 See, for example, Jalāl al-Dīn al-Suyūṭī, *Al-Durr al-Manthūr* (Beirut: Dār al-Fikr, 1993), Vol. 6, pp. 57–58; Muḥammad ʿIzzat Darwazah, *Al-Jihād fī Sabīl Allah fī al-Qur'ān wa al-Ḥadīth*, 2nd ed. (Beirut: Al-Nāshir, 1990), p. 45; ʿAbdur Raḥmān I. Doi, *Sharīʿah: The Islamic Law* (London: Ta Ha, 1984), p. 438; Bernard K. Freamon, "Martyrdom, Suicide, and the Islamic Law of War: A Short Legal History," *Fordham International Law Journal*, Vol. 27, 2003, p. 314.

33 Translations of the Qur'ānic texts are mine.

34 See Sohail H. Hashmi, "Is There an Islamic Ethic of Humanitarian Intervention?," *Ethics and International Affairs*, Vol. 7, 1993, p. 55–73.

well as the study of the armed conflicts that took place between the Muslims and their enemies during the lifetime of the Prophet Muhammad make it abundantly clear that the Islamic *jus ad bellum* is defence against aggression, this question has been an extremely complex issue. Giving an adequate summary and analysis of the armed conflicts that took place during the Prophet's lifetime is beyond the scope of this chapter. However, a series of fighting incidents most of them are very minor and left a handful or sometime no casualties at all took place between the Muslims and their enemies until within about a decade Muslims overpowered their enemies and unchallengingly ruled over not only Medina, but also their hometown Mecca. As an indication of the amount of force used in these armed conflicts, the numbers of fatalities from both the Muslims and their enemies in all the armed conflicts that took place during the period studied here are estimated "between a minimum of 367 (170 Muslims and 197 among their enemies) and a maximum of 514 (222 Muslims and 292 among their enemies)."[35] Obviously, this limited number is due to the fact that certain primitive means and methods of warfare were used in these conflicts as well the restrictions discussed below.

But the controversy about the Islamic *jus ad bellum* is due partly, first, to the fact that premodern Muslim jurists have not paid enough attention to addressing this Islamic *jus ad bellum* question in the Islamic law books regulating armed conflict. They were dealing with the reality on the ground where war was the norm in international relations unless a peace treaty was concluded. They were more concerned with, and focused heavily on, the Islamic *jus in bello* (rules regulating the conduct of Muslims engaged in an armed conflict), as shown below. Second, the adversaries of the Muslims in the armed conflicts that took place during the Prophet's lifetime, namely, during the Medina city-state, are referred to by their religious affiliations i.e., Muslims against "polytheists"/"unbelievers" or "people of the book" which led some to mistakenly think that Muslims went to offensive wars against their Meccan enemies to convert them to Islam. Hence, often Qur'ānic phrases such as "And fight them wherever you find them and expel them from wherever they expelled you"[36] and "kill the polytheists wherever you find them"[37] are quoted to claim that Islam justifies a "holy war" against non-Muslims because of their unbelief in Islam.[38]

---

35 Al-Dawoody, *The Islamic Law of War*, p. 40.

36 Qur'ān 2:191.

37 Qur'ān 9:5.

38 See, for example, Majid Khadduri, *War and Peace in the Law of Islam* (Baltimore, MD.: Johns Hopkins University Press, 1955), p. 163; Suhas Majumdar, *Jihād: The Islamic Doctrine of Permanent War* (New Delhi: Voice of India, 1994), p. 16; John F. Whalen, "In

But it is not possible to accurately deduce the Islamic *jus ad bellum* from just cutting certain Qur'ānic verses out of context and without studying the armed conflicts that these texts address. There is a genre of Islamic historical writings specifically dedicated to studying and documenting these armed conflicts that took place during the Prophet's lifetime know as *al-siyar* or *al-maghāzī was al-siyar*. In the Islamic historical literature, the term *al-maghāzī* refers to the Prophet's travels to, and military or non-military encounters with, non-Muslims, while they used the term *al-siyar* to refer to expeditions sent by him. The main purpose purpose behind this Islamic historical genre is documenting the life of Prophet Muhammad.

Likewise, some early seventh and eighth centuries Islamic jurists wrote legal works devoted to regulating armed conflicts and more generally relations with the enemies in times of war and peace. One of the earliest extant works written by the Iraqi Ḥanafī jurist al-Shaybānī (d. 805) is translated into English by Majid Khadduri (d. 2007) under the title *The Islamic Law of Nations: Shaybānī's Siyar*.[39] In the Islamic legal texts, the term *siyar* refers to the Islamic law rules developed, deliberated and negotiated by the Muslim jurists based on in accordance with the Qur'ānic ordinances and the practice and the precedents set by the Prophet Muhammad during Medina city-state period. The objective of the jurists was to regulate the conduct of the Islamic state practice and Muslim individuals' in the areas we call today international law and international humanitarian law.[40]

Previous studies show that the Muslims' engagement in the armed conflicts under discussion in this chapter was defensive.[41] These armed conflicts took

Search of Jihad: Toward a Policy of Constructive Islamic Engagement," *The Brown Journal of World Affairs*, Vol. V, Issue 1, Winter/Spring 1998, p. 281.

39 Majid Khadduri, trans., *The Islamic Law of Nations: Shaybānī's Siyar* (Baltimore, MD.: Johns Hopkins Press, 1966).

40 See, for example, Ahmed Al-Dawoody, "Al-Sarakhsī's Contribution to the Islamic Law of War," *UCLA Journal of Islamic and Near Eastern Law*, Vol. 14, Issue 1, 2015, p. 30; Al-Dawoody, *The Islamic Law of War*, p. 109; Muḥammad ibn Aḥmad ibn Abī Sahl al-Sarakhsī, *Kitāb al-Mabsūt* (Beirut: Dār al-Ma'rifah, n.d.), Vol. 10, p. 2.

41 See, for example, Al-Dawoody, *The Islamic Law of War*, p. 39; Al-Dawoody, "Armed Jihad in the Islamic Legal Tradition," *Religion Compass*, Vol. 7, Issue 11, November 2013, pp. 476–484; Aḥmad ibn 'Abd al-Ḥalīm ibn Taymiyyah, *Qā'idah Mukhtaṣarah fī Qitāl al-Kuffār wa Muhādanatihim wa Taḥrīm Qatlihim li-Mujarrad Kufrihim: Qā'idah Tubayyn al-Qiyam al-Sāmiyah lil-Ḥaḍārah al-Islāmiyyah fī al-Ḥarb wa al-Qitāl*, ed. 'Abd al-'Azīz ibn 'Abd Allah ibn Ibrāhīm al-Zayd Āl Ḥamad (Riyadh: N.p., 2004). pp. 96, 134; Sobhi Mahmassani, *Al-Qānūn wa al-'Alāqāt al-Dawliyyah fī al-Islām* (Beirut: Dār al-'Ilm lil-Malāyīn, 1972), p. 177; Wahbah al-Zuḥaylī, "Majālāt al-'Alāqāt al-Dawliyyah fī al-Islām," in Fārūq Ḥamādah, ed., *Al-Tashrī' al-Dawlī fī al-Islām*, Nadawāt wa Munāẓarāt, No. 70 (Rabat: Kulliyyah al-Ādāb wa al-'Ulūm al-Insāniyyah, 1997), p. 199; al-Sayyid Sābiq, *Fiqh al-Sunnah* (Cairo: Al-Fatḥ

place as a "result of normal developments of events arising from the political and cultural systems in place in the war-torn Arabia of the time."[42] Despite the irrelevance of the issue of the Islamic *jus ad bellum* in contemporary armed conflicts, except in cases of certain (NSAGs), both modern Islamic and Western literature still focus primarily on it while paying too little attention to the Islamic *jus in bello* rules: their relevance and impact on the protection of civilian persons and civilian objects in contemporary armed conflicts in Muslim contexts. The remaining sections of this chapter studies the Islamic *jus in bello* rules in an attempt to show how the Islamic humanitarian principles underpinning these rules may influence the behavior of Muslim arms-carriers in relevant contemporary armed conflicts.

V Restrictions and Prohibited Acts

The restrictions and prohibitions the Muslim jurists and soldiers deliberated, negotiated and developed in the context of the armed conflict under discussion reinforce the above understanding of the Islamic *jus ad bellum*. They show that the core objective is the protection of civilian persons and objects, while ensuring that these restrictions and prohibitions will not lead to the defeat of the Muslim army.

a *Protection of Civilians and Non-Combatants*

Islamic law makes it abundantly clear that all fighting on the battlefield must be directed solely against enemy combatants. Civilians and other non-combatants must not be deliberately harmed during the course of hostilities. Here the Qur'ān 2:190 is often quoted: "And fight in the way of God those who

---

lil-I'lām al-'Arabī, n.d.), Vol. 3, pp. 18–19; Muḥammad al-Ṣādiq 'Afīfī, *Al-Mujtama' al-Islāmī wa al-'Alāqāt al-Dawliyyah* (Cairo: Mu'assasah al-Khānjī, 1980), p. 148; 'Umar Aḥmad al-Firjānī, *Uṣūl al-'Alāqāt al-Dawliyyah fī al-Islām*, 2nd ed. (Tripoli, Libya: Dār Iqra', 1988), pp. 77, 82–83; Yūsuf al-Qaraḍāwī, *Fiqh al-Jihād: Dirāsah Muqāranah li-Aḥkāmih wa Falsafatih fī Ḍaw' al-Qur'ān wa al-Sunnah* (Cairo: Maktabah Wahbah, 2009), Vol. 1, pp. 339–364, 380: C.G. Weeramantry, *Islamic Jurisprudence: An International Perspective* (Basingstoke: Macmillan, 1988), p. 147. Rudolph Peters indicates that modern Muslim writers "show that all military campaigns, raids and expeditions of Mohammed and the first Caliphs were purely defensive". See Rudolph Peters, "Djihad: War of Aggression or Defense?," in Albert Dietrich, ed., *Akten des VII. Kongresses Für Arabistik und Islamwissenschaft* (Göttingen, Aug. 1974) (Göttingen: Vandenhoeck & Ruprecht, 1976), p. 286.

42 Al-Dawoody, *The Islamic Law of War*, p. 39.

fight against you and do not transgress." Hence, Muslims are permitted to engage in hostilities against enemy belligerents only, otherwise it is a violation of this Qur'anic injunction. Based on this text and several hadiths attributed to the Prophet Muhammad in which women, children, the aged, the clergy and the *'usafā'* (those hired by the enemy to do supporting services in the battlefield, but do not engage in the fighting) are mentioned as examples of protected categories that cannot be tagged during hostilities. Examples of other categories of civilians are given in the Islamic law books such as farmers, traders, craftsmen, the blind, incapacitated etc. Needless to say that, members of these categories will lose their protection from attack if they take part in hostilities. Interestingly, medieval-context cases of indirect participation in hostilities were deliberated whereby the jurists disagreed between those who adhered to the textual prohibition and those who lifted the prohibition because soldiers have to defend themselves in such cases. Still some jurists would prefer not target civilians in such case of indirect participation in hostilities if they could be captured.[43]

b *Prohibition of Destruction of Property and the Natural Environment*

In Islam, everything in this universe is the creation of God,[44] and human beings are entrusted with the duty of protecting it and contributing to the development of human civilization.[45] Hence, as a rule, attacks against enemy property and the natural environment whether during peace time or during armed conflict which is not required by imperative military necessity is prohibited. In fact, the Syrian jurist al-Awzāʿī (d.774) argued that *takhrīb* (wanton destruction) of enemy property during the course of hostilities falls under the criminal act described in the Qur'an (e.g., 2:205; 5:32–33) as *fasād fī al-arḍ* (literally, 'destruction/mischief in the land').[46] This rule generally applies to animate and inanimate property alike. Nonetheless, targeting horses and similar

---

43 See, for example, Al-Dawoody, *The Islamic Law of War*, pp. 112–116; Ahmed Al-Dawoody, "Islamic Law and International Humanitarian Law: An Introduction to the Main principles," *International Review of the Red Cross*, (2017), 99 (3), pp. 1002–1004.

44 Fazlun M Khalid, "Islam and the Environment" Vol. 5, *Social and economic dimensions of global environmental change*, in Peter Timmerman (ed) *Encyclopedia of Global Environmental Change* (Chichester: John Wiley, 2002), pp. 332–339.

45 Qur'an 2:30; 11:61. See also 'Abd Allah Shiḥātah, *Rū'yah al-Dīn al-Islāmī fī al-Ḥifāẓ 'alā al-Bī'ah* (Cairo: Dār al-Shurūq, 2001), pp. 13–14, 17–20; Sarie Zaid Al-Kailany, "Tadābīr Ri'āyah al-Bī'ah fī al-Sharī'ah al-Islāmiyyah," *Dirāsāt: 'Ulūm al- al-Sharī'ah wa al-Qānūn*, Vol. 41, issue 2, p. 1213.

46 Ahmed Al-Dawoody, "International Terrorism and the Jurisdiction of Islamic Law," *International Criminal Law Review*, Vol. 15, Issue 3, Spring 2015, p. 580.

animals during the course of hostilities was permitted only if enemy soldiers were mounted on them while fighting.

The Prophet Muhammad prohibited cutting down trees except those that block the Muslims from engaging in the fighting and prohibited destruction of houses.[47] Following the same logic, the first caliph Abū Bakr (d. 634 CE) gave the well-known 10 instructions to his army commander Yazīd ibn Abī Sufyān which include: "do not cut down fruit-bearing trees or destroy buildings; do not slaughter a sheep or a camel except for food; do not burn or drown palm trees; do not loot; and do not be cowardly."[48] Furthermore, from a pure utilitarian perspective, medieval Islamic State practice would not normally resort to wanton destruction of enemy property because of the customary practice for enemy possessions to be seized as war booty in international armed conflicts. The armed conflicts discussed in this chapter and the deliberations of the premodern Muslim jurists indicate that when required by military necessity, damage to enemy property may only be carried out with one of two aims in mind: to force the enemy to surrender or to put an end to the fighting. In other words, Muslim soldiers must not deliberately cause the destruction of enemy property for the sake of it.

c *Humane Treatment of Prisoners of War* (POWs)

Most of the rules under Islamic law that concern POWs are based on the treatment of the 70 enemy combatants captured during the battle of Badr in the second year of the Islamic calendar (March 624). There are two main issues that are of specific importance here: treatment of prisoners of war during captivity and the termination of captivity.

As for the treatment of POWs during captivity, following the precedents set by the Prophet Muhammad and his instructions: "Observe good treatment towards the prisoners,"[49] Islamic law, guarantees that POWs shall be treated humanely and with respect. They must be fed and given water to drink, clothed if necessary, and protected from the heat and the cold and from cruel treatment. Their families which include parents, grandparents and children would

47 See hadiths numbers 18155 and 18156 in Aḥmad ibn al-Ḥusayn ibn ʿAlī ibn Mūsā al-Bayhaqī, *Sunan al-Bayhaqī al-Kubrā*, ed. Muhammad ʿAbd al-Qādir ʿAtā (Beirut: Dār al-Kutub al-ʿIlmiyyah,3rd ed. 2003), Vol. 9, pp. 154–155.

48 Al-Dawoody, "Islamic Law and International Humanitarian Law," p. 1003.

49 Muhammad ibn Jarīr al-Ṭabarī, *Tārīkh al-Ṭabarī: Tārīkh al-Umam wa al-Mulūk*, (Dār al-Kutub al-ʿIlmiyyah, Beirut, 2001), Vol. 2, p. 39.

remain with them, so as to protect family unity. Torturing prisoners of war to obtain military information is prohibited.[50]

As for the end of captivity, classical Muslim jurists fell into three groups:

(a) releasing POWs unilaterally or in exchange for captured Muslim soldiers.

(b) The State should decide, based on what serves its best interests, whether to execute, enslave or release within Muslim State.

(c) The State should decide, based on its best interests, between all of the above.

The jurists who argued that it was permitted to execute POWs based their opinions on reports that three POWs had been executed during the Prophet's lifetime: Al-Naḍir ibn al-Hārith and 'Uqbah ibn Mu'ayṭ at the battle of Badr in March 624 and Abū 'Azzah al-Jumaḥī at the battle of Uḥud in March 625 AD. Examination of the historical record shows that if all or some of these reports were true, these three prisoners of war were singled out for crimes they had committed before joining the war and not because of being POWs per se.[51]

d *Prohibition of Mutilation*

Among the Prophet Muhammad's instructions to the Muslim soldiers: "Do not loot, do not be treacherous and do not mutilate," ["*lā taghlū wa lā taghdurū wa lā tumathilū*"].[52] The prohibition of mutilation of enemy corpses demonstrates respect for dignity and humanity. In another hadith Prophet Muhammad prohibited the torture and mutilation of animals, even of the body of *al-kalb al-ʾaqūr* (a rabid dog).[53]

---

50 See, for example, Joseph Hoelz, "Islamist Terrorism and the Classical Islamic Law of War," *International Law Studies*, Vol. 97, Winter 2021, p. 1650; Ahmed Al-Dawoody, "Detention in Armed Conflict under Islamic Law," in Ahmed Al-Dawoody ed., *IHL and Islamic Law in Contemporary Armed Conflicts* – Experts' Workshop Geneva, 29–30 October 2018 (Geneva: ICRC, November 2019), pp. 52–53, available at https://shop.icrc.org/ihl-and-islamic-law-in-contemporary-armed-conflicts-experts-workshop-geneva-29-30-october-2018-pdf-en-1; Al-Dawoody, *The Islamic Law of War*, pp. 138–140; Al-Dawoody, "Islamic Law and International Humanitarian Law," pp. 1010–1014; Wahbah al-Zuḥaylī, *Āthār al-Ḥarb fī al-Islām: Dirāsah Muqāranah*, 3rd ed., (Damascus: Dār al-Fikr, 1998), p. 415.

51 Al-Dawoody, *The Islamic Law of War*, pp. 138–140; Al-Dawoody, "Islamic Law and International Humanitarian Law," pp. 1010–1014; Al-Dawoody, "Detention in Armed Conflict under Islamic Law," pp. 52–53.

52 Mālik ibn Anas, *Al-Muwaṭṭa'*, ed. Muḥammad Fū'ād 'Abd al-Bāqī (Beirut: Dār Iḥyā' al-Turāth al-'Arabī, 1985), Vol. 2, p. 448.

53 Muḥammad ibn Aḥmad al-Sarakhsī, *Kitāb al-Mabsūt* (Beirut: Dār al-Ma'rifah, n.d.), Vol. 9, pp. 135, 196; Vol. 10, pp. 129, 131; Vol. 16, p. 145; Vol. 26, p. 145.

The prohibition against mutilation includes burying the dead bodies of the enemy in case the adversary does not bury its own dead, otherwise it will be tantamount to mutilation, as advocated by the Andalusian jurist Ibn Ḥazm (d. 1064). The Islamic legal and historical sources confirm that at the Battle of Badr, the Muslims buried the corpses of all enemies killed.[54]

e *Prohibition of Looting*

The prohibition of *ghulūl* (looting) mentioned in the hadith above refers to when a Muslim soldier takes or steals an item from the war booty before it is divided up, or allocates part of the war booty to themselves without handing it over to be distributed by the army chief.[55] In cases when it is not possible for the Muslims to buy food supplies in the battlefield, the jurists permitted the Muslim soldiers to take as much of the enemy's supplies as they required to feed themselves and their animals, provided that no more than the necessary quantity is taken.[56]

f *Prohibition of Perfidy*

The prohibition of *ghadr* (perfidy, treachery) obliges Muslims to respect their contracts and agreements, but it does not mean that ruses are prohibited in war. In fact, the Prophet said: "war is ruse."[57]

VI Means and Methods of Warfare

The Muslim soldiers who were engaging in the conduct of hostilities under discussion as well as subsequent generations of premodern Muslim jurists deliberated the permissibility of using certain means and methods of warfare that may cause incidental harm to civilian persons and civilian objects. Their deliberations were motivated by two main concerns: namely, the likelihood of the indiscriminate killing of non-combatants as collateral damage – usually specifying women and children, and the destruction of enemy property. The process of deliberating these means and methods has been a complex and

---

54 Wahbah al-Zuḥaylī, *Mawsūʻah al-Fiqh al-Islāmī wa al-Qaḍāyā al-Muʻāṣirah* (Damascus: Dār al-Fikr, 2010), Vol. 7, p. 495.

55 Al-Dawoody, "Islamic Law and International Humanitarian Law," pp. 1008–1010.

56 Muḥyī al-Dīn ibn Sharaf al-Nawawī, *Al-Majmūʻ: Sharḥ al-Muhadhdhab*, ed. Maḥmūd Maṭrajī (Beirut: Dār al-Fikr, 2000), Vol. 21, p. 109.

57 Muḥammad bin Ismaʻil al-Bukhārī, *Saḥīḥ al-Bukhārī* (Riyadh: Bayt al-Afkār al-Dawliyyah lil-Nashr, 1998), p. 579.

controversial one and has led to conflicting Islamic legal rulings in many cases. This is partly explained by, first, the fact that there have been different interpretations about the text and context of these battles. This is further complicated by certain Islamic (NSAGs) use of and/or interpretations of Islamic legal rulings developed by premodern Muslim jurists, discussed below, to justify the permissibility of indiscriminate means and methods of warfare. Second, understandably some jurists give priority to the restrictions provided in the precedents set during the armed conflicts under discussions, while other give priority to the pragmatic considerations of avoiding defeat at the hand of the enemy.

When it comes to the deliberations over the means and methods of warfare used in the armed conflicts under discussion, it is interesting to note that the location of some of the battles was chosen outside of the city and populated areas. For example, the first two big battles in Islamic history took place in the desert partly to avoid incidental harm to civilian persons and civilian objects. The battle of Badr (March 624) was chosen nearby the famous well 153 kilometers outside of Medina which the battle carries its name and the battle of Uḥud (March 625) was chosen in the strategic location of the mountain which the battle carries its name about 5 kilometers north of Medina.

The battles under discussion as well as those of subsequent generations mainly consisted of two scenarios. The first scenario involved one-to-one combat where enemy combatants used weapon such as the sword, lance, bow and spear usually until one party submitted or left the battlefield.[58] This is a relatively non-controversial situation since the use of these weapons in the battlefield is unlikely to cause harm to civilians in case they are present at the battlefield especially in light of the prohibitions on targeting civilians and noncombatants discussed above. Concerning the use of arrows which can be used in this and the second scenario, the jurists of the Mālikī school of law discussed the permissibility of using poison-tipped arrows.[59] Some prohibited the use of poison-tipped arrows, while others merely disliked the idea of it, on the basis that the enemy could shoot the arrows back at the Muslims and also because

58 See, for example, Muḥammad Khyr Haykal, *Al-Jihād wa al-Qitāl fī al-Siyyāsah al-Shar'iyyah*, 2nd ed. (Beirut: Dār al-Bayāriq, 1996), Vol. 2, p. 1343; Al-Dawoody, *The Islamic Law of War*, p. 122; Al-Dawoody, "Islamic Law and International Humanitarian Law," pp. 995–1018.

59 Sohail H. Hashmi, "Islamic Ethics and Weapons of Mass Destruction: An Argument for Nonproliferation," in Sohail H. Hashmi and Steven P. Lee, eds., *Ethics and Weapons of Mass Destruction: Religious and Secular Perspectives* (Cambridge: Cambridge University Press, 2004), p. 329.

there was no precedent for this action in the age of the Prophet.[60] However, the renowned Ḥanafī jurist al-Shaybānī permitted the use of weapons tipped with poison, fire or oil because they were more effective in defeating the enemy.[61]

The second scenario included where the enemy retreats and fights from behind fortifications and strongholds. Here, Muslim jurists deliberated the permissibility of shooting mangonels or fire at, or flooding, the enemy fortifications. The objective of using such indiscriminate primitive weapons was to ensure the victory of the Muslim army by forcing their enemy to surrender, while the rationale behind deliberating them is delineating the Islamic position on the permissibility of causing incidental harm to civilian persons and objects. The deliberations on the use of mangonels started when Salman al-Farisi (a Persian convert to Islam) introduced and suggested the use of this weapons to the Prophet during the battle of al-Ṭā'if (630), the last battle in the lifetime of the Prophet as follows: "we use mangonels in Persia to shoot at [enemy] fortifications."[62] Although apparently the Muslims did not manage to shoot mangonels at the enemy's fortress in this battle, the jurist permit the use of mangonels and justified the anticipated incidental harm by the military necessity.[63] In his time, Ibn Qudāmah (d. 1223) permitted using mangonels "because it is commonly used in fighting and, therefore, became similar to the shooting of arrows."[64]

But when it comes to shooting fire at enemy fortifications, the jurists are more nuanced and restrictive. As Sohail H. Hashmi aptly puts it, "the deliberate burning of persons, either to overcome them in the midst of battle or to punish them after capture, is forbidden."[65] However, directing fire at enemy

60 See, for example, Hashmi "Islamic Ethics and Weapons of Mass Destruction," p. 329; Khalīl ibn Isḥāq ibn Musā al-Jundī, *Mukhtaṣar Khalīl fī Fiqh Imām Dār al-Hijrah*, ed. Aḥmad 'Alī Ḥarakāt (Beirut: Dār al-Fikr, 1994), p. 102; Al-Dawoody, *The Islamic Law of War*, p. 112; Al-Dawoody, "Islamic Law and International Humanitarian Law," pp. 1004–1005.

61 See, for example, Muḥammad ibn al-Ḥassan al-Shay bānī, *Sharḥ Kitāb al-Siyar al-Kabīr*, commentary by Muḥammad ibn Aḥmad al-Sarakhsī, ed. Abī Abdullah Muḥammad Ḥassan Muḥammad Hassan Ismā'il al-Shafi'ī, (Beirut: Dār al-Kutub al-'Ilmiyyah, 1997), Vol. 4, p. 277: Al-Dawoody, *The Islamic Law of War*, p. 112; Al-Dawoody, "Islamic Law and International Humanitarian Law," pp. 1004–1005.

62 Muḥammad ibn 'Umar al-Wāqidī, *Kitāb al-Maghāzī*, ed. Muḥammad 'Abd al-Qādir 'Aṭā (Beirut: Dār al-Kutub al-'Ilmiyyah, 2004), Vol. 2, p. 332; Al-Dawoody, *The Islamic Law of War*, p. 123.

63 Al-Dawoody, *The Islamic Law of War*, pp. 123–124.

64 *Muwaffaq al-Dīn 'Abd Allah ibn Aḥmad ibn Mu*ḥammad ibn *Qudāmah, Al-Mughnī*, eds. *'Abd Allah ibn 'Abd al-Mu*ḥsin al-Turkī and *'Abd al-Fattaḥ Mu*ḥammad al-Ḥilu, 3rd ed., (*Riyadh: Dār 'Ālam al-Kutub*, 1997), Vol. 9, p. 230.

65 Hashmi, "Islamic Ethics and Weapons of Mass Destruction," p. 328. See also Ibn Qudāmah, *Al-Mughnī*, Vol. 9, p. 230; Muḥammad ibn 'Abd Allah al-Zarkashī, *Sharḥ al-Zarkashī*

fortifications was also prohibited by some jurists,[66] while considered merely reprehensible by others such as Ibn 'Abbās (d. 668) and Mālik ibn Anas (d. 795).[67] Furthermore, al-Awzā'ī (d. 774), Sufyān al-Thawrī (d. 778), al-Shaybānī (d. 805), and Ibn Qudāmah permitted directing fire at enemy fortifications provided that this was the only way to overcome the enemy.[68] While Ibn Rushd (d. 1189) permitted it in case of reciprocity,[69] al-Qarāfī (d. 1285) permitted it only if combatants – not women and children – are inside.[70]

It is interesting to note that these deliberations by the premodern Muslim jurists on the permissibility of the use of such primitive incendiary weapons are echoed in the contemporary Islamic modern discussions on the acquisition and use of weapons of mass destruction (WMD). Despite the significance and seriousness of the issue, it is unfortunate that it has not been adequately studied by modern Muslim scholars.[71] But generally the Islamic contemporary positions on WMD can be divided into three main attitudes.

- First, a total prohibition on the acquisition and use of WMD grounded on the Islamic prohibition on the indiscriminate killing of civilians and causing unnecessary destruction of civilian objects.[72]
- Second, permission to possess and/or use WMD in case the enemy possess and/or use them. This is grounded on the principle of reciprocity similarly utilized by the classical Muslims jurists in the examples given above.[73]

'alā Mukhtaṣar al-Khiraqī, ed. 'Abd al-Mun'im Khalīl Ibrāhīm (Beirut: Dār al-Kutub al-'Ilmiyyah, 2002), Vol. 3, p. 202; Hilmi M. Zawati, *Is Jihad a Just War? War, Peace, and Human Rights under Islamic and Public International Law*, Studies in Religion and Society, Vol. 53 (Lewiston, NY: Edwin Mellen Press, 2001), p. 41.

66 Aḥmad ibn Idrīs al-Qarāfī, *Al-Dhakhīrah*, ed. Muḥammad Būkhubzah (Beirut: Dār al-Gharb al-Islāmī, 1994), Vol. 3, pp. 208–209.

67 Muḥammad ibn 'Alī ibn Muḥammad al-Shawkānī, *Nayl al-Awṭār: Min Aḥādīth Sayyid al-Khyār Sharḥ Muntaqā al-Akhbār* (Beirut: Dār al-Jīl, 1973), Vol. 8, p. 76.

68 Ibn Qudāmah, *Al-Mughnī*, Vol. 9, p. 230.

69 Muḥammad ibn Aḥmad ibn Muḥammad ibn Rushd, *Bidāyah al-Mujtahid wa Nihāyah al-Muqtaṣid* (Beirut: Dār al-Fikr, n.d.), Vol. 1, p. 281.

70 Al-Qarāfī, *Al-Dhakhīrah*, Vol. 3, pp. 209–210.

71 Sohail H. Hashmi, "Interpreting the Islamic Ethics of War and Peace," in Sohail H. Hashmi ed., *Islamic Political Ethics: Civil Society, Pluralism, and Conflict* (Princeton: Princeton University Press, 2002), p. 213.

72 Ibrāhīm Yaḥyā al-Shihābī, *Mafhūm al-Ḥarb wa al-Salām fī al-Islām: Ṣirā'āt wa Ḥurūb 'am Tafā'ul wa Salām?* (N.p.: Manshūrāt Mu'assasah Maī, 1990), p. 76; Muḥammad 'Arafah, *Al-Khaṭar al-Nawawī fī Mirāh 'Ālim 'Āzharī*, supplement to *Majalah al-Azhar*, June 2004; Shmuel Bar, *Warrant for Terror: Fatwās of Radical Islam and the Duty of Jihād* (Lanham, MD: Rowman & Littlefield, 2006), p. 72.

73 See, for example, Muḥammad Abū Zahrah, *Al-'Alāqāt al-Dawliyyah fī al-Islām* (Cairo: Al-Dār al-Qawmiyyah lil-Ṭibā'ah wa al-Nashr, 1964), p. 102; Aḥmad Ghunaym,

- Third, permission to use WMD even before the enemies use them because already some States have stockpiled and used WMD.[74]

Although all the three positions confirm the Islamic prohibition on the use of WMD, the prohibition is lifted by the proponents of the second and third positions because of the enemy's acquisition and/or use of such weapons. Here also modern Muslim scholars, like their predecessors, negotiate between the Islamic humanitarian restrictions on the use of certain means of warfare and the pragmatic considerations of winning the war. The majority, however, have tended to override these Islamic restrictions under the guise of reciprocity. Obviously, committing crimes and violating Islamic law cannot be justified by the principle of reciprocity, and hence compliance with relevant international treaties will prevent the adoption of such positions.

The protection of civilians surfaced in the discussion above on the permissibility of using certain indiscriminate weapons. For the same reason, two methods of warfare were specifically deliberated: *al-bayāt* (night attacks) and *al-tatarrus* (human shield). Part of the rationale behind deliberating the permissibility of engaging in hostilities during the night in that premodern context is that Muslim soldiers would not be able to engage in one-to-one combat during the night and therefore incidental harm to civilian persons and objects might take place as a consequence of the use of indiscriminate weapons such as those discussed above. Depending on two hadiths, the jurists reached conflicting opinions. A prohibition on night attacks based on a hadith reported by Anas ibn Malik to the effect that Prophet Muhammad never engaged in hostilities during the night and used to wait until the morning.[75] Nonetheless, permission of night attacks is understood from a hadith narrated by al-Sa'b ibn Jaththāmah in which Prophet Muhammad did not prohibit night attacks when he was asked about their permissibility bearing in mind that they might cause incidental harm among women and children.[76]

As for the second methods of warfare, the question is whether it is permissible to shoot back at the human shield if enemy combatants take as human

Al-Jihād al-Islāmī: Dirāsah 'Ilmiyyah fī Nuṣūṣ al-Qur'ān wa Ṣiḥāḥ al-Ḥadīth wa Wathā'iq al-Tārīkh (Cairo: Dār al-Ḥammamī, 1975), p. 80.

74 Haykal, *Al-Jihād wa al-Qitāl*, Vol. 2, pp. 1353–1354.

75 Hadith number 2785 in Muḥammad ibn Ismā'īl al-Bukhārī, *Al-Jāmi' al-Ṣaḥīḥ al-Mukhtaṣar*, ed. Muṣṭafā Dīb al-Baghā, 3rd ed. (Damascus; Beirut: Dār ibn Kathīr, 1987), Vol. 3, p. 1077.

76 See, for example, hadith number 2850 in al-Bukhārī, *Al-Jāmi' al-Ṣaḥīḥ al-Mukhtaṣar*, Vol. 3, p. 1097; hadith number 1745 in Muslim ibn al-Ḥajjāj al-Qushayrī, *Ṣaḥīḥ Muslim*, ed. Muḥammad Fū'ād 'Abd al-Bāqī (Beirut: Dār Iḥyā' al-Turāth al-'Arabī, n.d.), Vol. 3, pp. 1364–1365; hadith number 2839 in Muḥammad ibn Yazīd ibn Mājah, *Sunan Ibn Mājah*, ed. Muḥammad Fū'ād 'Abd al-Bāqī (Beirut: Dār al-Fikr, n.d.), Vol. 2, p. 947.

shield, in one case, their women, children, the aged etc., or in another case, Muslim POWs or *ahl al-dhimmah* (permanent non-Muslim citizens of the Islamic State). In short, "all of the jurists permit shooting at the human shields in these two cases if required by military necessity, provided that Muslims aim to direct their attack at the combatants and avoid hitting non-combatants as far as possible."[77] They disagree however on defining the military necessity in these cases. For some the military necessity here means avoiding the defeat for the Muslims, while for others avoiding a greater number of fatalities among the Muslims if they do not shoot back at the human shield.[78]

VII Conclusion

The above discussion has shown that the modern IHL core principles of distinction, proportionality and precautions are echoed in the deliberations of the premodern Muslim jurists over what is permissible and what is prohibited in their primitive war contexts. These principles are innate to human civilizations and are reflected in various cultures and traditions throughout history. But what is needed now is to unearth the equivalence of these principles in other traditions in order to enhance compliance of IHL. It is essential that IHL is seen as globally owned, or at least not antithetical to the norms of arms-carriers in contemporary armed conflict. Many of the issues covered by modern IHL were addressed in these medieval Islamic law provisions to achieve some of the same objectives as those of IHL, namely alleviating the suffering of the victims of armed conflict and protecting certain persons and objects. The Islamic law of war was a self-imposed framework that regulates the Muslim soldiers conduct during armed conflict to humanize armed conflict by protecting the lives of non-combatants, respecting the dignity of enemy combatants, and forbidding deliberate damage to an adversary's property except when required by imperative military necessity. Ensuring respect for IHL by arms-carriers requires a genuine belief in its objectives, continues training and discussions over its challenges.

77 Al-Dawoody, "Islamic Law and International Humanitarian Law," pp. 1006.

78 'Alī ibn Muḥammad ibn Ḥabīb al-Māwardī, *Kitāb al-Aḥkām al-Sulṭāniyyah wa al-Wilāyāt al-Dīniyyah*, ed. Aḥmad Mubārak al-Baghdādī (Kuwait: Maktabah Dār ibn Qutaybah, 1989), p. 57; Ibrāhīm ibn 'Alī ibn Yūsuf al-Shirāzī, *Al-Muhadhdhab: Fī Fiqh al-Imām al-Shāfi'ī*, ed. Zakariyyā 'Imīr at (Beirut: Dār al-Kutub al-'Ilmiyyah, 1995), Vol. 3, p. 287.

CHAPTER 5

Eastern Native American Laws of War

Wayne E. Lee

1 Introduction

War was fundamental to Native American (Indian) culture in the eastern woodlands of North America.[1] Young men could gain status and authority through demonstrated courage and aptitude in war. Groups could gain or protect territory at the expense of others, incorporate prisoners into their population as kin or as labor, and even impose tribute on other peoples. Above all, the killing of a member of one group mandated revenge on the perpetrator's people. Blood demanded blood. The rewards and requirements of war were so thoroughly entwined in Native American societies that irrespective of the arrival of the Europeans a nearly endemic state of war existed throughout much of the eastern seaboard and beyond. Equally thoroughly entwined within Native American societies, however, were structural and cultural limitations on the scale and devastation of warfare.

This Chapter looks to explore the exact cultural mechanisms of escalation and de-escalation. In doing so, it must grapple with the level of violence in pre-contact Native America. Despite some romantic imaginings, Indians had not balanced war into harmony with their other cultural values and thus scaled down warfare into some kind of ritualized, non-lethal, nonentity. Given the opportunity and the right motive Native Americans were prepared to wage intensely lethal violence on another people. Much of the time, however, structural restraints built in to Native American social organization combined with their own values about war and interpretations of its meaning to restrain its scale and intensity. Contact with Europeans dramatically affected the nature of their social organization as well as their beliefs about the meaning of war. Not all of those changes happened at once. Nor can any one moment or incident

1 Much of the material for this chapter was originally published as Wayne E. Lee, "Peace Chiefs and Blood Revenge: Patterns of Restraint in Native American Warfare in the Contact and Colonial Eras," *Journal of Military History* 71 (2007): 701–41 and is published here in modified form with permission. It will also appear in a modified form as Chapter 4 in Wayne E. Lee, *The Cutting-Off Way: Indigenous Warfare in Eastern North America, 1500-1800* (Chapel Hill: University of North Carolina Press, forthcoming).

 | DOI:10.1163/9789004473218_007

be identified as that when restraints were cast off. Native Americans continued to try regulate war, and they tried to preserve the traditional nature of their social organization, all while trying to adjust to the opportunities presented and damage caused by the presence of Europeans.

There are some important caveats to this study. One is that the nature of the sources severely limits our ability to comprehend the probable changes in Native American ways of war at the very outset of contact. Sixteenth-century sources are sparse and interpretively debated, while the earliest seventeenth-century descriptions of Native American war are more voluminous but may reflect a society that had already markedly changed.[2] The second caveat is about the nature of the generalizations used here. There was of course no such thing as "Native American society." There was variation and difference from Maine to Florida, or even from one valley to the next. But with some caution we can generalize about Native American society in the eastern woodlands because those societies shared many characteristics, especially in war. Societies regularly at war with each other tend to converge, although never absolutely, in their techniques and values of war, partly from military necessity and partly from mutual self-interest.[3] This study is necessarily synthetic, and faces the task of trying to explain traditional restraints on warfare within a context of constant flux aggravated by European contact. Furthermore, the analysis here is primarily structural and cultural, rather than about how specific political configurations may have restrained or unleashed war. Nevertheless, focusing on the periods of contact and of competitive imperial colonialism (roughly 1500 to 1800 AD) lends a certain coherence.[4] In short, this

2 The argument for rapid and largely unseen change as a result of European contact is now well-rehearsed, but its implications for military behavior are still not clearly understood or agreed upon. See: Keith F. Otterbein, "A History of Research on Warfare in Anthropology," *American Anthropologist* 101 (2000): 794–805 and the follow up commentaries in the same journal by Neil Whitehead, 102 (2000): 834–37; Leslie E. Sponsel, 102 (2000): 837–841; Otterbein again, 102 (2000): 841–844; R. K. Dentan, 104 (2002): 278–280; R. Brian Ferguson and Neil L. Whitehead, eds., *War in the Tribal Zone: Expanding States and Indigenous Societies* (Santa Fe, N.M.: School of American Research Press, 1992); R. Brian Ferguson, "Violence and War in Prehistory," in *Troubled Times: Violence and Warfare in the Past*, eds. Debra L. Martin and David W. Frayer (Amsterdam: Gordon and Breach, 1997), 339–42.

3 Barbara Ehrenreich, *Blood Rites: Origins and History of the Passions of War* (New York: Henry Holt and Co., 1997),132–43.

4 Essentially this is another caveat. During much of the competitive imperial colonial period, many Native American peoples limited the impact of war by manipulating their position at the crux of competing European empires, playing one side against the other to limit their own exposure. Although in part such a diplomatic role was made possible because of native

Chapter generalizes and looks specifically in eastern Native American styles of war.[5]

Before examining the structures of restraint themselves, it will be useful to provide four specific examples of Native Americans at war to serve as foundations for the more diverse evidence that will follow. While some of these examples are well-known, others are obscure incidents chosen simply for their clear descriptions of activities typical to Native American warfare.

II Means & Methods of Warfare – Four Case Studies

There were three basic functions of war in Native American society. The broadest, and hardest to interpret, was the use of war to administer political "lessons" in proper relationships between groups (as will be argued for the Powhatans in 1622). Although the existence of political war is generally acknowledged, it is less clear to what extremes Native Americans would press war in a political cause. For example, could such political adjustments through warfare include outright conquest?

The other two functions for war, both broadly "cultural," are more clearly understood. A great deal of Native American conflict was filtered through the demand for blood revenge coupled with the expectation of achieving personal status through war. The mandate that relatives take blood revenge for the killing of one of their own was arguably the single greatest factor in patterning violent relationships both within a people and between nations. Furthermore, young men in virtually all Native American societies looked to success in war to assert not only adulthood, but also to increase their status within the group. Warriors returned home bearing enemy scalps or prisoners as their individual possessions, and although sometimes such prizes were redistributed upon

political structures discussed herein, the specific nature of the imperial standoff is not considered. Daniel K. Richter, "Native Peoples of North America and the Eighteenth-Century British Empire," in *The Oxford History of the British Empire: Vol. II The Eighteenth Century*, ed. P. J. Marshall (Oxford: Oxford University Press, 1998), 357–60.

5 The reader should assume from this point on that all references to Native Americans refer to peoples living in the eastern woodlands between 1500 and 1800 unless otherwise specified. Specifically excluded, therefore, are the peoples of the great plains, arctic and sub-arctic, the Pacific northwest, and the desert southwest. Warfare patterns in these places were very different.

arrival in the village for the benefit of all, for that moment, possessing trophies redounded solely to their own credit as men.[6]

These three motives or functions for war did not exist in isolation from each other. Even if war arose from material or political causes, it was frequently enacted through the blood feud. To put it another way, the recruitment of individuals for a succession of raids that might have political or material consequences still relied on blood feud and status rhetoric to motivate young warriors.[7] Of course the problem with these latter two motives for war is their potential endlessness. There are always new young men in need of proving themselves, and each act of revenge typically begets a fresh desire for revenge from the other side. In fact, however, although extraordinarily awkward to contain, the seemingly endless loop of the blood feud had both structure and restraint.

The basic principle of blood debt was simple. The killing of any person, accidental or otherwise, placed an obligation on the dead person's kin to exact revenge on the people of the killer. It is crucial to note the two open-ended facets of this belief. The timing and intent of the original killing were irrelevant. An accidental killing, a deliberate murder (as a European would define that term), or death in battle all equally mandated vengeance. The other open-ended component was the lack of specificity in who should be on the receiving end of the revenge. Any member of the killer's people would do- in the case of an intra-group killing, the killer's "people" meant himself and his relatives. If the killer were from outside one's own people (the tribe), then any member of his people would suffice.

a *The Powhatans and the 1622 "Massacre"*

English settlers arrived in the Chesapeake area of Virginia in 1607, and within a few weeks had built themselves a town and a fort at Jamestown. Almost immediately they became embroiled in conflict with the local paramount chief Wahunsenacawh, often referred to as Powhatan (who was both a war & peace chief) largely because of the colonists' persistent inability to feed themselves. Apparently, Wahunsenacawh had only relatively recently become *the* Powhatan, having led the nation of the same name to dominate an array of

6 In many peoples, a fourth motive functioned in parallel with the political, blood feud, and status motives, and that was the acquisition of prisoners for adoption. This is discussed more fully below.

7 Anthony F. C. Wallace, *The Death and Rebirth of the Seneca* (New York: Vintage books, 1969), 44.

peoples within a wide arc around the Chesapeake Bay.[8] His "empire" was unusual for its size and the extent of his personal control, although it had some parallels with the earlier paramount chiefdoms of the Mississippian cultures to the south and west. Some have even suggested that Wahunsenacawh was motivated to this level of conquest as a defensive measure against an expectation of further European arrivals. The natives of the region, and perhaps even Wahunsenacawh himself, had had some unpleasant experiences with earlier abortive English and Spanish settlement.[9]

At any rate Wahunsenacawh quickly perceived the English both as interlopers within his sphere of influence and as potentially useful allies. He therefore sought to bring the tiny, struggling Jamestown community within his orbit. From his point of view that process involved creating both familial and political ties, the first through marriage and adoption, the second through rituals of submission by the English. The English were unclear about the meaning of these activities, and frankly thought that they were leading Wahunsenacawh through rituals of submission to the English. In a classic scene of partially understood meanings, the English brought a crown to Wahunsenacawh in 1608 with which they hoped to mark him as a vassal of James I. Wahunsenacawh repeatedly ignored their signals for him to kneel and accept the crown. Finally one of the English pressed hard on his shoulders, Wahunsenacawh "a little stooped," and Christopher Newport put the crown on his head.[10]

Partly through this lack of understanding, and partly through the settlers' single-minded pursuit of quick riches, the two peoples remained in periodic

8 To the extent possible, I attempt to use Native American personal names (Wahunsenacawh *vice* Powahatan) and the nations ethnonym *vice* an exonym (Haudenosaunee *vice* Iroquois). Some nations have adopted their exonym and use it to this day, and in those cases I will continue to use it (e.g. Mohawk or Tuscarora). This matters because many if not *all* exonyms began as a derogatory nickname used by their enemies and passed to the Europeans. Personal names are more difficult since many nations had a tradition of name changes at key life stages, and even a seeming European name could have been authentically taken on. And, as with Powhatan, titles were often confused with names in European sources. It has taken generations of careful research to tease out the actual names, and I will try to honor that work here. I will indicate alternative names, since very many scholarly works use them in their titles.

9 Frederic W. Gleach, *Powhatan's World and Colonial Virginia: A Conflict of Cultures* (Lincoln: University of Nebraska Press, 1997), 88–105; J. Frederick Fausz, "Patterns of Anglo-Indian Aggression and Accommodation along the Mid-Atlantic Coast, 1584–1634," in *Cultures in Contact: The Impact of European Contacts on Native American Cultural Institutions, A.D. 1000–1800*, ed. William W. Fitzhugh (Washington: Smithsonian Institution Press, 1985), 235–36.

10 *The Complete Works of Captain John Smith*, ed. Philip L. Barbour (Chapel Hill: University of North Carolina Press, 1986), 1:237.

conflict until the diplomatic marriage of John Rolfe and Pocahontas in 1614. Frederic Gleach has interpreted these early years of conflict as a continuous effort by Wahunsenacawh to use war to bring the colonists' behavior into line with his perception of their subordinate status. He had no desire to exterminate, only to control.[11] Wahunsenacawh's daughter Pocahontas fell into English hands in 1613 as a hostage, leading to peace negotiations. Within a year Pocahontas and Rolfe were married and peace achieved. Peace through marriage was a diplomatic technique understood in both societies, and that connection maintained an uneasy peace until 1622.

The breakdown of the peace has been handed down to history as the "Massacre" of 1622, but the Powhatan attack in that year needs to be considered within their vision of war. Several things had happened since 1614. Pocahontas had died in 1617 while visiting England. The numbers and extent of the English settlement had expanded dramatically from what Wahunsenacawh might have guessed in 1614, and Wahunsenacawh himself had "resigned" in 1617. With Wahunsenacawh's abdication the chiefdom reverted to the dual leadership of a "peace chief" and a "war chief."[12] This division of authority was common to many Native peoples, and Wahunsenacawh's possession of both roles may have been a further mark of his unusual status. The new war chief, Opechancanough, was more suspicious of the expanding English than Powhatan had been. After trying and failing to persuade the English to help him in one of his own wars to the west, Opechancanough changed his name to Mangopeesomon, a name change often being a signal of coming war, and prepared to administer what he thought would be a decisive "lesson" in the proper subordination of the English to his control. They would strike at the English, punish them for their transgressions, and await the re-stabilizing of the relationship in the proper roles.[13]

The attack came on March 22, 1622. The Powhatans went about their business normally at the beginning of the day. By this time many of them had regular personal or economic contacts within the English settlements, and at the prescribed moment, all around the English colony, the Native Americans, already

11 Gleach, *Powhatan's World*, 130.

12 Gleach, *Powhatan's World*, 142; Karen Ordahl Kupperman, *Indians and English: Facing Off in Early America* (Ithaca, N.Y.: Cornell University Press, 2000), 102.

13 Gleach calls the attack a "coup" in an effort to emphasize the limited goals of this style of warfare. Gleach, *Powhatan's World*, 148–58. This is not a reference to the "counting coup" practices of Plains Indians. For other narratives of the 1622 attack and the subsequent war see: Edmund S. Morgan, *American Slavery, American Freedom* (New York: W.W. Norton & Co., 1975), 98–101; William L. Shea, *The Virginia Militia in the Seventeenth Century* (Baton Rouge: Louisiana State University Press, 1983), 25–50.

intermingled with the populace, picked up various agricultural tools (having come in unarmed) or appeared from the surrounding woods and set upon the English. They killed all those who came within reach that day, probably more than 350 people, completely wiping out some settlements. Tellingly, however, there was no follow-up. Having administered their lesson, the Powhatans went home. They surely expected retaliation, even as they would from another native society, but they would not be caught unawares, and probably expected to be able to prevent any kind of equivalent damage to themselves. They prepared for a war of raid and counterraid, but presumed that their initial successful attack would give them the advantage in the long run.

The Powhatans' targeting of the outlying settlements for the main brunt of the attack may provide the "text" of the lesson – that the English should remain within their proper area. Furthermore, the overall damage to the settlements was limited by warnings of the impending attack given by Native Americans living among the English, particularly the warnings provided to Jamestown by a Christianized Pamunkey Indian named Chanco (or Chauco) and another unnamed Indian living with the English.[14] As we will see, the exchange of residents between communities often served to limit the possibility of surprise and its consequent high level of fatalities.

The English, however, did not respond to the lesson in the expected manner. They prepared to fight war according to their own model of continuous campaigning: not raiding, but taking, destroying, and hopefully exterminating- largely in the hope of establishing their control over more land. In this the colonists succeeded to a horrifying degree, usually failing to catch very many Native Americans, but deliberately and thoroughly destroying their towns and crops. Native American efforts to negotiate a peace were repeatedly rebuffed until the war crept to a close in 1632.

b *Wendat (Huron)-Haudenosaunee (Iroquois) War of 1648/49*

The second example is perhaps the most famous and most interpretively debated of all the intra-Indian wars. It has also been called one of the most decisive. The scholarly debate centers around the motivation for the Haudenosaunee confederacy's successful attack on the Wendat confederacy in 1648 and 1649.[15] Some scholars have argued for essentially material causes: the

14 Gleach, *Powhatan's World*, 49–53; Kupperman, *Indians and English*, 196.

15 For reviews of the development of this debate see: José António Brandão, *'Your Fyre Shall Burn No More': Iroquois Policy Toward New France and Its Native Allies to 1701* (Lincoln: University of Nebraska Press, 1997), 5–18; Thomas S. Abler, "Iroquois Policy and Iroquois Culture: Two Histories and an Anthropological Ethnohistory," *Ethnohistory*, 47

Haudenosaunee sought to dominate the fur trade with the Europeans and therefore they attacked and drove out their most serious competitor. Others have at least partially accepted this explanation, but only in the context of European influence, arguing that such materialist-motivated warfare did not exist prior to contact. The dominant interpretations of the war suggest that there was no (or very little) material motivation, and in fact the Wendat and Haudenosaunee were engaged in traditional warfare based on an old enmity and a desire to gain captives for adoption, but admitting that their warfare had become more decisive and destructive due to European technology.

The permanent arrival of the French in the St. Lawrence region in the early seventeenth century eventually brought them into contact with the powerful Wendat confederacy on the far northeastern extremity of Lake Huron. For the Wendat this contact meant the arrival of missionaries and new material goods, purchasable through the sale of beaver and other furs and the Wendats quickly became significant trading partners with the French. The restrictive French trading system, however, limited their ability to trade for firearms. In 1614 the Dutch established a trading post at Fort Orange (now Albany) on the Hudson River, where they cultivated a similar trading relationship with the Haudenosaunee confederacy, ancient enemies of the Wendat. The Dutch proved more willing to trade guns and powder and eventually the Haudenosaunee, for whatever reason, determined to take advantage of their edge.[16]

In 1648 the Haudenosaunee began a series of major offensives into the Wendat home territories. They had been attacking outlying Wendat villages for a number of years, but beginning in 1648, and especially in the attack of 1649, the conflict became a much more concerted affair.[17] The Haudenosaunee cut off and destroyed two frontier towns in the summer of 1648. Then in the summer of 1649 a thousand Haudenosaunee warriors "well furnished with

---

(2000): 483–91; William A. Starna and José António Brandão, "From the Mohawk-Mahican War to the Beaver Wars: Questioning the Pattern," *Ethnohistory* 51 (2004): 725–750.

16 For the Iroqouis' success in obtaining guns and their impact, see: Keith F. Otterbein, "Why the Iroquois Won: An Analysis of Iroquois Military Tactics," *Ethnohistory* 11 (1964): 58; Bruce W. Trigger, ed., *Handbook of North American Indians-v. 15 Northeast* (Washington: Smithsonian Institution, 1978), 352 (hereafter HNAI 15); Bruce G. Trigger, *The Children of Aataentsic: a History of the Huron People to 1660* (Montreal: McGill-Queen's University Press, 1976), 2:627–633.

17 This account follows Keith F. Otterbein, "Huron vs. Iroquois: A Case Study in Inter-Tribal Warfare," *Ethnohistory* 26 (1979): 141–152, who is basically summarizing the French Jesuit account found in Reuben Gold Thwaites and Edna Kenton, eds., *Jesuit Relations* (Toronto: McClelland & Stewart, 1925), 34:123–137 (hereafter abbreviated JR).

weapons, – and mostly with firearms … arrived by night" without warning outside the Wendat town of St. Ignace (Taenhatentaron). After a winter-long approach march of hundreds of miles, the Haudenosaunee warriors crept up to the weakest point in the town's palisade wall (a fifteen foot high stockade and ditch), breached it and entered the town before the Wendats became aware of their presence. All but three men among the 400 Wendats in the village were captured or killed.

Those three warned the next village, St. Louis, some three miles away, and many of its inhabitants immediately fled, leaving only about eighty defenders. The Haudenosaunee force shortly arrived and assaulted the palisade around St. Louis. After two or three attempts they cut their way through the stockade, overwhelmed the defenders and burned the town to the ground (while preserving the palisade wall for their own uses). That night other towns of the Wendat confederacy, alerted, rushed to the French Jesuit post at Ste. Marie, and the next morning lay in wait to ambush the approaching Haudenosaunee and defend the French fort.

The second day of battle proceeded in a see-saw fashion as each side in turn gained an advantage, but fundamentally the Haudenosaunee had lost the advantage of surprise. They made an attempt on Ste. Marie, took heavy casualties, and chose to return home. Facing a long march, and presumably worried about the arrival of more Wendat reinforcements, they burned St. Ignace, killed many but not all of their captives, and headed south. In typical fashion, the Wendats of yet another town dispatched a pursuit force, but it failed to catch up. Although the Haudenosaunee had suffered more casualties than they had hoped for, they had successfully destroyed two towns (in addition to the two of the previous summer), and had killed perhaps as many as 700 Wendats.

There is much in this narrative that is "typical," but there is a scale and level of destructiveness that stands out. The use of surprise to attack a fortified village was a standard raiding technique, but the size of this raiding force meant that once they were inside the walls, they were able to succeed in killing and capturing to a startling degree. Emboldened, and unusually, the Haudenosaunee immediately attacked a second village. It was only after that success that the normal rallying of reinforcements from other nearby villages occurred. The raid completed, the raiders departed, pursued by the defenders. Although it was a "normal" raid on a larger than usual scale, in combination with previous years' successes and continued raiding, it was decisive in forcing the Wendat to disperse. They no longer felt safe in their home territories; the separate clans headed in separate directions, putting themselves under the protection of other groups.

c *The Creek-Cherokee War, 1715–1753*

A similar long-standing enmity between large native groups resulted in a continuous if episodic war in the mountains of the southeast between 1715 and 1753. The outbreak of this particular war is both well-documented and illustrative of the role of codes of war and diplomacy, as well as of the more usual alternative to conquest: endemic raid and counterraid. Although the Creeks of Georgia and Alabama and the Cherokees at the junction of Tennessee and North and South Carolina had had a long history of occasional violent conflict, this particular conflict (and our knowledge of its origins) resulted from the diplomatic needs of the English.[18] In 1715 the Yamasee Indians of Piedmont South Carolina had risen against their former English allies, and in the process had persuaded a host of other peoples to join them, including the powerful Creek confederacy. The hard-pressed South Carolinians also sought Native American allies, winning the Tuscaroras to their side, but they particularly aspired to gain the Cherokees' assistance. To help convince them, Colonel Maurice Moore marched a small expedition into the Cherokee towns to force serious diplomatic negotiations. Although hospitably received, the English quickly found themselves confined to a relatively passive role as witnesses to internal Cherokee debate and factionalism over how to respond to the English request.

The Cherokees, like most other native societies, were not a unified political body. Each town grouping, or even each town, had its own say in whether they would be willing to help the English. The "Lower" towns were initially reluctant to help against the Creeks (too close and therefore too threatening), or the Yamasees (too closely related), but they would help against some of the other small piedmont nations. Meanwhile, representatives from the Cherokee "Overhill" towns were pushing for war with the Creeks, and in fact some had already been to Charlestown to promise their support to the South Carolinians.

While the English emissaries were touring the towns trying to rally support, the Cherokees requested that the Creeks send an embassy for talks. A Creek delegation duly arrived in the Lower towns, but while in the town of Tugaloo

18 The main source for the outbreak of this war is George Chicken, "Journal of the March of the Carolinians into the Cherokee Mountains, in the Yemassee Indian War, 1715–16," *Yearbook of the City of Charleston* (1894): 315–354. See also Tom Hatley, *The Dividing Paths: Cherokees and South Carolinians Through the Revolutionary Era* (Oxford: Oxford University Press, 1995), 24–5; John Phillip Reid, *A Better Kind of Hatchet: Law, Trade, and Diplomacy in the Cherokee Nation During the Early Years of European Contact* (University Park: Pennsylvania State University Press, 1976), 61–73; *idem*, *A Law of Blood: The Primitive Law of the Cherokee Nation* (New York: New York University Press, 1970), 175; Verner Crane, *The Southern Frontier, 1670–1732* (Durham: Duke University Press, 1929), 162–186.

an anti-Creek faction within the Cherokees unexpectedly killed them. Our principal English witness, George Chicken, did not see the murder, but word of the incident spread like wildfire. The Cherokees realized that this violation of the sacred status of a diplomatic embassy, not to mention the deaths of several prominent personages, would bring swift Creek retaliation, and they prepared to meet it. Their short-term defensive strategy is as revealing about Native American warfare as is the fact that this decisive violation of the codes of diplomacy led to forty years of endemic warfare.

Expecting an attack from a large nearby Creek encampment, the Cherokees immediately put themselves and the English in a defensive posture, clustering close to the village the night of the killing, and the next day marching about three miles south of town "to waylay the pathe."[19] They waited in ambush all that day for the approach of any Creeks, took some prisoners, and then, fearing their intentions discovered, they abandoned their position and returned to the village for the night. The following day, realizing that the killing of the embassy was still undiscovered, the Cherokees, with their English allies, advanced still further south hoping to catch the main Creek force by surprise. They continued advancing in stages, each time getting closer to the Creek encampment, but by the time they arrived, the Creeks had abandoned it. Failing in their attempt at surprise, the whole Cherokee-English force returned to Tugaloo.

The Creeks eventually did find out about the murders, sought blood revenge, and the war began in earnest. Over the next ten years the Cherokees appear to have fortified a number of their more vulnerable towns, but in forty years of on-and-off warfare they could not always be alert, and several of those towns were surprised and destroyed (much like the Wendats at St. Ignace).[20] Many of the southernmost Cherokees abandoned the region entirely, joining with villages in the interior of their homeland. It is important to note, however, that the Creeks did not proceed to occupy the abandoned territory. Theirs was a war of prestige and revenge, not conquest. As the war dragged on, the South Carolinians pressed for peace out of a desire to trade with both sides. Finally, after a Cherokee victory at the battle of Taliwa and a highly successful series of Creek raids in 1752, both sides agreed to allow the British to mediate a peace.[21]

19 Chicken, "Journal of the March (1715)," 345.

20 Wayne E. Lee "Fortify, Fight, or Flee: Tuscarora and Cherokee Defensive Warfare and Military Culture Adaptation," *Journal of Military History* 68 (2004): 753–57.

21 For Taliwa, see Hatley, *Dividing Paths*, 93; for the Creek attacks of 1752 and the subsequent peace, see David Corkran, *The Cherokee Frontier, 1740–1762* (Norman: University of Oklahoma Press, 1962), 35–37.

d *A "Typical" Raid*

The last example is simpler, but deliberately more detailed, and is presented here as an effort to move beyond simple verbs like "attack," "raid," or "besiege" to see the inner workings of an Native American war party of average size. In 1725, power dynamics and Native American alliances having shifted from the Yamasee-Creek alliance just described, the English asked the Creeks to help them against the Yamasees. The Creeks agreed, and sent out a war party, but were disappointed to find the Yamasees alert and inside their fortifications. The Creeks then went:

> to a Fort in a Town Where we thought the Yamases were, and we fired at the Said Fort, Which alarmed ten Men that was Place[d] To Discover us which we [had] past [passed] when they were asleep. Our fireing awaked them and they Ran round us and gave Notice to the Yamasees Who was Removed from this town Nigher the Sea and had there Build a new fort which we found and Attacked but with litle Success [though] it happen'd the Huspaw Kings Family was not all got in the fort and we took three of them and fired Several Shott at the Huspaw king and are in hopes have killed him. There Came out a party of the Yamases who fought us and we took the Capt. We waited three days about there Fort, Expecting to get ane oppertunity to take some More but to no purpose. We then Came away and the Yamases pursued us.

Turning on their pursuers, the Creeks drove the Yamasees into a pond and were about to press them further when they were distracted by the arrival of a Spanish force. When the Creeks resumed their march home, the Yamasees pursued and attacked again, and it was in this "Batle in which they did us [the Creeks] the most Damnadge." All told, the Creeks killed eight Yamasees, and brought home those scalps, nine prisoners and some plunder. The Creeks lost five killed and six wounded.[22]

The pattern here replicates on a smaller scale much of what happened between the Wendat and the Haudenosaunee, but without the Haudenosaunees' overwhelming initial success. A raiding party attempted surprise, but was foiled by fortifications and the belated alertness of a defending ambush group. The Creeks attacked individuals they could find outside the

22 Tobias Fitch, "Captain Fitch's Journal to the Creeks, 1725," in *Travels in the American Colonies*, ed. Newton D. Mereness (New York: Macmillan Co., 1916), 202–05.

fort, and then offered battle to the defenders. The Yamasees, perhaps to maintain prestige (see the discussion of "battle" below) accepted the offer but lost their "captain" in the ensuing fight. The Creeks then lurked around the fort hoping to snipe at the occasional exposed person, and after three days headed for home. The Yamasees immediately pursued, hoping to take advantage of a party spread out on the march. A series of running battles damaged the Creeks and sped them on their way home.

Each of these examples highlights several issues central to a discussion of the restraints, and the lack thereof, in Native American warfare. Note in particular the role of blood revenge, the political divisiveness within peoples, the importance of resident visitors from other peoples, the reliance on the raid with possibly dramatic results if surprise was achieved, the willingness to besiege towns, the importance of prisoners and prestige, and finally the tendency to engage in endemic, although not *continuous* warfare—war parties did not move into enemy territory and stay there for months.

III Restraints

War, no matter how well-regulated, is by its nature destructive. Consequently, the first issue facing any culture in its efforts to restrain war is to set limits on its frequency and duration. The phrase "to set limits" implies conscious choice, and in moments of actual diplomacy there could certainly be deliberate recognition of the problem of "too much war." In general, however, what concerns us here is how Native American social organization and cultural visions of war drew boundaries around its frequency and duration. Once war is under way, the remaining problem is to find ways to regulate its destructiveness, primarily to one's own side but, for various reasons, also more generally. The remainder of this Chapter uses the preceding examples of war and additional evidence to examine these two questions. The organization is roughly step-by-step within the framework of an imaginary war. We will begin with the causes of war, and discuss how Native Americans provided some alternatives to war. We will then turn to ritual preparation, warrior mobilization, and the style of war itself.

As discussed above, the blood revenge system remained at the heart of the motivational complex, and two different systems developed to cope with this mandate: one for intra-people killing and one for killings between nations. If the blood debt was within a people, the general expectation was that the relatives of the killer would either withdraw their support from that individual, acknowledging that revenge against him was justified, or they would offer to pay a blood gift to the family of the dead person.[23] The situation became more complicated when the killer came from outside the nation. First, the possibility of a blood gift sufficing to calm relatives was reduced dramatically, although not completely. Diplomatic overtures could avoid the outbreak of war, but success depended on the willingness of the clan council and the dead person's relatives to accept it.[24] Second, there could be no expectation that the killer's relatives would stand aside, and in fact, the individual identity of the killer ceased to matter. Furthermore, in inter-people blood revenge, there was no expectation that the other side would simply accept the second, revenge killing as evening the debt. The suggestion could be made that one killing had balanced another, but convincing the other side to accept it proved difficult. The Cherokees of the town of Keowee, for example, threatened the Catawbas that a failure to accept a recent killing as squaring the balance would lead to escalation:

> As the Catawbas were coming home … finding one of our Women there, they kill'd her in Revenge, … that was the Reason why We in Return kill'd one of their Women in this Place. This is only the Talk of this Town, and if the Catawbas continue to take Revenge, we will not only go against them Ourselves, but draw the whole People of our Nation against them: but if they are satisfied we are also, for as they began first, and laid our People in heaps, we have kill'd two of them, and laid them on our own; and now we are satisfied, if they will be so; but if they are not, we will soon go

23 A sophisticated and detailed discussion of the blood feud is Reid, *Law of Blood.* Among many others, see: Charles Hudson, *The Southeastern Indians* (Knoxville: University of Tennessee Press, 1976), 230–32, 239–40; Richard White, *The Middle Ground: Indians, Empires, and Republics in the Great Lakes Region, 1650–1815* (Cambridge: Cambridge University Press, 1991), 80; Gordon M. Sayre, *Les Sauvages Américains: Representations of Native Americans in French and English Colonial Literature* (Chapel Hill: University of North Carolina Press, 1997), 279–80.

24 Hudson, *Southeastern Indians,* 242, based on James Adair, *History of the American Indians,* ed. Samuel Cole Williams (New York: Argonaut Press, (1930) 1966), 407. See also Cadwallader Colden's description of the possibility of such inter-people resolution of blood feud between the Adirondacks and the Iroquois. Cadwallader Colden, *The History of the Five Indian Nations of Canada* (London: n.p., 1747), 22. For other examples of inter-group attempts to assuage a blood feud before it got started see: Kupperman, *Indians and English,* 106; Fitch, "Captain Fitch's Journal," 203; Reid, *Law of Blood,* 171–72; James Merrell, *Into the American Woods: Negotiators on the Pennsylvania Frontier* (New York: Knopf, 1999), 116–121; Colin G. Calloway, *The Western Abenakis of Vermont, 1600–1800: War, Migration, and the Survival of an Indian People* (Norman: University of Oklahoma Press, 1990), 165, 189–90; Wendell S. Hadlock, "War among the Northeastern Woodland Indians," *American Anthropologist* new Ser. 49 (1947): 213–14.

> against them, as we think nothing of them, and as it was intirely their own Fault.[25]

This difficulty of "balancing blood" arose from the nature of a war party. A war party mobilized to avenge a blood debt, even a small one, was unlikely to be able to contain its damage to one person- even if they wanted to.

This is where the blood debt system overlapped with the use of war for personal status to produce endemic states of conflict. A war party ostensibly mobilized for revenge, but comprised of individuals hoping for status, especially young men, had no desire to limit their attacks to one person. Once in contact with an enemy group, individual desire for success in war quickly led to the taking of as many scalps and/or prisoners as could reasonably be accomplished–because in those prizes lay status.

There follows an obvious response. Any deaths inflicted by the first war party created a need in the targeted group for their own retaliatory strike. This cycle was the weak link within Native American restraints on war. The cultural mandate for revenge proved extremely difficult to overcome. Historian John Reid summarized the problem: "A [Cherokee] warrior who had recently lost a brother in a Creek raid might tell a Creek peace delegation that he would bury the bloody hatchet after he had taken one Creek scalp. If he succeeded, it would be for the brother of his Creek victim to decide if the war would continue. Peace negotiations therefore were largely promises to forgive and forget."[26] In some cases the original source of enmity between two groups might be lost in the depths of time, but endemic raiding back and forth continued nonetheless, as each new killing reinvigorated the blood debt.

There were, however, certain restraints within the need for revenge. The scale of the avenging party, and thus its destructive potential, was limited by the mobilization process. Decisions for war were reached by consensus, and Native American leaders lacked the capacity to coerce participation.[27] As indicated in the Cherokee-Catawba conflict quoted above, it was unusual to mobilize warriors from outside the family or from members of other towns. Unless the dead person was a prominent figure, it was unlikely that his or her death would stimulate a multi-town mobilization. An influential leader with a

25 Talk of Tistoe and The Wolf of Keowee to Governor Lyttelton, March 5, 1759, William Lyttelton Papers, William L. Clements Library, University of Michigan, Ann Arbor.

26 Reid, *Better Kind of Hatchet*, 9.

27 Ferguson argues that this lack of coercive structures was the most fundamental limitation on pre-state warfare. Ferguson, "Violence and War in Prehistory," 336.

significant following could possibly expand the pool of recruits, but he could do so only as long as his reputation held out.

While a lack of coercive political structure limited the scale of war, another fundamental limitation was the Native American ideology of revenge. The revenge motive did not carry with it the motivation to pursue the wholesale destruction of the enemy people- a few scalps and prisoners would suffice. This "tit-for-tat" understanding of war was unfocused in its targeting since any victim would do, but it was limited in its scale. This limited notion of revenge differed dramatically from the European ideology of revenge in war. The Europeans also had notions of retaliation, but were much more lethal.[28] It was just this kind of ideology that the Virginia colonists unveiled in their response to the 1622 attack. Materially they may have been seeking land, but ideologically they justified their efforts at wholesale destruction by citing the "treacherousness" of the Native Americans. Edward Waterhouse summed up the Virginians' explanations, writing, "Our hands, which before were tied with gentelnesse and faire usage, are now set at liberty by the treacherous violence of the Savages, not untying the Knot, but cutting it: So that we ... may now by right of Warre, and law of Nations, invade the Country, and destroy them who sought to destroy us."[29] In this light the blood revenge system seems much less destructive.

When we turn from the blood feud as a cause of war to the question of political and economic causes, we enter one of the most contentious issues in the study of Native American warfare. There are well-rehearsed arguments that Native American societies did not pursue conquest, or economic/territorial gain in their waging of war, or that if they did so, it was only because of European-induced changes – particularly the introduction of new trade items. This is not an argument limited to the North American continent.[30] There is strong evidence to the contrary, however, particularly in the chiefdoms of the late prehistoric Mississippian southeast who appear to have demanded tribute from submitted peoples.[31] There is also Wahunsenacawh's apparent conqueror

28 For one example of this ideology at work see: John Winthrop, *The Journal of John Winthrop, 1630–1649*, unabridged ed., eds. Richard S. Dunn, James Savage, Laetitia Yeandel (Cambridge, Mass.: Harvard University Press, 1996), 252.

29 Edward Waterhouse, *A Declaration of the State of the Colony in Virginia* (London: n.p., 1622; reprint, New York: Da Capo Press, 1970), 22–23.

30 See Samuel White & Ray Kerkhove, 'Indigenous Australian laws of war: junkarti, milwerangle & makaratta' (2021) 102 *International Review of the Red Cross* 959–978.

31 Lawrence H. Keeley, *War Before Civilization* (New York: Oxford University Press, 1996), 116; David H. Dye, "Warfare in the Sixteenth-Century Southeast: The de Soto Expedition in the Interior," in *Columbian Consequences, Vol. 2: Archaeological and Historical Perspectives on the Spanish Borderlands East*, ed. David Hurst Thomas (Washington: Smithsonian

status in the Chesapeake at the beginning of the seventeenth century. Even without certainty regarding the Native Americans' ultimate motives, however, they do appear to have distinguished between "grand" and "little" war.[32] On occasion, sufficient motivation existed – whatever it might be – for large parties of warriors, perhaps 600 to 1000, to attack their enemies "in the name of the tribe," rather than as part of a limited blood feud, apparently in the hope of inflicting damage well beyond the norms of the "little war."[33] Expeditions such as these were at least intended to force a reformation in relationships between groups, if not to conquer territory or impose tribute. They attested to the power and vitality of the attackers, and sought to arm-twist their enemy into modifying their behavior in some way. In that sense they *were* "political" wars, but with limited goals. As Neal Salisbury described the motivations of the Narragansetts of New England: "to the Narragansett warfare was a contest in which one sought to intimidate and scatter one's enemies through a combination of physical and supernatural weapons. The result might be a favorable shift in the balance of power but certainly not the elimination of any existing communal entities."[34] This interpretation has been applied to many of the larger attacks on the European settlements, but also applies to significant inter-Indian wars. The Haudenosaunee attack on the Wendat in 1648–49 described above was one example of the "grand" war on a large scale and so, in its own way, was the Powhatan attack of 1622.

This delineation between grand war and little war is not necessarily one that Native American societies would recognize, or at least not as a strict duality.

Institution Press, 1990), 211–22; *idem*, "Warfare in the Protohistoric Southeast, 1500–1700," in *Between Contacts and Colonies: Archaeological Perspectives on the Protohistoric Southeast*, eds. Cameron B. Wesson and Mark A. Rees (Tuscaloosa: University of Alabama Press, 2002), 131–2; Karl T. Steinen, "Ambushes, Raids, and Palisades: Mississippian Warfare in the Interior Southeast," *Southeastern Archaeology* 11 (1992): 132–39; David G. Anderson, "Fluctuations between Simple and Complex Chiefdoms: Cycling in the Late Prehistoric Southeast," in *Political Structure and Change in the Prehistoric Southeastern United States*, ed. John F. Scarry (Gainesville: University Press of Florida, 1996), 245–6.

32 HNAI 15:315; Leroy V. Eid, "'National War' among Indians of Northeastern North America," *Canadian Review of American Studies* 16 (1985): 125–54. For Mississippian conquest warfare see note 57.

33 Quote is from Joseph François Lafitau, *Customs of the American Indians Compared With the Customs of Primitive Times*, eds. William N. Fenton and Elizabeth L. Moore (Toronto: The Champlain Society, 1974), 2:101.

34 Neal Salisbury, *Manitou and Providence: Indians, Europeans, and the Making of New England, 1500–1643* (Oxford: Oxford University Press, 1982), 229. For other discussions of "political" goals for Native American warfare see: Gleach, *Powhatan's World*, 51–54; Thomas C. Parramore, "The Tuscarora Ascendancy," *North Carolina Historical Review* 59 (1982): 322–23.

The little war of the blood feud could escalate, through frustration, into larger attacks otherwise lacking the political or economic intent of "grand" war.[35] Conversely, a long series of small-scale "little" war style raids could have a larger political purpose, attempting in effect to achieve "conquest by harassment."[36] It was even possible to resolve disputes through single combat between champions; truly a "little war" but with larger political import.[37]

Nor did Native Americans draw a stark line between war and peace (perhaps in part due to the endemic nature of blood revenge needs). Peace did not exist as a formally declared state so much as it was achieved through the mollification of hostile feelings.[38] Since it was nearly impossible to completely erase hostile feelings within every individual, and centralized behavioral control in a social system with diffuse political authority was impossible, there was always the chance the members of a nation might launch their own raids. One Cherokee related to John Norton his own personal revenge raid from his boyhood, saying that they were "continually vexed by petty war parties from the Northern Tribes," so that once he and a friend went on a revenge raid against the Piankashaws on the Wabash River. They killed several and "brought off their scalps" and were pursued.[39] Not "politically authorized," but certainly culturally legitimate, his raid no doubt *did* inspire retaliatory raids in return, and thus had political impact.

This kind of behavior fleshed out a wide spectrum of violent behavior between the binaries of war and peace. Formal declarations of war did occur, such as sending the red stick, or flying the red flag of war, but there also existed a level of conflict between peace and outright war during which significant levels of violence could be in play, perhaps intended to carry a political message, or perhaps intended to let off young men's steam without a full commitment to war.[40] Essentially, there was another point on the spectrum between the poles

35 Thus the Keowee Cherokees' threat to draw in other towns as quoted above.

36 I greatly expand on this issue of the political outcomes of Native American war in my forthcoming *Cutting-Off Way*.

37 For example, the Montagnais and the Iroquois once agreed to "spare the blood of our followers" and submit to the judgment of a wrestling contest. JR 1:269–70.

38 Hudson, *Southeastern Indians*, 257; Daniel K. Richter, *The Ordeal of the Longhouse: The Peoples of the Iroquois League in the Era of European Colonization* (Chapel Hill: University of North Carolina Press, 1992), 40. See also below in the section on making peace.

39 Norton, *Journal of John Norton*, 141–42.

40 For examples of the red stick or red flag see Hudson, *Southeastern Indians*, 243; Adair, *History*, 408. Similarly, there is the famous story of the Narragansett chief, Canonicus, sending a clear warning of impending war to the Plymouth colonists in the form of a rattlesnake's skin wrapped around a bundle of arrows. Governor Bradford's response of returning the skin stuffed with powder and shot sufficiently impressed Canonicus that

of peace and war, which for lack of a better phrase, I call the "not quite war" level of conflict.[41] The "not quite war" was politically motivated as an effort to effect relations between groups, but employed only the small-scale methods of "little war." It might perhaps even have been deliberately disavowable *as* little war (a personal grudge only) if peace was determined to be a better alternative. Furthermore, the "not quite war" functioned very well within the imperial context, helped along by the autonomy of individual towns within the larger groups, and making it easier for Native American headmen to "capitalize on [their] decentralized, kin-based politics to cultivate connections with rival colonies and so avoid dependence on a single European power."[42]

As another example of such behavior, consider Tom Hatley's analysis of a Creek attack on the English trader John Sharp's home near the Cherokee town of Nayowee in 1724. The Creeks approached his house, fired several volleys, wounded Sharp in the leg, and then plundered his house. All of this was done within sight of the Cherokee town whose residents declined to interfere. Hatley interprets Sharp's survival as proof that the Creeks were merely making a point, "a symbolic statement about the strength of Creek men to the onlooking Cherokee villagers."[43] They could equally as well have been making a point to the English and the traders, but at any rate Sharp was neither killed nor captured, nor were the Creeks then "at war" with the English.

The Cherokees engaged in a similar round of "not quite war" with the English in 1758. Nominally allied with the British during the French and Indian War, some of their warriors returning home from Pennsylvania were attacked and killed by Virginia militia in a dispute over stolen horses. As a matter of course, the relatives and townsmen of the men sought blood revenge, and were aided by anti-British factions within the Cherokees who hoped to join with the French. Small groups of warriors began to raid the white frontier in Virginia and North Carolina, and in fact continued to raid the frontier throughout

---

he backed off from his challenge. William Bradford, *Of Plymouth Plantation, 1620–1647* (New York: Random House, 1981), 106; Alden T. Vaughan, *New England Frontier: Puritans and Indians, 1620–1675*, 3rd ed. (Norman: University of Oklahoma Press, 1995), 79–80.

41 For modern parallels consider the United States' bombing of Libya in 1986, the cruise missile strikes in Sudan and Afghanistan in 1998, or so-called "grey zone" operations. For the last see Samuel White, 'Colouring in the Grey Zone: An Australian Case Study' (2022) 21(2) *Journal of Military and Strategic Studies* 77–106.

42 Richter, "Native Peoples of North America," 357.

43 Hatley, *Dividing Paths*, 44–45. The original document is available as: John Sharp to Governor Nicholson, Nov. 12, 1724, in *Calendar of State Papers, Colonial Series, American and West Indies, 1574–1739*, CD-ROM, eds. Karen Ordahl Kupperman, John C. Appleby and Mandy Banton (London: Routledge, 2000), Item 429v, 34:280.

the summer and fall of 1759. Strikingly, at the same time all remained peaceful around the British forts in the Cherokee towns. Trade and relations there continued, if with greater worry and tension. There was no sense of the two peoples being "at war," even while some Cherokees were undeniably wreaking havoc elsewhere. When diplomatically confronted the Cherokee leadership downplayed the violence, describing it as young men out of control. The conflict thus was both simple blood debt and political at the same time, all while the Cherokees tried to avoid a broadening of the conflict.[44]

Once "at war," whether at the "Grand," "little," or even the "not quite war" level, a number of factors built into Native American society tended to limit the extent of the conflict's lethality and overall destructiveness- for both the attacker and the defender. These structures were not absolute, and they may or may not have originated as deliberate efforts to restrain war, but there is little doubt that they served that function in practice.

To begin with, Native American war demanded a certain level of ritual preparedness and sacred purity. Although much of Native American warfare was at least nominally motivated by the desire for revenge, ostensibly one of the more "bloody-minded" and unlimited approaches to war, it still occurred within a cultural framework that carried certain spiritual expectations. Those expectations reined in the potentially unrestrained attitudes arising from revenge-based warfare. Prior to the departure of any war party the community, the leadership, and the warriors partook in a series of ritual activities designed to insure the success of their endeavor. Southeastern Indians retired to the war chief's winter house, remaining there for three days and nights, fasting and drinking potions, intended both to purify them and protect them from danger.[45] John Gyles, captured by the Abenaki in 1689, described a feast in preparation for war that served both ritual purposes and to identify those willing to volunteer.[46] Mary Rowlandson, captive among the Wampanoags, witnessed a ritual dance prior to the departure of a war party that seemed in its details to embody the classic pre-hunt dance in which the warriors enacted the events of a successful raid.[47] The preparatory

44 Lee, "Fortify, Fight, or Flee," 761–62.

45 Hudson, *Southeastern Indians*, 243–44; Adair, *History*, 167–78.

46 John Gyles, "Memoirs of Odd Adventures, Strange Deliverances, etc.," in *Puritans among the Indians: Accounts of Captivity and Redemption, 1676–1724*, ed. Alden T. Vaughan and Edward W. Clark (Cambridge: Harvard University Press, 1981), 120.

47 Mary Rowlandson, *The Sovereignty and Goodness of God*, ed. Neil Salisbury (Boston: Bedford Books, 1997), 100.

rituals of the Miamis lasted for a full five days and nights and attendance was mandatory.[48]

Common to many of these pre-war rituals was the expectation that proper access to spiritual power would provide protection in war.[49] Such a belief attested to the Native American outlook that the spiritual and material world were in fact coterminous. Spiritual power was immanent in the world and only required ritual skill to tap it.[50] Such a powerful belief in the importance of ritual to the successful outcome of war meant that an offensive could easily be derailed by bad omens, whether natural or deliberately manufactured. The sensitivity of a small-scale society to casualties enhanced this probability. If the spirits seemed unwilling to support the nation's attack, the people could not afford to ignore them and risk defeat. Attakullakulla (Little Carpenter), a Cherokee leader in 1758, explained that their expedition to aid the British war effort could not go on because the "Conjurers" had produced omens of a "Distemper" which would afflict them after the first two months of the expedition.[51] A raid by the Native American people living on the Gaspé peninsula in 1661 saw half of its participants depart when one of their number "just now recalled" the command of a dying relative (and therefore spiritually significant) not to participate in the raid.[52]

Other purity expectations included a prohibition on sexual intercourse during or in preparation for a campaign. Crucially, the prohibition precluded the rape of enemy women. Although as we will see, women were targets in other ways – for capture, adoption, and possible marriage – there appears to have

48 HNAI 15:685–6. Examples can expand almost infinitely. For the Haudenosaunee, see HNAI 15:315–16.

49 Alfred A. Cave, *The Pequot War* (Amherst: University of Massachusetts Press, 1996), 22; J. Frederick Fausz, "Fighting 'Fire' with Firearms: The Anglo-Powhatan Arms Race in Early Virginia," *American Indian Culture and Research Journal* 3 (1979): 41–42; Corkran, *Cherokee Frontier*, 155.

50 Gregory Evans Dowd, *A Spirited Resistance: The North American Indian Struggle for Unity, 1745–1815* (Baltimore: The Johns Hopkins University Press, 1992), 1–22 contains an extensive discussion of the relationship of the spiritual, the material, and war.

51 George Turner to Governor Lyttelton, July 2, 1758, in William L. McDowell, Jr., ed., *Documents Relating to Indian Affairs, 1754–62* (Columbia, S. C.: Colonial Records of South Carolina, Series 2, 1970), 2: 471 (hereafter abbreviated DRIA). Colin Calloway records a similar instance of the Creeks delaying a war party until the completion of the Green Corn ceremony. *The American Revolution in Indian Country: Crisis and Diversity in Native American Communities* (Cambridge: Cambridge University Press, 1995), 62.

52 JR 47:227. War parties also carried medicine bundles or other sacred objects whose loss could send the warriors home. Hudson, *Southeastern Indians*, 244, 247; Adair, *History*, 409; Gleach, *Powhatan's World*, 53; HNAI 15:685, 695–6.

been no equivalent in Native American societies to the European soldiers' propensity to indulge in rape as a perquisite of war.[53] There is not much direct evidence on the subject, but there was certainly one example of English soldiers raping Cherokee women that contributed to starting a war.[54]

Finally, acknowledging the fundamental spiritual harm caused by the taking of life, some societies expected returning warriors to undergo a period of purification prior to their full reentry into society. Anthropologist Charles Hudson described the general process for the southeastern Native Americans as a process much like that before setting out: three days of fasting under the guidance of the war chief, accompanied each night by the women singing songs outside the war chief's home.[55] The Shawnees practiced a similar post-raid purification through isolation and fasting.[56] This need for purification after a raid created a basic limitation on the frequency of war, since it at least nominally prevented those warriors from simply resupplying and returning to the attack.

Where the needs of the spirit world provided a kind of halting, awkward, and unpredictable restriction on warfare, the more immediate and loudly voiced expectations of the people on their leadership created a different and more abiding set of limitations. As noted above, the coercive power of Native American leaders was extremely limited, and it was thus difficult to raise large armies or to maintain one's leadership position after a defeat. Authority within a nation usually derived from the consensus of the elders channeled through a peace and a war chief, the former of which restrained the usually more aggressive tendencies of the war chief. Furthermore, the group's religious figure or shaman himself wielded a separate authority through his more extensive contact with the spirit world.[57] In military terms this divided structure of

53 James Axtell, "The White Indians of Colonial America," *William and Mary Quarterly* 3d Ser., 32 (1975): 67; Rowlandson, *Sovereignty and Goodness*, 107 note 82; Thomas S. Abler, "Scalping, Torture, Cannibalism and Rape: An Ethnohistorical Analysis of Conflicting Values in War," *Anthropologica* 34 (1992): 13; Dowd, *A Spirited Resistance*, 9–10; Armstrong Starkey, *European and Native American Warfare, 1675–1815* (Norman: University of Oklahoma Press, 1998), 28, 81; Cave, *Pequot War*, 20; Elizabeth Hanson, "God's Mercy Surmounting Man's Cruelty," in *Puritans and Indians*, 242 (see also the editors' comments in *Ibid*, 14); Adair, *History*, 171–72.

54 Hatley, *Dividing Paths*, 107; Adair, *History*, 260–61. Richard White reports another instance of Indians taking revenge for the rape of women in the 1760s. White, *The Middle Ground*, 345.

55 Hudson, *Southeastern Indians*, 252. See also Starkey, *European and Native American*, 28.

56 HNAI 15:628. See also the Miamis' post-raid ritual, which although not as directly confining, deprived the warriors of their personal sacred bundles for several days, presumably preventing them from returning to war immediately. HNAI 15:685.

57 Native American societies that had combined, or partially combined, this tripartite power structure into one person were typically more militant and aggressive. Frederic

leadership which in turn rested on group consensus imposed two significant limitations. The first was the inability to coerce warriors to go to war–the mobilization problem. We have seen how grieving relatives could persuade others, usually young men in search of status, to join them in a blood feud. To raise troops for more "political" warfare required an almost identical, and therefore equally fragile process. As hinted in the preceding discussion of ritual preparation, warrior mobilization and purification were an intertwined process. James Adair, a trader and traveler in the eighteenth-century southeast, described the process of mobilization:

> In the first commencement of a war, a party of the injured tribe turns out first, to revenge the innocent crying blood of their own bone and flesh, as they term it. When the leader begins to beat up for volunteers, he goes three times round his dark winter-house, contrary to the course of the sun, sounding the war whoop, singing the war song, and beating the drum. Then he speaks to the listening crowd with very rapid language, short pauses, and an awful commanding voice. ... Persuad[ing] his kindred warriors and others, who are not afraid of the enemies bullets and arrows, to come and join him with manly cheerful hearts. ... By his eloquence, but chiefly by their own greedy thirst of revenge, and intense love of martial glory ... a number soon join him in his winter house [and commence the three day fast].[58]

The emphasis here is on volunteers, motivated by desires for revenge and status, and presumably supported in their hopes by the reputation of the war leader. A similar process of ritual volunteering occurred among the northern Iroquoian and Algonquian peoples as well.[59] One should immediately note

---

Gleach has made this argument for Powhatan's power in Virginia: that for reasons unknown, Powhatan had successfully combined civil, military and religious authority in his person, and thus was able to embark on building a paramount chiefdom. Gleach, *Powhatan's World*, 31. Similarly, the more centralized and urbanized Mississippian societies of the late prehistoric southeast were ruled by "priest-kings" who combined civil, military and sacred functions, and waged aggressive conquest warfare in competition with each other and with surrounding less centralized peoples. Hudson, *Knights of Spain*, 17; David H. Dye, "The Art of War in the Sixteenth-Century Central Mississippi Valley," in *Perspectives on the Southeast: Linguistics, Archaeology and Ethnohistory*, ed., Patricia B. Kwachka (Athens: University of Georgia Press, 1994), 54–56; *idem*, "Warfare in the Sixteenth-Century Southeast," 213–14.

58 Adair, *History*, 167–68.

59 Colden, *History*, 6–7; Gyles, "Memoirs," 120; JR 47:221–31; Sayre, *Les Sauvages Américains*, 275–76.

that these recruitment processes by their very nature were confined to one town at a time. Efforts to raise warrior volunteers from other towns required extensive negotiations, travel, and even gift-giving to convince other towns to join in.[60] Despite a generalized martial enthusiasm among the young men, such mobilization techniques among an already demographically limited society further restrained the size of war parties on most occasions. In turn, a smaller war party could inflict only limited damage.

Furthermore, the fragile authority of the war chief tended to limit the risks he could take while on campaign. High levels of casualties were ill-afforded, and generally defined a war party as unsuccessful. The Haudenosaunee believed that "a victory bought with blood is no victory."[61] The blame in such a case fell squarely on the war leader, usually on an assumption of his lack of ritual purity. Adair noted that "they reckon the leader's impurity to be the chief occasion of bad success; and if he lose several of his warriors by the enemy … he is degraded by taking from him his drum, war-whistle, and martial titles, and debasing him to his boy's name."[62] The Illini apparently systematized the process: two failures simply ended a war leader's career.[63] Serious disasters put the war leader's very life in jeopardy. After the English destruction of the Pequot village of Mystic in 1637, the Pequots very nearly killed their leader Sassacus.[64] Such punishments combined with the minimal standards for success (a few scalps or prisoners would do) encouraged the war leader to avoid risk, thus limiting the likely destructive potential of any given raid.

In practice, to "avoid risk" meant pursuing a limited repertoire of tactical techniques. A casualty-averse war party's best option was surprise. If they achieved surprise, either by ambushing a smaller party, or by attacking a sleeping village, then the relative casualty count for the defender could be quite

60 See, for example, Richter, *Ordeal*, 34–5; Cave, *Pequot War*, 3; Trigger, *Children*, 69; Claudio Saunt, *A New Order of Things: Property, Power, and the Transformation of the Creek Indians* (New York: Cambridge University Press, 1999), 21; Hadlock, "War," 211.

61 Pierre Francois Xavier de Charlevoix, *Journal of a Voyage to North America* (London, 1761), 1:360 cited in Stephen Brumwell, *Redcoats: The British Soldier and War in the Americas, 1755–1763* (New York: Cambridge University Press, 2002), 204. See also the Iroquois mobilization process described in José António Brandão, ed., *Nation Iroquoise: A Seventeenth-Century Ethnography of the Iroquois* (Lincoln: University of Nebraska Press, 2003), 67, 73, 75.

62 Adair, *History*, 416.

63 HNAI 15:676. See also: Stephen Aron, *How the West Was Lost: The Transformation of Kentucky from Daniel Boone to Henry Clay* (Baltimore: Johns Hopkins University Press, 1996), 34; Sayre, *Les Sauvages Américains*, 270.

64 Cave, *Pequot War*, 157.

high. There was no lack of willingness to kill large numbers of the enemy.[65] As the Cherokees once explained to George Chicken, "it was not plunder they wanted from them but to go to war with them [the Creeks] and cut them of[f]," that is, to kill them.[66] To successfully kill very many, however, depended on surprise, and surprise was difficult to achieve. An alert enemy, or one informed by "resident aliens" as discussed below, would be prepared, leaving the attacking war party with the options of returning home, offering open battle, or if the defenders remained behind a palisade, of laying siege. Each of these choices involves some interpretive controversy, so we need to consider each in some detail, and their relation to each other.

For many decades the usual argument about Native American tactical techniques was that they were relatively innocuous and bloodless prior to the arrival of the Europeans. Some have argued more specifically that Native Americans preferred to engage in linear pitched battles fought in a ritualistic manner, and with a great deal of mutual firing and dodging of missile weapons, and not many casualties.[67] The corollary to this interpretation was that the arrival of European technology and more lethal metal arrowheads, rapidly followed by clumsy but lethal guns, led Native Americans to abandon the pitched battle, and revert to the old alternative (never entirely absent) of ambush. This line of thinking has occasionally been taken to extremes, arguing that the Europeans introduced the Native Americans to torture and scalping, and even to the deliberate killing of enemies in battle.[68] One of the most frequently cited works on native warfare, after describing the loss of fifty Mohawks in a 1669 battle, asserts the unknowable: "such heavy losses in a single action were unheard of before the arrival of the white man and his weapons."[69] Recent

65 Some anthropologists and ethnohistorians would disagree with this statement, arguing that the casualty counts documented in the historic era (such as the 1649 Iroquois attack) resulted from European influence. See below.

66 Chicken, "Journal of the March (1715)," 342.

67 Richter, *Ordeal*, 35; Trigger, Bruce G. Trigger, *The Huron: Farmers of the North*, 2nd ed. (Holt, Rinehart and Winston, Inc.: Fort Worth, 1990), 54; Adam J. Hirsch, "The Collision of Military Cultures in Seventeenth-Century New England," *Journal of American History* 74 (1988): 1191; Fausz, "Fighting Fire," 34; Patrick M. Malone, *The Skulking Way of War: Technology and Tactics Among the New England Indians* (Lanham, Md.: Madison Books, 1991), 29–31.

68 Nathaniel Knowles, "The Torture of Captives by the Indians of Eastern North America," *American Philosophical Society Proceedings* 82 (1940): 151–225; Daniel P. Barr, "'This Land Is Ours and Not Yours': The Western Delawares and the Seven Years' War in the Upper Ohio Valley, 1755–1758," in *The Boundaries Between Us: Natives and Newcomers Along the Frontiers of the Old Northwest Territory, 1750–1850*, ed. Daniel P. Barr (Kent, OH: Kent State University Press, 2006), 32.

69 Malone, *Skulking Way of War*, 65.

anthropological work has offered a more complex, and more convincing, understanding of this style of war.[70] Their basic argument is that both highly lethal and highly ritualized warfare could coexist, with one superseding the other depending on circumstance.

It was true, however, that the technological and tactical balance of the offense and the defense both in siege warfare and in open battle meant that warfare prior to the arrival of Europeans would usually be a relatively mild affair. Successful surprise, however, overcame that limitation, and could immediately produce huge *per capita* casualty ratios.[71] The European arrival did not introduce the concept of lethality in warfare, what it did do was to introduce new technologies that upset the parity of offense and defense, making the open battle more lethal and a successful siege and assault possible. The better-equipped Haudenosaunee, therefore, could use metal axes to cut through the palisade walls of the Wendats, even after surprise had failed (as they did at St. Louis). In the face of the inability to either dodge bullets or heal bullet wounds, the ritual battle, probably never the true centerpiece of Native American warfare, rapidly disappeared.[72] It still happened, of course, that large war parties

70 Otterbein, "A History," 800; William Tulio Divale, *Warfare in Primitive Societies: A Bibliography*, (Santa Barbara, Calif: ABC-Clio, 1973), xxi–xxii; Thomas B. Abler, "European Technology and the Art of War in Iroquoia," in *Cultures in Conflict: Current Archaeological Perspectives*, eds. Diana Tkaczuk and Brian C. Vivian (Calgary: University of Calgary Archaeology Association, 1989), 278–79. Lawrence Keeley's emphasis on the *per capita* lethality of primitive warfare in general is an important stimulus to this argument, *War Before Civilization*. Dye, *War Paths, Peace Paths: An Archaeology of Cooperation and Conflict in Native Eastern North America* (Lanham, MD: AltaMira, 2009), 8–11, 67, 111–13; Richard J. Chacon and Rubén G. Mendoza, eds., *North American Indigenous Warfare and Ritual Violence* (Tucson: University of Arizona Press, 2007); Azar Gat, *War in Human Civilization*, (Oxford: Oxford University Press, 2006), 116–32. For a continued assertion of the paucity of evidence for prestate warfare, see R. Brian Ferguson, "Archaeology, Cultural Anthropology, and the Origins and Intensification of War," in *The Archaeology of Warfare: Prehistories of Raiding and Conquest*, ed. Elizabeth N. Arkush and Mark W. Allen (Gainesville: University Press of Florida, 2006), 469–523.

71 George R. Milner, "Warfare in Prehistoric and Early Historic Eastern North America," *Journal of Archaeological Research* 7 (1999): 126–27; Patricia M. Lambert, "The Archaeology of War: A North American Perspective," *Journal of Archaeological Research* 10 (2002): 227–29; Maria Ostendorf Smith, "Osteological Indications of Warfare in the Archaic Period of the Western Tennessee Valley," in *Troubled Times*, 241–66.

72 This does not mean that "ritualism" disappeared, just the ritual battle. Fausz, "Fighting Fire"; Starkey, *European and Native American*, 24–25; Richter, *Ordeal*, 54; Otterbein, "Why the Iroquois Won," 59–60. Note that these sources argue for the shift in tactics due to firearms. My argument, with significant influence from Otterbein and Divale, is for a broader shift from a duality of war styles (ritual battle and deadly ambush) to a stricter reliance on the ambush based on the shifting balance of offense vs. defense.

could encounter each other while far from their villages with neither side having the benefit of surprise. In that eventuality, battle might follow, but not the linear open battle described by the early sources. Instead individual warriors "took to the trees," firing from cover and endeavoring to outflank their enemy with a "half-moon" formation, negating the enemy's use of a single tree as cover.[73] Roger Williams's dictionary of the Narragansett language contains only a few phrases with tactical implications, but they give a good impression of the most important issues in Native American warfare: "They fly from us / Let us pursue"; "They lie in the way"; "They fortifie"; "An house fired"; "An Halfe Moone in war"; and probably most important of all, "Keep Watch."[74]

All of these tactical issues and their possible lethality relate to a larger and even more controversial topic, the question of a Native American "total war." Again, the usual understanding of Native American warfare prior to European contact is that warriors did not seek the indiscriminate destruction of the old, the women, and the children, nor did they usually burn villages or crops in the European tradition of laying waste the countryside. Francis Jennings and Patrick Malone have even argued that Native Americans were taken aback by the European destruction of villages and crops.[75] In one instance some Pequots literally queried the English about their style of war, asking "if we did use to kill women and children?" The English reply that they "should see thereafter" may have been a bit of a shock.[76] Later in the conflict the Narragansetts, although allied with the English against the Pequots, sent a message through Roger Williams expressing their desire that the killing of women and children be avoided.[77] And, most famously, when the English and the Narragansetts utterly destroyed the Pequot village at Mystic, killing hundreds of all ages and sexes, the Narragansetts "came to us, and rejoiced at our victories, ... but cried Mach it, mach it; that is, is is naught, it is naught, because it is too furious, and slays too many men."[78]

---

73 Leroy V. Eid, "'A Kind of Running Fight': Indian Battlefield Tactics in the late Eighteenth Century," *Western Pennsylvania Historical Magazine* 71 (1988): 147–71; DRIA 2:467, 468; Gleach, *Powhatan's World*, 43.

74 Williams, *Key into the Language*, 184–186. As an indication of its importance, there is a single word for the half-moon formation: "Onúttug."

75 Francis Jennings, *The Invasion of America: Indians, Colonialism, and the Cant of Conquest* (New York: W. W. Norton & Co., 1975), 152–53; Malone, *Skulking Way of War*, 103–4.

76 Lion Gardiner, "Relation," 131–32 cited in Cave, *The Pequot War*, 133.

77 Paul A. Robinson, "Lost Opportunities: Miantonomi and the English in Seventeenth-Century Narragansett Country," in *Northeastern Indian Lives, 1632–1816*, ed. Robert S. Grumet (Amherst: University of Massachusetts Press, 1996), 22–23.

78 John Underhill, *Newes From America* (London, 1638; reprint, New York: Da Capo Press, 1971), 42–43.

Contrary to this oft-quoted passage expressing Native American horror at an all too thorough European way of war, there is substantial evidence that they were themselves well-prepared to carry out fairly indiscriminate destruction. Fire by definition was an indiscriminate weapon, and we find early Wendat and Haudenosaunee fortifications designed with fire prevention in mind, while Le Moyne provided a very early engraving of Native Americans firing an enemy village.[79] There is no denying the occasional killing of women and children during the historic era, although as we will see many of them could be adopted instead of killed. As early as 1540 the Spanish reported both sexes and children being scalped in the southeast, and the same Pequots who queried whether the English killed women and children, upon hearing the Englishmens' vague answer, immediately replied that they would go to Connecticut to "kill men, women, and children, and we will take away the horses, cows, and hogs."[80] The subject remains contentious, however. The basic counter-argument is that this level of violence arose only in reaction to European methods of war. There is much to be said for that argument, but it may be that more is explained by understanding such killings within the context of a style of war that so highly valued prisoners.

One way to interpret the Narragansetts' "mach it, mach it" complaint about their English ally's destruction of the Pequots at Mystic is that such destructiveness denied them the opportunity to take prisoners for prestige or adoption. It is in the Native American attitude toward prisoners that one paradoxically finds both the most and least restraint in the overall violence of their warfare.

Prisoners served three and sometimes four overlapping purposes. Bringing prisoners back to the home village certified the overall success of the mission, and warriors gained individual glory by pointing to particular prisoners as "theirs." Scalps were also a mark of success and prestige, but were considered a poor second best to a live prisoner. The preference for prisoners over scalps arose from prisoners' other three functions. A prisoner, particularly an adult male, became the target for their captors' rage and grief at their other losses.

79 Keener, "Ethnohistorical Analysis," 783, 785; Hulton, *The Work of Jacques Le Moyne*, 1:149 and plate 123. Compare: Malone, *Skulking Way of War*, 14; Vaughan, *New England Frontier*, xxv.

80 D. Owsley and H. Berryman, "Ethnographic and Archaeological Evidence of Scalping in the Southeastern United States," *Tennessee Archaeologist* 31 (1975): 41–60; Gardiner, "Relation," 131–32 cited in Cave, *The Pequot War*, 134. There is also strong archaeological evidence for prehistoric killing of women. Richard G. Wilkinson, "Violence against Women: Raiding and Abduction in Prehistoric Michigan," in *Troubled Times*, 21–44. The extent of such killing is debated, but it certainly occurred. See Brian Ferguson's summary essay, "Violence and War in Prehistory" in the same volume, pp. 321–55.

Elaborate and extended rituals of torture unto death existed in many of the Eastern Woodland cultures. Scholars continue to struggle to understand their exact meaning, but it is clear that at the center of the process was a tremendous outpouring of violent grief, an outpouring in which the whole town- men, women, and children- participated. Native prisoners were well aware of what awaited them, and sought to remain impassive in the face of excruciatingly inventive torture. Not crying out certified their personal bravery, and some captor tribes sought to partake of that bravery through a ritual cannibalism in which they imbibed the courage and spirit of their prisoner.[81]

The third function of the prisoner was that of the adoptee. Adoption of prisoners may have been less universal than torture, but some incorporation into the captor group, either as kin or as a kind of servant, remained extremely common. Most familiar are the processes most often associated with the nations of the Haudenosaunee confederacy, in which the taking of prisoners in war was designed both to assuage grief and to restock their own population. In this "mourning war" complex Haudenosaunee families adopted prisoners to replace dead kinspeople, while torturing those not selected in a venting of their grief. Daniel Richter, Jose Brandão, and Jon Parmenter have rooted most if not all of the Haudenosaunee wars, particularly of the seventeenth century, in the temporarily successful but ultimately vain pursuit of sufficient prisoners to replace their losses in war and from disease.[82] Prisoner adoption was by no means exclusive to the Haudenosaunee; the process is simply most clearly understood for them. Among other trends it is well known that the demographic disaster of disease and war over the centuries of contact forced many peoples to reconfigure themselves through assimilation of other peoples; included in that process was prisoner adoption or incorporation.[83] In addition, recent scholarship is making increasingly clear that for some nations captives

81 Karen Anderson, *Chain Her by One Foot: The Subjugation of Native Women in Seventeenth-Century New France* (New York: Routledge, 1991), 169–78; Richter, *Ordeal*, 35–36; Hudson, *Southeastern Indians*, 254–55. Hudson also indicates that intertwined with torture as an expression of grief was a spiritual component. That is, torture also served a ritual purpose. Cf. Trigger, *Children*, 1:73–74. For a survey of the different torture rituals see: Knowles, "The Torture of Captives."

82 Brandão, *Your Fyre*, *passim*, 130–131; Richter, "War and Culture"; Jon Parmenter, *The Edge of the Woods: Iroquoia, 1534–1701* (East Lansing: Michigan State University Press, 2010), 103.

83 See, for example: Helen C. Rountree, "The Powhatans and Other Woodland Indians as Travelers," in *Powhatan Foreign Relations, 1500–1722*, ed. Helen C. Rountree (Charlottesville: University Press of Virginia, 1993), 50; Starkey, *European and Native American*, 29–30; James Merrell, *The Indians' New World* (Chapel Hill: University of North Carolina Press, 1989) 30–31; Colin G. Calloway, *New Worlds for All: Indians, Europeans, and the Remaking of Early America* (Baltimore: Johns Hopkins University Press, 1997), 142–51.

could become something much closer to a slave than a replacement relative, even when terms associated with fictive kinship might continue to be used. Brett Rushforth's linguistic analysis of the Anishinaabe-speakers and Miami-Illinois speakers of the Pays d'en Haut, for example, finds a strong sense of captives being degraded as "dogs," being marked by mutilation to indicate their lower status, and even to have been considered individually owned.[84]

The final role of the prisoner was as a source of ransom. Native Americans quickly became aware of the lengths to which European families would go to retrieve prisoners, and the successive imperial wars between France and England from the 1688 to 1763 formalized the process of redemption through ransom. James Axtell has argued that the whole prisoner-taking complex of Indian warfare shifted in response to this economic possibility.[85] Prisoners could still bring honor, but now they brought material reward as well- but only if returned. Adoption or incorporation never disappeared, but was substantially replaced by ransom (until the departure of the French) through the opposite imperial power's good offices.

This over-determined desire for prisoners limited the total level of destructiveness of Indian war.[86] In battle it was difficult to seize a prisoner at all, and if one succeeded, one was unlikely to return to the fray to take another, leaving the first prisoner either unguarded or subject to competitive confiscation by one of his fellow warriors.[87] While some of the prisoners would be tortured to death, others would survive as adoptees (or ransomees) limiting the total lethality of the conflict. Furthermore, the most likely adoptees were women and children, and so the goal of prisoner adoption, if not a generalized revulsion against total war, tended to limit the killing of the defenceless. Finally, and most speculatively, the extremity of torture practiced on individual prisoners

---

84 Brett Rushforth, *Bonds of Alliance: Indigenous and Atlantic Slaveries in New France* (Chapel Hill: University of North Carolina Press, 2013), 35–72. Also Christina Snyder, *Slavery in Indian Country: The Changing Face of Captivity in Early America* (Cambridge, Mass.: Harvard University Press, 2010).

85 Axtell, "White Indians," 59–61.

86 For a good discussion of the various uses of prisoners see Ian K. Steele, "Surrendering Rites: Prisoners on Colonial North American Frontiers," in *Hanoverian Britain and Empire: Essays in Memory of Philip Lawson*, eds. Stephen Taylor, Richard Connors, Clyve Jones, and Philip Lawson (Woodbridge, Suffolk, UK: Boydell Press, 1998), 138–42. Richter argues that the whole nature of Iroquois warfare (reliance on surprise, avoidance of assaulting forts, ritualized battles) was determined by this desire to take prisoners. *Ordeal*, 37–8.

87 Increase Mather, "Quentin Stockwell's Relation of his Captivity and Redemption," in *Puritans among the Indians*, 81; Ian K. Steele, *Betrayals: Fort William Henry & the 'Massacre'* (New York: Oxford University Press, 1990), 121.

may have played a role in limiting the need for further warfare. Since much warfare was originally motivated by a desire for revenge, the lengthy and elaborate rituals of torture practiced on a few individuals supposedly "responsible" for the original death may have forestalled or obviated the need for killing greater numbers of the enemy group.[88]

The logic of taking prisoners and its apparent limitations on overall violence had a flip side, however, and that was the side usually emphasized by Europeans. The targeting of women and children as preferential prisoners for adoption violated European norms of war that nominally (and I stress, nominally) preferred to exempt women and children from the theater of conflict at all.[89] Furthermore, the torture of prisoners, particularly the communal public torture of prisoners, also violated European norms.[90] In John Lawson's otherwise sympathetic description of southern Native American life in 1709, he called it the one thing "they are seemingly guilty of an error in."[91] Finally, the long and difficult return marches after a successful raid, often under pursuit, meant that the captors ruthlessly weeded out the unfit or incapable: in their minds this was a mercy killing to be preferred to slow starvation.[92] The logic of war for prisoners, however, extended beyond this simple calculation of fitness. While in theory a successful surprise of an enemy village could result in hundreds of prisoners, as after the Haudenosaunee capture of St. Ignace in 1649, logistically there was almost no way to guard that many prisoners for the long trip home. Fearing pursuit, and not wanting to release their enemies, the Haudenosaunee on that occasion summarily killed many of their prisoners.[93]

The end of an offensive, however, did not mean the end of hostilities. The resumption of peaceful relations required complex diplomacy. The full range of diplomatic activity and techniques lies beyond the scope of this Chapter, but there are some structures and practices designed to facilitate the process of peacemaking that are worth elaborating here. First, Native Americans typically extended protections over enemy embassies to facilitate the beginning of

---

88 Richter, *Ordeal*, 40.

89 See Samuel White, 'The Late Middle Ages' in Samuel White (ed.) *The Laws of Yesterday's Wars* (Brill NIjhoff, 2021) 101–127.

90 James Axtell, "The Scholastic Philosophy of the Wilderness," in *The European and the Indian: Essays in the Ethnohistory of Colonial North America* (Oxford: Oxford University Press, 1981), 138–50; Wayne E. Lee, *Crowds and Soldiers in Revolutionary North Carolina: The Culture of Violence in Riot and War* (Gainesville: University Press of Florida, 2001), 119–29.

91 John Lawson, *A New Voyage to Carolina* (London: n.p., 1709; reprint, Chapel Hill: University of North Carolina Press, 1967), 207.

92 John Demos, *The Unredeemed Captive* (New York: Vintage Books, 1994), 24, 29, 33, 38–39.

93 JR 34:135–37.

negotiations. We have already seen how the Cherokees' violation of this code in 1715 brought lasting enmity with the Creeks.[94] This fundamental need to allow for the safe passage of negotiators was almost the *sine qua non* of limiting warfare among Europeans, and its role was perhaps even more important in an environment of endemic, revenge-based, warfare.

The attack on the Creek embassy notwithstanding, the more normal protections for diplomatic parties can be seen in the peace negotiations between the Haudenosaunee and the French and their allies in 1644 and 1645. The French-allied Indians released an Haudenosaunee prisoner to return to his people to carry a message about the possibility of peace. Alternatively, a third party could be invoked to serve as an intermediary for this initial and most dangerous establishment of contact.[95] In this case, the Haudenosaunee sent back three negotiators and also released a French prisoner as their own gesture of good faith. The three negotiators were then hosted as eminent guests and treated with more than kindness.[96] Similarly suggestive of the process through which Native American peoples sought to end war was the Pequots' approach to Lion Gardiner's fort on the Connecticut River in 1637, "calling to us to speak with them." Gardiner and a translator went out to negotiate, and the Pequots asked if they had "fought enough." Although no peace was forthcoming at this attempt, both sides obeyed the dictates of the negotiating truce.[97]

Of course the approach of one side asking for peace did not mean that the other had to accept it, but the divide between civil and military authority within a people helped the process of choosing peace. Civil chiefs, especially in those peoples where the civil chief's authority passed through hereditary

---

94 Chicken, "Journal of the March (1715)," 345–46. Roger Williams's dictionary is again helpful in imagining this process, including such phrases as "let us parley" or "let us cease Armes." Williams, *Key into the Language*, 189. See also, JR 70:195.

95 A third party would not be implicated in the ongoing cycle of blood revenge, and therefore could approach the warring sides in greater safety. The English often saw themselves as filling this third party role, but usually for their own economic reasons, since they preferred to trade with all comers. See for example the Pequots appeal to English in 1634. Cave, *Pequot War*, 69–70. Similarly, the Indians sought to use Rhode Island as an intermediary between themselves and the other New England colonies at the outset of King Philip's War. John Easton, "A Relacion of the Indyan Warre," in *Narratives of the Indians Wars, 1675–1699*, ed. Charles H. Lincoln (New York: Charles Scribner, 1913), 8–9.

96 JR 27:246–73. See Richter, *Ordeal*, 41 and Hudson, *Southeastern Indians*, 257 for more details on the peacemaking process.

97 Quotes from Gardiner, "Relation," 131–32 cited in Cave, *Pequot War*, 133. For another example of the protection of embassies, see Rowlandson, *Sovereignty and Goodness*, 102–03, especially where the Wampanoag leadership expressed regret that some "Matchit" [bad] Indian had stolen provisions from the English embassy.

succession, did not have their personal prestige or power vested in successful war.[98] Where the war chiefs, supported by eager young men, might prefer to continue to pursue opportunities for victory, or to overcome recent reverses, those pressures did not apply to the civil chiefs in the same way. The Creeks went so far as to force their White, or peace, chiefs to take an oath that they must always be devoted to the white path of peace and that they must never shed human blood.[99] Furthermore, the ruling council tended to be made up of older men, respected for their wisdom, and already possessed of war honors.[100] Unfortunately, over the course of the colonial era, the power of the war chiefs tended to rise. European traders and diplomats almost invariably conducted negotiations with war chiefs, or younger members of the council who served as spokesmen for the real power behind the curtain.[101] As conductors of those negotiations, they both received the diplomatic gifts presented by the Europeans, and were assumed to be the real authority of the group. European bestowal of titles like "emperor" or "king" did not make it so, but over time this process weakened the influence of the civil and/or religious authority.[102] One can speculate that this decline made it more difficult to move from a state of war to one of peace as dealing with Europeans grew increasingly important.

In a similar way, Europeans affected the role of women within Native societies and their ability to restrain warfare. The political power of women varied widely among Native Americans, but some of the most prominent peoples, including the Haudenosaunee, the Shawnees, and the Cherokees, allotted a substantial political role to women. In many instances their desire

---

98 HNAI 15:314–15; Gleach, *Powhatan's World*, 34–35; Aron, *How the West*, 34.

99 Hudson, *Southeastern Indians*, 223–24.

100 "The Examination of James Quannapaquait," in Rowlandson, *Sovereignty and Goodness*, 124–5; Lafitau, *Customs*, 2:101–3; Calloway, *Western Abenakis*, 172; Saunt, *A New Order*, 23–25.

101 HNAI 15:192, 314–15. One European observer, for example, exactly reversed the real power relationship among the Cherokees: "Every Town has a Head Warrior, who is in great Esteem among them, and whose Authority seems to be greater than their Kings, because their King is looked upon as little else than a Civil Magistrate, except it so happens that he is at the same Time a Head Warrior." Sir Alexander Cuming, "Journal of Sir Alexander Cuming (1730)," in *Early Travels in the Tennessee Country, 1540–1800*, ed. Samuel Cole Williams (Johnson City, Tenn.: The Watauga Press, 1928), 122.

102 Rennard Strickland, *Fire and the Spirits: Cherokee Law From Clan to Court* (Norman: University of Oklahoma Press, 1975), 47–48; Hudson, *Southeastern Indians*, 222; HNAI 15:192, 315; Wallace, *Death and Rebirth*, 40; James Axtell, "Making Do," in *Natives and Newcomers: The Cultural Origins of North America* (New York: Oxford University Press, 2001), 139; Fred Gearing, *Priests and Warriors: Social Structures for Cherokee Politics in the 18th Century* (American Anthropological Association, Memoir 93, 1962); Calloway, *New Worlds for All*, 111. See also the theoretical discussion of this issue in Ferguson, "Violence and War in Prehistory," 336.

for vengeance, to grieve, or to replace their lost kin, could start a war, but in other instances they could prove a driving force to end one.[103] In some ways women could shift more easily from war to peace, since they, like peace chiefs, did not derive their social status or authority from success in war. European failure to understand women's roles, and their preference for dealing with war chiefs in general, helped to undermine the potentially (although not universally) ameliorative role of women.[104] As did European technology, so did European diplomacy upset certain balances within Native societies that had helped to contain the capacity for endemic warfare. Claudio Saunt's comment about the Creeks is more generally applicable: "Though Europeans observed only inconstancy and disorder, Creeks saw a healthy tension between female and male, old and young, and peace and war."[105]

If making peace was difficult, and required a minimal level of trust, keeping the peace was perhaps even harder. Peace was more a temporary lack of hostile feelings, than a permanent, preferred, state of being. According to John Reid, it simply meant less looking over one's shoulder.[106] The elders of the council realized that they could not fully control the desires of their young men to seek glory- and perhaps continued revenge- and thus in their creation of a peace they also had to seek ways to make such adventuring both less likely, and less likely to be successful. One component of the solution was a varying combination of hostages and resident aliens, the latter often created by marriage between peoples. Even to use the word "hostage" is to imply a forced residence among an enemy people that does not always fit. Powhatan, for example, deliberately took in and developed personal attachments to several young Virginia colonists.[107] To the English they were captives or runaways who naturally needed to be restored to their own people. To Powhatan the exchange of people was supposed to be both more lasting and a carrier of information between the two peoples. Powhatan regretted the flight of the English boy Thomas Savage, saying that he was "my child, by the donative of Captain Newport, in lieu of one of my subjects Namontacke, who I purposely sent to King James his land, to see

103 For pushing men to war: Wallace, *Death and Rebirth*, 101; Richter, *Ordeal of the Longhouse*, 60, 224. For pushing an end to war: Saunt, *New Order of Things*, 25; Hudson, *Southeastern Indians*, 187.

104 The role of Europeans in diminishing women's influence within Native societies forms a substantial literature: see Anderson, *Chain Her by One Foot*; Calloway, *New Worlds for All*, 191.

105 Saunt, *New Order of Things*, 25.

106 Reid, *Better Kind of Hatchet*, 10; Richter, *Ordeal*, 40, 44–45.

107 Kupperman, *Indians and English*, 197–99.

him and his country, and to returne me the true report thereof."[108] Englishmen living with the Powhatans served both as hostages at risk in the event of an English attack, but also as sources of information warning Powhatan of such an attack (and thus lessening the likelihood of a highly fatal surprise).[109] The Europeans and the Powhatans were closer to the same understanding of the diplomatic role of marriage, but differed on the details. Both sides clearly saw Pocahontas's marriage to John Rolfe as a marriage of peace, and the English even sought another of Powhatan's daughters for that purpose. Powhatan refused in frustration, pointing out that he only had so many daughters, and that he dealt with many nations.[110]

Marriage, adoption/incorporation, or hostages were not the only ways that visitors were introduced into the villages. It was common practice for members from many nations to live in, or lengthily visit, another people for trading or political reasons. At the simplest level, the presence of visiting Creeks in a Cherokee town, for example, made it less likely that the Creeks would try to attack another Cherokee town for fear of the fate of the visiting Creeks.[111] More systemically, resident aliens or long term visitors maintained interests in both camps. They frequently served as conduits of information between the groups, both formally and informally.[112] Themselves fearing the total destruction of either group in which they now had a vested interest, they warned of impending attacks, preventing the horrifying casualty rates of a successful surprise,

108 Ralph Hamor, *A True Discourse of the Present State of Virginia (1615)* (London: n.p., 1615; reprint New York: Da Capo Press, 1971), 38.

109 Gleach, *Powhatan's World*, 152–54; Rountree, "The Powhatans and Other Woodland Indians," 50.

110 Kupperman, *Indians and English*, 198–99. For a discussion of diplomatic marriages in another context see: Hudson, *Southeastern Indians*, 234. For the broader role of interlocking familial ties helping to keep communications open between peoples, see Stephen Brumwell, *White Devil: A True Story of War, Savagery, and Vengeance in Colonial America* (Cambridge, Mass.: Da Capo Press, 2005), 193–4.

111 Reid, *Better Kind of Hatchet*, 9–10; Cave, *Pequot War*, 157 (for the Pequots' killing of English-allied Mohegans living among them after the disaster at Mystic).

112 Ian K. Steele, "Surrendering Rites," 138; Hatley, *Dividing Paths*, 94; Richter, *Ordeal*, 111; Reid, *Better Kind of Hatchet*, 111; Trigger, *Huron*, 53; Cave *Pequot War*, 66–67; Wayne E. Clark and Helen C. Rountree, "The Powhatans and the Maryland Mainland," in *Powhatan Foreign Relations*, 132. R. Demere to Gov. Lyttelton, July 23, 1757; *idem*, June 26, 1757; White Outerbridge to Gov. Lyttelton, March 8, 1757, all in William Lyttelton Papers, William L. Clements Library, University of Michigan, Ann Arbor. Reid points out, however, that such resident aliens could also be loose cannons, acting on their own needs and thus creating trouble for the community in which they lived. *Law of Blood*, 163–72.

if not derailing an attack completely.[113] Resident aliens could also step into the role of peace negotiator. Lacking the taint of blood revenge, they were a safe choice to send to the enemy to open negotiations. Chanco (or Chauco) who warned Jamestown in 1622, apparently also later served as an emissary from the Powhatans proposing peace, bringing with him a released prisoner.[114] James Quannapaquait and Job Kattananit, both Christian Nipmucs, expected to fulfill this role from their position as resident aliens among the English during King Philip's War. They offered to go to King Philip to "suggest somthing [sic] in order to the enemies submission to the English & making peace if they found the enimy in a temper fit for it."[115] This "resident alien" system is in fact the system into which the Europeans at first fit relatively naturally. Traders and later forts and garrisons were desirable both for their role as conduits for material goods, but also for their certification of good feelings between the two peoples.[116]

IV Escalation

The structures of keeping the peace naturally merged with those which helped to prevent or limit the frequency of war. The first was the Haudenosaunee Confederacy, an elaborate governmental device designed to keep the peace between its five (later six) members (Mohawk, Cayuga, Oneida, Onondaga, Seneca and later Tuscarora). It seems to have originated to quell blood feuds among those groups that at the time were deemed out of control. It was not necessarily designed to conduct diplomacy with outside groups, but to preserve

113 The Jesuit Jean de Brébeuf saw this warning function as the main intent of sending and receiving visitors to and from the village. JR 10:229. See also the warnings passed along by one of Robert Rogers's Indian scouts to the target of Rogers's impending attack. Calloway, *Western Abenakis*, 178. There is a similar example in *Ibid*, p. 212. Karim Tiro has argued in a similar vein for the warnings passed back and forth between the divided members of the Iroquois Confederacy during the American Revolution. Karim M. Tiro, "A 'Civil' War? Rethinking Iroquois Participation in the American Revolution," *Explorations in Early American Culture* 4 (2000): 148–165, and personal communication.

114 Gleach, *Powhatan's World*, 49–53; Kupperman, *Indians and English*, 196.

115 "The Examination of James Quannapaquait," in Rowlandson, *Sovereignty and Goodness*, 120.

116 Lee, "Fortify, Fight, or Flee," 757. The Europeans viewed such "go-betweens" much differently. For an extended treatment of the initial successes and ultimate failures of intermediaries beteen Europeans and Indians see Merrell, *Into the American Woods*. Note, however, that I am treating "resident alien" as a much more specific category than Merrell's "go-betweens."

peace internal to the Confederacy.[117] The second was the ball game, known to posterity as lacrosse. There is some suggestion that inter-tribal lacrosse matches, known as the "little brother of war," may have served as an outlet for young men's aggression, although it did not seem to deal with revenge issues or serve as a substitute for "grand" or national war.[118] But it is important to note that restraint was not necessarily the dominant characteristic of Native American war. Peace chiefs (male or female) might play a role in limiting the resort to war, or help bring a war to a halt, but the more persistent and durable drive was blood revenge reinforced by the desire for personal status. That was the driving circle of Indian war, where one act led to retaliation, and that retaliation demanded yet another response, and so on. Breaking the cycle of vengeance proved extremely difficult in a society ill-suited to top-down coercion.

Nevertheless, if war was endemic, it was also usually conducted on a small scale, and usually without the more destructive goal of outright elimination of an enemy people. Where European warfare of the era was persistent, thorough, and when believed necessary, all-consuming, Native American warfare was usually episodic and personal, with easily satisfied goals, although it was no less fatal than its European counterpart.

As a general rule, the success of systems of restraint depends upon a minimal level of congruence between both sides' understanding of those systems.[119] Over time in North America, Europeans and Native Americans learned about each other, and moved to a certain level of understanding. Diplomacy became possible; intermarriage took place; wars ended. But in a deeper sense neither side ever fully came to terms with the other culture's overall vision of war, and thus never succeeded in meshing their systems of restraint. Failing that, war became more extreme and more destructive.

117 Richter, *Ordeal*, 30–49; Wallace, *Death and Rebirth*, 44–47.

118 Thomas Vennum, *American Indian Lacrosse: Little Brother of War* (Washington, D.C.: Smithsonian Institution Press, 1994).

119 Karr argues in a similar vein about the failure to establish "reciprocity" in "Why Should You Be So Furious," *passim*, esp. 888.

CHAPTER 6

Japanese Laws of War

Anna Kretowicz

1 Introduction

The first thing to observe about the samurai is that they are a group about which there is a dual body of knowledge: fact and fiction. In doing this historical study, one must begin by dispelling a number of incorrect assumptions about the rules that governed them -[1]

1. That samurai ethos derived directly from the values of medieval warriors;
2. That those rules or practices influenced the actions of the early twentieth-century Japanese Imperial Army; and
3. That samurai ethos embodied unflinching, brutal loyalty and an obsession with death.[2]

'Bushidō' was a term that only really gained currency in the Tokugawa period (1603–1867 AD) and wasn't used to denote any behavioural code until the nineteenth century, despite samurai having been around for many centuries prior. Because of that, and the breadth of time over which the samurai existed, this chapter will largely focus on how they acted and were depicted in the Tokugawa period, but with some broader consideration in respect of conduct in battle to appreciate the contrast. As a preliminary point, it has been observed that many of the contemporary texts on the subject should be viewed with a degree of restraint, or at least not taken as entirely historically accurate.[3]

The laws of war of the samurai has been described as 'the way of the warrior', or *bushidō*. It was – and indeed still is – a philosophy or self-discipline

1 Karl Friday, 'Bushidō' in Gordon Martel (ed), *Encyclopedia of War* (Blackwell Publishing Ltd, 2012) vol 1, 1.

2 G Cameron Hurst III, 'Death, Honor and Loyality: The Bushidō Ideal' (1990) 40(4) *Philosophy East and West* 511, 513–4; Karl F Friday, 'Bushidō or Bull? A Medieval Historian's Perspective on the Imperial Army and the Japanese Warrior Tradition' (1994) 27(3) *The History Teacher* 339, 341–2.

3 Hurst (n 2) 515; Friday (n 2) 340; Chris Goto-Jones, '*Bushidō* and Philosophy: Parting the Clouds, Seeking the Way' in Bret W Davis (ed), *The Oxford Handbook of Japanese Philosophy* (Oxford University Press, 2019), 311.

 | DOI:10.1163/9789004473218_008

that regulated the warrior culture of the samurai caste.[4] That is to say, to be a samurai in pre-modern Japan was a way of life (in fact, '*dō*' means 'way', similar to the Greek 'ethos'),[5] whether one was in battle or not. To that end, *bushidō* aimed to balance the civil and martial aspects of personal, social and political organisation so that war wouldn't simply degenerate into aggression. Samurai had to develop and display both moral and intellectual talent and martial supremacy.[6] That all being said, historians have discouraged viewing *bushidō* as a normative system or code of conduct, or a description of the actual behaviour of the samurai.[7]

II Historical Context

This chapter will focus on the samurai as they were in the Tokugawa period (1603–1867 AD), so it is germane to begin with some historical context.

The Tokugawa (or Edo) period corresponds to early modern Japan, distinguishable by the 'daimyō phenomenon' and characterised by significant social and political change.[8] Daimyō were local military lords who were semi-independent regional rulers and had the support of local loyal samurai. They would commonly war among themselves for national hegemony.[9] The transitory moment signifying the beginning of this period was when two lords, Oda Nobunaga (1534–1582 AD) and Toyotomi Hideyoshi (1536–1598 AD) united all daimyō under a single military command, thereby establishing a new shogunate – military government – in Edo. It was this shogunate that saw the period of great peacetime that is so characteristic of the Tokugawa period.[10] The shogun, or chief military commander, was appointed by and answerable to the emperor, although practically he held the balance of power. In this period, the empire was ruled by Emperor Tokugawa Ieyasu and the Tokugawa clan.[11]

---

4 Thomas Cleary, *Samurai Wisdom: Lessons from Japan's Warrior Culture* (Tuttle Publishing, 2009) 9.

5 Damon A Young, 'Bowing to Your Enemies: Courtesy, Budō, and Japan' (2009) 59(2) *Philosophy East and West* 188, 190–1; Goto-Jones (n 3) 308, 310.

6 Cleary (n 4) 9–10.

7 Goto-Jones (n 3) 313.

8 John Whitney Hall, 'Introduction' in John Whitney Hall (ed), *The Cambridge History of Japan* (Cambridge University Press, 1991) vol 4, 1, 3.

9 Michael Wert, 'Tokugawa *Bakufu* Political System' in Louis G Perez (ed), *Japan at War: An Encyclopedia* (ABC-CLIO, 2013) 433; Hall (n 8) 1.

10 Hall (n 8)1.

11 Cleary (n 4)13.

Legally, the Tokugawa period fell within the period of Japanese feudalism, and more specifically it was a time of centralised codified law. The two main sources of law were written feudal laws and customary private law. As to the former, in Tokugawa Japan there were four main sources: *Kuge Hoshiki* (the code for the Imperial Court Nobles, 1615); *Buke Shohatto* and *Shoshi Hatto* (the codes for the warrior classes, 1615 and 1632); *Kosatsu* (the laws for commoners); and the *O-Sadame-Gaki-Hyakkajo* (the 'Edicts of 100 Articles"', which were rules for guidance of the officials on criminal matters).[12]

In contrast to earlier periods, the empire wanted a 'total monopoly on violence' to ensure its continued rule; Maruyama Masao famously described it as a 'garrison state' (*heiei kokka*), in the sense that it was militarily poised and fully armed, so that it could instantly defuse any hint of insurrection or armed rebellion.[13] The difficulty was maintaining this with the daimyō system, because that system had the effect of partially decentralising power and an effective regime therefore depended on amicable cooperation between the shogunate, daimyō and the emperor. Evidencing this concern was the 'one country, one castle' directive issued by the Tokugawa shogunate, which sought to control castles across Japan. Especially in the latter part of this period, castles were symbols of authority but militarily obsolete, because of the near-complete lack of conflict. The shogunate therefore used them to legitimise and delimit the authority of the daimyō who occupied them, by ordering for the destruction of many so that daimyō were limited to one castle each. The 'Code for Warriors Houses' (*Buke shohatto*), published in 1615 AD, declared:

> Whenever it is intended to make repairs on a castle of one of the feudal domains, the [shogunate] authorities should be notified. The construction of any new castles is to be halted and stringently prohibited. 'Big castles are a danger to the state'. Walls and moats are the cause of great disorders.[14]

12 Dan F Henderson, 'Some Aspects of Tokugawa Law' (1952) 27 *Washington Law Review and State Bar Journal* 83, 88, 90.

13 Denis Gainty, 'The New Warriors: Samurai in Early Modern Japan' in Karl F Friday (ed), *Japan Emerging: Premodern History to 1850* (Taylor & Francis, 2012) 345; Maeda Tsutomu, 'Heigaku and Bushidō: Military Thought in the Tokugawa World' in Gary P Leupp and Demin Tao, *The Tokugawa World* (Routledge, 2021) 903.

14 Oleg Benesch and Ran Zwigenberg, *Japan's Castles: Citadels of Modernity in War and Peace* (Cambridge University Press, 2019) 23–4.

This turned out to be an important, and effective, part of the shogunate's strategy to maintain balanced power structures and minimise violence. Relevantly, this was the social and political structure within which samurai operated, and were recruited and promoted. In the Tokugawa period, there were approximately 22,500 samurai, with some 17,000 working within the shogunate's bureaucracy. Perhaps distinct from most other types of warrior cultures, the samurai (at least in the Tokugawa period) had a dual role as both soldiers and civil servants.[15]

III Philosophical Influences on the Bushido Code

Bushidō, being in part a philosophy, is a synthesis of three doctrines: Confucianism, Buddhism and Shinto.[16] Together, they foster a mindset that allowed samurai to remove what was physically and ethically compromising about war and to attain martial perfection.[17]

a *Confucianism*

Classical Confucianism was brought into Japan from Sung China, particularly during the Kamakura period (1192–1333 AD) when increasing overseas trade expanded contact with the continent. It spoke to the samurai in their capacity as civil servants, encouraging the development of leadership skills. The belief system encouraged development of personal character and conduct, and intellectual, emotional and moral abilities. It propounded that duties should be discharged impartially and peacefully, with the aim of gaining the respect of one's peers and people. A key tenet of Confucianism is that humans are essentially social beings.[18] It identified both a sense of personal and communal responsibility, to the extent that people were responsible for their own destiny, rather than deferring to any particular god.

This philosophy manifests in the concern that samurai had for filial piety and loyalty, as well as the belief that their morality was their responsibility. It is particularly apparent in the discussion around conduct in battle and the perception of death.[19]

15 Wert (n 9) 433–4.
16 Cleary (n 4) 10, 28; Young (n 5) 193.
17 Young (n 5) 206; Goto-Jones (n 3) 312–3.
18 Cleary (n 4) 10–11.
19 Young (n 5) 198–9, 200–1.

Classical Confucianism was the dominant form of the philosophy, designated as the official tradition of the warrior class by Oda Nobunaga, one of the most powerful warlords of the Tokugawa period (1536–1598 AD), and a core part of samurai education. To that end, Nobunaga's legal code, *Katto hanto* (*Laws for Eastern Japan*), which was promulgated in 1583, cited the Confucian philosopher Mencius to assert that the social order should be founded on compassion and equality.[20] Characteristic of the samurai was this emphasis on having a strong philosophical grounding for their conduct, so as much as they were taught military skills, they had to have an appreciation of the philosophical underpinnings. Neo-Confucianism also played a role, the feature distinguishing it from Classical Confucianism being that it elevated the ideological status of the social order to that of natural law. It 'cemented its views in the individual by the practice of sustained mental concentration', and that can be seen in many famous bushidō texts.[21] Legalistic Confucianism was the final strand, which was associated with primary production, military power and the rule of law. It operated on the premise that human nature is inherently bad.

However, there was also an underlying tension between Confucianism and the bushidō code. While the former emphasised honesty and transparency, the martial culture of the latter called for, to an extent, deception and inscrutability.[22] Thus, Confucianism could not be the sole source of samurai philosophy.

b *Zen Buddhism*

Like Confucianism, Zen Buddhism became more influential in the Kamakura period. It should be noted that the Zen school is different from the Shingon and Tendai schools, which tended to be preferred by the aristocracy.[23] However, Nobunaga was less welcoming of organised Buddhism, so the Tokugawa leadership legislated strict controls on Buddhist institutions to dampen their independence. The Zen school was particularly popular with samurai because it focused on self-efforts and personal insight (*jiriki*), and it also encouraged them to mingle more with court nobility, as it promoted the importance of scholarship and intellectual development.[24] What this strand of philosophy uniquely contributed to the samurai tradition was what it said about self-transcendence and acceptance of death.[25]

---

20 Cleary (n 4) 14–15.

21 Ibid 14.

22 Ibid 17–18.

23 Ibid 23–24.

24 Marius B Jansen et al, 'Medieval Japan', *Encyclopaedia Britannica* (Web Page, 25 March 2021) <https://www.britannica.com/place/Japan/Medieval-Japan>; Young (n 5) 204.

25 Cleary (n 4) 18; Young (n 5) 202, 204.

Inazō Nitobe (1862–1933 AD), the prominent Japanese statesman and author of *Bushidō: The Soul of Japan*, considered that this philosophy brought 'a sense of calmness in Fate, a quiet submission to the inevitable, that stoic composure in sight of danger or calamity, that disdain of life and friendliness with death'. That mindset of emptiness allowed samurai to become devoid of anger, hate and lust, which supports what the other philosophies required, that battle be humane and respectful.[26]

Buddhism had its own notions of 'just war' – the ethics and legitimacy of using aggressive force against other human beings – but as will become evident, those beliefs don't seem to fully permeate the samurai mentality to regulate their conduct in battle. Buddhism strongly condemns war and conflict, and 'attests to utter futility in gaining a meaningful resolution of any conflict'.[27] Non-violence, or *ahimsa*, is the first of the five precepts in the Buddhist ethical code, and strictly requires the non-injury of living or sentient beings. Buddhism also operates on the presumption against the use of indiscriminate and/or excessive force, and considers that the consequences of actions are relative to the motives and intentions behind them, and the nature of acts performed on whom and how. The preferred method of conflict resolution is conciliation, although there are some examples where Buddhism permits recourse to violence, such as the defence of honour and military aggression propounded by Zen Roshi, Shaku Soen, who was prolific in the 'New Buddhism' movement in the Meiji period (1868–1912 AD).[28] Similarly, Buddhist ethics are generally governed by the principle of moral autonomy, so it was considered that soldiers had full individual responsibility for their actions; nothing could be overridden by 'military necessity'.[29] So although the complete ban on violence and conflict is inconsistent with the samurai tradition, other elements can readily be seen as influential in shaping conduct in battle, particularly the emphasis on personal responsibility and justified action.

c *Shinto*

The final philosophical strand is Shinto, which was a comparatively late development, coming through more in the 17th and 18th centuries. It represents a stronger sense of Japanese national identity and tradition, which was critical to having an orthodox rationale for permanent and stable military rule.[30] For

---

26 Young (n 5) 205.

27 Laksiri Jayasuriya, 'Just War Tradition and Buddhism' (2009) 46(4) *International Studies* 423, 428.

28 Ibid 429–30.

29 Ibid 428–9.

30 Cleary (n 4) 25; Young (n 5) 193–4.

example, the notable philosopher and military strategist Yamaga Sokō (1622–1685 AD) insisted on referring to Japan as the 'Central Civilisation' or 'Central Nation', in contrast to somewhere like China, which was a foreign country.[31] The greatest virtue this philosophy propounded, apart from a strong sense of nationalism, was sincerity of self or purity. This would derive from having a very intense focus on things and a lack of contradiction in one's beliefs. It manifested in the martial arts for samurai as sincerity in action[32] – arguably evident in the 'anything goes' attitude to battle, as will be discussed later.

Nitobe considered that Shintoism imported '[s]uch loyalty to the sovereign, such reverence for ancestral memory, and such filial piety as are not taught by any other creed … imparting passivity to the otherwise arrogant character of the samurai'.[33] Shintoism, as a belief system, asserted the innate goodness of the human soul and focussed on the loyalty element of bushidō. Together with its emphasis on nationalism and sincerity in action, it can be seen how it provided a strong philosophical foundation to guide warrior behaviour.

IV Goals of Warfare

a *Samurai in the Social Order*

To elucidate the goals of samurai warfare, the proper role of the samurai in Japanese society must first be understood; the socio-political climate of Tokugawa Japan was crucial to shaping their approach to and justifications for battle – when it occurred. This is important because it is suggested that it takes the samurai conception of war beyond the classic Western dichotomy of *jus ad bellum* and *jus in bello*. Rather, samurai theories of just warfare relied more heavily on Chinese, particularly Confucian, principles. Tracing back to medieval Japan, Friday observes that the Imperial court viewed warfare with foreign powers and peoples 'as an extension of domestic law enforcement and justified it accordingly'.[34] Looking through to the Tokugawa period, this emphasis on domestic policy did not seem to change; the Imperial rulers remained

31 Cleary (n 4) 25.

32 Young (n 5) 195–6.

33 Inazō Nitobe, 'Bushido: The Soul of Japan', *Project Gutenberg* (eBook, 21 April 2004) <https://www.gutenberg.org/files/12096/12096-h/12096-h.htm>.

34 Karl Friday, 'Might Makes Right: Just War and Just Warfare in Early Medieval Japan' in Torkel Brekke (ed), *The Ethics of War in Asian Civilizations: A Comparative Perspective* (Taylor & Francis Group, 2005), 160–1.

concerned with internal peace, rather than managing external conflicts and expanding the domain of their rule.

To contextualise, samurai first appeared in the eighth century in the Heian period (794–1185 AD) following a shift in Imperial court military policy. They held a 'near-monopoly' on arms and armed combat until the 12th century, when Minamoto Yoritomo (1147–1199 AD) created the shogunate – the military government, distinct from the emperor and sovereign rule.[35] But while the samurai existed, they were better conceptualised as private warriors serving the court rather than a public military force. This was important socio-political context for the samurai, because Japan at this time was characterised by a general and gradual privatisation of government functions. That supported the samurai developing their identity as an order of private, organised warriors but also with an element of civil service.[36]

At the same time, the organisation of the public military force was reformed (influenced by Tang China) so that it was controlled by the emperor and supervised by the court. The Ministry of Military Affairs (*Hyōbushō*) administered the armed forces at a central level and delegated to governors in the provinces. There were two guiding principles: first, central control and direction of all military affairs; and secondly, public conscription (relating to all free male subjects aged between 20 and 59, other than rank-holding nobles and those unfit for duty).[37] Conscripted men were largely peasants. However, the regimental system was abolished in 792 AD because provincial officials and regimental officers were found to have been abusing the system and using conscripts for their private labour since around 719 AD. The government considered that it would be more efficient to rely on privately trained and equipped elites instead, and that was an important shift that helped define the samurai.[38] However, no guidelines for drafting or raising troops emerged once that system had been abolished; the samurai remained largely a privately-run group, operating in accordance with private chains of command. The concept of privatisation, though, put a gloss on military service as a path to the civil service and aristocracy, a duality that persisted throughout the samurai existence.[39]

---

35 Friday (n 1) 1.

36 Karl F Friday, 'The Dawn of the Samurai' in Karl F Friday (ed), *Japan Emerging: Premodern History to 1850* (Taylor & Francis Group, 2012), 178–9.

37 Friday (n 36) 180.

38 Friday (n 36) 182; Friday and Humitake, *Legacies of the Sword: The Kashima-Shinryū and Samurai Martial Culture* (University of Hawai'i Press, 1997) 13; Karl Friday, 'Valorous Butchers: The Art of War During the Golden Age of the Samurai' (1993) 5(1) *Japan Forum* 1, 2.

39 Friday (n 36) 183, 185, 187.

The Tokugawa period, which demarcated the transition from medieval to early modern Japan, was a significant period of institutional change for the samurai. Medieval warriors were more flexible and permeable as a group and were more true warriors, in the sense that most of the time they were engaged in battle. Early modern samurai, by contrast, were a 'legally defined, legally privileged, hereditary class' and were clearly separate from the peasants. This was consistent with the Tokugawa period as a time of relative peace, but resulted in a sort of 'samurai identity crisis'.[40] The samurai were 'codified as an elite and exclusive social class', but because the shogunate was rebellion-averse, they had to grapple with justifying that position without reference to military operations as a significant part of their activities.[41] That is not to say that samurai always had a clear-cut warrior role. In medieval Japan, they were still a relatively flexible and permeable group as they served individual daimyō across the provinces and operated in a feudal hierarchy. It is true that they were primarily fighters, but their duties in serving their lord would also go beyond that.[42]

Under the Tokugawa regime, samurai constituted around six per cent of the total population. Within that group, there were different classifications or types of samurai. This was quite a strict order, which reinforced the samurai as a hereditary class:

- *Hatamoto* ('bannermen' or 'liege vassals'), who were wealthy warriors that served the Tokugawa clan – that is, the Imperial family – directly;
- *Gokenin* ('house men'), who were less privileged warriors in the clan's employ; and
- *Rōnin* ('wave men'), who were free-floating and deprived of land and status because they served daimyō who had no title.[43]

In the broader social order, samurai were part of the *shi* ('gentlemen') class, as they were considered scholarly and well-read in Confucian teachings, and in that sense, an example for the rest of society. So, despite the aforementioned narrower classifications, samurai were all expected to comport themselves in the same way.[44] Additionally, because their occupation was not predominantly military-focussed, from the Tokugawa period onward they were more

40 Friday (n 1) 2; Cleary (n 4) 30. See further Oleg Benesch, *Inventing the Way of the Samurai: Nationalism, Internationalism, and Bushidō in Modern Japan* (Oxford University Press, 2014) 35–42.

41 Gainty (n 13) 344–5; Friday (n 2) 340.

42 Friday (n 1) 2.

43 Gainty (n 13) 346; see also Wert (n 9) 434.

44 Gainty (n 13) 347–8.

commonly employed in the civil service and in administrative or bureaucratic positions, such as tax collectors and census takers, managers of households and economic advisers.[45] This allowed for some resolution of the identity crisis, because samurai could justify their relatively elite position by reference to these new roles in society. They cultivated their knowledge through education and worked in essential roles within the government. As a class, the samurai carved out a new niche for themselves as the learned 'all-rounders', where their way of living and their mentality became something that required training, in a sense, and therefore became their new duty. As will be discussed, legislation was a useful tool for the Tokugawa shogunate to entrench this class difference.[46] Consequently, the concept of class became an important lens through which the samurai and their 'rules' of warfare can be understood. But that is not to say it is flawless; changing economic conditions in the Tokugawa period and the gradual poverty of some samurai meant that concepts like 'class' and 'status' were not always as clearly applicable.[47]

The status as a samurai was also meaningful in other ways, because the group retained benefits like the right to carry two swords and the right to kill non-samurai (known as *kirisute gomen* or *bureiuchi*, literally meaning 'pardon for cutting and throwing away').[48] The latter right reflects the importance of hierarchy in Tokugawa Japan, more so than having any military utility. That the military prevailed over the civilian class was a basic precept of Tokugawa law, which was exacerbated by the fact that the government was dominated by the military. The law of *kirisute gomen* reflected the belief that farmers, townsmen and peasants were not just inferior, but existed for the military class.[49]

After the Tokugawa period came the Meiji Restoration (1867–1868 AD), which was another significant historical event for the samurai; it is considered to signal the end of them as a class. They lost their monopoly on military activity, were stripped of badges, privileges and status, and the Japanese army shifted its constitution and operation to the more westernised form that it approximates now. While the samurai as a group still held great political sway – still working in government positions – in practice, they were more 'homesteaders', in that they were encouraged to give up their weapons and develop a more self-sufficient, agricultural lifestyle.[50]

---

45 Ibid 348; Friday and Humitake (n 38) 42–3.

46 Benesch (n 40) 18.

47 Ibid 18–19. See further Kozo Yamamura, 'The Increasing Poverty of the Samurai in Tokugawa Japan, 1600–1868' (1971) 31(2) *The Journal of Economic History* 378.

48 Gainty (n 13) 350–1.

49 Henderson (n 12) 95.

50 Friday (n 1) 3–4; Gainty (n 13) 353–4.

From that point on, the concept of bushidō was developed in popular discourse and most of the texts that historians rely on nowadays to understand the samurai were written in the Tokugawa period and onward. This is problematical, in that the authors of these texts that propounded bushidō discourse tended to romanticise it and the samurai class. The scholarship has even been characterised as a 'selective nostalgia' of earlier times, involving an idealisation of the samurai as an exclusive class and portraying their entire being as dictated by loyalty and clear martial and ethical canons. Some of the texts even explicitly limited their scope to certain domains or samurai families.[51] As the discourse of bushidō developed, it also became a general attitude adopted by the Japanese population, in that it was sold as the 'essence of Japaneseness itself'.[52] For example, Nitobe wrote that all Japanese people were warriors at heart.[53] Acknowledging these difficulties, this chapter will nonetheless consider the texts insofar as they apply to Tokugawa Japan.

b *Public vs Private*

Japanese warfare fell into one of two categories: public or private.

Public warfare was the dominant form of conflict in early and medieval Japan. At that time, conflict was largely externally focussed and the court was hesitant to engage in internal warfare. Any warfare or battles tended to demarcate historical eras and signify broader change. For example, the efforts to pacify parts of north-Eastern Honshu in the late 7th to early 9th centuries were done with the goal of controlling the criminals and rebels in that region, and Emperor Go-Daigō waged a civil war from 1331–1333 AD to found the Kenmu regime and overturn the Kamakura regime.[54] Any conflict, therefore, had to be sanctioned by the state in advance, and that attitude persisted until the 14th century.[55] The reality of the Tokugawa peace meant that public warfare on this scale was virtually non-existent.

More significantly for the Tokugawa period, battle could be pursued for private reasons, which related to a samurai's political status and their dual role as military officers and civil bureaucrats. Because war could be allegedly waged in pursuance of honour, vengeance or loyalty, the battles were smaller-scale and

51 Benesch (n 40) 16–18.

52 Friday (n 1) 4; see also E Taylor Atkins, '*Bushidō*' in Louis G Perez (ed), *Japan at War: An Encyclopedia* (ABC-CLIO, 2013) 46.

53 Gainty (n 13) 353–4.

54 See Friday (n 34) 161; Friday (n 2) 346.

55 Friday (n 34) 161; Thomas D Conlan, 'Medieval Warfare' in Karl F Friday (ed), *Japan Emerging: Premodern History to 1850* (Taylor & Francis Group, 2012) 244.

reflected the decentralised and feudal organisation of the samurai. Viewed this way, however, it is questionable whether the term 'warfare' is accurate, given its connotations of large, organised armies going into battle in pursuance of a larger, often common, goal. The majority of samurai activity in the Tokugawa period may therefore more accurately be described as conflicts, but the question that this chapter explores – how that was regulated – remains the same. There is evidence of privately justified conflict across multiple periods,[56] not just the Tokugawa, and it could be justified in five ways.

First, where it had been sanctioned by some higher authority. This is evident from an anecdote involving Minamoto Yorinobu in around 990 AD: 'Yorinobu was a retainer of [Fujiwara Michikane]. Now and then he would say, "If I were to be ordered by my lord to kill [his rival, Michitaka], I would take up my sword and run to his home; who could defend him against me?" When [Yorinobu's father] Yorimitsu heard this, he was greatly surprised, and restrained Yorinobu, saying, "In the first place, the likelihood of successfully killing him would be exceedingly small. In the second place, even if you were to succeed, this evil deed would prevent your lord from becoming Chancellor. In the third place, even if he were to become Chancellor, you would have to protect him unerringly for the rest of his life, which would be all-but impossible".'[57]

The second reason was to pursue and protect one's personal honour,[58] which as will be discussed, was both a justification for conflict and a regulating force of samurai conduct. The third reason was in the name of filial piety and family honour – the latter being a slightly broader concept – where the idea was to avenge minor slights against family members. Fourthly, and less commonly, it could be a response to overt attempts of self-aggrandisement. Finally, samurai could be drawn into battle by virtue of their service to their vassals or retainers.[59] To an extent, the fifth reason is similar to the first, where the higher authority that the samurai was answering to was their lord.

A good example from the Tokugawa period, which illustrates most, if not all, of these justifications, is the Akō Incident of 1703 AD, considered to be a 'fulcrum for attempts to excavate a Japanese warrior ethic'.[60] It began when the lord of the Akō domain, Asano Naganori (1667–1701 AD), drew his sword

56 Conlan (n 55) 245.

57 Kobayashi Yasuharu (ed), *Kojidan: Koten bunko* (Gendai shichosa, 1981) vol 60-62, tale #317.

58 Eiko Ikegami, 'Shame and the Samurai: Institutions, Trusthworthiness, and Autonomy in the Elite Honor Culture' (2003) 70(4) *Social Research* 1351, 1359–60.

59 Friday (n 34) 164.

60 Benesch (n 40) 23.

and lightly wounded Kira Yoshinaka (1641–1703 AD), the shogunate's chief protocol officer, in the course of an imperial ceremony. Asano was arrested for the crime of drawing his sword in the castle and condemned to *seppuku*. His domain was confiscated by the shogunate, leaving his retainers as masterless samurai. Nearly two years later, approximately 47 of these samurai, under the leadership of Ōishi Yoshio (1659–1703 AD) attacked Kira's residence in Edo and beheaded him. The head was taken to Asano's grave, where 46 of the samurai notified the shogunate and apparently calmly awaited arrest. They were all sentenced to death by *seppuku*.[61]

While the evidence is not clear on the reasons for the original feud between Asano and Kira and there is significant scholarly debate about the incident in general, there is more evidence to support that, regarding the attack on Kira's mansion, the Akō samurai were motivated by vengeance for the death of Asano and considered themselves to be fulfilling their samurai duty. Viewed in this simplistic way, it is therefore a classic example of a revenge killing, underpinned by concepts of honour and loyalty. The reality of the Tokugawa system, though, is that it was essentially peaceful, and the Akō Incident is unique.[62] Accepting that, and the debate surrounding the Incident, it is suggested that this displays merely some justifications for battle rather than a consistent and clear warrior ethic.

v Means and Methods of Warfare

a *Conduct Outside Battle*

The samurai teachings were passed down in a number of ways: orally, practically, and through text, although the emergence of the samurai pre-dates when we see the first texts.

The first texts date from the mid-13th century and were written by Hojo Shigetoki (1191–1261 AD). These outlined advice on navigating the court and Kamakura politics, how to handle retainers and allies, the importance of maintaining military reputation, and etiquette.[63] So, it can be seen that the 'way of the warrior' was not just focussed on the military aspect but extended to general conduct. Other texts, called house precept texts, also circulated, but were directed towards warrior aristocrats (as opposed to warriors in battle). They advised the warrior as a ruler, balancing military prowess and statesmanship

61 Ibid 24.
62 Ibid 24–28.
63 Friday (n 1) 1–2.

(‘*bunbu ryodo*’, or the twin path of military and civil arts), and the ‘warrior ceremonial’ of how to care and maintain for weapons and etiquette.[64]

The *bun-bu* binary continued into the Tokugawa period and has been suggested to be a more useful concept for understanding samurai thought and motivations, rather than looking to concepts like honour, vengeance and loyalty as justifications for battle.[65] It had two defining characteristics in the Tokugawa period: a shift away from the practical to the metaphysical, and its use as a political or philosophical binary rather than a civil-martial dichotomy. Confucian scholar Nakae Tōju (1608–1648 AD) likened it to *yin* and *yang*, writing that '[*b*]*un* is correctly practising the way of filial piety, brotherliness, loyalty, and trustworthiness. *Bu* is striving to eliminate things that obstruct filial piety, brotherliness, loyalty, and trustworthiness'.[66] Tōju’s conception affirms that the Tokugawa samurai had a more cerebral and less bloodthirsty understanding of loyalty and honour that guided their actions, but it also suggests that honour and loyalty were nonetheless important and manifested in ways other than through violence. Indeed, that the concepts of *bun* and *bu* were intertwined, like *yin* and *yang*, indicates a belief that one could not have martial prowess without a sense of peace.

Interestingly, the concepts of *bun* and *bu* were largely criticised by the end of the Tokugawa period, because scholars from different schools of thought each had their own beliefs about the proper balance of *bun* and *bu* and how samurai should practise it in a time of peace. So while the *bun-bu* dichotomy is useful to understanding samurai thought in the Tokugawa period, the most that can be said is that there was broad consensus on the importance of maintaining a balance between *bun* and *bu*. To that extent, it should not be oversold as representing a unified samurai ethic.[67]

Most of the texts that we know nowadays, and consider as emblematic of the samurai, actually arose from the Tokugawa period and were instrumental in grappling with the ‘samurai identity crisis’, because they looked to justifying the samurai’s place in society when there were no longer any real wars to fight. Prominent texts include *Hagakure, Budō shoshinshū, Shidō,Yōjōkun,* Nitobe’s *Bushidō: The Soul of Japan.* [68] Friday identifies three key observations from those texts -

64 Ibid 2.
65 Benesch (n 40) 29.
66 Ibid 30.
67 Ibid 34.
68 Friday (n 1) 3; Atkins (n 52) 44; Gainty (n 13) 351-2; Young (n 5) 190; Hurst (n 2) 521.

1. First, the term 'bushidō' was rarely used before the 20th century, perhaps mostly attributable to Nitobe's, *Bushidō: The Soul of Japan* (written in 1899).
2. Secondly, even as a historiographic term, bushidō identifies a "'vast array of competing ideas' rather than a single, identifiable code of conduct – and in that way, similar to terms like 'masculinity' and 'femininity'.
3. Thirdly, few of the ideas that emerged from this debate actually derived from the behavioural norms of samurai warriors in earlier times.

Further, the texts also each take slightly different views on what the 'way of the warrior' means, but a common thread is that there was always a balance between the civil and military identity of the samurai. While the scope of this chapter is not to conduct an in-depth analysis of each text, it is germane to summarise what each depicted bushidō as. Yamaga Sokō, author of *Shidō*, focussed on the samurai's responsibility to exhibit moral conduct to commoners; Yamamoto Tsunetomo, author of *Hagakure*, considered mental preparation for meeting death without hesitation and etiquette and good manners,[69] and Kaibara Ekken, author of *Yōjōkun*, wrote on the proper observance of ritual hierarchy and the importance of study. Although having their differences, there was a common thread ofselflessness.[70] An illustrative extract, showing the emphasis on 'martial virtues' is when Ekken wrote:

> Warriorhood has roots and branches. Loyalty, filial piety, duty, and courage are the roots of military science; these are martial virtues. Discipline and strategy are military sciences. Discipline refers to the disposition of troops and the way to carry out a military campaign, or what is referred to as martial law. The techniques of weaponry, such as sword, archery, spear, and so on, are the branches of military science; these are martial arts. It is best to include both roots and branches. Martial arts are rooted in military science, military science is rooted in humanity and justice. It is imperative to know these three elements, understand their order, and know their relative importance.[71]

Similarly, Nitobe identified eight key characteristics of the samurai. These traits were considered essential to samurai in their general behaviour, but also carried across to when they were engaged in conflict.

69 Young (n 5) 189.
70 Atkins (n 52) 44–5; see also Goto-Jones (n 3) 322–4.
71 Cleary (n 4) 16–17.

Nitobe, also conceptualised of bushidō as an ethical system. He said: '*Bushi-do* means literally Military-Knight-Ways – the ways which fighting nobles should observe their daily life as in their vocation; in a word, the 'Precepts of Knighthood', the *noblesse oblige* of the warrior class'. This text is considered as having taught the West about bushidō, but Hurst identifies it as problematic to that extent. Nitobe wasn't a very good 'bridge' between the East and West because he had a very shallow understanding of the culture, history and literature behind the movement. This text therefore tends to be ultra-nationalistic and misleadingly suggests that bushidō was a binding code.[72]

Tsunetomo's *Hagakure* famously opens with a line equating the way of the samurai with finding death and set the tones for behavioural guidelines as such. However, that was based on an idealised view of warfare and an over-emphasis on the relative importance of samurai within the overall class structure. Tsunetomo considered that samurai were innately superior to others because of their dedication to the military craft.[73] Gainty suggests that Tsunetomo's *Hagakure* 'is best understood not as a coherent code for samurai conduct, but as a bitterly nostalgic critique of the overly philosophised, rationalised, and domesticated role of samurai in Tokugawa Japan, set against Yamamoto's own wistful depiction of the "good old days"'.[74] However, that did not stop it from being one of the most influential texts of the Tokugawa period.

Sokō also wrote *The Way of the Samurai*, which similarly took an exalted view of the samurai. He endorsed the duality of their duty: to be outwardly prepared through their military training, especially swordsmanship, and to be inwardly prepared by constant reflection and a focus on what is ethical and moral behaviour. Time to do the latter, in particular, was what Sokō considered justifiably separated the samurai from farmers, artisans and merchants. 'The Way' was said to be a samurai's exclusive duty.[75] Sokō wrote: 'Within his heart [the samurai] keeps to the ways of peace, but without he keeps his weapons ready for use'. Appreciating that Sokō was likely exaggerating to an extent and not necessarily describing, but idealising, samurai practice, this nonetheless supports the notion that samurai never stopped considering themselves as warriors, and had to temper it during periods of relative peacetime.[76]

Stepping back from what each text individually says about bushidō, the essential point is that the thought landscape was complex and nuanced.[77]

72 Hurst (n 2) 512–13.
73 Benesch (n 40) 21.
74 Gainty (n 13) 352. See also Goto-Jones (n 3) 324.
75 Ibid 21–22.
76 Friday and Humitake (n 38) 2.
77 Goto-Jones (n 3) 324.

While the texts portray it as a uniform mentality, the reality of being a samurai was highly dependent on social, cultural and economic factors. It can also be understood that the way of the warrior was ritualistic in the sense that there was a great emphasis on teaching and self-cultivation – at least from the Tokugawa period onwards.

Turning now to samurai training, there were four words used to describe the traditional military disciplines: 'bugei', '*hyōhō*' (or *heihō*), '*budō*', and '*bujutsu*' – meaning a generic term for fighting arts, strategy, and the warrior's way, respectively.[78] Samurai trained and developed their skills in a more organised fashion in 'bugei schools' (*ryūha*) – the oldest, for example, is the Kashima-Shinryu which was founded in the 15th century, but more were developed after this period. These schools claimed to foster both physical fighting skills and to support samurai fulfilling their human potential, the latter done through incorporation of music, painting, calligraphy and tea ceremonies. Physical training was considered the first step, because it prepared the body to be the receptacle for the teachings on the intuition and spirit. This is consistent with Buddhist influences on samurai thought, which stressed that the physical practice alone could never lead to true mastery; it had to be complemented by a sound doctrinal understanding.[79]

Bugei schools provided a means for the systematic passing down of knowledge.[80] As they became more 'institutionalised' throughout the Tokugawa period, they would issue diplomas and licenses to students to mark when they were considered to have mastered the teachings. There were some 700 schools and while each was unique in terms of its organisation, history, strategy, philosophy and technique, it is suggested that there is enough similarity that understanding the nature and functioning of one can allow for reasonably accurate interpolation about the others.[81]

Overall, this highly structured and rigorous style of training ensured a perpetual readiness for battle. To be a samurai, or at least an ideal samurai, was a state of being. Samurai did not train for battle as such, they trained for their existence. This mentality was reflected in certain pedagogical texts that the samurai were required to study when training in the ryūha. The *Ryū no maki* ('Dragon's Scroll'), an example from the Kashima-Shinryu tradition, said: 'Men wear swords. Although they proclaim this to be distinct from using them, there are none who are completely outside the need for military readiness. Those

78 Friday and Humitake (n 38) 7.

79 Ibid 100–1, 139.

80 Ibid 3–4, 14–15, 58–9; see further 55–6.

81 Ibid 9–10, 51.

who fail to learn this are ignorant of combat'.[82] To truly master the art of being the warrior was when you could perform your best 'at any time, in any place, and under any circumstances'.[83] Again, this reflects the philosophical influences. Zen Buddhists believed in working towards a state of 'oneness of body and mind' (*shinshin ichinyo*) or 'congealing of body and mind' (*shinshin gyōnen*), because superseding the dichotomy was the way to enhance your physical performance.[84]

b *Conduct in Battle*

The Mindset

The other side of the coin of samurai teachings is that the behaviours samurai practiced outside of conflict also governed how they were to act in conflict. But importantly, there was a clear division between medieval and early modern battle styles. At least in medieval Japan, the religious establishment was highly fragmented across many schools and sects, so there was no uniformity in the teaching of ethics of warfare.[85]

Early sources – chronicles and literary tales, such as *Hogen monogatari, Heiji monogatari, Heike monogatari* – focussed on the warriors' preoccupation with reputation and personal honour. For the most part, military conduct was deeply entwined with a concern for one's reputation.[86] Samurai texts would also describe it as ritualistic or formalistic, but as already discussed, this is suggested to be more the product of creative nostalgia; Kamakura and Heian warriors, at least, were much more 'anything goes' in their fighting style in the pursuit of honour.[87] Friday observed that 'medieval Japanese concepts of honor and honorable conduct in battle were flexible enough to permit successful warriors to rationalize almost any sort of behaviour'.[88]

For example, there was a clan of samurai called the Aizu samurai, who fought for the Tokugawa shogunate in the Edo period. The first clause of the Aizu Creed (1668 AD) read: 'Always serve the shōgun with single-minded loyalty and never conduct yourselves by the examples of other domains'.[89]

---

82 Ibid 145–7.
83 Ibid 152.
84 Ibid 152–3.
85 Friday (n 34) 175.
86 Friday (n 1) 1; Ikegami (n 58) 1353, 1358–9.
87 Friday (n 34) 167–8; Friday (n 38) 1, 15.
88 Friday (n 1).
89 Guohe Zheng, 'Aizu Samurai Spirit' in Louis G Perez (ed), *Japan at War: An Encyclopedia* (ABC-CLIO, 2013) 4.

The corollary of honour and reputation was shame (*haji*), an important concept for samurai. It covered both external honorific status and a sense of personal pride and dignity – at least what we understand from the famous samurai Yoshida Shōin's writings (1830–1859 AD). In that way, it was never a passive emotion purely about failing to conform to external expectations. Samurai always ultimately respected decisive action and moral autonomy, a sort of 'honorific individualism'.[90] Pertinently, Shōin wrote that '[s]hame (*haji*) is the most important word in a samurai's vocabulary. Nothing is more shameful than not understanding shame'. Further, '[o]n one occasion, someone asked me: Which is more serious, crime (*tsumi*) or shame (*haji*)? I answered: Crime belongs to the body, but shame lies in the soul'. It should be noted, however, that Shōin's writing was heavily influenced by the Tokugawa period, where vassal samurai were directly loyal to their daimyō.[91] To that extent, it may display an abnormal level of concern with loyalty and overstate the level of shame for any breaches of it.

So understood, the concepts of loyalty and shame appear consistent with the element of Buddhist ethics, particularly as described by Shaku Soen, that violence may be justified in some circumstances. Soen specifically identified Zen Buddhist ethics as consistent with the samurai culture and Japanese spirit.[92] Where personal reputation or loyalty called for protection, recourse to violence was permitted. Conflict, a very physical phenomenon, seemed a justifiable remedy for the contrastingly cerebral and internal feeling of shame.

Later sources, notably the texts arising in the early modern period, placed much greater emphasis on the concepts of honour, loyalty, courtesy and benevolence as conditioning samurai conduct. Relevantly, courtesy can be seen as encompassing all the concepts of respect, deference, sensitivity and tact; it was about recognising others and overcoming self-interest.[93] For example, Nitobe considered that chivalry was central to Japanese warfare and samurai behaviour. He wrote: 'If military interests had operated alone, without higher moral support, how far short of chivalry would the ideal of knighthood have fallen!' That indicates that honour served an important purpose, being to provide a moral foundation for what was presumably otherwise considered an immoral action.

That being said, modern scholars have been cautious to not overstate the importance of loyalty. Friday observed that the early focus on loyalty reflected

90 Ikegami (n 58) 1351–2, 1357–8. See also Tsutomu (n 13) 908.
91 Ikegami (n 58) 1353, 1356.
92 Jayasuriya (n 27) 430.
93 Young (n 5) 188–190.

basic tenets of Confucianism and was a focus in government before the samurai emerged. And in any case, they were more aspirational/normative than a documentation of actual behaviour: 'In practice, samurai loyalty was a commodity predicated on adequate remuneration, not an obligation transcending self-interest, and warriors were reliable only in proportion to their dependence'.[94] So, all of what is said must be taken with a degree of restraint.

The notion of respect also conditioned battle tactics. For example, there was a tactic called *gekokujō* ('lower attacking the higher'), illustrated by the Mei'ō coup d'etat, which arose out of a dispute over a line of succession to the empire.[95] So even though conflict was all-or-nothing in a way, it was still structured and not a complete 'free for all'. Respect also took on greater significance in the early modern period, as the samurai began to function in a near-exclusively peaceful environment. Coming back to what was taught in the bugei, the Kashima-Shinryu school considered that the highest form of martial and moral power (*shinbu*) was *tatazu-no-kachi* ('victory without a stand'). That meant to diffuse a confrontation without recourse to physical violence. Similarly, samurai were encouraged to 'become one with the opponent', in that they should embrace them and flow with their physical movements. And even when they won, if they had to 'defeat' an enemy, they should 'delight naught in the unavailing joy of felling an enemy, of destroying evil'.[96]

Finally, coming back to the underlying philosophical influences, the samurai operated on the basis that there was a path to ultimate spiritual attainment or enlightenment. The commonality between the three – Buddhism, Shintoism and Confucianism – was a 'totalistic notion of human perfection'. This self-cultivation was considered to enhance the samurai's fighting ability, because a focussed and trained mind allowed them to overcome physical fear and therefore be undistracted in battle.[97]

Taken together, that battle was conditioned by loyalty, respect, honour and the like – whatever the time period – consistently allowed samurai to approach it from a place of moral detachment. Samurai were, in that way, instrumental; they facilitated the events of war and battle, but were not considered individually responsible for deaths, casualties and other outcomes.[98] This takes on some significance, and has great explanatory power, when we look at how samurai treated non-combatants and prisoners of war.

94 Friday (n 1) 3.
95 Conlan (n 55) 250.
96 Friday and Humitake (n 38) 64–7.
97 Ibid 15–1 7.
98 Ibid 67.

The Weaponry

The Tokugawa period saw fundamental changes to combat. Because it was a period of relative peacetime, samurai were more likely to engage in duels and street brawls wearing ordinary clothing, rather than full armour, and the sword was the primary weapon, as opposed to the spears and bows from earlier periods,[99] or guns. Fighting without armour required a shift in tactics and battle style.[100] This can be seen in what the bugei schools taught. Friday and Humitake explored the Kashima-Shinryu school, which again serves an example that can be generalised from. The bugei schools not only taught with slightly different weapons from what was used in earlier periods, but more broadly, they taught in a structured and organised manner; a marked change from the privately trained warriors of the earlier periods.

The Kashima-Shinryu bugei taught twelve military disciplines, divided into two broad groups: the omote (outside) arts, consisting of kenjutsu (swordsmanship), battō-jutsu (sword drawing), *naginata-jutsu* (use of the *naginata*), sōjutsu (spearmanship), *kenjutsu-tachiai* (use of the sword against other weapons) and *shuriken-jutsu* (use of throwing darts); and the ura (inside) arts, including jūjutsu (grappling), *kenpō* (striking and kicking), *bōjutsu* (use of the long staff), *jōjutsu* (use of the short staff), *kaiken-jutsu/tanto-jutsu* (use of knives and short swords) and *tasuki-dori/hōbaku-jutsu* (tying or binding an opponent). Although separated in these two categories, each drew upon the other and had to be combined to form a single budo.[101] In addition, particular techniques were taught, such as[102] –

- *Nukiuchi* ('extricating strike') techniques aimed at 'silent victory' (*otonashi-no-kachi*), where one defeated their opponent without blocking or striking his weapon with one's own
- *Ichi-no-tachi* (roughly translating to number one sword stroke), which was a very subtle sword technique that, if performed properly, was virtually impossible to counter – based on the swordsman's timing, the position to which he stepped, and the angle at which he strikes
- *Katsujin-ken*, a concept that involved drawing out the opponent, inducing him to strike, and then going inside his technique, countering it either at the moment of its origination or at its most complete extension. Compare this to *setsunin-tō*, which was considered much more 'egostic and risky' and focused on using force of will to overpower, immobilise and strike down an

99 Friday (n 38) 3–6, 12–13.
100 Friday and Humitake (n 38) 15.
101 Ibid 61–2.
102 Ibid 23, 27, 31, 45.

opponent before he can react – there was the risk that you would walk into the opponent's counter-attack
- *Musōken* ('the unbeheld sword'), an extension of ichi-no-tachi, where the swordsman would stop the opponent's technique by positioning himself so as to distort the opponent's perception in a way that would prevent him from completing the attack.

So at least for the Kashima-Shinryū, the sword was the primary weapon, supplemented by knives, iron fans and other smaller weapons, and eventually spears and staffs.[103] These weapons were more appropriate for foot soldiers, consistent with the shift away in the Tokugawa period from armed horsemen of the medieval era.

It may be observed, from the way these techniques are described, that fighting was considered an art. It was about efficiency and matching energy, and movement was to be done with the utmost care and consideration. Moreover, the ryūha would not simply convey the knowledge of how to use weapons. Rather, there were three essential types of knowledge to be conveyed:: *hyōhō* ('strategy'), *te-no-uchi* ('skill') and *waza* ('techniques'). These referred to the general principles of combat, how those principles and strategies operated (that is, timing and posture), and how they would apply to specific situations.[104] Thus, the law of war for the samurai was more about the art of war. The rules of battle were not so much regulated, as the style.

Arguably consistently with this, Nitobe considered that the sword was 'the emblem of power and prowess' for the samurai. It assisted them to carry out their duties, which were always done in the name of virtues like honour and loyalty. The corollary was that samurai had to be careful to use their swords properly; any misuse or promiscuity was denounced. That was consistent with the ultimate ideal of knighthood being peace: 'The best won victory is that obtained without shedding of blood.'

The next notable military innovation, and accompanying tactical shift, was the introduction of firearms by the Portuguese when they arrived in 1542 AD. The Japanese military swiftly incorporated them into their forces, and by the time that Tokugawa Ieyasu established his shogunate in 1603, there were hundreds of thousands of firearms in use, with some estimating around 150,000–200,000.[105] The dominant type was the matchlock musket, which used a small

103 Ibid 120–1; see further 68–89.

104 Ibid 104.

105 David L Howell, 'The Social Life of Firearms in Tokugawa Japan' (2009) 29(1) *Japanese Studies* 65, 66; David B Kopel, 'Japanese Gun Control' (1993) 2(2) *Asia Pacific Law Review* 26, 31; Shigeo Sugawa, *The Japanese Matchlock: A Story of the Tanegashima* (Shigeo Sugawa, 1991) 43.

piece of cord – the match – to ignite the charge. Produced in lesser quantities, as dictated by the shogunate, were handguns and small cannons. Guns alone were not responsible for transforming military tactics, but one notable effect was a 'lengthen[ing] the battlefield'.[106] An example of this is the famous battle of Nagashino in 1575, where the forces of Lord Odu Nobunaga purportedly fired in volleys of three. This was underpinned by trickery tactics and allegedly hiding behind wooden posts – not an especially honourable way of fighting, but highly successful.[107] Guns eventually gained popularity and greater use, so that they decided many battles in the 16th century. They had the advantage of being able to be deployed *en masse*, destroying armoured knights with relative ease compared to the one-on-one combat that the samurai would typically have engaged in. In that sense, guns were considered weapons of the unskilled peasantry, while 'true' samurai still preferred to use swords or spears.[108]

Firearms fell into disuse following the rise of the Tokugawa shogunate in 1603 AD, because samurai did not need much more than their swords.[109] It began in 1588 AD, when on 29 August, Hideyoshi, a peasant who gradually rose in the ranks and took control of Nobunaga's army, declared the 'Sword Hunt' (*taiko no katanagari*). Hideyoshi intended this as a measure of control; it banned the possession of swords and firearms by anyone except the noble classes, and he sent the heads of provinces, official agents and deputies to collect all such weapons and turn them in to the government. This exacerbated the hierarchical divide between peasants and samurai, leaving the former at the mercy of the latter and vulnerable to the exercise of *kirisute gomen* should any disrespect be shown. In addition, the Tokugawa shogunate required that all gun and powder production be done in Nagahama from 1607, and orders were almost exclusively fulfilled for the government, granting them an effective monopoly on firearms.[110]

From 1657 AD, the shogunate began making concerted efforts to regulate firearms in the countryside by issuing edicts that called for the confiscation of illicit weapons. This likely had a greater impact on peasants than samurai, but would have included many of the petty warriors rusticated during the Tokugawa peacetime.[111] It is suggested that such strict gun control succeeded because it

---

106 Conlan (n 55) 252.

107 Kopel (n 105) 32.

108 Ibid.

109 William Johnston, 'Firearms in Premodern Japan' in Louis G Perez (ed), *Japan at War: An Encyclopedia* (ABC-CLIO, 2013) 86–7.

110 Kopel (n 105) 32–4.

111 Howell (n 105) 66–7.

was consistent with the cultural needs of Japanese society at the time.[112] That has force, acknowledging the uniquely peaceful time that Tokugawa Japan was, combined with the principles of bushidō that governed the samurai. The sword, rather than the gun, embodied bushidō: craftsmanship, skill in its use, responsibility for action, and control.

Cannons were also introduced in the 1560s, brought over from Europe, and that encouraged changes in military architecture – stone walls were preferred to earthen ones, for example, for their sturdiness.[113]

Tactics and Strategy

Tactics and strategy were very important in Japanese warfare, but may best be appreciated by looking slightly beyond the peaceful Tokugawa period.While battle was a 'free-for-all' in the sense that the ends justified the means in pre-Tokugawa Japan,; there was almost always a clear tactical strategy underpinning the fighting. For example, the Ōnin War of the 15th century 'devolved into a tactical stalemate'. Pike formations had started coming into use, meaning that horsemen no longer were the dominant player on the battlefield. Defensive tactics were more apparent, as the pike-wielding infantry occupied territory, dug trenches and manned watchtowers.[114]

Unlike many of their European counterparts, the samurai did not have any prohibition on surprise attacks. Rather, this was a very common and popular technique. Contemporary texts would describe warriors as 'highly skilled in the conduct of battles, night attacks, archery duels on horseback and ambushes'[115]. Noting the relatively simple weaponry of earlier periods (horses, archery, long-distance), it offered a way for opposing sides to create a kind of advantage where all else was essentially equal.

Friday cites the battle between Taira Koremochi and Fujiwara Moroto, two late 10th century warriors, as '[o]ne of the most revealing accounts' of the extent to which the tactic of surprise was used. Koremochi and Moroto had agreed on a date for a battle (over a land feud) but as the day approached, Moroto realised that he was outnumbered and fled to a nearby province. When Koremochi learned of this and considered the environment to be safe, he demobilised his men and sent them home. Moroto, however, took advantage of this and ambushed Koremochi and his household one night and set fire to

112 Kopel (n 105) 35.

113 Conlan (n 55) 253.

114 Ibid 250.

115 Friday (n 34) 169, citing *Shin Sarugakki,* Kodai seiji shakai shiso in *Nihon shiso taikei,* (Iwanami shoten, 1986) vol 8, 138; Friday (n 38) 8; Friday (n 2) 341.

the buildings and surrounds. Although some 80 people died, Koremochi actually survived, unbeknownst to Moroto, who was travelling back and celebrating his victory. Koremochi then made his own surprise attack on Moroto, and he emerged victorious.[116] The use of surprise attacks, Friday suggests, was perhaps considered justified because warriors were always expected to be on their guard. So, taking them by surprise could not be seen as taking unfair advantage of them any more so than attack in an ordinary battle if they have slipped their guard.[117]

Aside from coordinated surprise attacks, there were no real other sorts of large-scale tactical manoeuvres. That was a product of warriors operating in smaller groups, as opposed to large, public armies; and the early conception of samurai as privately equipped professionals with individual responsibility.[118] Perhaps also connected to the smaller-scale nature of conduct, there was a focus on efficiency, in the sense that the ends were considered to almost always justify the means. That is consistent with the use of surprise attacks, at least in medieval Japan.[119] As has been discussed, the relative peacetime of Tokugawa Japan saw samurai conduct themselves in a vastly different way.

What happened when samurai captured enemies, or were captured themselves? The samurai had few customs on how to treat prisoners of war, unlike Europeans, and the fate of each individual, if captured, was entirely circumstantial.[120] It is worth comparing this to the current position, when in 1942, the then Japanese Foreign Minister, Minister Tōgō Shigenori formally announced Japan's intention to abide by the Geneva Prisoner of War Convention of 1929. Friday cites three reasons for the lack of regulation in early medieval Japan. First, capture was relatively rare, largely because the kinds of weapons used in any large-scale battles (archery and cavalry, in medieval times) were more likely to result in death than injury and capture. Second, as discussed in relation to goals of warfare, wars were more properly described (at least in the early medieval period) as public, rather than private. Samurai were acting 'for' the State and warfare had a more criminal focus, so any captives were treated as such; winning was the goal. And thirdly, unlike European knights, samurai didn't occupy a distinct position in the social hierarchy – at least until the Tokugawa period. Friday concludes that that confluence of factors resulted in war being more 'sport-like', so there was no need to conceptualise of prisoners

116 Friday (n 34) 169–70.
117 Friday (n 38) 10.
118 Ibid 13–14.
119 Friday (n 34) 170–1; Friday (n 38) 8.
120 Friday (n 34) 171; Friday (n 2) 347.

as something to be traded. In the 13th and 14th centuries, prisoners tended to be executed because they were seen as a liability and potential threat. But the essential point is that there were few rules around treatment of prisoners of war. This is probably most inconsistent with Buddhist influences and teachings, but is arguably attributable to the fact that samurai were not strictly faithful.[121]

As to the treatment of non-combatants, that may be analysed from two perspectives: those that were coincidentally present during a defined military attack or battle, and how the samurai would treat civilians any time outside of that. As to the former, non-combatants were treated in a way similar to prisoners of war. There was no strict immunity, rule or custom dictating that they should be left unharmed, and on top of that, because the rules of warfare were already somewhat loose, any separate treatment that they would receive would have been unique to the circumstances and samurai involved. For the most part, non-combatants present in battle were slaughtered along with enemies, the exception being if there was a special reason to preserve their life. For example, and this appears consistent with the values of honour, hierarchy and familial respect, lives may have been spared to avoid making trouble with a particular family. While such treatment may seem cruel, and perhaps even inconsistent with the philosophies underlying bushidō, it can be viewed as an extension of the consequentialist samurai mindset and their pragmatic approach to battle in earlier periods. Samurai were as willing to kill as they were to die.[122]

As to the latter, how samurai treated civilians outside of 'strict' battle, we return to the (unwritten) laws of *kirisute gomen*, or *bureiuchi*. As previously discussed, samurai had the authority to kill those below them in the social hierarchical order, most commonly in the name of respect. In *Hagakure*, Tsunetomo wrote that the martial nature and readiness to serve that samurai displayed gave them a right to determine the life or death of non-samurai.[123] Respect and honour thus continue to be an important theme to understand how samurai regulated themselves. Because the social hierarchy was so strict, what might now appear to be mere disrespect or rudeness was not a petty offence; it signalled a disregard for the fundamental social order. For a samurai to kill a non-combatant or civilian in such circumstances was entirely justifiable, because it was effectively enforcing the unwritten law and values of bushidō.[124] That being said, there is little documentary evidence for *kirisute gomen* occurring

121 Friday (n 2) 347; Friday (n 34) 171–4.
122 Friday (n 2) 346; Friday (n 34) 174–7.
123 Benesch (n 40) 20–1.
124 Claudia Marra, 'The Regulation of Disrespect-Killings Within the Framework of Tokugawa Legislation' (2018) 22 *The Journal of Nagasaki University of Foreign Studies* 101, 102–3.

during the Tokugawa period, so it may be more furphy than fact.[125] Indeed, one must question how this really sat consistently with the careful and rigorous training that the samurai undertook in respect of both their body and their mind, and their dual role as bureaucrat-soldiers. It arguably would have undermined the concerted efforts of the shogunate to maintain peace if those in positions of authority, who were supposedly educated and cultured, could cut down citizens in this manner.

To the extent that there was evidence of any regulation of the unwritten practice of *kirisute gomen*, in 1742 AD, the shogunate enacted the *Kujikata Osadamegaki*, a compendium of criminal laws that purportedly regulated it. Generally, and consistent with the contemporary philosophical traditions, it advised samurai to abstain from unnecessary violence and attempted to delineate between murder and excusable killing. It was to be reserved for more serious transgressions, such as publicly slandering a samurai's domain, family or reputation, or preventing a samurai from performing his duties. When a citizen was killed, the matter had to be reported to local authorities and the circumstances of the killing were investigated. While the investigation was pending, the samurai concerned would be furloughed and temporarily relieved from his duties. If the killing were found unlawful, the samurai would be the one facing punishment instead.[126] This is consistent with the prohibition against drawing weapons in public without proper justification. Although samurai were required, at the same time, to always be armed, taught to be perpetually ready for battle and retained the right to carry two swords, the practical reality of the Tokugawa peacetime meant that the readiness for battle was more a state of mind, and the carrying of swords a status symbol.

VI Defences

To complete the picture, there was an apparent grasp of the principles of defence. But again, appreciation of such tactics arises from how they were used in earlier periods, before tapering off in the Tokugawa peacetime. Defence tactics would include choosing topographically strong positions and buttressing with entrenchments. That would make successful attacks by opposing forces difficult, but also allow for defence by way of giving the army a place to hide and refuse to come out, leaving the opposing side exhausted and unable to maintain an attack for long.[127]

125 Ibid 102.

126 Ibid 107–8.

127 Friday (n 38) 10–11.

An example of this was the Battle of Osaka Castle (1614–1615 AD), which was the last incidence of large-scale fighting by samurai armies in Japanese history. It was between supporters of Tokugawa Ieyasu and supporters of Toyotomi Hideyori, and came from a background of a power struggle between Ieyasu and Hideyori. Hideyori was at Osaka Castle and had about 90,000 defenders, with a castle fortified by walls, a moat and armaments. Although Ieyasu had about 180,000 supporters, the first month of battle was relatively ineffectual because the defences of the castle were too strong. In the event, the parties turned to negotiations.

While that illustrates the strength of defences, the end of that battle also indicates the use of surprise tactics, discussed earlier. The negotiations resulted in a settlement (in January 1615 AD), so Ieyasu began to act as if withdrawing his forces. Hideyori, in response, ordered his samurai to begin levelling the castle's defences, e.g., filling in the moats. Ieyasu took advantage of this trickery and recommenced hostilities in May 1615, as defences had been weakened. His forces ultimately prevailed.[128]

Death

All of these techniques and tactics of battle sit against the samurai's preoccupation with death and dying, and that it had to be done in the proper way. To some extent, this tempered the co-existing restriction on conflict that the ends justified the means.

When it came to killing others, unlike the way that prisoners-of-war or non-combatants were treated, at least in the early modern period and onwards, bugei teachings indicate that samurai were required to be considerate in *how* they killed their enemies, and how they treated the corpse afterwards. Using the Kashima-Shinryu bugei as an example, samurai were taught to treat corpses of slain enemies in particular ways in order to stay their spirits and prevent them from returning into the world (*todome*). Stemming from Chinese folklore, it was believed that an improperly treated body that had been subjected to a violent or premature death may have a portion of their soul trapped in the mortal world, or otherwise seek to return and exact vengeance. A samurai might have slain an enemy for one of three principal reasons, and for each, Kashima-Shinryu lore dictated how the corpse should be treated afterwards.[129]

First, it may have been on the order of his superior (*gyoi-uchi*, 'striking for the honourable will'), where upon death the samurai would present the

---

128 Philip Streich, 'Battle of Osaka Castle (1614-1615)' in Louis G Perez (ed), *Japan at War: An Encylopedia* (ABC-CLIO, 2013), 301–2.

129 Ibid 87–9.

victim's head to the superior. Damage to the corpse should be minimal, so the appropriate *todome* was to stab in the sole of the left foot. Secondly, it may have been to kill an enemy of the samurai's parents on grounds of filial piety (*teki-uchi*, 'striking for vengeance'). The proper *todome* was to stab the victim below his left ear. This severed the carotid artery, and because of the way in which the blood would drain, the victim's face would not become distorted and the head remained presentable to give to the parent or place on their grave. And thirdly, killing may have originated from the warrior themself (*ishu-uchi*, 'striking of one's own accord'). This demanded special caution because the warrior was not acting instrumentally, and therefore had greater ethical responsibility. For that reason, the *todome* required stabbing the victim just below the left nipple and twisting the blade from edge up to edge downward as it was withdrawn. In all cases, the slain should fall forward so as not to bring undue dishonour to them; facing upward in death was considered by samurai to be the proper posture for women, not men (to ensure this in *seppuku*, the samurai would tuck the sleeves of their kimono under their knees).

When it came to their own death, the notion of honour also conditioned the manner of it; samurai had to die honourably, so that their personal reputation was not sullied by having been captured or defeated in battle. It would also be used to avoid death by execution, and to follow one's lord or master into death (*junshi*).[130] It was also considered a reward for all their training.[131] A key means of ensuring this was ritual suicide, or *seppuku* (also called hara-kiri). It was performed by cutting open the abdomen and could also be used as a way to ensure an honourable death outside of battle. The focus was on the abdomen because it was the core of the physical body, and according to Asian thought, it is where the soul is located.[132] Nitobe wrote: 'i]n our minds this mode of death is associated with instances of noblest deeds and of most touching pathos, so that nothing repugnant, much less ludicrous, mars our conception of it'. This apparently sits inconsistently with Shinto and Buddhist beliefs, because neither openly approved of suicide, but they didn't outrightly condemn it either. In this way, *seppuku* was a marker of samurai status.

The origins of *seppuku* can be traced to the Minamoto clan during the Gempei Wars. The first recorded act was by bowman Minamoto Tametomo in

130 RW Purdy, '*Hara-kiri* (*Seppuku*)' in Louis G Perez (ed), *Japan at War: An Encyclopedia* (ABC-CLIO, 2013) 110; Nicholas WMull, 'The Honor of War: Core Value of the Warrior Ethos and Principle of the Law of War' (2018) 18(1) *Chicago-Kent Journal of International and Comparative Law* 1, 22; Ikegami (n 58) 1361.

131 Atkins (n 52) 46.

132 Purdy (n 130) 110.

1177 AD. He had been banished to the island of Oshima following the Hōgen War of 1156 AD, and his enemies had cut the tendons in his forearms to render him harmless. He couldn't seize power, so rather than face defeat, he killed himself.[133] Another good example comes from the aforementioned Battle of Osaka Castle. After Tokugawa forces had penetrated the Castle, Hideyori retired into the castle's keep and committed suicide on June 3, 1615.[134] Presumably, this is because it had been such a long-running battle and Hideyori considered this a failure as he had ordered the Castle's defences be taken down. That may have added to the shame of defeat, so to retain honour, this was the only way for him to die.

From 1600 AD onwards, however, this became less common. There was not such a need because of the relative decrease in battles, but it was nonetheless permitted by the Tokugawa bakufu as a way for samurai to avoid execution. It was eventually outlawed because of a fear that the suicides of a deceased lord's retainers could lead to political instability,[135] and as aforementioned, the Tokugawa rulers were especially concerned to maintain peace. The practice of *junshi*, specifically, was outlawed by the shogunate in 1663 AD, and the ban was enforced by punishing the family members of the person who had committed the suicide. Samurai, however, avoided the ban by practising other forms of ritual suicide, including *memboku* (*seppuku* performed to prove one's innocence), *kanshi* (in protest against some action taken by a samurai's lord) and *inseki* (performed to assume responsibility for some mistake).[136]

VII Conclusion

To speak of the samurai and the laws that governed their conduct in battle, the *bushidō* code, is to describe a system distinctly different from the modern laws of war and international humanitarian law. Not only did the term *bushidō* only really emerge in the Tokugawa period, but, as this chapter sought to elucidate, it is best understood as a code by which those in the samurai caste regulated their conduct, whether in or out of battle.

As sections II and III of this chapter discussed, the way that the samurai regulated themselves, particularly from the Tokugawa period onward, was

133 Ibid.
134 Streich (n 128) 302.
135 Purdy (n 130) 110.
136 Constantine Vaporis, 'The Samurai in Tokugawa Japan' in Gary P Leupp and De-min Tao (eds), *The Tokugawa World* (Routledge, 2021) 147.

inextricably bound up with the social and political structures of Japanese society. The Tokugawa period saw an identity crisis amongst the samurai, where they had to justify their traditional military role when the shogunate was actively suppressing rebellion and war. That may be seen as the time when *bushidō* as 'the way of the warrior' gained traction, as demonstrated in the many texts (from which our current understanding of samurai) that were then published, such as *Hagakure* and *Bushidō: The Soul of Japan*.

Sections IV and V examined the military aspects of *bushidō*. The use of particular weapons, the strategies and tactics employed in battle, and the purposes of warfare can all be traced to the philosophical foundations of *bushidō*, so that it may be said that what 'laws' of war did exist had a deeper foundation and concern than regulating battle. That concern was to maintain the essence of the samurai as a particular social class, who abided by particular philosophical teachings and engaged in battle largely in the name of honour, reputation and loyalty.

All that being said, what this chapter drew out must be remembered to be a product of the contemporary samurai texts. It has been recognised amongst scholars in this field that what emerged from the samurai texts written in the Tokugawa period and after was an idealised, smoothed-out conception of the samurai. That is, *bushidō* was not necessarily a strict normative code or a reflection of actual behaviour. Nonetheless, an understanding of the samurai and ancient Japanese 'laws of war' at least emphasises the extent to which the modern legal landscape developed, and provides a contrast to the Western and Eurocentric norms that so heavily influence it.

CHAPTER 7

East African Laws of War

Kenneth Wyne Mutuma and Eve Massingham

Introduction

Most African communities have always been peace loving people, and peaceful coexistence remains the cornerstone of their communal way of life.[1] In fact, a sense of humanity is one of the permanent and most prized values of most African communities.[2] To many African communities, war was not a normal state of affairs but a last resort since they were profoundly devoted to peace.[3] That said, resorting to armed conflict was not completely foreign to these communities. As a result, even the conduct of war, where it was necessitated, had to be regulated. Most African communities came up with rules of warfare to govern them during conflicts with other communities to ensure that the loss of human life was minimised and human suffering was diminished. While precolonial African communities had deep rooted customs and systems for the protection of people during periods of conflict, it is worth noting that this view of African communities is only more recently emerging. Suffice it to say, no significant efforts had been made to study African communities and their customs extensively before sweeping conclusions were made that they not only did not have humanitarian principles but that they were incapable of understanding them.[4]

This Chapter therefore seeks, in Part I, to outline East African traditional war customs and juxtapose the same to contemporary IHL principles, thereby revealing these communities to have long since formulated pragmatic traditions and customs that resemble modern IHL norms.[5] While the East African

---

1 Kariuki Muigua, *Traditional Conflict Resolution Mechanisms and Institutions* (2017).

2 Emmanuel G Bello, 'Shared Legal Concepts between African Customary Norms and International Conventions on Humanitarian Law' (1984) *23 Mil. L. & L. War Rev. 285*, 290.

3 Yolande Diallo, 'Humanitarian Law and Traditional African Law' (1976) 16(179) *International Review of the Red Cross (1961–1997)* 57.

4 Jack Donnelly, 'Human Rights and Human Dignity: An Analytic Critique of Non-Western Conceptions of Human Rights' (1982) 76 American Political Science Review 303.

5 Emmanuel G Bello (n 2), 289; See also, Mutoy Mubiala, 'International Humanitarian Law in the African Context' in Monica Kathina Juma and Astri Suhrke (eds), *Eroding Local Capacity; International Humanitarian Action in Africa* (The Nordic Africa Institute, 2002) 37–49.

 DOI:10.1163/9789004473218_009

region geographically refers to Kenya, Uganda, Tanzania, South Sudan, Rwanda and Burundi – collectively known as the East African Community; as well as Djibouti, Eritrea, Ethiopia and Somalia, the examples herein are by and large drawn from Kenya, Uganda and to a lesser degree, Ethiopia.

In Part II, this Chapter turns to look at East African contributions to IHL showing the voice that East Africa has had at the negotiating table of IHL and related treaties in the 21st Century and the inclusion of IHL principles and concepts in institutional frameworks of the region. While there is certainly no evidence of the region *always* being an exemplary model when it comes to IHL, there is evidence that the region does make a strong contribution to IHL, and must be emboldened to continue to do so.

Why did East African Groups go to War?

Despite the peaceful nature of most traditional African communities, some factors necessitated going to war, often times as a last resort after all other forms of dispute resolution had failed. One such factor was the need to establish chieftaincy, kingship or other forms of leadership over a community. Such situations more often than not divided the community in question into factions of those who endorsed a particular leader and those who were against his or her leadership at times leading to war.[6] In other instances, war was a result of an outcry by a group of people against actions they consider unjust such as skewed distribution of resources or the enrichment of some factions of the community to the detriment of others.[7] In some cases, this involved leaders and the elite taking prime and fertile lands for themselves or the imposition of high taxes which impoverished other members of the community.

Moreover, warfare often arose as a result of intrusion by communities that were comparably stronger.[8] In such cases, the stronger community would be looking to expand its territory and/or gain control over other regions. Such intrusions often lead to war, whereby communities felt the need to protect its territory and prevent a takeover as a matter of honour and pride. Communities who boasted of vast natural resources such as minerals and fertile lands were

6 Nancy Annan, 'Violent Conflicts and Civil Strife in West Africa: Causes, Challenges and Prospects' (2014) 3 Stability: International Journal of Security and Development Art. 3.

7 MSW, 'Early Warfare and Weapons in Africa' (*Weapons and Warfare*, 14 April 2018) <https://weaponsandwarfare.com/2018/04/15/early-warfare-and-weapons-in-africa/> accessed 29 November 2021.

8 MSW (n 7).

often a target for such kinds of intrusions by neighbouring communities that wanted to take control.[9] In other cases, wars arose in retaliation or defence, for instance when women and children, livestock, food, natural resources or weapons had been stolen by neighbouring communities.[10]

Additionally, war was often announced when communities wanted to decide who was stronger than the other in terms of political organisation and military prowess.[11] Announced and planned wars gave the communities time to prepare and such preparations included military trainings on techniques, storage of food and other basic resources and making arrangements for the women, children, persons with disabilities and elders.[12] Preparations also included setting up designated zones to cater for the wounded soldiers.[13] However, some attacks came as a surprise where one community wanted to catch the other unaware so as to easily conquer them when their defences were down. This was common in cases of hostile takeovers to gain control of natural resources.

I Shared Concepts between African Customary Norms and International Conventions on Humanitarian Law

At this stage, there is a need to look at some of the basic principles of IHL embodied in the Geneva Conventions of 1949 and Additional Protocols. As Bello points out, '[t]he study of the rules of African armed conflict makes it abundantly clear that there were no universal or commonly accepted laws which applied in every conflict situation amongst all the tribes and villages in the continent'.[14] However, as we will see in this chapter, there were many rules that are today reflected in the Conventions and Protocols, including those which require that persons who are *hors de combat* (outside of combat), and those who are not taking part in hostilities in situations of armed conflict (e.g., neutral nationals), shall be protected in all circumstances.[15] Furthermore, the

9 'History and War' (*Weapons and Warfare*, 23 February 2021) <https://weaponsandwarfare.com/history-and-war/> accessed 29 November 2021.

10 Ibid.

11 SC Ukpabi, 'The Military in Traditional African Societies' (1974) 9 Africa Spectrum 200.

12 'African Values in War: A Tool on Traditional Customs and IHL' (*International Committee of the Red Cross*, 24 May 2021) <https://www.icrc.org/en/document/african-customs-tool-traditional-customs-and-ihl> accessed 29 November 2021.

13 Ibid.

14 Ibid 3.

15 International Committee of the Red Cross (ICRC), *Geneva Convention for the Amelioration of the Condition of the wounded and sick in armed forces in the field* (First Geneva Convention), 12 August 1949, 75 UNTS 31; International Committee of the Red Cross

wounded and the sick shall be cared for and protected by the party to the conflict which has them in its power.[16] The emblem of the "Red Cross", or of the "Red Crescent," shall be required to be respected as the sign of protection.[17] Captured persons must be protected against acts of violence and reprisals and they shall have the right to correspond with their families and to receive relief.[18] In addition, no one shall be subjected to torture or to cruel, inhuman, or degrading treatment or punishment.[19] Parties to a conflict do not have an unlimited choice of methods and means of warfare.[20] Parties to a conflict shall at all times distinguish between combatants and non- combatants. Attacks shall be directed solely against legitimate military targets.[21] In the sections that follow, we will mainly be focusing on those traditional practices in the East African region which reflect IHL principles; that is certainly not to say that all do, and some examples of contrary practices are included.

Traditions of warfare from all corners of the globe include practices that have caused horrendous suffering not in-keeping with modern IHL principles. Many of these practices have in fact informed prohibitions – such as the practice of poisoning food and wells in the Middle Ages and the use of the plague and smallpox against enemies in the 1700s[22] ultimately informing restrictions

---

(ICRC), *Geneva Convention for the Amelioration of the Condition of Wounded, Sick and Shipwrecked Members of Armed Forces at Sea* (Second Geneva Convention), 12 August 1949, 75 UNTS 85; International Committee of the Red Cross (ICRC) *Geneva Convention Relative to the Treatment of Prisoners of War* (Third Geneva Convention), 12 August 1949, 75 UNTS 135; *Geneva Convention Relative to the Protection of Civilian Persons in time of War* (Fourth Geneva Convention), 12 August 1949, 75 UNTS 287; International Committee of the Red Cross (ICRC), *Protocol Additional to the Geneva Conventions of 12 August 1949, and relating to the Protection of Victims of International Armed Conflicts* (Protocol I), 8 June 1977, 1125 UNTS 3, art 41; International Committee of the Red Cross (ICRC), *Protocol Additional to the Geneva Convention of 12 August 1949, and relating to the Protection of Victims of Non-International Armed Conflicts* (Protocol II), 8 June 1977, 1125 UNTS 609, art 4; Common Article 3.

16 First Geneva Convention (n 7) art 15, Second Geneva Convention (n 7) art 18, Fourth Geneva Convention (n 15) art 16, Additional Protocol II (n 15) art 8.

17 Geneva Convention I (n 15) art 38.

18 Geneva Conventions and Additional Protocol II (n 15) common article 3; Third Geneva Convention (n 7) art 4(b); First Geneva Convention I (n 15) art 28(2); Additional Protocol I (n 15) art 44.

19 Geneva Conventions (n 15) Common Article 3.

20 International Committee of the Red Cross (ICRC), 'Methods and Means of Warfare' (Blog Post, 29 October 2010) https://www.icrc.org/war-and-law/conduct-hostilities/methods-means-warfare.htm.

21 Additional Protocol I (n 15) art 48, 51(2) and 52(2).

22 Robert J Mathews, 'Chemical and biological weapons' in Rain Liivoja and Tim McCormack (eds), *Routledge Handbook of the Law of Armed Conflict* (Routledge, 2016) 212.

on biological and chemical weapons – while others that have taken place outside the Euro-centric formation of modern IHL are equally reflective of prohibited conduct.

Protection of Civilian Persons and Property

The African customs of war on the conduct of belligerents just like in modern IHL, protected certain individuals and the environment in times of armed conflict. This is pursuant to Geneva Convention IV, Relative to the Protection of Civilian Persons in Times of War whereby persons who are outside of combat, and those who are not taking part in hostilities in situations of armed conflict, shall be protected in all circumstances.[23] Consequently, parties to a conflict are expected, at all times, to distinguish between combatants and non-combatants and to attack only military targets.[24]

In the Buganda Kingdom in Uganda as well as among the Maasai community in Kenya and Northern Tanzania, there were rules concerning treatment of certain persons during times of war and after war.[25] Such protected people included mediators, envoys, priests, medicine men, the elderly, the disabled, children, diviners, women, and the rainmakers.[26] Such categories of persons were regarded as non-combatants and enjoyed immunity from direct attacks.[27] Among the Kikuyu of Central Kenya, women and children could be moved to safer locations as the young warriors went to war.[28] Further, the attacking community, for example the Nilotic Maasai community which often raided the Kikuyu territory, knew not to attack women and children even when they had knowledge of their hideouts, due to their frequent interactions.[29] It is however not clear whether or not there were previous agreements between communities to ensure that specific places were excluded from attacks or raids.[30]

---

23 Geneva Conventions, common Article 3, Additional Protocol I, Article 41, Additional Protocol II, Article 4.

24 Ibid.

25 Robert L Tignor, *Colonial Transformation of Kenya: The Kamba, Kikuyu, and Maasai from 1900–1939* (Princeton University Press, 2015).

26 'Political Organization of the Maasai', *Tutorke.com* (Web Page, 2000) https://www.tutorke.com/lesson/3876-political-organization-of-the-maasai.aspx accessed 19 April 2021.

27 Godfrey Muriuki, 'A History of the Kikuyu to 1904' (PhD Thesis, SOAS University of London 1969).

28 Ibid.

29 John Lonsdale, 'Contests of Time: Kikuyu Historiography, Old and New' (2002) *A Place in the World: New Local Historiographies from Africa & South Asia* 201.

30 Ibid.

Observing this rule, regardless of how fierce the war was, alleviated its consequences by protecting the defenceless and preserving life. In fact, Muriuki observes that:

> despite the Maasai and Kikuyu communities being at war, there was a tacit pact to spare the womenfolk. It was thus a spectacle to see Maasai women walking with impunity in a battlefield while their kin could be engaged in the fierce war.[31]

Even among tribes with approaches to warfare that bear little resemblance to modern IHL in many ways, such as the traditions of the Guji peoples of Southern Ethiopia,[32] a man who killed a woman would be 'highly despised'.[33] Women were not targeted or captured and had an important role to play in the peace process.[34] Among the Somali, a Cushitic community in East Africa, women, children, the elderly and men of religion were protected in their rules of warfare. According to the Somali community, it was generally agreed that:

> those oblivious to the war should not be finished off, wounded enemies should not be killed but it is better to leave them alone, prisoners of war should be delivered to the commanders, inhumane means of killing like strangulation should not be used and dead bodies should not be mutilated.[35]

This embodies the first principle of IHL which is the protection of non-combatants.

There were also rules to ensure the protection of sites and property that had symbolic value to the communities – such as sacred forests, shrines, burial grounds, sculptures, monuments, idols representing their ancestors and resources such as crops, animals, and water sources.[36] Protection of cultural property and the environment is rooted in the rules of ancient civilization,

31 Muriuki (n 27).

32 Taddesse Berisso, *Traditional warfare among the Guji of Southern Ethiopia* (ProQuest Dissertations Publishing, 1988) 7–46.

33 Ibid 31.

34 Ibid 41–42.

35 Musa Yusuf Hussein, Mohammed Abdilaani Riraash and Ibrahim Haji M. Wa'ais, 'Spared from the Spear – Traditional Somali Behaviour in Warfare' *International Committee of the Red Cross* (Online Report, 1998) 5 https://blogs.icrc.org/somalia/2015/09/21/spared-from-the-spear/.

36 Yolande Diallo (n 3).

which are similar to those codified in the 1954 Hague Convention for the Protection of Cultural Property in the Event of Armed Conflict, which protect among others, movable or immovable property of cultural heritage of every people, monuments of architecture, museums, libraries, art or history, religious or secular sites; archaeological sites; groups of buildings which, as a whole, are of historical or artistic interest; manuscripts, books and other objects of artistic, historical or archaeological interest, among others.[37]

In the African traditional setting, the protection of persons and property was based on the belief that certain persons and property fulfilled a social role of prime importance. For instance, in the Kalenjin community, priests (also known as the *Tisiik*) accumulated wisdom and strength in performing religious rites. They could interpret the will of their gods and regularly performed the rites that entailed the sacrifice of a cock or any other animal in a burial ground to appease the dead.[38] The priests benefited from double protection since the sites at which they performed their duties were sacred and therefore protected. Moreover, the elderly people were custodians of the cultural and historical knowledge and hence they were protected. Amongst the Kamba community in Kenya, the medicine men were protected as they were able to detect disease through invocations and cure the sick by giving them herbal medicine while also casting evil spirits from people and averting bad omens.[39] Properties such as land (which was collectively owned), water sources, cattle and crops were spared from despoliation and destruction due to their role of ensuring survival and continuity of the community. Direct attacks to animals and crops were strictly prohibited amongst the Maasai community.[40]

Methods and Means of Warfare

Whilst specific rules were put in place to protect non-combatants, equally strict rules existed between the combatants themselves. For instance, among the Buganda, young warriors were taught to never kill an enemy who has

37 United Nations Educational, Scientific and Cultural Organisation, '1954 Hague Convention of Cultural Property in the Event of Armed Conflict', *UNESCO Armed Conflict and Heritage* (Web Page) http://www.unesco.org/new/en/culture/themes/armed-conflict-and-heritage/convention-and-protocols/1954-hague-convention/ accessed 19 April 2021.

38 Florence J Chelimo and Kiplagat Chelelgo, 'Pre-Colonial Political Organization of the Kalenjin of Kenya: An Overview' (2016) 5(13) *International Journal of Innovative Research and Development* 6.

39 Tarsis B Kabwegyere and Judith Mbula, *A Case of the Akamba of Eastern Kenya* (No. 5) (Canberra: Australian National University, 1979).

40 Elizabeth Mrema, Carl Bruch and Jordan Diamond, *Protecting the environment during armed conflict: an inventory and analysis of international law* (UNEP/Earthprint, 2009).

surrendered or who was seriously injured.[41] The historical culture that instilled the importance of humanity among the Bantu in Kenya taught that, "*brothers do not kill each other*"; such ethics were taught at a very young age.[42] As a result, war was the last resort when it came to settling a dispute. Other forms of dispute resolution like negotiations were applied first before a war was declared. Additionally, ambushes were generally not allowed as a method of warfare.[43] In fact, amongst the East African communities like the Baganda, Maasai and Kikuyu, negotiations had to be undertaken first in an attempt to resolve the dispute in question. It was only when these failed that war could be declared. It was the council of elders/kings/political leaders who were tasked to declare war. In countries such as Uganda, Kabaka (chief) of Buganda, was charged with the role of declaring war.[44]

Moreover, military establishment varied from one community to another in the East African region and their response to armed conflict also differed. Communities such as the Maasai of Kenya evolved from simple military communities to battle empires. Africans were known for crafting unique weapons during the pre-colonial era, which were then used for war. Most notable weapons were the spears made using a long wooden sheath and a metallic head as well as bows, arrows, shields often made from animal hide and the swords crafted by some communities such as the Maasai.[45] The development of the military arts moved from simple to the more sophisticated as technology led to the introduction of weapons such as gunpowder, though such weapons were frowned upon by the African communities. Well established traditional kingdoms, such as the Buganda Kingdom, had armies with three distinguishable military organisations.[46] There was the citizen army, currently known as the *Levée en masse*. It was composed of able-bodied men who were eligible for

---

41 Dorothy L Hodgson, *Being Maasai, Becoming Indigenous: Postcolonial Politics in a Neoliberal World* (Indiana: Indiana University Press, 2011).

42 Lloyd A Fallers, *Bantu Bureaucracy: a Study of Integration and Conflict in the Political Institutions of an East African People* (Cambridge: East African Institute of Social Research, 1959).

43 'Discover Maasai Tribe and Culture in Kenya Safari Experience – CWC', *Campi Ya Kanzi* https://maasai.com/conservation/maasai/ accessed 19 April 2021.

44 Annie Barbara Chikwanha, 'The Anatomy of Conflicts in the East African Community (EAC): Linking Security with Development' (Keynote Speech, Development Policy Review Network – African Studies Institute. Leiden University, The Netherlands, 2007).

45 Discover Maasai Tribe and Culture in Kenya Safari Experience – CWC (n 43).

46 Richard Reid, 'The Reign of Kabaka Nakibinge: Myth or Watershed?' (1997) 24 *History in Africa* 287.

military service during unprecedented warfare.[47] There was also a group of professional soldiers who were supplemented by the citizen army whenever necessary and a category that included young warriors who had just been initiated into adulthood through circumcision and who were responsible for protecting the community from any attacks along their boundaries.[48]

The African traditional communities, like in Buganda Kingdom and the Kalenjin community of Kenya, restricted the choice of both the weapons and methods to be applied during hostilities.[49] There were often some acceptable choices of weaponry. For instance, during the emergency of the Chagga political identity in Kilimanjaro in the 1940s, various chiefdoms sought to expand and strengthen their chiefdoms with the wealth they acquired during different chiefdoms warfare.[50] Among other weapons the Chagga people used were swords with a double-edged, leaf-shaped spatulas blade, often made from spring steel.[51] The Maasai had a weapon named *Rungu,* which was a 20-inch narrow shaft with a large knob at the end. It was a core weapon during armed conflict. It was also considered as a symbol of Moran's (a Moran is a young man between the ages of 14–30 in the Maasai community) soldier status.[52]

African customs of war prohibited the use of dangerous weapons against adversaries from the same ethnic group as well as the use of poisoned arrows and spears.[53] The restriction of both the weapons and methods to be applied during hostilities mirrors the modern restrictions as stated in Article 35 of Additional Protocol 1 where belligerents are prohibited from the use of weapons and projectiles that can cause unnecessary sufferings or widespread long and short term damage to the environment.[54] The Protocol also prohibits the

---

47 Kenneth Ingham, Omari H Kokole, Maryinez Lyons and Kiwanuka M Semakula, 'Uganda – Bunyoro and Buganda' *Encyclopaedia Britannica* (Web Article, 18 June 2021) https://www.britannica.com/place/Uganda accessed 19 April 2021.

48 International Committee of the Red Cross (ICRC), 'War in Cities: An African Perspective' *ICRC* (Online Video, 6 July 2017) https://www.icrc.org/en/document/war-cities-african-perspective accessed 19 April 2021.

49 Kathleen Klaus, *Political Violence in Kenya: Land, Elections, and Claim-Making* (Cambridge University Press, 2020).

50 Thomas James Fisher, 'Chagga Elites and the Politics of Ethnicity in Kilimanjaro, Tanzania' *Edinburgh Research Archive* (Web Article, 29 June 2012) https://era.ed.ac.uk/handle/1842/6452 accessed 19 April 2021.

51 Matthew V Bender, 'Being "Chagga": Natural Resources, Political Activism, and Identity on Kilimanjaro*' (2013) 54 *The Journal of African History* 199.

52 'Discover Maasai Tribe and Culture in Kenya Safari Experience – CWC' (n 43).

53 Christof Heyns, 'Autonomous Weapons in Armed Conflict and the Right to a Dignified Life: An African Perspective' (2017) 33 *South African Journal on Human Rights* 46.

54 Fisher (n 50).

application of weapons incapable of discriminating between civilian and military objects, also referred to as indiscriminate weapons.[55] The Geneva Protocol of 1925 prohibits the use of biological, chemical weapons and blinding laser weapons, and being a customary international law it binds all states irrespective of whether they have signed or not.[56] The Convention on Certain Conventional Weapons of 1980 bans the use of weapons that cause injuries, fragments that are not detectable by x-ray, explosive remnants and weapons that cause burn injuries to a person (incendiary weapons).[57]

Other measures addressed by the 1949 Geneva Convention include official declarations of war, and a form of compensation at the end of the war.[58] Among the Maasai and Kikuyu who interacted with each other frequently due to trading expeditions, and fought just as often, the raids were conducted based upon well-established rules. Their war had no bitterness or hatred unless one party broke the rules, in which case the other would retaliate.[59] War was viewed as a sport, a fact which was strengthened by the few casualties in the aftermath. Between these communities, trading parties were the ones that were used to exchange challenges. For example, the Maasai warriors could send a message through a trading party to the Kikuyu community that they had plans to raid and invade a particular area or rescue a particular prisoner.[60] In addition to that, they would send offers or demands for ransom pertaining to prisoners of war. Peace treaties that lasted decades were also negotiated.[61] Efforts to enter into such treaties were mostly initiated by the Maasai who, like many pastoralist communities, fell victim to drought and famine and therefore needed the Kikuyu to supply them with food and water for their nutritional needs through trading.[62] Peace negotiations were in fact taken very seriously and involved protracted procedures that culminated in a solemn religious ceremony during which oaths not to initiate wars were taken. Public declarations like "*if we*

55 Henri Meyrowitz, 'The Principle of Superfluous Injury or Unnecessary Suffering: From the Declaration of St. Petersburg of 1868 to Additional Protocol 1 of 1977' (1994) 34 *International Review of the Red Cross* (1961–1997) 98.

56 Rodney J McElroy, *'The Geneva Protocol of 1925', the Politics of Arms Control Treaty Ratification* (Springer, 1991).

57 United Nations Office for Disarmament Affairs, 'The Convention on Certain Conventional Weapons' *United Nations* (Web Page, UN 2016) https://www.un.org/disarmament/the-convention-on-certain-conventional-weapons/.

58 Raymund T Yingling and Robert W Ginnane, 'The Geneva Conventions of 1949' (1952) 46 *The American Journal of International Law* 393.

59 Muriuki (n 27).

60 Lonsdale (n 29).

61 Ibid.

62 Fallers (n 42).

cause harm to them, may we be killed" would be made.[63] This fostered stronger friendships and calm between communities. Oaths were also taken to deter any initiation of violence.

Protection of the Sick and the Wounded

Chapter II of the Geneva Convention for the Relief of the Wounded and Sick in Armies in the Field deals with the wounded and the sick. According to article 12, members of the armed forces and other persons who are sick or wounded, should be protected, respected, accorded humane treatment by the party to the conflict in whose power they are. The emblem of the "Red Cross", or of the "Red Crescent," shall be respected as a sign of protection.[64] In pre-colonial Africa, although the mode of application was different, the principle was the same. It was customary practice in African communities for the sick and wounded to be carried away at the end of the battle. The groups in conflict made sure that the sick and wounded co-patriots of their fellow combatants were taken care of. Often there was an implied understanding that the invalids would be the responsibility of the opposing group.[65] The injured were thus taken care of by those who injured them. This was the case for the raids between the Kikuyu (Bantus) and Maasai (Nilotes) of Kenya in East Africa.[66] They took a humane approach in tackling the issue of the invalids during war. To start with, their reasons for going to war were already predetermined. This set the tone for the warfare as reckless killings were prevented. Further, at the end of the war, the sick and wounded would be carried off the battlefield to be catered to while the dead were left on the battlefield to be eaten by animals and to fertilise the soil.[67]

Treatment of Prisoners of War

Pursuant to the Geneva Convention III, Relative to the Treatment of Prisoners of War, persons captured must be protected against acts of violence and reprisals.[68] They shall have the right to correspond with their families and to receive relief. No one is to be subjected to torture or cruel, inhumane, or degrading

63 Muriuki (n 27).

64 François Bugnion, 'The Red Cross and Red Crescent Emblems' (1989) 29 *International Review of the Red Cross Archive* 408.

65 Muriuki (n 27).

66 William L Lawren, 'Masai and Kikuyu: An Historical Analysis of Culture Transmission' (1968) 9(4) *Journal of African History* 571.

67 Emmanuel G Bello (n 2) 291.

68 Geneva Convention III (n 15).

treatment or punishment.[69] In pre-colonial Africa, in the Kikuyu community, prisoners of war were welcomed into the warriors' families and were treated as their brothers or sisters.[70] On this account, sexual contact with them would be deemed as incest. Moreover, once a Maasai woman or girl was captured, the rules required that a message be sent to her people for ransom.[71] If her family was willing to pay the ransom, then they would peacefully visit the Kikuyu community with tokens of peace, and the prisoner would be released to them. However, in case her family died in the raid and payment of a ransom was not possible, the prisoner would be integrated into the Kikuyu community. With time, if another Kikuyu man expressed his intention to marry her and she consented then her captor would willingly receive her bride price.[72] This signifies that integration was to such a great extent that a woman or girl was viewed as a daughter of the captor's family.

Treating a prisoner of war as a family member was the highest form of honour that could be accorded to one in the African context. Such a privilege came with benefits like being initiated into institutions reserved for family, intermarriage, and even the freedom to return to one's homeland if they wished to.[73] The Somali were guided by the concept of 'Nabsi' which basically mandated opposing parties to treat each other with dignity because if they did not, the same fate could befall them in the next war.[74] As a result, acts of torture or brutality were barely perpetrated by Somali warriors.[75] This practice embodies the IHL principle that requires captured persons to be protected from torture, to correspond with their families and receive relief.[76]

This is not to say that all traditions concerning the treatment of prisoners of war were in line with how modern IHL requires those detained to be treated. As has already been noted, some tribes were known for their warrior status and their practices did not reflect the ideals of the Third Geneva Convention. Bello's study of traditions of warfare in Africa notes the Oromo of Southern

69 Albert J Esgain and Waldemar A Solf, 'The Geneva Convention Relative to the Treatment of Prisoners of War 1949: Its Principles, Innovations, and Deficiencies' (1962) 41(3) *North Carolina Law Review* 537.

70 Lonsdale (n 29).

71 Muriuki (n 27).

72 Lawren (n 69).

73 Emmanuel Bello (n 2) 292.

74 Bogumil Witalis Andrzejewski, 'The Literary Culture of the Somali People' (2011) 23(1) *Journal of African Cultural Studies* 9.

75 Ibid.

76 Jonathan Crowe and Kylie Weston-Scheuber, *Principles of International Humanitarian Law* (Cheltenham: Edward Elgar Publishing, 2013) 96–115.

Abyssinia (today known as Ethiopia) as being particularly brutal with their prisoners and 'cutting off the genitals of their prisoners of war as trophies'.[77] The Oromo also denied their prisoners food and water for several days, and subjected them to torture as well as ill-treatment.[78] Moreover, some of the prisoners would eventually be killed. Notably, among the Oromo, killing was viewed as a satisfaction of natural order.[79] It mattered not whether the victim was delicate youth or an old person. The death of an enemy was accounted for as merit for the whole community.[80]

Consequences for the Breach of War Customs

There were serious consequences for the breach of war customs. For example, one could be given to the afflicted party for proper punishment. This was not an idle threat as was seen from the example of a warrior by the name of 'Wangai' who was handed over to the Maasai in the 1890s after breaching a peace treaty.[81] His fate and that of other warriors who were handed over to the offended parties was left in the hands of the latter. Additionally, natural calamities would befall the wrongdoer as a result of being unclean. Moreover, the issue of compensation for damages and losses arose at the close of hostilities.

Here, some belligerents would either form a truce, or the party that had won the conflict would occupy the land of the defeated party or of the one that had surrendered.[82] Amongst the East African countries, the chiefs/kings/leader/head of the belligerent parties met in the presence of a member of a neutral group to settle the matter by payment in kind. For instance, the Bakiga of Uganda demanded a specific herd of cattle, part of which was used to offer sacrifices to their ancestors.[83]

This concept of compensation can be compared to the modern, formally enshrined IHL principle of reparations.[84] Even though there were not enough sanctions at the time, since the principles were informal, it can be seen that in the case of war, there were laid down procedures which had to be followed

77 Emmanuel Bello, *African Customary Humanitarian Law*, (ICRC, 1980) 30.

78 Ibid.

79 Taddesse G Berisso, 'Traditional Warfare among the Guji of Southern Ethiopia' (PhD Thesis, Michigan State University 1988).

80 Ibid.

81 Muriuki (n 27).

82 Lawren (n 69).

83 'Bakiga People and Their Culture' *Ugandan Tourism Centre* https://ugandatourismcenter.com/place/bakiga-people-and-their-culture/ accessed 19 April 2021.

84 Emanuela-Chiara Gillard, 'Reparation for Violations of International Humanitarian Law' (2003) 85(851) *International Review of the Red Cross* 529.

and failure to follow these procedures would lead to some sort of sanction. However, apart from reprisals, modern IHL has brought with it codified sanctions such as the trial and prosecution of war criminals through proper trial tribunals and courts such as the ICC, where the Court has jurisdiction to try and prosecute persons who are suspected to have committed the crime of genocide, aggression, war crimes and crimes against humanity.[85]

Defenses to Breaches of Traditional Customs of War

By and large there are no clear known justifications that would be given by those who breached traditional customs of war. However, a common defence for breach was that the action served the best interest of the community.[86] The best interests of a community varied from economic to social benefits such as acquisition of slaves to provide labour. For instance, if warriors ambushed a community, instead of initiating negotiations first before declaring war, they could defend themselves by stating that more human capital was needed for economic gain.[87] As discussed earlier, some communities-initiated war to revenge on another for a fight they lost to the latter. The motivation was to regain back the resources that were stolen such as cattle, horses and farm proceeds, among others.[88] Other communities waged war to gain more land either for living space or agricultural uses.[89] The presence of such factors thus provided sound defences to breaches of the customs of war.

Places of Asylum and Truces

At the end of hostilities, there was a need to resettle the belligerents, victims of war and the protected elite to a resemblance of peace. Some people fled to neighbouring communities seeking asylum or to sacred places in their own communities which were regarded as inviolable places of asylum and varied from one tribe to another. For instance, amongst the Kikuyu of Kenya, sacred trees (known as Mugumo tree) were a classic place for asylum for the victims of war and the civilian population.[90] Areas where the Mugumo tree grew were

85 Mahnoush H Arsanjani, 'The Rome Statute of the International Criminal Court' (1999) 93(1) *The American Journal of International Law* 22.

86 Mr Zedekia Sidha and Michael Ntabo Mabururu, 'The Moral Justification of War: An African Case' (2016) 4(6) *Merit Research Journal of Education and Review* 60–64.

87 José Capela, 'Slave Trade Networks in Eighteenth-Century Mozambique' (2015) 30 *Networks and Trans-Cultural Exchange: Slave Trading in the South Atlantic 1590–1867* 31–70.

88 Fallers (n 42).

89 Neal W Sobania, *Culture and Customs of Kenya* (Greenwood Publishing Group, 2003) 159–187.

90 Ibid.

considered sanctuaries where no one could be pursued. The Maasai of Kenya and Tanzania had sanctuaries used for the yearly circumcision, where no one with belligerent intention could enter; equally, certain burial grounds for the members of the Rwandese dynasties were considered inviolable places of asylum.[91] Most ethnic groups also recognised truces during combat. For example, among the Lugbara of Uganda, the suspension of hostilities came just before the periods for sowing and harvesting the crops after making a truce with their adversary.[92]

II East African Contributions to International Humanitarian Law

Thus far in this chapter there has been a focus on looking at East African traditions and comparing them to the key principles of modern IHL. This is an important exercise[93] and one which allows reflection on the universal nature of principles enshrined in documents which were drafted by white European men in the late 1800s through the mid-1900s. However, given that this system of international legal governance is the one that has emerged in the global order, this chapter would not be complete without also considering the contributions made by East African states to other aspects of modern IHL and particularly to those instruments which have captured international attention this century.

This is particularly so because, previously, it was much easier and fashionable even, to denigrate traditional customs and activities in pre-colonial Africa.[94] African communities were assumed to be in a constant state of war with each other because they lacked institutional guarantees of peace.[95] European Christian missionary, Denys Shropshire, described Africans as, *"primitive and barbaric natives with no sociological or cultural development"*.[96]

91 Pieter Serneels and Marijke Verpoorten, 'The Impact of Armed Conflict on Economic Performance: Evidence from Rwanda' (2015) 59 *Journal of Conflict Resolution* 555.

92 Tignor (n 25).

93 Although the criticism of this approach is also well noted: see Karolina Aksamitowska, 'Traditional Approaches to the Law of Armed Conflict' (2020) 11(1) *Journal of International Humanitarian Legal Studies*; see also Francoise Hampson, 'Other areas of customary law in relation to the Study' in Elizabeth Wilmsurst, Susan Carolyn Breau (eds) *Perspectives on the ICRC Study on Customary International Humanitarian Law* (Cambridge University Press, 2007).

94 Ibid.

95 Emmanuel G Bello (n 2) 288.

96 Makau Mutua, 'Savages, Victims, and Saviors: The Metaphor of Human Rights' (2001) 42(1) *Harvard International Law Journal* 201.

Moreover, German philosopher, Georg Hegel, stated that before coming into contact with European culture, Africans had no history of their own.[97] It was thus widely thought that Africans could not therefore be left to their own devices and it was necessary to lead them to civilization. African communities were deemed basically incapable of having an awareness of IHL principles let alone incorporating them in their customs of war. Throughout the decades, this perception has had a ripple effect not only on the contribution of Africa to the development of IHL but also on its participation and involvement in the global IHL debate.

IHL Treaties

As Mutoy observes, there is 'extensive formal acceptance by modern African states of the principal instruments of contemporary [IHL]'.[98] Further, the contributions of African states to the 1977 Additional Protocols has been noted: with a focus on Protocol I and issues at the time such as decolonisation, apartheid and mercenaries, and resistance to Additional Protocol II discussions on non-international armed conflicts.[99] We can particularly point to a number of examples which show an East African voice on issues of IHL in recent years. The examples show East African states coming to the negotiating table and supporting a number of new IHL initiatives. As we will see, the results of this are mixed, and indeed the serious violations of IHL that continue to take place in many different conflicts across Africa show that even where support exists on paper, the implementation of it is often lacking.

A simple starting point is to note the speed at which South Sudan became a party to the Geneva Conventions of August 1949 and their Additional Protocols, in its own right, following independence from Sudan.[100] Accession to these documents was one of the earliest moves by the newly formed nation when it comes to international law engagement and was specifically noted by the then Minister for Justice in his speech to the United Nations in September 2012.[101] It is clear that such a step has not prevented conflict and huge numbers of IHL violations. Indeed, as South Sudan recently marked 10 years of

97 Ibid.

98 Mubiala Mutoy (n 5) 37.

99 Ibid 41.

100 '2016 ATT Academy East and Horn of Africa' *Control Arms* (Blog Post, 2016) https://controlarms.org/attacademy/ineastafrica/ accessed on 13 May 2021.

101 His Excellency Mr John Luk Jok, 'Statement' (Statement, high-level meeting on the rule of law at the national and international levels, 24 September 2012).

independence there was little to celebrate.[102] Yet, had South Sudan not prioritised this Convention, it would have been significant in so far as it would have put a small question mark on a series of documents that are widely accepted for their universality and understanding by people from all backgrounds.

Looking then to the IHL treaties of the 21st Century, we have to consider prohibitions on nuclear weapons and cluster munitions, and limitations on arms trades and protections for internally displaced persons.

On the subject of nuclear weapons, the broader African standpoint has long been very clear. The initiative of an African Nuclear-Weapon Free-Zone (the Pelindaba Treaty), which opened for signature on 11 April 1996 and entered into force in July 2009, is one that is supported by most African States including Ethiopia, Kenya, Rwanda and Tanzania from the East African region.[103] Further, Ethiopia, Kenya, Eritrea, Uganda and Rwanda have all ratified the 1996 Comprehensive Nuclear Test Ban Treaty.[104] However, only Tanzania is a signatory to the newly concluded Treaty on the Prohibition of Nuclear Weapons (2017), having signed in September 2019.[105] This is a very new treaty and so that may provide at least one reason for the low signature and ratifications rate. It should be noted that all the other East African states in attendance at the conference – Burundi, Djibouti, Eritrea, Ethiopia, Kenya, Uganda – voted in support of the draft treaty.[106] The healthy attendance from the region at the negotiating conference is in itself telling of the support for the prohibition in light of the pressure placed on many smaller states by nuclear-weapons-powers not to support the ban.[107]

Mweemba points out the involvement of East African states, as part of the Zambian coordinated African Group, in relation to the Convention on Cluster Munitions. Kenya and Uganda are noted as being 'actively engaged in the Oslo

---

102 'Kiir pledges peace as South Sudan marks decade of independence' *Al Jazeera* (News Article, 9 July 2011) https://www.aljazeera.com/news/2021/7/9/kiir-pledges-peace-as-south-sudan-marks-decade-of-independence.

103 African Nuclear Weapon Free Zone Treaty, Status as at 17 January 2020, African Union (Web Page, 19 August 2021) https://treaties.au.int.

104 Comprehensive Nuclear Test Ban Treaty, Status as at 19 August 2021, UNTC (Web Page, 19 August 2021) https://treaties.un.org/Pages/ViewDetails.aspx?src=TREATY&mtdsg_no=XXVI-4&chapter=26&clang=_en.

105 Ibid (n 98).

106 United Nations General Assembly Conference *to negotiate a legally-binding instrument to prohibit nuclear weapons*, A/CONF.229/2017/L.3/Rev.1, Rwanda, Somalia and South Sudan were not in attendance and did not vote.

107 Edith M. Lederer, 'US urges countries to withdraw from UN nuke ban treaty' *AP News* (Web Article, 22 October 2020) https://apnews.com/article/nuclear-weapons-disarmament-latin-america-united-nations-gun-politics.

Process'.[108] However, Kenya and Uganda have both not yet ratified their signatures.[109] Burundi, Rwanda and Somalia are the other State parties in the region. The Statement by South Sudan at the 2014 Fifth Meeting of States Parties on the Convention on Cluster Munition also demonstrates South Sudan's support, noting that although South Sudan, not existing at the time, was not a part of the negotiating process it 'applaud[s] the extraordinary efforts of states, NGOs and civil society that have made this convention a reality' and notes that its 'preparations are at an advanced stage for South Sudan to join the convention' (although we note that as at 2021 it has not yet done so).[110]

Another topic of particular interest in the region has been small arms and light weapons. The regulation of small arms and light weapons and the ease at which they could be procured is often argued to be a key driving feature of conflict within the region.[111] In 2004, States from the Great Lakes Region and Horn of Africa concluded the Nairobi Protocol to address the proliferation of small arms and light weapons in the region.[112] The Protocol required States to legislate to criminalise trafficking, illicit manufacturing, possession and misuse. As well as establishing import, export and transfer systems, it included provisions for marking, tracking and disposing of small arms and light weapons.[113] In addition to this regional instrument, the region contributed to global efforts towards arms control. Kenya was one of seven States (along with Argentina, Australia, Costa Rica, Finland, Japan and the United Kingdom) who co-authored the 2006 United Nations resolution calling for the UN to establish common international standards for the import, export and transfer of conventional arms.[114] Kenya also participated in the Group of Government Experts on the issue which reported to the UNGA in 2008.[115] However, some 8 years later, Kenya is not a party to the Arms Trade Treaty. The Arms Trade Treaty has

108 Sheila Mweemba, 'An African perspective on the Cluster Munitions Convention' (2008) 12(2) *Journal of Conventional Weapons Destruction*, 9.

109 United Nations Treaty Collection, 'Convention on Cluster Munitions' *UNTC* (Web Page, 13 August 2021) https://treaties.un.org/Convention_on_Cluster_Munitions.

110 Republic of South Sudan, 'Statement by South Sudan' (Statement, Fifth Meeting of States Parties of the Convention on Cluster Munitions, 3 September 2014).

111 Dr Esther Chelule, 'Proliferation of Small Arms and Light Weapons: Challenge to Development, Peace and Security in Africa' (2014) 19(5) *IOSR Journal of Humanities and Social Science* 82.

112 The Nairobi Protocol for the Prevention, Control and reduction of Small Arms and Light Weapons in the Great Lakes Region and Horn of Africa, signed 21 April 2004.

113 Ibid.

114 UNGA, Res A/Res/61/89 (6 December 2006).

115 'Arms Trade Treaty', *Reaching Critical Will* (Web Page, 2020) https://www.reachingcriticalwill.org/disarmament-fora/att/.

consequences for the East Africa region beyond the realms of armed conflict. One particular theme of interest in the region is that of poaching of wildlife and this has been the subject of some discussions at regional conferences such as those hosted by Control Arms and Pace University in 2016 at Lake Nakuru National Park in Kenya.[116] That said, while there is lots of discussion on this topic, and significant attempts to clarify any misconceptions about its interaction with the Nairobi Protocol in case that is the course of any hesitancy,[117] there remains a lot of actions still to be taken with no East African state yet a state party, and only Djibouti, Rwanda and Tanzania as signatories.[118]

Finally, we focus on the African Union Convention for the Protection and Assistance of Internally Displaced Persons, concluded in Kampala, Uganda, in 2009 (the Kampala Convention). This instrument is a global first in so far as it provides a specific framework for legal protection for internally displaced persons (IDPs). It has been rightly held up as a regional example.[119] The instrument is not purely an international humanitarian law one. Indeed, it provides quite broad protections for persons facing displacement for a range of reasons including 'displacement based on polices of racial discrimination or other similar practices',[120] 'forced evacuation in case of natural or human made disasters'[121] and 'displacement induced by [development] projects'.[122] That said, it has some very significant IHL obligations.[123] Djibouti, Ethiopia, Rwanda, Somalia, South Sudan, Uganda are States parties.[124] Burundi, Eritrea

116 '2016 ATT Academy East and Horn of Africa' (n 97).

117 See e.g. East African Community Press Release, 'Push for Ratification of the Arms Trade Treaty as EALA, ICRC hold seminar in Arusha' (Web page, 2018) https://www.eac.int/press-releases/1241-push-for-ratification-of-the-arms-trade-treaty-as-eala,-icrc-hold-seminar-in-arusha%20.

118 Arms Trade Treaty, 'Treaty Status' *ATT* (Web Page, 2021) https://thearmstradetreaty.org/treaty-status.

119 See Adama Dieng, 'Protecting internally displaced persons: the value of the Kampala Convention as a regional example' *International Review of the Red Cross* (2017), 99(904) 263–282.

120 African Union, *African Union Convention for the Protection and Assistance of Internally Displaced Persons in Africa ("Kampala Convention")*, 23 October 2009, art. 4(4)(a).

121 Ibid art 4(4) f.

122 Ibid art 10.

123 For a full list of comparative provisions between the Kampala Convention and IHL see, International Committee of the Red Cross, 'Stocktaking exercise: translating the Kampala Convention into Practice' *ICRC* (Web Article, 21 March 2018) https://www.icrc.org/en/document/translating-kampala-convention-practice-stocktaking-exercise annex 79–92.

124 African Union, 'African Union Convention for the protection and assistance of internally displaced persons in Africa (Kampala Convention)' *African Union Convention* (Web Page, 2020) https://AfricanUnionConventionfortheprotectionandassistanceofinternallydisplacedpersonsinAfrica.pdf.

and Tanzania are signatories. Kenya has not signed,[125] although it is noted that Kenya has its own IDP legislation.[126] The ICRC has pointed out a number of good practices which exist in the region in response to IDP concerns, but also strongly recommends further engagement both in terms of the legal instrument itself and its implementation.[127]

What we can see from this discussion is that the region's engagement with recent instruments designed to bolster the protections in times of armed conflict is mixed. Whilst the region has shown strong support, and indeed very active engagement on some topics, and often been present and vocal at international discussions, the follow through with international legal processes, including signature or ratification of international treaties and then subsequent domestication and implementation, has not always been forthcoming.

Institutional Frameworks

We will now consider the incorporation of principles of IHL into the institutional frameworks of relevance in the region. One observation made of the approach to the conduct of war in the region during pre-colonisation was the lack of institutions or offices of leadership, at least in the sense as understood in Western concepts.[128] As the evidence presented in this chapter has shown, there has in fact been a strong tradition of practices and processes for peace and conflict in traditions of warfare in Africa. The example of the Kikuyu and Maasai performing a ceremony at the end of the war 'symbolizing friendship' and ending the raids on one another's territory is given by Bello.[129] Another example is that of the practice of sending women to negotiate peace agreements, because of their status as protected persons allowing them to cross sides to facilitate a deal[130] or an exchange of prisoners.[131]

Today some of these practices and processes are more formalised as part of institutional frameworks that are globally recognisable. That this is the case is specifically stated as part of the legal framework for the region. Article 61 of African Charter on Human and Peoples' Rights (African Charter) states that the African Commission on Human and Peoples' Rights (African Commission), shall,

125 Ibid.

126 Ibid.

127 Ibid (n 117); See also, International Committee of the Red Cross, *The Kampala Convention: Key Recommendations Ten Years On* (ICRC, 2016).

128 Emmanuel G Bello (n 2) 20.

129 Emmanuel Bello (n 80) 51.

130 Taddesse Berisso (n 32) 31–2.

131 Taddesse Berisso (n 32) 33.

> take into consideration, as subsidiary measures to determine the principles of law, other general or special international conventions, laying down rules expressly recognized by member states of the Organization of African Unity, African practices consistent with international norms on human and people's rights, customs generally accepted as law, general principles of law recognized by African states as well as legal precedents and doctrine.

Although this is a human rights instrument and organisation, it is clear that there is significant overlap with IHL. For example, the African Commission makes calls for states parties to comply with IHL and its propensity to reference IHL in some detail has increased.[132]

To track back a little, the African Commission is one of two key bodies of the African Union specifically dealing with human rights issues. The African Union is the 55-member continental body launched in 2002, which as a successor to the Organisation of African Unity (OAU) (established 1963), and is focused on 'increased cooperation and integration of African states to drive Africa's growth and economic development'.[133] The Constitutive Act of the African Union includes in its objectives the promotion of 'peace, security and stability on the continent',[134] ideals that conflict is, of course, at odds with. The Constitutive Act references the African Charter, an instrument of the OAU, and the 1998 Protocol which establishes the African Court on Human and Peoples' Rights,[135] (intended to become the African Court of Justice and Human Rights following a merger of the African Court on Human and Peoples' Rights and the African Court of Justice) and the African Commission. The African Commission on Human and Peoples' Rights is concerned with the protection and promotion of human rights and the interpretation of the African Charter.[136]

It should be noted that in addition to taking into consideration African practices consistent with international norms, pursuant to the African Charter, the

132 Michaela Hailbronner, 'Laws in conflict: the relationship between human rights and international humanitarian law under the African Charter on Human and Peoples' Rights' (2016) 16 *African Human Rights Law* 348.

133 African Union, 'About the African Union' (Webpage, accessed 23 August 2021), https://au.int/en/overview.

134 Constitutive Act of the African Union, Art 3.

135 Organization of African Unity (OAU), *Protocol to the African Charter on Human and People's Rights on the Establishment of an African Court of Human and People's Rights*, 10 June 1998, Art 1.

136 ACHPR, 'About ACHPR', *African Commission on Human and Peoples' Rights'* (Web Page, 2020) https://www.achpr.org/aboutus.

African Commission 'shall draw inspiration from international law on human and peoples' rights' with a number of African and international legal instruments specifically mentioned.[137]

Significantly for the purposes of this discussion, the Protocol on Amendments to the Protocol on the Statute of the African Court of Justice and Human Rights (Malabo Protocol), negotiated in 2014, seeks to extend the jurisdiction of the African Court to include genocide, crimes against humanity, war crimes and various other international and transnational crimes. The idea of an African Court of this nature dates to the drafting of the African Charter in the early 1980s.[138] However, the Malabo Protocol has not yet entered into force with only 15 signatories and no States Parties.[139] The Malabo Protocol is controversial for a number of reasons including the immunity clause for heads of state,[140] the changes in makeup of judges with the transition to the African Court of Justice and Human Rights, the resources of the potential court and the interplay with the International Criminal Court.[141] However, the fact that it has not been ratified and does not look to have any prospects of coming into force is the more controversial element. Although a good number of African states (33), including Djibouti, Kenya, Uganda and Tanzania from East Africa,[142] are states parties to the ICC, the African story in relation to the ICC is not without controversy,[143] and the failure to agree on a clear jurisdiction regionally regarding war crimes only adds to this.

Additionally, within the African Union framework there is the Peace and Security Council, with conflict prevention and peace-making and peace building mandates.[144] However, again, no specific IHL mandate is articulated.

---

137 Organization of African Unity (OAU), *African Charter of Human and Peoples' Rights ("Banjul Charter")*, 27 June 1981, CAB/LEG/67/3 rev. 5, 21 I.L.M. 58 (1982) art 60.

138 Amnesty International, *Malabo Protocol: Legal and Institutional Implications of the Merged and Expanded African Court* (Report, 2016) 7.

139 African Union, 'Protocol on amendments to the protocol on the statute of the African Court of Justice and Human Rights' (Web Page, 20 May 2019) https://treaties/Protocol-on-amendments-to-the-protocol-on-the-statute-of-the-African-Court-of-Justice-and-human-rights.pdf.

140 African Union, *Protocol on the Statue of the African Court of Justice and Human Rights*, 1 July 2008, art 46A bis.

141 Amnesty International (n 135).

142 'The States Parties to the Rome Statute' *International Criminal Court* (Web Page, 2021) https://asp.icc-cpi.int/thestatespartiestotheromestatute.aspx.

143 See for example, Jadranka Petrovic, Dale Stephens and Vasko Nastevski, 'To arrest or not to arrest the incumbent head of state: the Bashir Case and the interplay between law and politics' (2016) 42(3) *Monash University Law Review* 740.

144 'The Peace & Security Council', *African Union* (Web Page, 2000) https://au.int/en/psc.

Taking a more regionalised approach we can only see a more general reference to human rights and peace and stability. No specific reference is made to IHL, and the relevant regional bodies do not specially have this as a focus. However, as Hailbronner points out, with so many conflicts in the region and so much involvement in peacekeeping operations, these regional bodies 'can play an important role in sanctioning violations of international humanitarian law'.[145]

The East African Community comprises Kenya, Uganda, Tanzania, Rwanda, Burundi and South Sudan.[146] Article 6 (b) and (d) of the Treaty for the Establishment of the East African Community (EAC), for example, notes the fundamental principles of the EAC as including the 'peaceful co-existence and good neighbourliness' and the 'recognition, promotion and protection of human and people's rights in accordance with the provisions of the African Charter on Human and Peoples' Rights'. The EAC also has its own judicial branch, the East African Court of Justice, which has jurisdiction over the application of the EAC Treaty. The potential for a broader jurisdiction including human rights that has not yet been enacted.[147] The Intergovernmental Authority on Development (IGAD), whose vision is achieving peace, prosperity, and regional integration in the region, has Djibouti, Eritrea, Ethiopia, Kenya, Somalia, South Sudan, Sudan and Uganda as members. The organisation has a strong focus on food security and environmental protection (having succeeded an earlier iteration focused on severe drought and other natural disasters) as well as 'economic cooperation and integration'.[148] That said, there are topics that overlap with IHL issues. For example, a key area of work for the EAC, for example, has been projects in cooperation with the Regional Centre for Small Arms which have included the measures for controlling small arms and light weapons which contributes to peace and stability including through reducing violations of IHL. These include marking of military and police weapons and national control plans.[149] IGAD also has a focus on 'peace and security and humanitarian affairs',[150] and has a Regional Peace and Security Strategy

145 Hailbronner (n 129) 341.

146 East African Community, 'Overview of EAC', *EAC* (Web Page, 2019) https://www.eac.int/overview-of-eac.

147 *Treaty for the Establishment of the East African Community*, opened for signature 30 November 1999, (entered into force 7 July 2000) art 27.

148 Intergovernmental Authority on Drought and Development, 'About Us' *IGAD* (Web Page, 2021) https://igad.int/about-us.

149 'Promotion of peace and security in the East African Community' *GIZ* (Web Page, 2014) https://www.giz.de/en/worldwide/15668.html.

150 Ibid.

(guided by the Africa Peace and Security Architecture).[151] IGAD has played a role in peace negotiations in the region – including various peace agreements with respect to South Sudan.[152]

As Hailbronner observed in 2016, 'both the African Commission and the African Court are only just beginning to address questions of the application of humanitarian law, and even when they do so, it is often in vague and unclear terms'.[153] However, Hailbronner argues that 'there are no reasons why the African Commission and Court should not be successful in elaborating a strong interpretive approach to the relationship between human rights and international humanitarian law in situations of armed conflict'.[154] The 'interpretative approach' of using the central role of human rights which the African Commission and Court can offer may well be preferable to the direct application of IHL.[155] 'Their expansion to cover ever newer fields of life and newer questions has made it inevitable that they be flexible and adaptable to new challenges and situations'. This may well be so, and indeed a very valuable contribution to be made, but it does seem that this cannot be the full picture without some changes to ensure that IHL is not a side product of other clearly specified roles such as 'peace and security' and 'human rights', but rather given its own specific frame of reference. The Malabo Protocol would be one avenue for this (although its weaknesses are noted). But it may not be the only one needed.

Importance of IHL in Africa Today

The need for a wider compliance with IHL principles in Africa today is self-explanatory. The cost of armed conflict within the continent has been catastrophic.[156] Despite such prevalence of armed conflict in the continent, Africa and African issues have remained largely absent from global IHL debates[157] even while the region 'has been an experimental laboratory for the legislative

151 IGAD, 'IGAD Regional Strategy: Strategic Plan Development Process', *Intergovernmental Authority on Development* (Web Page, 2020).

152 For example, IGAD, 'Revitalised agreement on the resolution of the conflict in the Republic of South Sudan', *Intergovernmental Authority on Development* (Agreement, 12 September 2018).

153 Hailbronner (n 129) 341.

154 Ibid 363.

155 Ibid.

156 Gus Waschefort, 'Africa and international humanitarian law: The more things change, the more they stay the same' (2016) 98(902) *International Review of the Red Cross* 593.

157 Karolina Aksamitowska (n 90) 5.

and operational activities of the United Nations in the humanitarian sphere'.[158] It is likely that such exclusion is but a symptom of colonialism, which excluded them from the formative negotiations of IHL.[159] IHL is thus perceived primarily as a product of Western thought. Indeed, increasingly, anti-Eurocentrism acts as a stumbling block to the wider acceptance of IHL principles on the continent.[160] Another challenge to a wider acceptance of IHL is the 'African Solution for African Problems' slogan.[161] IHL and other international laws and institutions are perceived by Africans as being used by Western countries to perpetuate racialised norms that subordinate non-European states to European ones.

This notwithstanding, it is important for Africa to engage more in the global IHL debates for the reason that international oversight and assistance will catapult efforts to combat armed conflict to the next level. There is also the need to more clearly incorporate IHL into African institutional frameworks so that it is at the forefront of decision makers' minds. Hiding behind the banner of 'African Solutions to African Problems' and using the same to satisfy selfish political interests is not only a perversion of the slogan but also derails efforts to eradicate armed conflict in the continent. Receding to regional limitations denies Africa an opportunity to implement global solutions to armed conflict on the continent. Leaders on the continent thus lack greater insight into overcoming hurdles experienced in the region. This limited pool of solutions without a doubt, significantly reverses the gains achieved over the years. Further, engaging more in the global IHL debate will give Africa an opportunity to contribute to global solutions aimed at ending armed conflict. However, to promote wider acceptance on the continent, it is important for European countries to seek to understand the African context and take into account their values and customs as IHL is discussed.[162] Traditional warfare incentives such as reciprocity, self-interest and reputation 'still matter for inducing the willingness to comply with the law'.[163] While this might not be so different in other parts of the world, as Bello notes, 'there is a need to locate oneself in the African context' to recognise the psychological and cultural 'differences between Africans

158 Mutoy Mubiala (n 5) 56.

159 Waschefort (n 153).

160 Mutoy Mubiala (n 5) 48–49.

161 See Remofiloe Lobakeng, 'African Solutions to African Problems: a viable solution towards a united, prosperous and peaceful Africa?' (2017) 71 *Institute for Global Dialogue*.

162 Emmanuel Bello (n 80) 48.

163 Heike Krieger, *Inducing compliance with International Humanitarian Law: Lessons from the African Great Lakes Region* (Cambridge University Press, 2015) 505.

and the western world'.[164] This will debunk the idea of Eurocentrism within the continent and enhance cooperation in the implementation of IHL.

Conclusion

African customs and traditions are replete with principles that are strongly reflected in the Geneva Conventions and other modern-day articulations of the laws and customs of war. The traditional warfare customs of several communities in East Africa, specifically the Maasai and Kikuyu of Kenya, the Baganda of Uganda as well as the Somali of Somalia, among others, are evidence that due to the peace-loving nature of these communities, they conducted wars with utmost humanity. As a general rule, traditional African customs protected non-combatants and the vulnerable like women, children, and the elderly. The laws of warfare also ensured that the use of excessive force and dangerous weapons were prohibited. Further, prisoners of war were treated with dignity and humanity. They were even integrated into their captors' families. At the end of every war, compensation for the loss of life and property was discussed. More importantly, in order to ensure that everyone in society adhered to the laid down war customs, breach was punished by the community. All these traditional practices are imbued with modern IHL norms.

There are examples, as set out in the second part of this chapter, which show that voices from the region have been a part of more recent global processes to develop IHL. Even then, Africa does not feature prominently in the global IHL debate. This is in part due to historical inequalities, but also is due to increased anti-Eurocentrism and the notion that Africa should develop its own solutions to its problems. This notion advocates for autonomy and independence but unfortunately, at the same time, often marginalises Africa in the global debate. Owing to the devastating consequences of war on the continent, Africa should aim at finding ways to increase the implementation of IHL principles which have been shown not to be entirely foreign ideas but rather a reflection of all of our common humanity. By better integrating IHL principles into armed conflict debates within the continent, Africa will also be able to infiltrate the global debate thereby contributing meaningfully to the same, it's leadership with the Kampala Convention being one example. Moreover, European countries should couch their debates in a manner that shows recognition of the

---

164 Emmanuel Bello (n 80) 48.

African context and its customs. This is likely to ensure that African states embrace IHL and guarantee their cooperation as well.

Acknowledgement

The authors wish to thank Kirsten McRuvie for her research assistance relating to Part II of this Chapter.

Conclusion

> If you have no more to tell us than that one barbarian succeeded another on the banks of the Oxus or Ixartes, what use are you to the public?[1]
>
> VOLTAIRE

∵

I started the conclusion to Volume 1 with the above quote, and do so again for the powerful reminder it gives us that there is little merit in merely recounting history. In order for the true benefit of the work of the contributing authors to be realised, it is necessary to demonstrate the *so what*.

One of the many benefits of a comparative study methodology is the research gains with extra datasets. Volume 2 has provided an additional seven cultures through which the 'golden thread'[2] can be traced through. These norms of war, moreover, provide valuable non-Western insights into modern issues that European cultural developments did not have the opportunity to grow towards. There are many different concepts that can be covered: the power of law as a weapon; how the laws of war can evolve in the face of the dated Mediterranean concept of peace and war. Yet this Chapter will focus on one topic that seems to have escaped debate so far but is increasingly important in an area of spectrum of competition: whether the laws of war unnecessarily promote suffering through legitimising war.

1 Sharp War, Soft War

Francis Lieber made a passing assurance that brutality in 'short and sharp'[3] wars was, paradoxically, more humane that the soft wars caused by the legalisation and legitimisation that the laws of war bring. Military necessity – *kriegsraison* – has always had its advocates and continues to exist as a domestic legal

1 I. Berlin, *The Crooked Timbre of Humanity* (New York, 1991) 52–3.

2 Samuel White, 'Conclusion' in *Laws of Yesterday's Wars* (Brill Nijhoff, 2021) 209.

3 William A. Blair, *With Malice Toward Some: Treason and Loyalty in the Civil War Era* (University of North Carolina Press, 2014) 96.

 | DOI:10.1163/9789004473218_010

remedy in many jurisdictions. Admiral Williams Rebolledo, Commander-in-Chief of the Chilean Navy, justified his bombardment campaign of unfortified Peruvian towns, though the following statement:

> [t]he people of Peru, and perhaps even a portion of our own, have forgotten in the current contest that a war is all the more humanitarian when it is crueller, and that only by making the belligerents feel all the rigours of war is that we will promptly reach peace.[4]

This was a point recently raised in Samuel Moyn's' new book: *Humane: How the United States Abandoned Peace and Reinvented War*.[5] Relying on the fictional characters in Tolstoy's seminal work, *War and Peace,* we are forced to consider whether or not war really should be left in a State of Nature. Volume 1 touched on this indirectly when canvassing shock arising from the clash of British and Maori cultures. The result was the degradation of the Maori 'first wave' customs of war, in the face of British 'second wave' warfare.[6] The point was perhaps most aptly stated by the 1930s British Prime Minister, Stanley Baldwin, who remarked on attempts to regulate the use of bombers in the inter-war periods of the 1930s:

> if a man has a potential weapon and has his back to the wall and is going to be killed, he will use that weapon whatever it is and whatever undertaking he has given about it. Experience has shown us that the stern test of war will break down all conventions.[7]

Špicová's expert translation of the *Mahābhārata* makes clear that Ancient Indian authors believed it virtually impossible to win a war using only just means. The main battle of the *Mahābhārata* lasts 18 days; during the first ten days, the general of the Kauravas is Bhisma who only uses the *dharmayuddha,* but after his death, warriors from both sides start to use the means of the *kutayuddha,* and the war becomes much swifter: the second general is killed after five days, the third after two, and the fourth in a single day. The final act

4 Juan Williams Rebolledo, *Operaciones de La Escuadra Chilena Mientras Estuvo a las Órdenes del Contra-Almirante Williams Rebolledo* (Imprenta del Progreso 1882) 30.

5 (Macmillan, 2021).

6 Per the methodology offered by Alvin Toffler, *The Third Wave* (Bantam, 1991).

7 Prime Minister Stanley Baldwin, United Kingdom, House of Commons, *Debates* (November 10, 1932) Cols 631–38.

of the war is the night carnage of Asvatthaman where no rules apply anymore; after that, the text focuses on re-building of dharma.

Moyn moreover follows the progression of the legitimisation of the laws of war and draws analogies between the legitimisation, through the legalisation, of slavery. There are important and powerful linkages to be made. Moyn, through the perspectives of Clauswitz and Tolstoy, highlights the risks of allowing soft war – that is, war regulated by law. Clauswtiz is cited as having warned against the 'kind-hearted fiction that a national could wage war without too much bloodshed'.[8] Indeed, says Moyn through Clausewitz:

> the fact that slaughter is a horrifying spectacle must make us take war more seriously but not provide an excuse for gradually blunting our swords in the name of humanity ... Sooner or later someone will come along with a sharp sword and hack off our arms.[9]

Clausewitz was more worried by pacifists than international law. The sole reference to international law is in one dismissive sentence: '[a]tached to force are certain self-imposed, imperceptible limitations hardly worth mentioning, known as international law and custom, but they scarcely weaken it'.[10] To that end, Lieber – a support of Clausewitz's sharp war construct – codified the right to deny quarter to captured persons. This act of lawfare, as Chris Bailey noted in Volume 1, was without precedent in its time.[11]

Denial of quarter, a particularly brutal concept only recently regulated, has remerged again in the recent Russian-Ukrainian war. On 02 March 2022, Ukrainian Special Forces announced it would no longer capture Russian Ukrainian artillerymen, but would kill them in response for their 'brutal shelling of civilians and cities'.[12]

Yet Moyn through Tolstoy notes that even the mere act of codifying the laws of war would suggest a softening; just how the humanising of slavery had insulated it against criticism and abolition so too did Lieber's work support the system of warfare. It is an interested argument and one that gives pause

8 Moyn (n 5) 34.

9 Carl von Clausewitz, *On War*, (trans. Michael Howard and Peter Paret; Princeton: Princeton University Press, 1989), 260.

10 Ibid, 75.

11 Christopher M. Bailey, 'A Code of Necessity' in Samuel White (ed.) *The Laws of Yesterday's Wars* (Brill Nijhoff, 2021) 187–209.

12 Facebook post, reported in: https://www.youtube.com/watch?v=5cqlJp3lW_w&ab_channel=news.com.au.

for thought and reflection. Can we exist in a system without war? Or is war a natural part of the human condition? The author's personal feeling is towards the latter, grounded in the evidence that the abolition of formal slavery has not resulted in a world without. It has merely outsourced and evolved the use of human labour to a system without limitations – as globalisation and sweat shops have demonstrated.

There is risk then in deregulating warfare, just as there has been risk in deregulating slavery. It is a difficult discussion to be held. Should we remove the laws, and sharpen war to resolve conflicts quicker? Does the deregulation of warfare really speed up its resolution? The move by Ukrainian Special Forces would seem based in this theory; but just as readily it may incentivise Russian artillerymen to win. The subsequent backtracking of Ukrainian Special Forces to the ambiguously worded threat they 'would not spare'[13] Russian artillerymen would appear more backed in maintaining the legal and moral legitimacy than soft war theory.

These two volumes, however, have demonstrated that those cultures canvassed have naturally gravitated towards mitigating and controlling the violence of warfare. Some cultures, like Indigenous Australians, created a complex structure of cultural norms that prohibited bloodshed in many instances without sacrificing their sovereignty. Others still divided the responsibility for peace and war into separate commands. Rome had a very simple structure based around one concept: *fides.* This might come as a surprise to some, for the solemnity of Latin hides the fact that the *jus ad bellum* and *jus in bello* are not millennia old concepts.

Sharp wars (those without the straightjacket of laws) have often been used to justify campaigns of terror. As this work has demonstrated, however, is that there has always been an attempt to humanise combatants – in a literal sense. Homer recognised the dividing line between humans and animals throughout the *Iliad.* Humans, unlike animals, can be both savage and compassionate. Achilles, in his *ariestia,* comments to Hektor:

> ... I will have no talk of pacts with you, ...
> As between men and lions there are none,
> no concord between wolves and sheep, but all
> hold one another hateful through and through
> so there can be no courtesy between us ...[14]

13 News Source (n 12).

14 *The Iliad* (trans. Robert Fagles, 1990) 22.308ff.

This scene, of Achilles transformed into an animal, is laden with Homer's implied view of what it means to be human: to be willing to parley, to consider self-restraint, to respect others as possible friends.[15] Achilles is not a hero in the story. He is a lesson in Fate, and in the excesses of war. Indeed, the *Iliad* starts with a forewarning of the purpose of the tale:

> Rage – Goddess, sing the rage of Peleus' son Achilles,
> murderous, doomed, that cost the Achaeans countless losses,
> hurling down to the House of Death so many sturdy souls,
> great fighters' souls, but made their bodies carrion, feasts for the dogs
> and birds ...[16]

Homer is warning us of what can occur when the laws of war – which, as David Feany noted, were well recorded for the Hellenes – are broken. Yet he also talks to us of the importance of these regulations, lest we end up doomed.

This latter concept – of humanising the foe – is critical in international humanitarian law, and the historic laws of war to a certain point. Yet there is a clear dividing point where the foe has transitioned from an equal, to lesser, and it is this degradation of the enemy that modern international humanitarian law has sought to reintroduce and codify.

The two volumes in this series so far seem to suggest that the jump from equals to lesser is first reflected in the Old Testament. Specifically, the story of David and Goliath highlights the use of degrading language to dehumanise, and to vilify the enemy. Goliath, vested in the contemporary symbols of wealth and prestige – mail armour, shield bearer, sword and spear – is met with David, a shepherd and armed with a sling. Often the story ends there; but a literary analysis of the language demonstrates the layers that this choice of weapons means to Goliath.

> And David said to Saul, Let no man's heart fail because of him [Goliath]; thy servant will go and fight with this Philistine.
>
> And Saul said to David, Thou art not able to go against this Philistine to fight with him: for thou art but a youth ...
>
> [David answered,] *Thy servant slew both the lion and the bear; and this uncircumcised Philistine shall be as one of them*, seeing he hath defined the armies of the living God

15 Jonathan Shay, *Achilles in Vietnam* (Simon & Schuster, 1995) 83.

16 *The Iliad*,1.1.

> David said moreover, *The* LORD *that delivered me out of the paw of the lion, and out of the paw of the bear, he will deliver me out of the hand of this Philistine*

David, who did not need armour to fight animals, dismisses the weapons in lieu of a sling and stave. He approaches Goliath:

> And when the Philistine looked about, and saw David, he disdained him ...
> And the Philistine said unto David, *Am I a dog, that thouh comest to me with staves?*

Goliath immediately grasps that David defines and intends to treat him sub-human – an animal, to be fought without honour. This Abrahamic origin story – shared by those of the Christian, Jewish and Islamic faith – is perhaps more shaping than is often given credit for. As Jonathan Shay, classicist and combat trauma psychologist notes:

> Twentieth-century nationalism has taken over the biblical tendency to measure loyalty by how vehemently one dehumanizes the enemy. When American soldiers and their commanders in Vietnam debased the enemy, they echoed very ancient proofs of their faith in God and of their own religious merit ... The Judeo-Christian (and Islamic) world view has triumphed ... that dishonouring the enemy now seems natural, virtuous, patriotic, pious.[17]

Shay is, with respect, not utterly correct in this statement. As Chapter 4 highlighted, Islam has always tried to mitigate the cruelty of wars even against those who are Dar Al-Hab. The Prophet Muhammad instructed: "Observe good treatment towards the prisoners".[18] Islamic law guarantees that POWs shall be treated humanely and with respect – fed and watered, clothed if necessary, and protected from the heat and the cold and from cruel treatment. Their families which include parents, grandparents and children would remain with them, so

---

17 Shay (n 16) 115.

18 Muhammad ibn Jarīr al-Ṭabarī, *Tārīkh al-Ṭabarī: Tārīkh al-Umam wa al-Mulūk*, (Dār al-Kutub al-'Ilmiyyah, Beirut, 2001), Vol. 2, p. 39.

as to protect family unity. Humanising the enemy even extended towards the body of *al-kalb al-'aqūr* (a rabid dog).[19]

Judeo-Christians also seek to honour the enemy. Central to medieval public warfare were tactics designed to compel the other party to accept the validity of their claim. Such means and methods included forced contributions, arson, plunder, and injuries against certain individuals, destruction of property, ransom, and use of lethal force. As noted by Girat, Duke of Burgundy (an independent sovereign, therefore capable of public war) discussing the use of burning and plundering around him:

> If my neighbour starts a quarrel with me,
> With fire burns my lands to cinders;
> And I, his, on all sides;
> If he steals my castles or keeps,
> Then so it goes until we come to terms,
> r he puts me or I put him in prison.[20]

Procession through hostile territory – to *chevauchee* – demonstrated the justice and moral superiority of one's claim, and further undermined the position of an impotent noble unable to defend what they claimed theirs. Although some tactics evolved that sought to introduce sharp war – such as the *chevauchee* – there were rules that regulated it, such the right of captives to ransom rather than execution.[21]

Even if we take the rules away, and promote sharp war, societies will always try to regulate themselves. This is, indeed, the underlying assumption of Hobbes' state of nature and emergence of the State. Roman warfare, with its emphasis upon *fides publica populi Romani*, demonstrates a society without peer (after the collapse of Carthage) that still sought to regulate itself.[22] But of course this *bona fides* only extended to those who were recognised by the Roman State as deserving it – such as those across the Middle Sea but not those across the Rhine. This, of course, is not unique: just see the experiences

19 Muḥammad ibn Aḥmad al-Sarakhsī, *Kitāb al-Mabsūt* (Beirut: Dār al-Maʿrifah, n.d.), Vol. 9, pp. 135, 196; Vol. 10, pp. 129, 131; Vol. 16, p. 145; Vol. 26, p. 145.

20 Quoted in Richard W. Kaeuper, *Chivalry and Violence in Medieval Europe* (Oxford University Press, 1999) 177.

21 Michael Bryant, *A World History of War Crimes: From Antiquity to the Present* (Bloomsbury, 2016), 58.

22 Of course, many contemporary as well as modern historians have remarked that the fall of Rome led to its eventual corruption.

of Indigenous Australians against the legal rhetoric of the British Empire,[23] those of the Mexica (Aztecs) against the Spanish *conquistadors,*[24] Native Americans and European colonisers, or those of the Japanese against China after adopting European laws of war.[25] In many ways, whilst still in its isolationist period, Tokugawa Japan adopted a similar approach to Romans. Like Rome, 'medieval Japanese concepts of honor and honorable conduct in battle were flexible enough to permit successful warriors to rationalize almost any sort of behaviour'.[26] As Anna notes in Chapter 6, samurai were acting 'for' the State and warfare therefore had a more criminal focus. Yet it is the Aztecs, not the Romans, who perhaps give the best examples that lethality in war need is not undermined by humanitarian law.

Aztec warfare represented 'pre-metallurgic warfare in the most refined and one of the most eccentric forms it could take'.[27] So too were the restrictions they placed on themselves, although the true extent of their customs and norms can only be guessed at, through implications and fragments of text. It is an area that demands further attention and revision. However, it raises a more pertinent point of the inherently Eurocentric nature of international humanitarian law, with its European notions of chivalry.[28] As Soustelle wrote:

> The Aztec's intention was not to force the enemy to yield by ruining the country or massacring the population, but to make manifest the will of [H]uitzilopochtli ... Nothing would have seemed more incomprehensible to the ancient Mexicas, nor more atrocious, than the characteristic features of our modern war: huge destruction, the systemic extermination of whole nations, the annihilation of states or their overthrow.[29]

23 Henry Reynolds, *Truth-Telling* (UNSW Print, 2021).

24 See an excellent example of lawfare in Shoshana Zubkoff, *The Age of Surveillance Capitalism* (Profile Books, 2019) 177 where we remarks about how *conquistadors* would quickly utter legal doctrine, as a whisper while laying in ambush, to satisfy the requirement of taking all feasible precautions in an attack.

25 Susumu Yamauchi, 'Civilization and International Law in Japan During the Meiji Era' (1868–1912) (1996) 24 *Hitotsubashi Journal of Law and Politics* 7.

26 Friday, 'Bushido' in *The Encyclopedia of War.*

27 John Keegan, *A History of Warfare* (Hutchisons Publishing, 1993) 114.

28 Samuel White, 'The Late Middle Ages' in Samuel White (ed) *The Laws of Yesterday's Wars* (Brill Nijhoff, 2021) 101–127.

29 Jacques Soustelle, *Daily Life if the Aztecs – On the Eve of the Spanish Conquest* (trans. Patrick O'Brian) (Weidenfeld and Nicholson, 1961) 211–212.

Once an individual was captured, they were not sacrificed on the spot but were housed by, fed by and cared for by their captors for nearly a year. They sacrificed at the first gathering of the agricultural harvest, at the onset of the Aztec seasons of war, called the Feast of the Flaying of Men.[30] Eight days after the harvests began, the less important warriors in the previous year were sacrificed; eight days after that they were followed by the more important warriors. 'Ideally they were meant to go leaping up the steps of the [sacrificial] pyramid, shouting the chants of their city as they went, and some did; others had to be dragged up by the priests'.[31] For the most revered captured warriors was reserved a ritualistic trial by combat at the top of the pyramid, the catch being that they were equipped with a sword of feathers whilst their executioners – two Jaguar Warriors and two Eagle warriors – were equipped with a obsidian-studded swords.

For the more important warriors, the evening before their sacrifice would be spent in vigil with their captor, culminating in his *piochtli* being removed – thus began the transition from warrior to sacrifice; and the transition from the human to the sacred.[32] It was, however, a time for mourning for the Aztec warrior, like his captive, had been long prepared for this fate. Every young man in training was taught of the two ways to enter the House of the Sun – death in battle (which was rare), and death on the pyramid of another. For this reason, when their flesh was issued to the family of the captor for consumption, the captor would omit to eat it, saying "Shall I perchance eat my very self?"[33] Failing to abide by this prohibition would have been viewed as a serious breach of the laws of war. Core to it, even amongst a society that executed nearly all prisoners, was empathy for their enemy.

This familial status in captured persons is reflected in the cultures of East Africa. The historical culture that instilled the importance of humanity among the Bantu in Kenya taught that, 'brothers do not kill each other'.[34] Mutuma and Massingham highlighted in the Kikuyu community, prisoners of war were welcomed to the warriors' families and were treated as their brothers or sisters.[35]

30 Inga Clendinnen, 'The Cost of Courage in Aztec Society' (1985) 107 *Past & Present* 44, 50.

31 Ibid, 69.

32 Ibid.

33 *Florentine Code*, Bk 2, Chap 21, p 54.

34 Lloyd A Fallers, *Bantu Bureaucracy: a Study of Integration and Conflict in the Political Institutions of an East African People* (Cambridge: East African Institute of Social Research, 1959).

35 John Lonsdale, 'Contests of Time: Kikuyu Historiography, Old and New' (2002) *A Place in the World: New Local Historiographies from Africa & South Asia* 201.

Sexual assault of a captive woman, therefore, amounted to incest.[36] If the right of ransom was not exercised, the woman integrated into the Kikuyu community. It is perhaps for this reason that such strongly held forms of dispute resolution were applied before a war was declared, and peace treaties were often concerned with reintegration into society.[37]

So too are East African cultures illuminating when it comes to the notion of non-combatant, and the cultural rules applied to who was offered protection. In an globalised era where the academic analysis of 'direct participants in hostilities' has created an academic field where it is easier to say who *is* a combatant, it is important to look outside the European continent. The approach of the Somali is perhaps the most useful test to apply: are the individuals oblivious to the war? Such a position is reflected in Melanesian warfare[38] and the *Mahābhārata*.

It may also help address the issue of third-party contractors. Private Military Contractors (PMCs), security consultants, professional military personnel or defence contractors are being increasingly relied. The current conflict (at the time of writing) in Ukraine just highlights this: fighters are being publicly crowdsourced,[39] or recruited from other battlefields.[40]

Nowhere is this clearer than Iraq and Afghanistan, although the trend towards privatisation of militaries has existed long before that. The attacks of September 11 were the catalyst for the United States to declare a 'Global War on Terror' who found themselves rapidly mobilising but without sufficiently trained troops and logistical nodes. In a subsequent U.S. Senate Estimates, it was calculated that the replacement of PMCs in Iraq in 2008 would have required approximately nine brigades.[41] Of the 150,000 private contractors, only 8000 were categorised as 'shooters' – the rest provided non-lethal effects.[42] Table 1, utilising American military force elements, demonstrates this.[43]

36 Godfrey Muriuki, 'A History of the Kikuyu to 1904' (PhD Thesis, SOAS University of London 1969).

37 Samuel White, 'Does Justice Come from the Briefcase of the White Man?' (2018) 3 *Perth Journal of International Law* 19–32.

38 *Protection under the Palm: Wars of Dignity in the Pacific* (ICRC, 2009).

39 ABC News, 'Foreign Fighters await weapons' – https://abcnews.go.com/International/wireStory/foreign-fighters-ukraine-await-weapons-chaos-war-83452681.

40 Reuters, 'Russia Wants Syrian Fighters' https://www.reuters.com/world/some-syrian-veterans-ready-ukraine-fight-commanders-say-2022-03-20/.

41 Jack Bell, US Deputy Under Secretary for Defense for Logistics and Readiness, *Jane's Defence Weekly*, 9 July 2008, 24.

42 Ibid.

43 Alexander Tabarrok, 'The rise, fall, and rise again of privateers' (2007) 11(4) *Independent Review* 566–567.

TABLE 1 Civilians contracted to support military operations

War/Conflict	Contracted personnel	Military	Raito
American Revolution	1,550 (est)	9000	1:6 (est)
Mexican/American	6,000 (est)	33,000	1:6 (est)
Civil War	200,000 (est)	1,000,000	1:5 (est)
World War I	85,000	2,000,000	1:20
World War II	734,000	5,400,000	1:7
Korea	156,000	393,000	1:2.5
Vietnam	70,000	359,000	1:6
Persian Gulf War	5,200	541,000	1:100
Rwanda/Somalia/Haiti	No Records Kept	N/A	N/A
Balkans	5,000–20,000	(Varied) 20,000	Up to 1.5:1
Iraq	95,461	95,900	1:1
Afghanistan	112,092	79,100	1.42:1

The notion of mercenary service has blurred since the Second World War, with increasing globalisation and interconnected alliances resulting in officers and soldiers 'seconded on loan service' from third country Regiments to military advisors.[44] Although Hellenistic and Roman law recognised the right of mercenaries on the battlefield (the term finds its roots in the Latin *mercanarius,* which meant 'working merely for monetary or other reward; actuated by self-interest'[45]). So too did Renaissance Europe, with its paid forces on land[46] and sea.[47] However in modern military operations, and the common vernacular, the term mercenary contains a pejorative element that has largely arisen from a deeply held, if imperfectly understood, feeling that service in the military should be morally defensible, and accordingly, be linked to a *casus belli* and a State (just war). In turn, it is only the State which can authorise the

44 Ian Wing, *Private Military Companies and Military Operations,* (Land Warfare Studies Centre, 2011, Working Paper No. 138) 2.

45 Ibid.

46 Kyle Walker, 'The Renaissance' in Samuel White (ed) *The Laws of Yesterday's Wars* (Brill Nijhoff, 2021) 127–150.

47 Andrew Read, 'Pirates and Privateers in Elizabethan England' in Samuel White (ed) *The Laws of Yesterday's Wars* (Brill Nijhoff, 2021) 171–187.

taking of life, outside of self-defence. Thus, the killing of others – a core component of the *rason d'etre* of a military force – should always be by the citizen soldier.[48]

Should these modern soldiers be targeted? Under Islamic law, there is precedent to exclude them from targeting. These were the *usafā* – those hired by the enemy to do supporting services in the battlefield, but do not engage in the fighting (those who wield the sword, not those who sharpen it). It is left to the reader to decide which philosophy outlined in this Chapters that they think should apply for a globalized battlefield.

Importantly, nearly every culture has exceptions to their laws of war (including non-combatants). Of the 15 cultures canvassed in Volumes 1 and 2, only Indigenous Australian nations seem to have had a taboo on the spilling of non-combatant blood (women, and Elders) even if they participated in conflict. It may be that the Aztec porters (*tlamemeh*) were also sacrosanct, but the sources are not clear. However, Buddhist ethics are governed generally by the principle of moral autonomy, so it was considered that soldiers had full individual responsibility for their actions; it was not overridden by "military necessity". The use of surprise attacks, Friday suggests, was perhaps considered justified because warriors were always expected to be on their guard. So, taking them by surprise could not be seen as taking unfair advantage of them, any more so than attack in an ordinary battle if they have slipped their guard.

As I covered in Volume 1 and elsewhere,[49] despite popular fiction, surprise was also a valid tactic in many European cultures. What was not acceptable, and core in the argument against sharp war, was the breaking of trust. It is here that Moyn's assertion is, with respect, the weakest. People always have, and always will, seek to leave the state of nature. This is achieved, says Bentham, when people demonstrate obedience to an authority.[50] What these volumes have demonstrated is that this obedience is often not to an individual, but to an idea: that of chivalry, *fides*, community, *bushido*, *milwerangel*. These are the customs and laws of war which individuals have created rituals around and which some individuals will always wish to shape and change – sometimes

48 Samuel White, 'A Soldier By Any Other Name: A Reappraisal of the Citizen in Uniform Doctrine in Light of Part IIIAAA of the *Defence Act*' (2019) 57(2) *Military Law and Law of War Review*, 20–52.

49 Samuel White, 'Colouring in the Grey Zone: Lawfare as a Lever of National Power' (2022) 21(2) *Journal of Military and Strategic Studies* 77–106.

50 Jeremy Bentham, *A Fragment of Government* (Clarendon Press, 1776) 141.

through appeals to exceptionalism, or to that of necessity. Yet it is important to distinguish between those who agitate for a reform of the system, and those who argue for its entire dismantlement. Those in the latter camp may try use misinformed appeals to history and precedent; it is hoped that these and future Volumes may help inform and clarify the debate.

Index

East African Laws

Islamic Laws

Japanese laws

Native American (Eastern) Laws

Roman Laws

www.ingramcontent.com/pod-product-compliance
Lightning Source LLC
La Vergne TN
LVHW020635300926
849161LV00004B/706
* 9 7 8 9 0 0 4 4 7 3 2 0 1 *